Iván Szelényi

From State Socialism to Post-Communist Capitalism

Iván Szelényi

From State Socialism to Post-Communist Capitalism

Critical Perspectives

2022
Harrassowitz Verlag · Wiesbaden

Bibliografische Information der Deutschen Nationalbibliothek
Die Deutsche Nationalbibliothek verzeichnet diese Publikation in der Deutschen Nationalbibliografie; detaillierte bibliografische Daten sind im Internet über https://dnb.de/ abrufbar.

Bibliographic information published by the Deutsche Nationalbibliothek
The Deutsche Nationalbibliothek lists this publication in the Deutsche Nationalbibliografie; detailed bibliographic data are available in the internet at https://dnb.de/.

Informationen zum Verlagsprogramm finden Sie unter
https://www.harrassowitz-verlag.de/

Gedruckt auf alterungsbeständigem Papier.
Druck und Verarbeitung: Memminger MedienCentrum AG
Printed in Germany

ISBN 978-3-447-11858-3 eISBN 978-3-447-39289-1

Contents

Foreword

I am delighted that Harrassowitz Verlag has taken up my suggestion to publish in this volume the collected writings of the social scientist Iván Szelényi. At the same time, I would like to thank Szelényi for assembling a selection of solely or jointly authored publications for this book and for writing an introduction to accompany them. No other author has been as qualified as Szelényi to compare the societal conditions in Communist Hungary with those of the post-Communist era, through his own perception, his academic career, and the research he has undertaken.

He became known in Germany in 1978 when he published, in Hungarian and German, the book *Die Intelligenz auf dem Weg zur Klassenmacht* (Frankfurt/Main: Suhrkamp) with the Hungarian author György Konrád. After the publication of the book the two authors had to leave Hungary. For Szelényi, this was the starting-point for an increasingly successful academic career at a series of highly regarded universities in Australia and the United States. Throughout his academic career, he has been recognised with important honours and awards. He currently lives in the US and in Budapest, becoming an honorary citizen of the Hungarian capital in 2008.

The aim of the introduction and the selection of texts is to provide readers with new knowledge and to prompt them to reflection through the unfamiliar perspectives presented to them. That this will be the case, I am most certain.

I thank Mr. Fetkenheuer and his team for eliminating the conversion errors in the texts and the footnotes. Mrs. Elke Kühne for her kind courtesy in looking through the entire text because of the conversion errors that occurred.

Hannover/ Autumn 2021
Hubert Treiber

From State Socialism to Post-Communist Capitalism: Critical Perspectives

Iván Szelényi

Introduction

I published my first scholarly paper in 1962, almost 60 years ago. I first published in English in 1969, just over 50 years ago. During this 50–60 years I published in English some 9 monographs and about 100 papers in English. When I was asked to put together a collection of my English language papers I was humbled and challenged.

The world changed around us so much. In 1962 Hungary was still a neo-Stalinist country, which tuned soon into Janos Kádár's "goulash communism". Its disintegration started in the 1980's and in 1989–90 the transition to "market capitalism" began on a trajectory what appeared to be a bourgeois liberal democracy. In 2014 Viktor Orbán announced his dream to build an "illiberal regime" and indeed this proved to be political trend not only in Hungary, but in many European countries (and elsewhere in the world, even under Donald Trump in the USA). Many countries in the world seem to be moving away from "liberal democracy" towards illiberalism. How much coherence can one expect from the works of a social scientist in this fast changing world? Not much... and I am not one who claim "I knew it all along". I did not, and I made many predictions which never happened. So is there any chance for me to justify this collection of essays? Is there any coherence to these 10 papers?[1]

I have to leave the judgement to the readers, but my best self- defense is that in all of these papers and in all of my work I had a commitment to critical social science, mainly in the Weberian tradition. But I have to start with a qualification. I distinguish between two types of critical analysis, one I call "teleological", the other "immanent". A teleological critique assumes that the analyst has a critical vintage point. Hence the critical analysis of "actually existing socialism" during the 1960's or 1970's often started – at least in Eastern Europe – from an ideal conception of "socialism". Especially Marxist critical social scientists usually claimed "actually existing socialism" is not really "socialism"... this is not what Marx or even Lenin intended to create. By the 1980's a different kind

1 My Bulgárian colleagues for my 80th birthday published a volume in Bulgarian language with 14 of my papers (Sofia: Iztok-Zapad, 2019). For this volume I added 2 more recent papers and cut 6 from the Bulgarian language edition.

of "teleological criticism" appeared: here the critical vintage point was the ideal type of capitalism. The same logic of teleological criticism can be applied for post-communist capitalism: either it is not "really" capitalism", or yes, it is capitalism, but its problems will only be fixed with a "socialist solution". (In Eastern Europe there are not too many "true socialists" believing in this, but there are still a few). In all of my work I was committed to develop an immanent critique, be it socialism or capitalism. Immanent critique means I am not critical of state socialism because it is not "real socialism" or it is not "capitalism". It is socialism all right and the problems I identify comes from its socialist features. Will it solve those problems by turning the system into a capitalist one? No, since a capitalist system will have its own contradictions and whether those contradictions are better or worse than contradictions of socialism can only be solved in a political way, there is no "theoretical solution" to this dilemma.

David Stark astutely called my "immanent critique" the method of "mirrored comparisons". If I solve in capitalist ways the problems of socialism I create the problems of capitalism. I also called this method "ironic". The purpose of irony is not to give answers or solutions, but to pose questions. Over the past half century I tried to develop an immanent critique, or ironic view of state socialism and post-communist economies. Both systems have their problems and I want to leave it to social actors to decide which one they prefer or oppose. As social analyst it is not my task to make such choices for society. Society needs to find democratic ways to evaluate the "costs and benefits" of any policy solution. There is never a "free lunch"... To put is brutally simply: if one wants more freedom (that's what capitalism is likely to offer) you have to pay a price for it in terms of reduced security, if you prefer security you may have to give up some of your freedoms (that's what socialism promises).

Before I present the structure of this book I better make a few autobiographical notes. I was born in 1938 and I received my first degree at Karl Marx University of Economics in Budapest in 1960. My first job was at the Hungarian Central Statistical Office, where I started to publish after 1962 sociological articles. In 1963 a Sociological Research Group was created at the Hungarian Academy of Sciences and I was recruited there as a part-time researcher. The Hungarian Academy of Sciences nominated me to be a post-doctoral fellow in the United States, which was supported by the Ford Foundation. I spent a semester at Columbia and one at UC Berkeley and visited many other sociology departments, including University of Michigan where I met Eugene Litwak. My first empirical research in Hungary was on the question when people have to rely on primary groups in case bureaucracies cannot meet their needs. Eugene was working on the same subject, so we decided to collect data with the same methods in the US and Hungary and this resulted in my 1969 ASR article with Litwak. Upon returning to Hungary I got involved in empirical research on urban (and eventually rural communities) and I became interested in the kind of inequalities bureaucracies create (as distinct from inequalities created by markets). After 1971 this put me on collision course with the Hungarian regime so in 1975 I had to leave Hungary and spent almost forty years abroad. (England, Australia, the United States, United Arab Emirates). I was in "exile" for seven years, but I got back my Hungarian passport in 1982 and I became an "outside" observer of the decline of socialism and the transition to post-communist capitalism. In 2014 I moved back to Hungary, so the past few years I have lived on my "research field" again. The papers in this book follow this "Gypsy trajectory".

The structure of this book is the following (it follows by and large the dates of publication, but not mechanically):

I. Towards a Critical Political Economy of State Socialism

- I.1 "Primary Group Structure And Their Functions" (1969)
- I.2 "Social Inequalities in State Socialist Redistributive Economies" (1978)

II. Social Structure of Socialist and Capitalist Societies

- II.1 "The Intelligentsia in the Class Structure of State Socialist Societies" (1982)
- II.2. "Circulation or Reproduction of Elites during Post-Communist Transformation" (1995)

III. Transition from Socialism to Capitalism

- III.1 "On Irony: An Invitation to Neoclassical Sociology" (2003)
- III.2. "The new Capitalism in Eastern Europe" (2005)

IV. Critical Theory of Post-Communism

- IV.1 "Weber's Theory of Domination and Post-Communist capitalism" (2016)
- IV.2 "Drifting from Liberal Democracy" (2015)
- IV.3. The Role of Rents in the Transition from Socialist Redistributive Economies to Market Capitalism (2017)
- IV.4. Karl Polanyi: a Theorist of mixed Economies (2020)

V. Revolt of the Masses and the Ukrainian Crisis

- V.1 Back to Max Weber: the concept of "Der Wille der Beherrschten"
- V.2 Sovereignty: Uses and abuses

Let me make a few brief comments on each of these papers, starting with the **first block, towards a critical political economy of state socialism.**

In 1963 the new Sociological Research Group attempted to develop a "research agenda" to gain legitimacy in communist Hungary. In Hungary, much like in Bulgaria during the early times of communism sociology was a bourgeois "pseudo-science", historical materialism was the sociology of Marxism. To gain such legitimacy we needed to develop empirical research. The director of the Sociological Research group hence assigned a "branch" of sociology to every researcher, I was designated to become the "urban sociologist". I just started to read urban sociology literature and it appeared to me that in this field the key question is who lives where. In the early 1960's one fashionable topic was "neighborhood", study of communities where people live. I was involved in an empirical pilot study, I developed a questionnaire on people's relationships to their neighbors. But I cast my agenda more broadly so I was trying to measure what functions various primary groups – neighbors, relatives, and friends perform in people's life. In December 1964 I met Eugene Litwak in Ann Arbor, at the University of Michigan and it turned out he was just analyzing data he collected in Detroit on the same subject.

I became especially intrigued by the general theory Litwak was working on. The central puzzle for him was why primary groups survive against bureaucracies (and in market economies) when their fall was predicted by theory. Weber defined bureaucracies as the rational organization, with rationalization it was reasonable to anticipate that the more "archaic" organization, such as primary groups will lose their functions. Litwak offered an intriguing theory. After all Weber is correct about bureaucracies being efficient, but only when they are confronted with standardized, routine task. But in idiosyncratic situations bureaucracies will not work efficiently and one will have to rely on primary groups to solve such problems. I decided to re-conceptualize my work along these lines and in 1966 – in collaboration with George Konrád – in new housing estates in Pécs and Debrecen and as soon as those data were collected we wrote **"Primary Group Structure and their Functions" (I.1)**, published in 1969 in American Sociological Review (ASR). This paper has many shortcomings, nevertheless I decided to start this volume with it. It was my "entry" into the international scene and fifty years after it publications I still get quite a few citations for this article.

So what is the paper and what are its shortcomings? The paper somewhat narrowly focuses on different functions of various primary groups but in retrospect I wish we would have framed in into Litwak's general theory. It is only implicit in the paper. Kin, neighbors, friends perform different function, but all of those function are nor routine, or standard. In light of my later work I should have asked which are those function not performed by bureaucracies in socialist Hungary and why those needs are not met by markets and bureaucracies in the United States. Relying on primary groups on bureaucratically (I will use later the term: redistributively) coordinated economies as much as market coordinated systems would have framed the study in light of "mirrored comparisons". With reference to state socialism the "informal economy", reliance on primary groups became a major tool to compensate for bureaucratic failures. In my work during the 1980's this became my primary focus and led to my book "Socialist entrepreneurs" (Polity Press, 1988). While the informal economy is not as important in market economies as it was in bureaucratically coordinated socialist economies informality was gaining more and more attention even in studies of market economies.

There is another shortcoming of this first paper. In Hungary we studied new housing estates, consisting with public housing. When we published the ASR article we have not analyzed the structural characteristics of these estates and public housing in general. We just assumed that in socialism free new public housing will go the poorer people (and we make a reference to this in the article), though this hypothesis turned out to be utterly wrong.

My early work (1967–68) with George Konrad focused on housing allocation in socialist countries. We just started to use main frame computers for data analysis and one day in Konrad's apartment we just looked out computer outputs. While we were not communists we just operated with the assumption the system that it is at least in some way the dictatorship of the proletariat. Anyway, we just looked at occupational and educational composition of people on these new housing estates (the available new housing in these countries), compared it with census data and we could not believe our eyes. The occupants of this free public housing tended to be systematically higher both in occupation and education than urban population in Hungary. Our first reaction was: there must be a coding error, "1" is not high status occupation, but low status occupation. So we asked our programmer to double check. It turned out the error is not in coding but in the socialist social/housing system. I believe in "Housing system and social structure" (in English published in 1972 and not included in this volume)) I finally got it right. I still use here the term "bureaucracy". I discovered Karl Polanyi's distinction between market and redistributive integration just around this time and eventually decided "redistributive coordination" is the more precise term that "bureaucratic coordination" (there is plenty of bureaucracy in market integrated economies as well). Interestingly this paper did not cause me any trouble yet, but the book which came out of the same research and was written in 1973 could not be published in Hungary yet and came out later in English as "Urban Inequalities under state socialist redistributive economies" by Oxford University Press (1983). This article was also putting Konrad and me on the "road to dissent" and culminated in our last joint book, "The intellectuals on the road to class power" (written in 1974 and published in English in 1979) and my eventual departure to Australian – via England – in 1975.

And now let me turn to the second paper in this volume, to **„Social Inequalities in State Socialist Redistributive Economies" (1978) (I.2)**, my first major publication in "exile". Already "The intellectuals on the road to class power" and Karl Polanyi's idea of socialism as a "redistributively coordinated economy" are our major point of reference. Applying redistribution to a modern economy was, – I believe – a major innovation. Polanyi used the term to "ancient empires" and mentions only in passing that Soviet type of economies may also be redistributive. So while to use of redistribution" to construct a political economy of state socialism is "polanyian" it is unusual. Redistribution is normally used as activities of social democratic states to re-allocate resources from rich to the poor so our concept was met with a great deal of skepticism. In Hungary by the mid-late 1980's people started to use the term in Western sociology there was not much reception. Hence the purpose of „Social inequalities in state socialist redistributive economies" was to clarify the difference between "welfare redistribution", and the idea of "redistributively coordinated" economic systems. I see this paper as one of my most important ones (though the journal it was published was not a "high impact" outlet). The bottom line: in redistributively coordinated economies (socialism) inequalities are created by redistribution and those who are underprivileged have to use the markets to get by. The opposite is true for "market integrated economies" where inequalities are produced by the market; redistribution is the mechanism to reduce those inequalities. It took a long time to get an attention to this new theory of inequality. Victor Nee's 1989 article in the American Sociological Review (ASR) was a breakthrough, he understood my theory. He cited my paper and ever since "redistributive economy" has been widely used to describe socialist economies and my article was and still is also cited. I am grateful to Victor.

When socialism was in decline I became interested why socialist failed. I wrote an article "Why socialism failed?" (1994, written with my son Balazs Szelényi, what I did not include into this volume). The received wisdom around 1989 was that socialism failed since "it did not work". While I was fully aware of the economic challenges socialist redistributive economies faced (especially the difficulties to make a transition from "extensive" growth to "intensive" growth), I believed that especially in the extensive growth stage socialist economies had important achievements. The USSR for instance during the 1930s created a heavy-military industry (the bloody price for this was of course unacceptable) without which it would have been impossible to defeat Hitler's Germany. For us "socialism failed", since "socialism did not work" was economic reductionism. It is "politics, it is not the economy you stupid" – is the bottom line of this paper. Sure, with our perspective "market socialism" is contradiction is terms, but whether "democratic socialism" would be conceivable? In this paper we do not advocate "democratic socialism" we just ask in the socratarian way: what if socialism would have tried democratic reform instead of market reforms (or at least complementing it with political reform)? When we think about China today this question may be quite relevant. The Chinese economy (some call it socialist, whether it is can be debated) seem to be working fine, but will it be sustainable without democratic political reforms?

I can move now on the **second block of papers on social structure of capitalist and societies.** The "Intellectuals on the road to class power" after my "exile" was smuggled out of Hungary and published in English in 1979. It was well received both in the US and Germany, but I was not sure it was properly understood. The book was written in clandestine conditions without proper academic debate. The sources were also not properly cited, it was indeed an early example of "samizdat publications"[2]. My purpose in **"The Intelligentsia in the Class Structure of State Socialist Societies" (1982) (II.1)** was to clarify what the book tried to do and how it is linked to sociological scholarship.

The critical initiating question is: how is our analysis with Konrad related to Djilas "new class" theory? While teaching in Australia and in the US I learned from students they appreciate our book more when they see in what way and why it differs from Djilas. The book does not negates, it complements Djilas. In the paper the key proposal is that we offer two modification to Djilas new class theory. The first one: while we agree that during Stalinist times the bureaucracy was in total "command" but he uses the term "class" in a "cavalierish" way. Following Marx and Weber we believed class is economically constituted, while the roots of bureaucratic domination is rooted in politics. Hence is Stalinist times, yes the bureaucracy rules, but not as a class, but rather as an estate. Our second amendment to Djilas is that the rule of bureaucratic estate was eroded with the failure of Stalinism. Stalinism was Charismatic authority but as the Charismatic leader passed away the bureaucracy needed a new legitimacy. This legitimacy was "scientific socialism", a social order based on reason respectively on science. Given the le-

2 Term for non-conforming literature or scientific texts that were nevertheless distributed.

gitimation problems the bureaucracy needed allies and since the new emphasis was on science and was logical to try to open up to the intellectuals/professionals. This was the main trend during the 1960 even in the USSR, but more so in the satellite countries, Poland, Czechoslovakia, Hungary and I think also in Bulgaria. Radovan Richta's book "Scientific and technological revolution" (1967) was the Bible of state socialist intellectual reformers, and it paved the road to the Prague Spring. Actually Richta coined the term "socialism with a human face" as well. He eventually abandoned the Prague Spring, and made a compromise with the regime after Warsaw pact invasion of Czechoslovakia, became even the director of the Institute of Philosophy in 1969 in Prague. But the received wisdom during the 1960's was in Hungary – and I assume in many other socialist countries: "socialism is a good idea, the only problem that the right people are not on the right places". Hence the invitation by the bureaucracy to intellectuals to share power was welcome by many intellectuals.

In this paper I had to clarify what we did mean by intellectuals becoming a "new class"? Where the process of such a class- formation stood was not defined with enough clarity in the book, so I tried to correct this in the article: intellectuals were a new dominant class only in "statu nascendi", they were only flirting with the idea to become co-rulers with the bureaucracy, but by 1982 we all know this did not happen.

In what way would it be conceivable to think even with this qualification of intellectuals as a new class? In this paper I tried to make as accessible our very complex argument. Intellectuals are actors who claim power and privilege on the grounds of their monopoly of "trans-contextual orienting knowledge". The stated aim of economic reforms was to replace in the bureaucratic economic voluntarism with a system of "rational redistribution", scientific planning, where those with knowledge monopolies, the "teleological redistributors" would play a central role. We have been and we are still criticized for the term "rational redistribution", our critiques claim socialist redistribution was "irrational". There are two reasons for calling the project of economic reforms of the 1960's "rational". 1/ it was the Stalinist voluntarist economy which was "irrational", but the aim of reform was to make the management of the economy scientific and (in this sense) rational; 2/ we needed to clarify in what way we use the term "redistribution" differently from Polanyi. In "ancient empires" according to Polanyi the economy was coordinated by redistribution but this was legitimated by tradition.

Under reform communism the plan was too legitimated by the right of redistributors to dispose with surplus with reference to their science based (hence rational) teleological knowledge.

Let me just add one last point: neither in our book, nor in this paper advocated we that good society is only one which is "run" by intellectuals (to pout it with Plato: philosopher kings). Not at all. The book and the article is a radical critic (and in a way an auto-critic) of intellectuals. Our analysis is very similar to Foucault and his concept of knowledge/power. Knowledge is never innocent, knowledge monopolists always have aspiration for power, to tell those who are defined by them the "knowledge-poor" what they **should** do.

As Hegel put it: "the owl of Minerva spreads its wings only with the falling of the dusk". This is certainly true for our book on intellectuals and for Gouldner's book on the new class. The empirical "project" both books reflect on took place mainly in the 1960's, by the time the books were published the project were in serious trouble or even defeated. The story of state socialism and early communism is complicated. Intellectuals certainly abandoned their aspirations – if they ever had such aspiration – to rationalize socialism. They did play a critical role in bringing socialism down. Well, during the early years of post-communism in many countries, especially in Poland, the Czech Republic and Hungary intellectuals – writers, historians, sociologists, economists – occupied key power positions, but not as "rational redistributors", but as "liberals". They certainly never established themselves as a "class" but for a while they were key component of the rising new elite.

In 1988–1900" I was a keen observer of transition from socialism to market capitalism. I wrote the paper "**Circulation or Reproduction of Elites during Post-Communist Transformation**" **(1995) (II.2)** with my daughter Szonja Szelényi. It formulated the central hypotheses of the research project we carried out with Donald Treiman. This was a large international survey (Social stratification after 1989 in Eastern Europe) in several post-communist countries. Once data were collected I analyzed those with my graduate students at UCLA, Gil Eyal and Eleanor Townsley and we co-authored a book ("Making capitalism without capitalists") in 1998.

"Circulation or reproduction of elites during post-communist transformation," was mainly inspired by Pierre Bourdieu. Its key puzzle: what happens if you have a dramatic change in social structure? When – to put it with Bourdieu – there are substantially new "dispositions". Who will end up on the top of social hierarchies? Can those who were on the top in the old system end up on the top of the new system, though the habitus which was required to climb up in the old regime is sharply different from the habitus needed now to be in the elite. Following Pareto we posed this question sharply by asking: can we observe a circulation of elites, will new actors with new habitus constitute the elite, or does the old elite reproduce itself by modifying to some extent their old habitus to fit the new conditions. Will those who were the big communists became now the big capitalists? In 1988–90 the dominant view was one the "nomeklatura bourgeoisie". It was anticipated by scholars like Hankiss, Staniszkis or Szalai that the nomenklatura, or at least their technocratic fraction will be the key winners. We accepted this as a good hypothesis but we posed the alternative hypothesis: what if new agents will capture the new positions of power? We called for a theoretically informed empirical investigation to test which of these hypotheses will get more support from data. To be immodest, this turned out as a sort of agenda setter, for years to come post-communist social research was flooded with elite studies, mainly testing whether the old elite was reproducing itself, or is there a major recruiting of new agents into elite positions.

In 1992 we carried out I suppose the first and broadest empirical study on this topic. We identified in several post-communist countries those who were in elite positions in 1988 where were they in 1992 and where people in similar position in 1992 came from. We knew this is very early in the game (especially in Russia), but we hoped eventually we can replicate the study and test how it unfolds. This was an expensive project and with the disintegration of the Soviet system interest in Eastern European affairs declined among agencies which previously funded social sciences so the study was never replicated. In our book "Making capitalism without capitalists" (1998) we offered an answer empirical sociology usually does: the glass is half full and half empty. In some countries, like Russia or Bulgaria the reproduction of elites was dominant, in Poland or Hungary we documented a substantial circulation of elites.

By the end of the second decade of the 21st century the old communist guard who was in power in 1988 with few exception either retired are died. Hence reproduction of the "old elite" became irrelevant. Nevertheless this was replaced by a new question can the new elite pass their privileges on the next generation? In the most recent American literature, like Robert D. Putnam, "Our kids" (2015) and Richard V. Reeves "Dream Hoarders" (2017) the claim is made that a deepening gap is created between the upper middle class (the top 20 percent) on the basis of wealth, income and education and the remaining 80 percent. On my most recent book with Péter Mihályi, "Rent seekers, the top 20 percent" (Palgrave-MacMillan, 2019) we review this literature and in one chapter we pose the question if in advanced post-communist societies a similar reproduction of the privileged elite observable, if so where is the critical dividing line, the top 10 or the top 20 percent..

In the third block of this collection of essays I included two papers on "Transition from socialism to capitalism". The first paper in the block in is **"On Irony" (2003) (III.1)** was co-authored by Gil Eyal and Eleanor Townsley. This paper is a follow up with our exchange with my good friend Michael Burawoy. Michael published an excellent criticism on my "Making capitalism without capitalists" and it was a thoughtful criticism of the "varieties of capitalism" (VoC) paradigm – a paradigm we were and I am still deeply committed to. Michael as a committed Marxist (in the gramscian mode) is of course opposed to the VoC paradigm. There is ONE capitalism and VoC does not appreciate the fundamental logic of capitalism. According to Burawoy to see post- communism just as one version of capitalism is theoretically and politically misleading. His review was published in American Journal of Sociology (AJS) and the journal gave us a chance to respond. This was the greatest opportunity to promote the book, Michael is one of the leading sociologists in the world and to get his attention is valuable.

We greatly appreciated Burawoy's criticism, but we believed he is still working with a "utopian" notion of socialism (hence the opposite what we called "immanent critique" of a system). In AJS we did not have room to respond in substance. Nevertheless Burawoy's criticism raised a major methodological problem, one I have been struggling with all my life. Can one offer a critical theory of capitalism, if socialism as a realistic alternative is not on the agenda any more (at least for the time being)? In order to offer a critical theory of (various versions) of capitalism do I need an ideal concept of socialism, as a critical vintage point? This led me inevitably to the method of irony and Socrates (Foucault?).

As far as we can tell from the accounts of Plato Socrates mainly asked questions and tried to encourage doubt in his students (audience). Socrates did not have to have "solutions", his aim was to make his audience aware that there are other (several different) solutions to the question they are thinking about. It was not implied implication that those "other solutions" are better, they are just different and the audience had to decide which from the alternative solution is more appealing to them. This appeared to me (and my co-authors) as a wonderful way to proceed in post-socialist world with the critique of actually existing capitalisms. This was as different from Burawoy's belief in the "mission" of social scientists. So we are back at Weber: our task is not to tell people what they ought to do, but to alert them what they could do and what the prices are of their various courses of action. In fact Burawoy's more recent work on "public sociology" may not that different from our view. If public sociology merely implies that we make the public more aware what alternative strategies at what costs they can pursue. We enthusiastically support "public sociology" if interpreted this way.

Being familiar with Burawoy's oeuvre I suspect with his enlightenment project he wants to promote the "right solution", namely "genuine socialism" and this is where "ironic method" and "public sociology" diverge.

We published this piece in "Thesis eleven", an Australian journal stared in the 1970's. I love Marx's Feuerbach theses, except thesis eleven. Thesis eleven suggests philosophers so far interpreted the world, now the task is to change it. In my view this is the original sin of Marxism-Leninism and Bolshevism (and in post-communism of liberal intellectuals who now believed their task is to tell society how they ought to reconstruct the society and economy). Post-communist liberal intellectuals loved irony as it implied to be ironic about your opponents. Hence you could be ironic about "communists", but there is no room to be ironic about "liberal capitalism". The irony we suggested in this article – as we did in "Intellectuals on the road to class power" – is also "self-irony". Capitalism itself takes various forms, there is not one what we can recommend as the right form. We should leave it to the democratic political process to make choices between alternatives (this may even be socialism, though this does not seem to be on "the table" for the time being). Hence I am very close to Habermas (the need for domination free discourse) I am just skeptical about this like Foucault and Gouldner was: given the intimate link between knowledge/power it is doubtful whether domination free discourse possible at all. Probably not, but it is a noble goal to aim at.

But what is post-communist capitalism? With Larry King we tried to find an answer to this question in **„The new Capitalism in Eastern Europe" (2005) (III.2)** With Larry and Kathy Beckett we already published an article on the political economy of socialism for the first volume of the Smelser-Swedberg edited "Handbook of Economic Sociology" (1994). Second volume we were asked to write a paper on post-communism. This paper is still primarily about the various pathways of "transition" from socialism to capitalism. We identify three distinct pathways from communism to capitalism: capitalism from below, capitalism from above, capitalism from outside. I believe this was not a bad analysis of the dilemma early post- communism faced.

I have been a great admirer of Deng Xiao Ping and his strategy to reform the Chinese economy. Back in 2005 I called it still "capitalism from below" though the Chinese transition started to change trajectory by the late 1990's. Nevertheless, arguably during the first decade of Chinese reform, 1968–1978, China was close to Janos Kádár's goulash communism. The collectives were not dissolved, large corporation were not privatized but space for private initiatives was opened up. This worked miracles. The "economics of shortage" – just like after 1963 in Hungary disappeared almost over-night and without privatization the "family responsibility system" transformed agrarian economy, reduced poverty and created relative well-being in the country-side. Inequality between cities and the countryside was reduced. I interpreted 1979 as a revolution of urban population against the reforms they did not benefit much or at all. This first decade of reform in China could be hardly be called "capitalism", it was not like "socialism with Chinese characteristics", or was a socialist "mixed economy". After 1979 there was an intense struggle between reformers and anti-reformist fraction. After all reformers won, but they shifted their attention to the urban economy. The critical turning point took place during the late 1990's when "privatization" of state owned corporations became a priority.

We will do not know enough to tell whether indeed turned the Chinese economy "capitalist". Many of my esteemed colleagues, like Janos Kornai and Victor Nee believes yes (though Kornai having seen the way President Xi rules, changed recently his mind), I still have my doubts. In 2009 I presented a paper at a UNO-Wider conference in Helsinki "The new grand bourgeoisie under post-communism – Central Europe, Russia and China compared" which was only published as a working paper of UNO-Wider. I carefully analyzed data on the "top 10" lists (a few years earlier) and it turned out than many of the Chinese new dollar billionaires started with humble social origins. There were many of them, who were "self-made men", originally farmers or bricklayers who made their fortune by exploiting the opportunities of the "second economy". The East European and Russian story was strikingly different, many of the billionaires were coming from former managers or party cadres. This is again the story of the "owl of Minerva". While my data were rock solid my Chinese colleagues were aware what has been going on during the end of the first decade of the 21st century. They were mainly now talking about the "princelings", the children of high cadres who now became managers of large corporations. Whether these large corporations are really capitalist or not we still do not know. My friend Victor Nee – and he knows so much more about China than I do – believed the transformation of Chinese economy to capitalism did take place, but there are certainly counteracting tendencies. Especially under President Xi state control of the economy is increasing rather than declining so one can still debate, whether China today is "state capitalism", a "hybrid economy" or "socialism with Chinese characteristics". But certainly, China is not any more "capitalism from below" as I described it during the first decade of Deng Hsiao Ping's reforms.

We called the second pathway "capitalism from above" and we suggested post-Soviet Russia is the prime example for such a change.

It implied that high officials conducted privatization for their own benefits, or at least offered advantages in the privatization process to their clients. Russia under Yeltsin was a prime example, but in many ways Putin did stay on track in this respect. There were similar tendencies in many other countries, the Ukraine, Byelorussia, the central Asian republics and to some extent in Romania and Bulgaria. In the final block of papers, I will qualify this, identify the new features of Putinism and its extraordinary impact not only in Eastern Europe, but in many other European countries.

Yeltsin announced he will create capitalism in Russia in 500 days… it was of course madness and assumed the Chicago school most naïve assumptions. Once you change property relations everything else will fall in place and it even does not mean who the owners will be. If the "wrong" people (for instance former communists) become the news owners do not worry: the market will correct it and eventually proper entrepreneurs will gain property right. To make this worse it did not matter at what price public property is sold, the aim is to get rid of public property and this was legitimated with a quasi "socialist" ideology". We do not want a few millionaires, but we want millions of owners. The mechanism to achieve this was vouchers. The public property will be distributed among all citizens in equal shares as vouchers so it will be a kind of Proudonian socialism. This of course was rubbish. Voucher holders of course did not know what to do with vouchers, but many became unemployed, with hungry families and desperate need of cash so they sold their vouchers for trivial price to speculators, who had some initial investment fund, information and networks and in no time they became billionaires. This is the genesis of "oligarchy", the rule by new rich. Some call it crony capitalism, corruption. I was always careful to use these value loaded terms.

Once you decide you want to transform an economy from state socialism into market capitalism and once you believe the right way to do is to convert property rights from public to private in 500 days – or let's say in 5 years – you do not have too many options. You will have to "appoint" the new grand bourgeoisie and of course they will be either members of your staff or at least people you trust.

Let me qualify: there was a third pathway and this is what we called "capitalism from the outside". During the 1990's the classical example was Hungary where there was a massive inflow in FDI[3]. During the early 1990's Hungary had the highest per capita FDI. This sounded reasonable, foreign investors unlike domestic "entrepreneurs" did have capital to invest, hence one could hope that public good will sell on its price. Not quite and for a number of reason. First of all, foreign investors of course wanted to purchase the most valuable property. While half of the state owned sector in 1988 in Hungary produced some gains, the other half produced losses. Profit making firms of course were more attractive the rational foreign investors. In addition it was hard to tell, which firm is profitable and which is not. Only management knew the real value of the firms, hence prospective buyers had to rely on "socialist" managers to decide what to buy and what not to buy, and this created a sort of clientelism, now not between the state and its staff, or loyal followers, but the foreign investors and management. A third problem with this pathway was that investors occasionally purchased markets. State socialism economically was not an unmitigated disaster. Sure, it did not produce goods which were competitive with the better quality products of capitalist economy, but it had a market with probably lower quality, but still useful and reasonably inexpensive good. Hungary certainly had a market for instance on North Africa for refrigerators,

3 FDI = foreign direct investment = Ausländische Direktinvestitionen (ADI).

buses, trucks etc. (And of course there was a large COMECON market…). It made a lot of sense for multinational or at least large Western firms to buy such companies up, shut them down but capture their markets.

There was of course some concern that excessive FDI (German capital was especially important in early stages of privatization in Hungary) may create "dependency" as world system theory might have predicted it. One I discussed this with Petar-Emile Mitev, especially since Bulgaria initially was solidly on the "second pathway" and was not attractive to FDI. Petar-Emile assured me: "Don't you worry, once Germany bought Hungary up, they will start investing into Bulgaria." And indeed after 2000 Hungary started to fall behind in per capita FDI, Slovakia sky-rocketed.

And now I can turn to the last, **fourth block of papers** the **"Critical Theory of Post-Communism"**. These are all article I wrote after my return to Hungary and my concern is that they may report on "consolidated post-communist capitalism." When I am writing this Introduction, the late fall of 2020 I see former communist countries – Russia and Hungary in particular, and of course the Ukraine and Byelorussia – but in many ways also Poland, Slovakia, the Czech Republic, Romania, Bulgaria, Macedonia and many more – consolidated into an "illiberal regime" which for the time being shows great strength to keep reproducing itself.

In my paper – not included is volume "Capitalisms after communisms" (2015) – there are two important new contributions. First I suggest to use the logic of "varieties of capitalism" to communism itself. Hence in the title I use the terms communism in plural. This is of some importance certainly in Hungary, but probably in most post-communist countries. Since anti-communism is a common feature of both "liberal" and "national radical" wings of post-communist political regimes they tend to use the term "communism" as if it were a unified system so they all have to accept the blame for "gulag", Stalinism and "great leap forward" or "cultural revolution". Analytically – and politically – it is vitally important to see the rather extraordinary diversity what "communism" was. It varied from the "new economic policy" of the 1920's to Stalinist collectivization and show trials. Mao's early flirt with the Soviet model and later intriguing, in many ways anarchist searches for a Chinese version, the Stalinist epoch after WWII in Eastern Europe which turned into reform communism a la Gomulka, Nagy, after 1963 Kádár, Todor Zhivkov from the early, mid 1960's (who intriguingly after the fall of communism claimed he was never communist), during the first years of 1960's Gheorgiu-Dej and ironically for a while even Nicolae Ceausescu (until he tuned into a neo-Stalinist), the Prague Spring's "socialism with a human face" (and of course most importantly post Mao China) these all represented different versions of communism. It is vitally important to understand these differences to appreciate the "nostalgia" for state socialism (there is such a nostalgia surprisingly even in Romania after Ceausescu). The point is: the 1960's-1980's communist regimes experimented with paternalism, some degree of market reform even some democracy and most were not "Stalinist dictatorships".

The second innovation of the paper is the idea of "re-convergence". The paper offers a short summary of various pathways out of socialism, but the novel feature of the paper is to spot the significance of the turn Putin represented after the year 2000. Yeltsin's "capitalism from above" by the end of the 1990's was culminating in a disaster. The new grand bourgeoisie Yeltsin (and his beloved daughter Tatyana) as the "godfather (godmother?) of the Kremlin" appointed had political ambitions and began the "privatize the state itself", they turned into "oligarchs" from a "grand bourgeoisie". That was unacceptable for Putin, he did not want big money to tell him what to do, he wanted to recreate "order", not as a new Stalin, but as a new "tsar".

Putin is undoubtedly the greatest political genius of post communism. As he was elected as president of Russia he put all the oligarchs to loyalty test. Those who passed the test could carry on, those who failed were either sent to Siberia or to exile. He did break the power of oligarchs, political power was restored to the "tsar" and only those were allowed to keep their newly acquired wealth who gave up independent political ambition. This "reform" had long traditions in Russia in its way to feudalism to modernity. Ivan Terrible and Peter the Great are in some ways the predecessors of Putin much more so than Lenin or Stalin. Both Ivan the Terrible and Peter the Great created an effective executive power, by breaking the power of the boyars and replacing them with pomeshchiks. The boyars – much like the nobility and aristocracy in Western Europe – had substantial political power independent from the tsar. The property they owned were theirs (together with substantial political influence) and were inherited by their children.

Peter the Great replaced them with a "service nobility". Now property rights were granted depending on their loyal service to the tsar. Putin re-invented this system for post-communism, only those were allowed to retain the wealth their received from the "godfather" who delivered reliable services. Using Weber's terminology already in this paper I called this a shift from patrimonialism to prebendalism, the next article in this collection elaborates on these distinctions. New Left Review published this article right after submission, but intriguingly I am quite certain Perry Anderson –the editorial force behind New Left Review – who knows so much about Russian and East European history – added the term "prebendalism" to the title of the essay. I was happy to accept this change.

The first article in this block in this volume – **"Weber's Theory of Domination and Post-Communist Capitalism" (2016) (IV.1)** – is a somewhat complicated – arguably overcomplicated – interpretation of Weber's theory of legitimacy with particular attention to "traditional authority". The originating question is whether postcommunist regimes, like one by Putin or Orbán can be regarded as "legitimate" at all. Liberal or left-wing critiques of such regimes occasionally argue they are "illegitimate". The paper begins with a review of Weber's theory of legitimacy and arrives at a conclusion which may not be controversial among Weber scholars. Weber as an "interpretative sociologist" was slow in making value judgement. His project was not to classify regimes as "legitimate" or "illegitimate", but to understand, which are those "myths" upon which powerholders tried to justify their legitimacy. The terms as "illegitimate" or "non-legitimate" exists in Weber's vocabulary, but they are "extreme" cases. In my reading Weber would call a system illegitimate only if they have to use excessive and continuous coercive power to obtain obedience. Such would be Stalinism in the 1930's or the later years of Hitler's rule. In the paper I try to show that socialism, except Stalinist and Maoist extreme epochs did achieve some legitimacy. Some communist leaders were accepted as "charismatic" (Lenin for instance in the early years, especially Fidel Castro), others were seen (like Kádár) were "paternalistic" leaders.

This is almost trivial for Weber scholars so is mainly my account of Weber's typology of domination. Though here the paper aims to make a new contribution. In the new critical edition of Weber's collected works I found an article from 1917 in an Austrian newspaper which reported on his lecture that fall in Vienna. Much to the astonishment of those of us who taught Weber's "three types of legitimate authority" Weber in this lecture told the audience that there is a fourth type of authority: one by "Wille der Beherrschten" (by the will who of subjected to authority).[4] This is the most intriguing, since Weber did not seem to have a proper theory of democracy.

Legal-rational authority sounds the most like "liberal democracy", but it is not since the laws/rules which apply to all equally are established either by consent or by imposition. The question WHO the sovereign is put in the side. In my reading "Wille der Beherrschten" refers to majoritarian approval, but given Weber's views as a "liberal in despair" it is not the will of "free individuals", everyone is under some system of domination. Weber's somewhat ironic view about "democracy" as another system of domination rather than the real of freedom is important for the last paper in this block, on the emotionally discussed question whether an "illiberal democracy is possible at all". While I found the idea of "Wille der Beherrschten" original and fascinating it is equally puzzling while Weber in the spring of 1920 when he was re-writing the section of legitimacy "forgets" about the fourth type of authority. Is it in any way linked to his great disappointment with the outcomes of the Russian revolution or his skepticism about the emergent Weimar republic? I have no answer to this question.

This paper however intended to make an original contribution to Weber's description of traditional authority. Weber uses the terms patrimonialism and prebendalism often in his writings, but the definition of concepts changes. With due immodesty I tried to "get Weber right". I offered a definition in which patrimonialism refers to the system where the subjects receive property and authority from the "master", which as lasting power, property and often authority as well can be inherited. Prebendalism on the other hand refers to "service nobility", property and authority is given to subjects by the masters on condition of loyalty. If the master is dissatisfied with their services their property authority (or even their life) can be taken away from them. The most extreme case of prebendalism is sultanism, but I use the patrimonial/prebendal distinction for different

4 Weber used his concept as ideal types and therefore he changed definitions as he was faced with new empirical evidence. At the end of his life, in Volume I, Chapter 1–4 in Economy and Society, he made an effort to offer a coherent terminology, with partial success. This is true for his use of "will of the ruled". I was reminded by reviewers that Weber used his term already in his "Anti-authoritarian reinterpretation of charisma". This missed my attention – and I apologize for this – and also the attention of the editors of Weber's critical edition. But in his 1917 Vienna lecture the use of the term as the "fourth type of authority" is strikingly novel and basically contradict his earlier use as a subtype of charismatic authority. I am grateful for my reviewers to bring this earlier formulation to my attention, but my interpretation is novel and tried to clarify some of the contradictions is Weber's terminology.

stages of post-communism as well. Yeltsin's Russia was a patrimonial system, Putin invented post-communist prebendalism.

Well, there were some patrimonial elements in all types of post- communism, but some were rather close to legal-rational order/and democracy with only some elements of patrimonialism. And here we are back again on re-convergence. After initial flirts with liberal capitalism many post-communist countries are on their way to Putinism, I call the system of Viktor Orbán for instance Putin-light.

And now it is time to rap this up with a few comments on a follow up article on **"Drifting from Liberal Democracy" (2015) (IV.2)** (co-authored with my former NYUD student Tamás Csillag). In early summer of 2014 Viktor Orbán who is almost as capable as a politician as Vladimir Putin, but much more sophisticated as a theorist gave an incredible, agenda setting talk about his plans to build "illiberal democracy". The term "illiberal democracy" has been used in political science since the mid 1990's, but mainly with pejorative overtones, mainly on African authoritarian regimes. It implied a system without the "proper" rule of law[5], which nevertheless holds elections and makes at least the appearance of majority approval. Orbán turned this obscure poli-sci term[6] into an integral part of public discourse about regimes. Every other day you can read about "illiberalism", Orbán is often mentioned as his preeminent figure but next to Putin, Erdogan and recently Donald Trump. Orbán turned "illiberalism" from an obscure, pejorative political science term onto a political project, which is spreading like wild-fire in Europe, but even in the United States and elsewhere in the world.

The criticism of social scientists and politicians from the left were focusing their attention of the question whether democracy is possible in an illiberal regime. This is a legitimate question, but missing the key point in the Putin-Orbán project, namely "illiberalism". Orbán's criticism in his 2014 speech of liberalism was that it over-emphasizes individual freedom and interest and does not see the national interest, or to put it more broadly the "public good". (Since 2014 this public good increasingly became national, and in particular ethno-national interest driven by the 2015 refugee crisis, skillfully used by radical ethno-nationalists, like Orbán for their political purposes). This is a real dilemma (like migration is also a real dilemma). We agree there is such a thing as "public good", which is more than the sum total of individual wills. And this is indeed the weakness of liberalism. The big problem with illiberalism is: who knows what this public good is? Did you get a letter, from whom, so you can speak in the name of the public? Those who get the majority vote? Well, since Tocqueville and J. S. Mill we have enough reason to be concerned about the despotism of the majority… Especially in electoral system, where only 60–70% of electorate turn out to vote…[7]

5 When a system is rule of law is debated by illiberals. Liberals see rule of law as a system which is long lasting, changes in legal system are slow and difficult. Illiberal regimes changes laws simply by majorities if the legislature and the authority of constitutional courts to decide the constitutionality of laws is greatly reduced.

6 This is a common abbreviation for "illiberal democracy".

7 In some countries parties which do not get 3–5% of the votes at elections do not get any seats on the legislature and their seats often is added to the votes of the parties which won the election. In

Csillag started to write his senior thesis under my supervision in NYUAD. He wanted to write a thesis about the undemocratic nature of the Orbán regime. I warned him, it will be difficult, Orbán just won two third majority at election using the same rules as used by other elections since 1990. So I advised him to read Montesquieu.

Montesquieu makes a critical distinction between the manner people rule and how they were selected in to decision making positions. In my reading the manner to rule refers to liberalism/illiberalism, the way how people get into position of power has a lot to do with democracy (Wille der Beherrschten). I will accept every system where people in power have a majority approval (let qualify: majority of those who qualify under certain time and conditions have the right to express their will). Manner of rule means something quite different. Moderate rule assumes division of powers, it means control over the executive by other branches of the government. Even the idea of illiberalism is not evil as such. The important argument for an illiberal regime is the efficiency of the executive branch. As we have seen for instance during the last years of the Obama administration the actions of the executive branch was blocked time and again by the house or mainly the senate which during his second term was under the control of the opposition. Obama on some occasion used "executive orders". Hence he bypassed the "elective branch" in some very important issues (where Obama had my political sympathies, such as the deal with Iran and so called Obamacare) but he set a precedent this way to Trump. Hence the ability of the executive to act with political decision in the legislature and even more frustration with the "legalism" of the judiciary is frustrating, but that is the foundation of the "moderate" rule by the executive.

Especially in major crisis, like the 2015 refugee influx the executive does not want to be incapacitated by "silly", "word stewing" judiciary, but wants to be act in what the executive perceived as the "national interest". This is especially appealing in post-communist countries, where the citizenship is historically accustomed to "strong leadership" and wants stability and action and not legalistic is political deadlock. Nevertheless, deadlock imposed by the legislature and the judiciary on the executive power is often resented on it leads to illiberalism".

In this last paper we do not confront the issue, which is has been so central in the discourse since the Orbán speech: is this democracy or a democratic regime can only operate under a liberal separation of powers. Following Montesquieu we use a "minimalist" conception of "democracy". Democracy has little to do with the manner of government, but it defines the way how the "ruler" is selected. The system in which the properly qualified individual's majority select the "ruler" is "democratic". You may only allow "free men" to make such a decision like in Ancient Greece or 18th century US (slaves, women, who do not hold property may not qualify), but we still regard the systems as democratic. An ideal type of democracy does assume something like "domination free discourse" or to put it more simply "free press". But we know it does not exist. Of course even in my "ideal" democracy", the US major media outlets are under the control of

---

Hungary for instance just with 35% of votes a party may gain two third majority in parliament – hence they can change any.

big money and elections are driven by donation by major corporations. Arguably if big money does it rather than the government it is still preferable to political/government control, but let's not fool ourselves it is still "Wille der Beherrschten", it is not by the will of the "free individuals".

We do note nevertheless that the drift away from "liberal democracy" is dangerous and it may lead to autocracy or worse. While liberalism is not a precondition of democratic rule, but with Montesquieu we tend to believe that good governance is liberal democracy.

As a post-script to this paper we also have to acknowledge that Viktor Orbán is his 2014 and again in his 2018 speech, both delivered in Tusnádfürdő/Baile Tusnad in Romanian Transylvania spotted an important international trend. The most important event in this respect was the election of Donald Trump as president of the US. Put America first and his violent anti-migration campaign makes him the soul brother of Viktor Orbán (and Netanyahu with his new law which makes Israel the "state of Jews", hence an ethno religiously constituted state and NOT a community of citizens irrespective of their ethnic background or religious beliefs). Not only Hungary (Bulgaria, Poland, Russia etc.), or post-communist countries, but the whole world seems to be at a critical turning point: do we remain civil (to the extent we ever were) or are we returning to be ethnic. Orbán might not a bad forecaster in predicting the raise of illiberalism as we have seen recently in election in Austria and Italy and the rise of AfD in Germany and the "ethno-nationalist radicals" even the Netherland, Denmark or Sweden. Nevertheless the illiberal turn just did not happen – so far. A new epoch may be in the making. The struggle between liberalism and illiberalism, bilateralism or multilateralism, European United States, or the EU as a loose confederation of nations states continues, and who the winner will be is unpredictable.

Let me add to this volume two more recent papers, "**The Role of Rent in the Transition from Socialist Redistributive Economy to Market Capitalism" (2017), (IV.3)"** and **"Karl Polanyi: a Theorist of mixed Economy" (2020) (IV.4**) both co-authored with Péter Mihályi).

"The role of rent in the transition from socialist redistributive economy to market capitalism" takes a paper published on 2000 by Aage Sorensen as its point of departure. Adam Smith identified profits, rents and wages as the three sources of wealth. While Marx believed new wealth can be created only by labour he also emphasized that rent is only another form of profit. David Ricardo in sharp contrast with Smith claimed rent is not the source but only the symptom of wealth. The owner of land – by all three classical theorists – rent was understood as income coming from land ownership- and Ricardo pointed out, that landowners unlike owners of capital were not involved in the process of production, their income merely stemmed from the monopolistic ownership of land. Sorensen now generalized the concept of rent and defined it as "unearned income" and its sole source is limitation of competition.

With Péter Mihályi we also define "rent "as "unearned income", its source is limitation or absence of market competition. We distinguish two major forms of rents, "exploitation rent" (this term is also used by Stiglitz) and "solidarity rent" (this our addition to the theory of rent). Exploitation rent may be derived from economic sources or it can be the result of governmental restrictions of competition. Monopolies, oligopolies and cartel also generate exploitation rent since it makes impossible or at least very difficult to other owners of capital to enter competition (there is an "excessive accumulation" of capital at the hands of monopolists and those with less capital cannot compete. Monopolists can set the prices of their products and services higher than their efforts and this was collect "unearned incomes". Under liberal democracies governments are supposed to restrict the making of such monopolies. As the US government did when interrupted (or at least limited) the monopoly of John Rockefeller. By 1882 Rockefeller created the gigantic Standard Oil, which controlled about 90 percent of US oil industry. In 1980 the federal government passed to the called "Sherman anti- trust law" and in 1909 the fed sued Standard oil and forced it to break up into 34 companies and created at least some competition among them.

But government intervention into the operation of markets also occurs in capitalist economies. Nation states intervene in. A classic example was mercantilism, which aimed to maximize exports and minimize imports order to defend national capital from foreign competition (the dominant economic theory before Adam Smith), but its contemporary version – like Donald Trump's "make America great again" – are very much alive. Political elites can also interfere in favor of their clients in exchange for "kick-backs", this what we usually call "corruption".

Sorensen also calls all "unearned incomes", such as unemployment benefits, welfare payments etc. "rent". With Mihályi we make a critical distinction between "exploitation rents" and "solidarity rents". Exploitation rents are incomes collected by owners of productive assets (capital, land are prime examples) which are incomes higher than owners would collect without economic monopoly or without governmental intervention on their behalf. Solidarity rents are paid to those who do not earn incomes on the market what is regarded as "sufficient" in a "civilized" society. In liberal democracies solidarity incomes are defined though a democratic political process.

All capitalist societies do have actors who are rent-seekers. Even exploitation rents can serve important social or economic purposes. A good example is human capital. Supply of medical doctors is usually limited by governmental regulations in order to secure quality of medical services, but it typically provides rent to doctors, hence incomes which are higher than their incomes were in conditions where the supply of doctors would not be regulated (for instance everyone would be allowed to practice medicine). Copy right also generates rental income, but it usually is important to motivate innovation. Rent seeking on the other hand can become destructive when it replaces market defined profits and wages. If a society becomes rent seeking it led on many occasions to state failure, undermined economic efficiency and created social disturbances against earners who are seen as earning high unearned incomes. This can be the case even in solidarity rent. If a political system defines solidarity rents at such a level what taxpayers find excessive, may lead to capital flight or outmigration of highly skilled and heavily taxed labor.

Our paper deals with rent seeking behavior in the transition from socialist redistributive economies to market capitalism. In such situation rent seeking, mainly government induced rents to the new owners of capital or land tends to be widespread. After the fall of communism the neo-liberal economic doctrine tended to emphasize that the first and most important task is to fine "identifiable" (private) owners to previously publicly owned property. In principle privatization happened through competitive auctions. But there was not sufficient capital accumulation (or even reliable credit rating) during socialism hence competition at auctions could not be free and fair. Personal recognition and connections inevitably played a role for the privatizing agency decide who the winner of the auction will be.

In a way the political elites "appointed" the new bourgeoisie (occasionally having been rewarded by kick-backs – this is what Bálint Magyar called the "mafia state"). In many post-communist states this "intimate" connection between political elite and the new bourgeoisie became the system and it may cast some doubt on the sustainability of post-communist capitalism in countries like Russia, or Hungary.

One of the last papers in this volume is "Karl Polanyi: a theorist of mixed economy". As it is clear from several previous papers in this volume Polanyi had a deep impact on my scholarly work. But Polanyi – especially his "Great Transformation" is not an easy read. This paper contrasts a "hard" and "soft" reading of Polanyi. Polanyi in his scholarly life was in cross-fire between two people who dearly loved: his wife, Ilona Duczyńska, who for a while was a revolutionary communist and a sympathizer of the USSR and his brother – as accomplished in his scholarship as Karl – Michael Polanyi, a conservative and a merciless critique of the Soviet experience. It is not accidental, that Karl Polanyi did not offer any systematic analysis of the USSR, I started to use his theoretical framework for a critical analysis of actually existing socialism. Polanyi was obviously a critic of unregulated markets. He saw the self-destructive capacities of uncontrolled markets and sees a necessity for "counter-vailing" forces. What is less obvious to what extent he was a "revolutionary socialist", who wanted to eliminate markets and private ownership or to what extent he merely advocated a Scandinavian type of mixed economy. The hard reading of Polanyi sees him as a radical socialist. Chris Hann – an outstanding ethnographer – goes as far as to suggest that the late Kádár regime was the model Polanyi idealized. My paper with Mihalyi offers a soft reading of Polanyi, hence the theorist of mixed economies.

The last chapter V. "Revolt of the Masses and the Ukrainian Crisis" is presented as an Afterword, which can also be read as a foreword. In this chapter together with an introduction aspects are to be discussed that, on the one hand, have a direct connection to the concept of sovereignty and, on the other hand, have received too little attention.

Dear reader, you have the confessions of someone who wanted to be a social scientists and offer the possible most objective analysis what was possible at the turbulent times he lived in. I never believed what Giuliani, Donald Trump's recent legal adviser said: "truth is not truth". True, truth is always from a certain perspective, but we have a consensus to tell when someone tell un-truth. Over the past 50 years I was never afraid to admit when I was wrong in my diagnosis and forecast and I can only hope that the gloomy conclusions of this Introduction will be proven false by history.

And now let me turn to the papers in order I already outlined:

VI. Towards a Critical Political Economy of State Socialism

- I.1 "Primary Group Structure And Their Functions" (1969)
- I.2 "Social Inequalities in State Socialist Redistributive Economies" (1978)

VII. Social Structure of Socialist and Capitalist Societies

- II.1 "The Intelligentsia in the Class Structure of State Socialist Societies" (1982)
- II.2. "Circulation or Reproduction of Elites during Post-Communist Transformation" (1995)

VIII. Transition from Socialism to Capitalism

- III.1 "On Irony: An Invitation to Neoclassical Sociology" (2003)
- III.2. "The new Capitalism in Eastern Europe" (2005)

IX. Critical Theory of Post-Communism

- IV.1 "Weber's Theory of Domination and Post-Communist capitalism" (2016)
- IV.2 "Drifting from Liberal Democracy" (2015)
- IV.3. The Role of Rents in the Transition from Socialist Redistributive Economies to Market Capitalism (2017)
- IV.4. Karl Polanyi: a Theorist of mixed Economies (2020)

X. Revolt of the Masses and the Ukrainian Crisis

- V.1 Back to Max Weber: the concept of "Der Wille der Beherrschten"
- V.2 Sovereignty: Uses and abuses

I. Towards a Critical Political Economy of State Socialism

I.1 Primary Group Structures And Their Functions: Kin, Neighbors, and Friends*

Eugene Litwak and Iván Szelényi

Technological development leads to new forms of primary group structure. It demands differential mobility which makes traditional primary groups hard to maintain. However, it also provides mechanisms which permit new types of primary groups. Thus, contacts among extended family kin can be maintained despite breaks in face-to-face contact; neighborhoods can exist despite rapid membership turnover; and friendships can continue despite both of these problems. This is possible because technology permits rapid communication over distance and rapid group indoctrination. It is hypothesized that because of differences in structure, neighbors can best handle immediate emergencies; kin, long term commitments; and friends, heterogeneity. Data from Hungary and U.S.A. are used to illustrate the point.

Introduction.

Until recently, little attention has been given in sociology to a theoretical statement on the variety of "primary" group structures and their differential function in an industrial society. We would like to suggest that under the impact of modern industrial society primary group structures tend to assume a variety of structural forms.[1]

Furthermore, these different structures can handle different types of tasks more effectively. We shall attempt to illustrate this argument from comparative data gathered in Detroit and in two cities in Hungary. We shall confine our discussion to three types of primary groups-kinship ties, neighbors, and friends, and use Cooley's (1955) terminology (viz.: face to face, permanent, affective, non instrumental, and diffused) for primary

* We would like to acknowledge the aid of the Ford Foundation which permitted the two investigators to come together as part of their program of training. The Foundation is not, however, in any way responsible for the point of view taken here. We would also like to acknowledge the thoughtful comments of Irwin Epstein, Phillip Fellin and Tony Tripodi.

1 Goode (1963:1–86) points out that because of the many diverse kinds of pre-industrial societies and common pressures for industrialization, the historical trends may look quite different for each of them. Japan had a decreasing rate of divorce with industrialization while the United States had an increasing one because pre-industrial Japan had high rates of divorce and the U.S. didn't. The analysis in this paper assumes "Western" type societies.

groups, rather than Parson's equally useful pattern variables (particularistic, collective, diffused, affective and ascribed).

Until the late 1940's many sociologists had adopted the point of view that there was little need to study primary groups in modern industrial society because primary groups were doomed (Tönnies, 1940: Wirth, 1957: Simmel, 1957). The theoretical bases for this orientation is (1) industrial bureaucratic organizations are more effective than primary groups in achieving most goals, and.

(2) they required social conditions which were antithetical to primary groups. One of the major conditions so required was the need for primary group members to engage in differential geographical and occupational mobility. In the late 1940's, Parsons suggested the "isolated nuclear family" as a very special kind of primary group that could meet the conditions of urban society and avoid the problems of differential mobility. It did this by having one member in the labor force and restricting itself to a two-adult family unit. In the 1950's, a series of studies emerged which suggested that the extended kin relations could also survive in modern urban society but, unlike the Parsons solutions, these studies argued that primary groups could maintain cohesion despite differential mobility (Sussman and Burchinal, 1968 and Litwak, 1960a and 1960b). Continuing work in the field has further suggested that friendship groups, neighborhood groups, and work groups may also be viable in current society. But little, if anything, has been done to demonstrate in theory that these various forms of primary group relationship can deal with problems of differential mobility. Do these forms represent vestigial remains which will soon disappear; do they represent ineffectiveness in the operation of industrial society; or do they (as we hypothesize) represent groups consistent with industrial society? Most important, if these different types of primary groups are all viable, are they structurally the same and can they handle the same type of problems?

To clarify this point, we are advancing the following propositions: in order for extended kin to remain viable, they must learn to communicate and exchange services in other than face-to-face situations; in order for neighbors to remain viable, they must learn to exchange services and communicate despite short membership turnover; and for friendships to remain viable, friends must learn to do both, in addition to learning how to deal with the most idiosyncratic aspects of life. In terms of "small group theory," we are asking what mechanisms permit group cohesion under conditions of limited face to face contact or rapid membership turnover. In terms of stratification theory, we are asking under what conditions do people identify with primary groups across class lines. Most generally, we are asking, in terms of theories of urban society, what are the differential structures and functions which are performed by "primary type" groups in an urban society. Though at first blush this may seem a bit ambitious, many of these problems are so intertwined that solutions to one lead to solutions to others. Within this general frame work, we will undertake the analysis of specific primary groups.

Structure of Neighborhoods.

Neighborhoods are characterized by geographical proximity of members. Consequently, neighbors tend to be in face-to-face contact with one another. At the same time, industrialization demands that people in a given neighborhood have short tenure. If a neighborhood requires geographical proximity and industrialization requires short tenure, it follows that if neighborhoods are to survive in current industry they must stress face-to-face contact without one of the dimensions of a classical primary group, i.e., permanent membership.

To clarify this point, two thoughts will be elaborated, viz., to what extent does industrial society demand high neighborhood membership turnover, and to what extent does it provide mechanisms for primary group survival despite lack of permanence.

A. *Technological Pressure Forces High Neighborhood Turnover.* There are several ways in which technological developments in an industrial society force high membership turnover in neighborhoods. First, rational allocation of labor demanded by modern industry frequently means the labor force has to be shifted to where the work is. Jobs are mechanized or automated, causing shifts in geographical demands for labor (e.g., agriculture to industrial). Technology might create new industries as well as produce innovations which make previously undesirable areas habitable.

Technology also forces membership turnover, because land and housing, like labor, are subject to "rational" redefinition. Large residential areas have been turned into superhighways even as commercial areas have been redeveloped for residential use. Technology brings about rapid shifts in housing standards. Housing put up ten to twenty years ago may be viewed as currently obsolete. Technology makes it economical to shift houses and neighborhoods with family life cycle. It also leads to continuous rises in standard of living, giving people a continuous option to move to better housing. Finally, because technology leads to occupational specialization, members of a neighborhood are often differentially effected by automation and pressure to move.

B. *Technological Support for Neighborhood Cohesion Despite High Membership Turnover.* If, indeed, technology tends to force high membership turnover in neighborhoods, can neighborhoods survive as meaningful primary groups? Several recent works suggest that in principle neighborhoods can survive despite short membership tenure (Litwak, 1960c; Festinger, 1951; Whyte, 1956; Fellin and Litwak, 1963; Wilensky, 1961). The basic point is that short tenure can be partially compensated for by rapid means of group indoctrination. If an individual is rapidly accepted into the group (from the moment of his appearance), the group might survive considerable membership turnover (Fellin and Litwak, 1963). What are some of the mechanisms which permit groups to indoctrinate members rapidly? The movement between groups can be made without loss of cohesion where the movement is ordered, i.e., expected and planned (Wilensky, 1961; Fellin and Litwak, 1963). Thus, where the group norms state newcomers are to be welcomed and newcomers have norms that long-term residents are friends, speedy indoctrination is encouraged (Fellin and Litwak, 1963). Other devices for rapid indoctrination are: groups with special subunits formally designated to seek out newcomers and introduce them to their neighbors, e.g., welcome wagons, ministers, PTA[2] members, etc. (Fellin and Litwak, 1963); neighborhood voluntary organizations (i.e., consisting of neighbors) where group norms can be publicly stated and re-enforced, e.g., PTA block clubs, church related clubs, etc. (Litwak, 1961); extra economic resources which permit use of professional movers, freeing the newcomer to socialize. The fact that newcomers and long term residents already share many basic values, languages, and roles can speed up group socialization.

The question arises, how systematically are such mechanisms encouraged in a technological society. It has been suggested that the occupational milieu which is prototypical of the advanced technological society is that of the professional in large-scale bureaucratic organizations. In addition, the argument has been made that such occupations systematically require the development of ordered change while encouraging integration into primary-group-type work situations (Litwak and Fellin, 1963). As such, the occupational experience provides training for the development of norms welcoming strangers, as well as norms in which ordered change is accepted as good in itself. Furthermore, technological society encourages the development of nationally based industry, mass media, nationally based educational norms which in turn mean that individuals in such a society share a common language and a common culture even though they may have occupational specialties which differ. Technological societies, through their rising standards of living, permit more and more people to use professional movers. Finally, technological society encourages the development of education. This in turn enables the individual to take into account longer time spans (e.g., plan for ordered change) and to equip people interpersonally to run neighborhood voluntary associations with success.

To summarize, high membership turnover can be overcome where groups can evolve rapid modes of indoctrination, and this tends to be systematically the case in technological societies. However, to say it can survive does not mean that its structure will be the same as the "traditional" neighborhood primary group. For the fact remains that it is a group which does have a high membership turnover, and this key structural fact will, we hypothesize, limit the kinds of tasks it can best handle.

Structure of Kin Croups.

If the kinship structure (i.e., the relations between nuclear families) is examined, we find that central to its traditional historical meaning is the idea that people are related in semi-permanent biological or legal ways (e.g., mother-son relationship). At the same time, it is suggested that the kinship system, like the neighborhood, is faced with pressures for differential mobility in a technological society. If these two considerations, viz., permanent membership and differential mobility, are taken into account, then the kinship system can survive only by dropping the traditional primary group demand for face-to-face relations. It is hypothesized that this is possible in modem society because

2 PTA = Parent Teacher Association.

technological developments permit kinship exchanges over large distances. Before developing this point, a brief review will suggest that differential kinship mobility is intrinsic to modem technological development.

A. *Differential Kinship Mobility.* If we examine those preindustrial societies which stressed kinship cohesion, we see, generally, three factors which prevented differential kinship mobility: (1) the kin controlled the occupational system, (2) a norm that any movement of kin must involve the total kinship structure, and (3) a strongly centralized authority system within the kin structure. It is our view that all three of these have been undermined by modem technological development. Thus, technology has encouraged the development of bureaucracies and professions. These in turn have loosened the hold of the kin on the occupational structure.[3] Technological pressure for change means that father and son may have different jobs and be subject to differential pressures for mobility (e.g., father's job automated to a point where few opportunities are left for sons, or better educational opportunities for young lead to different occupational choices). The child may not be offered the same job, may not want it, or may not be trained for it. Furthermore, where labor was unskilled, it was easily interchangeable and large kinship groups could move together. With specialization, introduced by modem technology, kinship members who move together might find it more difficult to find a job at a common locality.[4]

Finally, it would be argued that the modern technological system undermines a highly centralized power structure within the kinship system. It is suggested that this erosion is brought about in the long run by the fact that the kinship system is no longer able to control completely the occupational market.

To summarize, a modem industrial society tends to offer maximal economic rewards to those willing to engage in differential mobility. It prevents the kin from using traditional means for halting mobility, and, as we shall point out, it lessens the cost of differential mobility to the kinship system.

B. *Mechanisms for Maintaining Kinship Ties.* The question arises as to whether a kinship system can survive the loss of face-to-face contact (i.e., differential mobility) in any meaningful way. It has been suggested elsewhere that kinship systems can maintain their viability despite breaks in face-to-face contact (Adams, 1967; Lansing and Muller, 1967; Litwak, 1960b). The general point is that modern means of communication – the telephone, car, and airplane – have made it increasingly easy for families and individuals

3 The various studies which show considerable social class inheritance in American societies do not contradict the assertions made herein. All such studies demonstrate is that the family can affect one's chances of entering the occupational world at a given level. But they do not assert that the family can control the child's being hired or fired. Nor can the family control the geographical re-location of the child, his rate of promotion, or whether he will be automated out of a job, etc., except as these processes are indirectly related to education. Since many of these attributes are inversely related to education, the families' control of a specific occupation for purposes of controlling the movement of their offsprings is very limited.

4 Gutkind (1962:93–112) provides some limited support for one aspect of our argument. He points out that in certain African states the extended family will move as a totality even when there are no jobs; i.e., they work against the rational distribution of labor.

to communicate with each other, even though not living within immediate geographical proximity of each other. Furthermore, our monetary economy (essential to a technologically advanced society) requires the use of money as a generalized means to most goals. Money can be easily and quickly transmitted, making it possible for kinship units to exchange aid over great distances.

Some have argued that estrangement between kin might arise, since differential economic success leads to a different cultural milieu. Without denying this point, it is only necessary to suggest that such differences take place within a larger context where society provides much in the way of common elements. The mass media, the large-scale mass education, etc., all lead to the evolvement of a common cultural and language base (Dahl, 1966:35–59; Adams, 1967; Streib, 1968:408–409; Litwak, 1960a). People have overlapping group memberships and so differences take place within a context of communality as contrasted to situations of complete group polarization (Dahl, 1966: 367–386; Williams, 1964:352–391). It is suggested that the communality will increasingly become a sufficient base for maintaining kinship identity across class lines (Streib, 1968:408–409; Adams, 1967).

To argue that kinship structures can exist despite breaks in face-to-face contact does not mean that such structures are the same as the traditional kinship structures. This difference is hypothesized to affect significantly the kind of tasks they can best perform.

Structure of Friendship Peer Croups.

With these thoughts on kin and neighbors in mind, let us now examine friendship relationships. In some ways, these are structurally the weakest ties of all. They do not have the permanence of the kinship link or the face-to-face contact characterizing the neighborhood. Nevertheless, they are confronted with the very same social pressure that both of these groups are faced with differential mobility. One would hypothesize that the major factor holding friendship ties together is affectivity. Unlike the other two groups, the individual has more options in choosing his friends. We suggest that because of this greater choice, friendship ties have affectivity as their major base of strength. The question arises as to how such affectivity can survive breaks in face-to-face relationships. To some extent, the answer would be the same as for the kinship group, e.g., modern modes of communication. However, friendship ties may be much more vulnerable to breaks in face-to-face contact than kin groups because there are no institutional pressures for permanence.

In any case, what we are suggesting is that friendship ties tend to rest on free choice and affectivity; neighborhood ties, face-to-face contact; and kinship structures, permanent relations. There is no reason at any moment in time why all these primary groups could not overlap – friends may be neighbors and family members at the same time. However, the main point of our discussion is that there are pressures in an industrial society for each of these groups to separate.

Structure of the Nuclear Family Croup.

Although we will not present empirical evidence on the isolated nuclear family, it is necessary to make a few remarks about it to highlight the role of the other primary groups. The isolated nuclear family is the husband, wife, and young children. Married children and relatives are excluded. The nuclear family comes closest to meeting the traditional demands of the primary group, e.g., face-to-face, permanent, affective, non-instrumental, and diffused. However, a key structural feature of the isolated nuclear family is its lack of human resources. By definition, it has only two adult members. Because of this limitation in size, the nuclear family often cannot handle crucial problems even though they fall within the province of primary group structures. Thus they find it difficult to deal with tension management problems where the source of trouble is disputes between themselves – husband and wife (e.g., neither adult is able to provide succor to the other). In addition, because of the intense affectivity, family members may not be able to diagnose objectively incipient states of mental illness (Landy, 1960). Finally, because of technological innovation, family members often cannot use their personal history as a base for handling all problems (e.g., newest techniques for handling children, how to deal with new norms on dating, etc.). In a rapidly changing society, it is not enough for two adults to have only each other to draw upon.

We feel that the chief virtue of the kin and neighborhood and friendship primary groups is their ability to provide supplemental resources to the isolated nuclear family. They are able to do this because structurally they are close enough in form to the traditional primary group to minimize problems of communication.

Functions of Neighborhood Peer Croups.

With these ideas as background, the analysis will focus on the unique capacities of the neighborhood, the kinship group, and the friendship group which might emerge because of their structural differentiation. We pointed out that the neighborhood has face-to-face contact as its distinguishing factor. The question now arises: what are the advantages of face-to-face contact? We suggest here three important advantages without claiming these are exhausted.

Perhaps the first advantage of face-to-face contact is speed of reaction. However, this would be true only if all other things were equal-knowledge, equipment, etc. We are talking about actions which are, on the one hand, simple enough for the ordinary person to handle and, on the other hand, so idiosyncratic that they cannot be programmed efficiently for large-scale equipment (Litwak and Figueira, 1968). For instance, the need to borrow a cup of sugar in the midst of preparing a meal, or having someone watch the baby for five minutes while one runs out unexpectedly to the store are both simple, widespread, yet idiosyncratic events. Such emergency situations range from the trivial matters to catastrophes. According to Form and Nosow (1958:54–82), as high as 75% of the people connected with major natural disasters may be rescued in the first few hours by neighbors or kin living nearby.

The second advantage involves all those services which are technologically based on people living in the same territory. For instance, all people living on the same street have common problems if the water supply, police protection, street pavement, schools, etc., are inadequate. Most certainly, the chances of improving these services are immeasurably increased if the neighbors act cooperatively (Davies, 1966).

Third, neighbors' face-to-face contact may play a role in situations where continuous observation is necessary for learning. It is possible that much in the way of socialization – how to be a good mother, whether children's peer groups encourage delinquent attitudes or low school achievement – takes place in the neighborhood because it depends so heavily on everyday personal observation (Whyte, 1956:296ff; Deutsch and Collins, 1951:78–103; Coleman, 1966:217–333).

To summarize, there are three tasks which are thought to be the special province of the neighborhood – time emergencies, services based on territoriality, and activities which require everyday observation to be learned.

Function of Family Kin Croups.

As noted, the kin structure is distinguished by its permanence. It would seem, therefore, (all other things being equal) such a structure would do best where the task involved long-term ties. It is frequently true that parents with young children will draw up wills making kin, rather than good friends, responsible for rearing their children. The kin, in addition to providing long-term medical help, may play a decisive role in shaping the long-term career and attitudes of the individual.

Function of Friendship Peer Croups.

We have suggested that modern society is characterized by overlapping memberships; this means that there are certain things that group members hold in common and others on which they differ (Dahl, 1966:260–284, 367–386; Williams, 1964:352–391).

What also characterizes modern society is continuous uncorrelated change; technology may introduce changes in the educational world with no matching change in the work world or leisure time one. If the preceding speculations are correct, then it should also be true that the number of elements which can be shared with a fixed group is definitely limited. To illustrate, an offspring who goes to college will be confronted by a series of problems which are outside the knowledge and interest of the parents, e.g., studying for examinations, dealing with peers, dating, etc. Even in the cases where the parents had also attended college before, it is quite likely that many of the norms will have changed so radically since the parents' stay in college that their knowledge base is limited.

The reader will recall that the family, because of its long-term biological and legal criteria, and the neighborhood, by virtue of its geographical definition, both provided a somewhat fixed and arbitrary definition of group. From all of the above, we concluded that the friendship groups can best handle matters involving continuous fluctuation while the others can handle the general communalities. It is not just because friendship groups provide the greatest options to choose matching group members but also because people with only ties of mutual affectivity may be more motivated to adjust to each other. Illustrative of some areas where friends would predominate would be the following: Clothing fashions are continuously changing within some common value set; a liberal or conservative political tradition still permits variations in choice of candidate, e.g., Goldwater, Reagan, Nixon, Rockefeller, etc.

Summary of Structure and Function of Types of Primary Croups.

The structure and function of different types of primary groups have been summarized in Table 1. Reading across the top line of the table, we see that the nuclear family has all of the classical dimensions of the primary group but is so limited in human resources that it frequently cannot perform all of the primary-group functions. The extended kin tends to be quite high on permanence and human resources but very low on face-to-face relations, but only moderately so on other dimensions of organization. The other lines may be read similarly. There are many logically possible types as well as concrete ones which we have not discussed, e.g., friendship groups which take place at the job site and are intimately bound to the job itself.

In sharp contrast to any of these primary group types of organizations are the non-primary groups, e.g., bureaucratic relations. Table 1 shows these groups as very low on all dimensions. This line is introduced to the reader to highlight explicitly the danger of dichotomizing social relations. To say that a group does not have all of the dimensions of the classical primary group does not automatically make it a secondary or bureaucratic one. Between these poles is much distance, and one way of describing the analysis is to say that we are attempting to specify the structure of some of these intervening groups which, though they differ from the classical primary group, are much closer in structure to it than to any other type of group.

Table 1: Level of Task Performance By Primary Group Structure.

	Nuclear Family	**Extended Kin**	**Friends**	**Neighbors**	**Non-primary Group**
Face to Face	High	Low	Low	High	Very low – significant amount of behavior ordered by rules
Permanent (Ascribed)	High	High	Moderate	Low	Very low – achieved
Diffused	High	Moderate	Moderate	Moderate	Very low – specific or specialized
Affective	High	Moderate	High	Moderate	Very low – affectively neutral or impersonal
Non-instrumental (Particularistic)	High	Moderate	Moderate	Moderate	Very low – universalistic or contractual
Human Resources	Low	High	High	High	Very high – any number more than 20*
Type of Task Optimally Done	All primary group tasks which require only two or fewer adults.	All primary group tasks which require low face-to- face contact, long-term commitments, and more than two people.	Those primary group tasks which require the closest manifest agreement to be accomplished but involve relatively. long-term. involvement.	Those primary group tasks which require everyday contact and more than two adults, e.g., time-urgent tasks, everyday socialization. tasks, etc. However, no task which requires long-term commitment.	All tasks requiring specialized training, large capital goods investments, or groupings of very large numbers. of people.

* This is, at best, only a rough guess. It can be as high as 1,000 or 100,000.

Some Empirical Documentation.

In order to present some initial evidence on these speculations, we present materials from two studies – one carried out in Detroit in 1961 and the other in two cities in Hungary in 1966. In the Detroit study, all women who lived in a new housing area (built in the last three years) and who had one child under 19 were interviewed.[5] Because of the new housing, this sample contained very few unskilled or very poor people. In the Hungarian study, new housing areas were also selected. All married couples and single persons with children under 19 were included; 90% of the people interviewed had at least one child. All told, there were 573 people interviewed in the Hungarian study.[6] Because new housing was supposed to be assigned by need rather than income, the chances are that the very poor could have been included. Clearly these are not representative samples. However, if the theory suggested above has any validity, it should predict for special subgroups as well as the general population.[7] Furthermore, we feel these samples are prototypic of the advancing industrial society consisting of movers.[8] As such, it may be more representative of future states of affairs.

To highlight the differences between kin and neighborhood groups, we asked the Detroit sample three questions, the first of which read, "Suppose you had an upset stomach and were laid up for the day, how much help, if any, would your neighbors be?"

5 This sample consisted of all people on the block who had lived in their houses not more than three years and who had children under 19. In addition, a special sub-sample of 34 entrepreneurs was taken from school lists in the designated areas in order to insure a sufficient number of entrepreneurs for the analysis. The blocks were selected at random from suburbs of Detroit which ranked among the first ten in building permits in the three years preceding the study in order to insure the inclusion of new housing in the sample. For complete details of the sampling, see Phillip Fellin (1961).

6 The data for the Hungarian study were gathered in 1966 in two cities. The housing from which the sample came in City Number 1 was started in 1957 and finished in 1963. Thus, some of the respondents could have been living there for as long as nine years while others could not have been there for more than three years. In the other city the housing was started in 1960 and finished in 1963. The housing in both cities consisted of very large apartment house projects. The investigators selected the apartments on a 10% probability sample base and then interviewed all people in the apartment who met the criteria of being married or being single but having a child 18 or under. Pecs and Debrecen, the two cities in the study, had populations around 200,000; 378 families came from Pecs, 195 from Debrecen.

7 A powerful theory should predict any elements within its presumed population universe no matter how they are selected. Put somewhat differently, it may be difficult to prove a theory by selecting special groups within the theoretical universe, but it should be useful for disproving or showing the limitations of a theory if one can show it does not account for special groups.

8 We are arguing throughout this paper that society is moving towards a situation where differential primary group mobility is typical. To test that aspect of our theory, we focus on groups which are subject to mobility. In addition, we are saying that if one wants to anticipate what the future primary groups will be like, it is a mistake to take a random sample of current groups and project them on to the future. Rather, one must take the groups which according to one's theory will be typical of the future, even though they are currently in the minority, and project their structure on to the future.

The same question was repeated twice, once for friends and once for relatives. A similar set of three questions was asked regarding help if the respondent were laid up for two weeks with an appendectomy.[9] Still a third set of three questions asked how much help she would get if she were laid up for three months or more with a broken leg.[10] According to our theory of differential roles, the neighborhood should play a dominant role in the first task, i.e., help with "upset stomach." This is because the first task stressed a time emergency which made face-to-face contact more imperative. For purposes of testing our theory, it would have been better to have an item which measured a much shorter span than a day.

In the Hungarian data, we had one item which rectified this omission. We asked, "Would you expect help from your neighbors if you would need some small service like borrowing something (not money) or having someone watch your children for an hour?" Similar questions were asked about friends and relatives.[11] A second type of question asked: "Would you expect to get help from your neighbors if you were away or sick for one week and needed someone to take care of the children, do the shopping, or do the housework?" Again, similar questions were asked about relatives and friends. These two sets of items, like their American counterparts, were intended to point up the different functions of relatives and neighbors as far as time urgency was concerned.

In Table 2 it can be seen that the hypothesis is borne out relatively in the American data and both relatively and absolutely in the Hungarian data. Thus, in the American data, both neighbors and relatives are thought of as equally helpful (46% and 44% respectively) when dealing with the one-day problem, while the family is by far the most helpful when dealing with the three-month problem (i.e., 32% and 73% for neighbors and family, respectively). We speak of this as a relative confirmation, because ideally we would have suggested that the neighbors should play a more important role than the family in time emergency problems. We think the confirmation would have been even more direct if we had used an item that measured a greater time emergency. If we look at the Hungarian data, we find in the item which suggested such an immediate short-term emergency (e.g., an hour), the neighbors are thought of as much more likely to be helpful (73%) as compared to the family (56%). However, when dealing with the one-week period, just the opposite occurs – with the neighbors thought to be helpful by 46% of the people, while the relatives are thought to be helpful in 66% of the cases.

The same point can be made more convincingly if the reader recognizes that our argument on the differential functions of neighborhood and kin rests on three factors – the immediacy of the task, the distance of kin from the nuclear family, and the level of technology available to communicate over distance. Thus, where kin are

9 "Suppose you were recovering from an appendectomy and were laid up for two weeks. How much help, if any, would your neighbors be?" Matching questions were asked about relatives and friends.

10 "Suppose you were laid up for three months with a broken leg. How much help, if any, would your neighbors be?" Matching questions were asked about relatives and friends.

11 These questions about the family were only asked of those respondents who indicated they had some contact with their family. Those respondents who said they had no contact at all with their families were automatically classified as expecting no help from their families.

in fact neighbors, one would expect them to handle the short-term immediate problems as well as the long-term problems. To test more fully our theories, it is necessary to vary all three elements, i.e., time emergencies, distance from kin, and technological capacity to communicate over distance. We have already suggested above a series of items which can be used to measure time emergencies. We propose to use the difference between Hungary and America as an index of technological advancement. To obtain data on geographical distance, we asked the respondent if she or her husband had any relatives living in the city or its immediate suburbs.

Table 2: *Percent* Who Say Group Will "Very Much" Give Help By Time Emergency.

	American				Hungarian		
	One-Day Stomach Ache	Two-Week Appen-dectomy	Three-Month Broken Leg	(N)	One-Hour Watch Children	One-Week Take Care of Children	(N)
Neighbors	46	45	32	(300)	73	46	(573)
Friends	30	40	28	(300)	33	47	(573)
Relatives	44	75*	73*	(300)	56*	66*	(573)

* Difference between neighbors and relatives significant at .05 level or higher. Unless otherwise noted, confidence intervals for proportions were used, assuming a single population.

If we examine those respondents in the more advanced technological community (i.e., the U.S.), whose relatives do not live in the city, we should find the ideal situation for primary-group differentiated structure and function. Neighbors should handle time emergencies and kin should handle long-term commitments. In Table 3 it can be seen that when no relatives live in town and one faces a time-urgent task, neighbors are viewed as helpful in 43% of the cases, while kin are viewed as helpful in only 5% of the cases. On the other hand, when long-term tasks are involved (i.e., help during a three-month period while recovering from a broken leg), only 25% of the people say neighbors are helpful while 63% say families are. Some would say the first finding is obvious – if no relatives are in town, how can they be helpful. However, what they overlook is the second finding: where time urgency is not the key issue, the kin are viewed as most helpful even when they are not in town.

Now let us examine Hungary, a society which is technologically less advanced than America. By this we mean that communication over geographical distance is much slower in many parts of Hungary than in the U.S. Here most families have cars and telephones; in Hungary, this is as yet not true. Consequently, making a long-distance call in Hungary might take some time as contrasted to the almost instantaneous direct dialing of the American system. Here most families who live 30 miles apart might be in direct contact by automobile in an hour or less. In Hungary, the dependence on a very good public transportation still means that individuals might have to take considerable time from the moment aid is first requested until the family members finally meet.[12] One can see in these cases what is typical of most other modes of communication. If we examine in Table 3 the Hungarian families who have no relatives in town, we find, like the American data, that most people (72%) view the neighbors as helpful for handling time emergency problems. Only 2% view the family as helpful on such matters. However, in contrast to the American data, we find that the Hungarian families do not even view their relatives as helpful for dealing with long-term problems (3%) as compared with neighbors (50%). Our hypothesis is that in Hungary, as compared to America, the technology does not permit as rapid communication over geographic distance.[13] [14]

Table 3: *Percent* Who Say Group Will "Very Much" Give Help By Time Emergency For Those With Relatives In And Out Of Town.

	American				**Hungarian**		
	One-Day Stomach Ache	Two-Week Appen-dectomy	Three-Month Broken Leg	(N)	One-Hour Watch Children	One-Week Take Care of Children	(N)
				No Relatives in Town			
Neighbors	43	41	25	(58)	74	50	(109)
Friends	35	44	33	(58)	27	48	(109)
Relatives	05*	53*	63*	(58)	02*	03*	(109)

12 The individual has to adjust his time schedule to that of the public transportation, and if transportation is limited to a given area it is difficult and expensive to arrange alternatives. Perhaps in the most obvious and immediate sense, public transportation in most large cities, with the exception of a few major lines, is closed during substantial parts of the night. One's only option is taxi cabs.

13 In general it would be argued that the wealthier the individual the more able he is to take advantage of technological means for maintaining primary group contacts over geographical distance. Thus, Adams (1967) indicates that middle class families maintain contact over large geographical distances more than working class families, while the material of Lansing and Mueller (1967) can be given a similar interpretation. Rosow (1967:172–175) has similar material on the family. What we are now suggesting is, at the time of our studies, the living standards of the skilled and middle class Americans (our American sample did not include very poor people) were higher than the Hungarian group. As a consequence, the American group had more access to technological modes of communication and more disposable income than even the wealthier Hungarian families in our study.

14 There are two additional hypotheses which might account for the material. First, this item referred to a one-week time period, whereas the items used for the U.S. referred to two weeks and three months. It is possible if we had asked the Hungarian population a question which covered the same period that they also would have more relatives who would help. There is a second objection which is a methodological one. The Hungarian sample was asked a screening question prior to the item on kinship aid. They were asked if they had any contact with their kin. If they said no they were not asked the questions on kinship aid. It is quite possible that even those who had no contact with their kin would have answered affirmatively our questions on kinship help. This will require further investigation.

Relatives in Town							
Neighbors	47	46	33	(242)	70	43	(464)
Friends	29	38	27	(242)	31	40	(464)
Relatives	53*	80*	75*	(242)	68	82*	(464)

* Difference between relatives and neighbors, significant at the .05 level or higher.

In that part of Table 3 where relatives are in town, we find a great similarity in the patterning of results in the American and Hungarian data. For short-term time emergencies the relatives and neighbors play the same role, while for long-term emergencies the family is much more likely to be chosen as the key source of aid. We would speculate that if our respondents could be further sub-classified as to distance families live from each other, the further apart they are, the more the pattern would resemble the part of Table 3 where relatives do not live in town. However, as families live closer and closer to each other, the advantages of technological society become less and less important. The two countries should resemble each other more and more in the traditional primary group structure. The resemblance of the two countries in that part of Table 3 where relatives live in town is consistent with the theory suggested herein. Differences in question wording restrict our comparisons to overall patterns rather than similarities in percentages.

There is yet another type of evidence which bears on the hypothesis. It is possible within each of our two countries to select subgroups which are more likely to be subject to the demands and privileges of a technological society. Those prototypic groups are the ones under technological pressure for mobility and at the same time have the educational and economic resources to deal best with these demands (e.g., communicating over large geographical distances) (Fellin and Litwak, 1963: 367–370; Whyte, 1956: 1–249). The prototypic groups we chose to examine are occupational-educational ones. Many have suggested that the group most prototypical of modern society is the highly educated managerial or professional bureaucrat. From the viewpoint of the traditional sociological theorist, he is the most subject to contractual, impersonal, segmental relations (Simmel, 1957:635–646; Wirth, 1957; Tönnies, 1940:18–28). This view would suggest that such people would be inclined to have less primary-group-type relations than others. By contrast, our formulation would suggest that these very same groups would actually encourage new forms of primary group development. Thus, if our theory is correct, it should turn out that within the highly technological society (American) the bureaucratic groups, because of their educational, occupational, and mobility pressures, should most clearly illustrate our hypothesis (i.e., use neighborhood groups more for time emergencies and relatives for longterm problems). On the other hand, if our hypothesis is wrong, the bureaucratic groups should be the least likely to use any form of primary groups, but insofar as they used them, they should not have differential functions. Table 4 shows that the bureaucrat [15] is most likely to use the neighbors for.

Table 4: *Percent* Who Say Primary Group Will "Very Much" Give Group Aid By Type Request And Occupation (American Sample)

	One-Day Stomach Problem			Two-Week Appendectomy			Three-Month Broken Leg			
	Neighbor	Friend	Family	Neighbor	Friend	Family	Neighbor	Friend	Family	(N)
Bureaucrat	50	32	38*	46	37	68*	35	26	70*	(99)
Entrepreneur	42	27	48	34	39	80*	23	29	65*	(84)
White Collar	46	29	46	51	40	78*	31	25	72*	(47)
Manual	44	31	46	53	41	74*	40	31	74*	(70)

* Difference between neighbor and family significant at .05 level or higher.

short-term emergency problems and the family for long-term problems. By contrast, the other occupational groups do not as clearly differentiate neighborhood and family. They use family and neighborhood equally for short-term problems and the family more often for long-term problems. What is also true is that the bureaucrat tends to use primary groups as much as other occupational groups – once the nature of task and the type of primary group is taken into account. If we examine the same occupational groupings[16] in the Hungary sample, we find very little difference between the prototypical and the other occupations. We think this is true because the level of technological development in Hungary is such that no group except a very small one has the technological capabilities to communicate across geographical distance. In addition, the bureaucrat's relatives would be less likely to have such capabilities. We can summarize our discussion thus far by saying that prototypical groups in the most advanced technological society are the

15 All husbands who were members of larger firms (over 500 employees) performed managerial or professional activities (as indexed by occupational title and education) and salaried employees were classified as bureaucrats. All individuals who either worked in smaller organizations but met the other criteria were classified as independent professional or entrepreneurs. In addition, people who did not meet the above criteria but were owners of a business were classified as entrepreneurs. All other individuals were classified by census job classifications into white collar or manual workers. For details see Fellin (1961:55–57).

16 In Hungary at the time the study was done there were virtually no entrepreneurs-owners of private businesses. Thus, people could only be classified into three groups: bureaucrats, white collar and manual workers. Manual workers could be split from white collar workers by the traditional occupational analysis. White collar workers were designated as bureaucrats in all cases where the job description demanded education beyond high school.

ones (as suggested by the theory) that most clearly differentiate the functions of neighborhood and family primary groups.

There is, finally one bit of evidence which can be brought to bear on the differential functions of neighborhood and family primary groups in an advanced technological society. In answer to a question which asked the American sample how often the following people are invited to their homes, it turns out that 43% invite neighbors in at least once a week or more, 9% invite friends in once a week or more, and 17% invite relatives in once a week or more. The reader will recall from Table 2 that respondents (depending on whether it was a time emergency or not) were as likely, or over twice as likely, to view their relatives as a source of aid rather than neighbors. By contrast, we now find that neighbors are more than twice as likely to be in the respondent's home as are relatives.

Table 5. *Percent* Who Say Primary Group Will "Very Much" Give Group Aid By Type Request And Occupation (Hungarian Sample)

	One Hour			One Week			
	Neighbor	Friend	Family	Neighbor	Friend	Family	(N)
High Bureaucrat	74	40	55*	47	56	65*	(156)
White Collar	73	24	54*	42	32	69*	(91)
Worker	69	30	58*	43	38	68*	(283)

*Difference between family and neighbor significant at the .05 level or higher.

This highlights our hypothesis that neighbors in a highly mobile and advanced technological society are in a better position to provide time-urgent services. It is also suggestive of modeling-type tasks which neighbors might best perform and which we have not explored in this paper. However, much evidence has been gathered by others which is very suggestive. Deutsch and Collins (1951:78–103) present some evidence that neighbors play a role in shaping racial attitudes. Reiss and Rhodes (1960:258–266), Maccoby *et al.* (1958:38–51), and Kobrin (1958:448–505) suggest that neighbors play a role in delinquent gangs; Wilson (1964: 217–235), Turner (1964), Sewell and Armer (1966:159–168), and various others, suggest that they play a role in the educational process; and Davies (1966) shows that they play a role in the decision of urban renewal.

Thus far, the discussion has centered on the comparison between the kin and the neighborhood group. What can be said about the friendship groups? If we re-examine the prior tables, we find that the friendship groups tend to form a pattern somewhere in between the neighbors and kin. For instance, in the American sample, friendship groups are most often expected to help on the two-week problem. On the one-day or the three-month problem, they are less likely to help. For the Hungarian data, the friendship groups are called upon for the one-week task more often than for the one-hour task. In other words, friends are generally not called upon to deal with the immediate time urgent problems or the long-term ones; it is either the neighbors or the kin. We think the non-linear relationship to time urgency in the American sample and the possible beginnings of such a relationship in the Hungarian sample might reflect that the friendship group does not have the degree of face-to-face contact of the neighborhood or the permanence of the kin group. It is structurally somewhere between the two groups. In addition, we suggested that one of the unique features of the friendship relationship is the freedom to choose one's peer groups. Such groups might be especially bound together by positive affect or in their common agreements around the fluctuating aspects of general goals, e.g., clothing fashions, household furnishing fashions, child-rearing fashions, etc. To explore this idea, we asked the individuals in the American sample the following question:

> Now a question about friends who do not live in this neighborhood. Would thinking about how your friends might handle problems like furnishing a house, controlling children or dealing with in-laws be helpful to you,' harmful, or wouldn't you think about friends?

A parallel question was asked about relatives and neighbors. What was characteristic of each of these questions is that there is no time urgency and no permanent contact assumed. Some of these problems do overlap with long-term commitments, but the question does not ask the respondent to make any. Most important, the questions tend to deal with issues which, in a modem society, are likely to be unique to a given phase in the family life cycle, a given level of income, and a given level and type of education and occupation. As such there are many unique configurations which would make it difficult for the respondent to find a kin or a neighbor with similar tastes or problems. With this in mind, Table 6 can be examined. It can be seen 'that in the American sample friends are as often referred to on such issues as the family and both more than neighbors. This is in sharp contrast to the earlier tables where friends were the least designated group. If we now examine the most prototypic situation for our hypothesis (where no relatives live in town), we see that friends are more often chosen than neighbors. Thus we can see that, given a situation subject to fluctuation, the friendship group tends to emerge as the most useful group, whereas.

Table 6: *Percent* Who Say Thinking About How Peer Croups Would Handle Problem Would Be Helpful By Type Primary Group And Relatives In Town (American Sample)

	Relatives in City	No Relatives in City	Total
Neighbors	54**	41**	51
Family	68	50	64
Friends	63	64.	63
(N)	(242)	(58)	(300)

*Difference between family and neighbor significant at .05 level or higher.
** Difference between neighbors and friends significant at .01 level or higher.

for the other tasks they tend to assume a lesser role. This is of course consistent with our theory.

For the Hungarian sample, we had a question which could be used to measure friendship but it had some problems. We asked the respondents: Do you have friends with whom you might discuss personal, family, and child-rearing problems? A similar question was asked about family and neighbors. We think such a question might be more contaminated with long-term family concerns and might imply less free choice (e.g., where the parents initiated contact, the respondent might well answer yes). Also, there is more direct aid implied which will entail both more permanent long-term commitments and greater stress on general solutions of aid rather than on specific ones. In Table 7, we find the family is most often chosen and the neighbors and friends are equally chosen. Can we say that this comparative lack of differentiation is related to the lower technological level of the Hungarian society? If we examine the prototype case of the group with relatives out of town, we find that on this item the Hungarian respondent behaves the same way as he does on the prior aid problems. He is very close to the neighbors while the relatives play a very minor role. If we can accept the item as a legitimate measure of friendship task, then the differences between America and Hungary would suggest both the differential functions of family and friendship as well as the impact of the larger technological milieu; i.e., in American society the differentiation has proceeded further.

There is finally one last point which should be made with regard to the friendship groups. If we examine the friendship item by each occupational grouping, we find little.

Table 7: *Percent* Who Discuss Problems With Primary Group Members By Relatives In Town (Hungarian Sample)

Who Discuss Problems With	Relatives in Town in %	Relatives Out of Town in %	Total
Neighbors	45	47	45
Relatives	74	02	61
Friends	47*	48*	47*
(N)	(464)	(109)	(573)

* Difference between friends and relatives significant at .05 level or higher.

difference among the American groups; i.e., the prototypical bureaucratic occupations behave the same way as the non-bureaucratic ones. In the Hungarian situation, the prototypical bureaucratic groups tend to differentiate mainly along the same lines as the American sample, while the less prototypical groups tend to select relatives as the group to which they would assign friendship functions. We think in general this is consistent with the theory proposed but involves additional considerations not discussed in this article.[17]

Selected Review of Literature.

The empirical evidence we have offered so far is more illustrative than definitive. Much more would have to be done to verify the conceptual scheme presented herein. Several studies show that in the American society extended family relations can be maintained over geographical distance (Sussman and Burchinal, 1968; Adams, 1967; Lansing and Mueller, 1967). In addition, we have already noted a series of studies which have demonstrated the important role of the neighborhood in education, delinquency behavior, interracial attitudes, leisure pursuits of the aged, urban renewal decisions, etc. (Fellin and Litwak, 1968). Our admittedly brief survey of the literature suggests that the functions of friendships have received the least attention, but there are important leads (Rosow, 1967:35–77; Kadushin 1966; Coleman et. al., 1966; Merton and Lazarsfeld, 1954; Blau, 1961). One of the outstanding characteristics reported about "friendships" is the extent to which they are based on similarities in sex, age, and stage of the family life cycle as well as income and education. This evidence is consistent with our view that friendships deal with the edges of change and fluctuation, because to deal with the changing aspects of our society it is often necessary to find others in almost matching circumstances.

Perhaps the single most impressive documentation of our general hypothesis on the differential functions of primary groups is a study by Rosow (1967, 194–245). He started with the hypothesis that friendship, neighboring, and kinship groups might be able to compensate for each other: where one was absent the other could take over its functions. (Implicit in such a hypothesis is a point of view which is opposed to the one advanced herein.) He assumed that these groups were sufficiently similar in structure to perform

17 There is a paradox in our data. When we look at the items on kinship exchange by occupation, we find that the group which is hypothesized to be most prototypical (the bureaucrats in American society) most closely matches our predictions. By contrast, when we look at friendship exchanges, we find that the bureaucratic groups in Hungarian communities most clearly match our prediction. Though we have no evidence, we would speculate that geographical distance between friends may generally be less than that between kin. In part it is because the friendship dyad is structurally weaker (e.g., only moderate degrees of permanency), and in part because the very function of the friendship group is to permit matching between people on somewhat idiosyncratic elements. We would suspect that such idiosyncrasies may often be related to geographical areas, if not to as small a unit as a neighborhood. If at the same time we argue – as we have already done – that lowest American groups in our sample (e.g., skilled workers) have more resources than the best off Hungarian group in our sample (e.g., middle level bureaucrats) then the paradox might be resolved. For we would speculate that to cover the relatively small distances of a community and its suburbs would be within the means of all the members of our American sample, and therefore there would be no sharp differences between bureaucrats and others. However, because of the lower state of technology and resources, it would be argued that in the Hungarian case to move within the community and its environs may constitute a substantial problem, in which case the differences between the bureaucrats and the manual workers may manifest themselves.

similar tasks. However, his data indicated that, contrary to his original hypothesis, these primary group structures were not generally compensatory, prompting him to revise his original hypothesis. His data and new hypothesis provide very strong independent evidence for the point of view suggested herein. We would further speculate that many of the current controversies over the role of family and neighborhood in education and delinquency would benefit from a closer analysis of the nature of tasks. Thus, on one extreme it is clear that young children cannot join gangs unless there are others in the "neighborhood" so inclined. The role of the neighborhood is less obvious but nevertheless apparent in teaching. Therefore, a teacher confronted by a class dominated by children poorly prepared for reading and mathematics may be in no position to teach advanced subjects to the small minority who are prepared. The role of the neighborhood may be very minor in shaping expectations or attitudes toward educational achievement in that such attitudes are not necessarily as territorially based as joining delinquent gangs and learning specific school subjects. Thus, over the long run the kin may provide a more frequent and continuous social stimulus for education expectations and aspirations than any single set of neighbors.

Summary and Conclusion.

At this point, we would like to briefly restate our main hypothesis as well as point out some of the research implications. The hypothesis advanced is that the processes of technological development have forced an increasing differentiation of primary-group structures. At the same time, the level of technology permits the survival of forms of primary group structures which could not remain stable in some earlier stages. Thus, the neighborhood as a primary group must often exist with high membership turnover, and the kinship structures must frequently exist without face-to-face contact, while friendship structures may exist with only moderate degrees of either. These forms of primary group structures are viable because technology provides rapid modes of integration as well as ways of communicating over distance. Because of their differences in structure, the various primary groups might each have their own area where they can perform tasks better than others. We supplied empirical data to show that neighborhood and family varied as to when they were called upon to perform tasks depending on the time urgency. We indicated that friendship groups were especially suited to dealing with explicit reference orientations.

We do not pretend that these particular empirical illustrations exhaust the repertory of tasks each group can perform. We meant only to point out the need to investigate this problem. For, if we are correct in our assertion and the investigator does not recognize it, he is likely to find that any data he gathers will have an inconsistent pattern. He will find in some instances the family is called upon more than the neighbors and friends, and in other instances just the opposite. The other error which the investigator could make is to take all items from one time perspective (e.g., those which involve long-term commitments) and on this basis argue that the family primary group is more often called upon than other types.

A second methodological point is that primary groups cannot be easily studied without the investigator's explicitly taking into account the technological level of the society or a given subgroup in the society. For, if our hypothesis is correct, at each technological level both different needs and capacities to deal with them exist. Thus, it would be an error to say that, because a primary group structures changes from one stage of historical development to another, it is moving to destruction. An investigator who assumes implicitly that only one type of primary group can exist will be making such an error. From a theoretical point of view this article suggests alternatives to those theories (Tönnies, 1940; Wirth, 1957; Simmel, 1957) which assert all primary groups tend to disappear, as well as those theories which suggest that only one type of primary group (isolated nuclear family) is viable in a modern technological society (Parsons, 1949). It does this by suggesting that technological demands for differential mobility do not disrupt kinship, friendship, and neighborhood groups as assumed by all of these theorists, as well as by painting out that primary groups other than isolated nuclear family have unique functions. As such this article supports an alternative theory of the organizational basis of technological society (Litwak and Figueira, 1968).

References.

Adams, B. N.
1967 Kinship in an Urban Setting. Chicago: Markham Publishing Company.

Blau, Z.
1961 "Structural constraints on friendships in old age," American Sociological Review 26: 429–439.

Coleman, J., E. Katz, and J. Menzel.
1957 "The diffusion of an innovation among physicians," *Sociometry* 20: 253–269.

Coleman, James S., Earnest Q. Campbell, and Carol J. Hobson.
1966 Equality of Educational Opportunity, United States Department of Health, Education and Welfare, Government Printing Office.

Cooley, Charles H.
1955 " 'Primary Groups' in Small Groups", A. Paul Hare, et al. (eds.), *Studies in Social Interaction*. New York: Alfred Knopf: 15–20.

Dahl, Robert A.
1966 "The American oppositions: affirmation and denial," in R. A. Dahl (editor), Political Oppositions in Western Democracies, New Haven, Connecticut: Yale University Press.

Davies, J. Clarence.
1966 Neighborhood Groups and Urban Renewal, New York: Columbia University Press.

Deutsch, Morton and Mary Evans Collins.
1951 *Inter-Racial Housing. A psychological evaluation of a social experiment*. Minneapolis: The University of Minnesota Press.

Fellin, Philip.
1961 "A study of the effects of reference group orientations on bureaucratic careers on neighborhood cohesion." Unpublished Ph.D. dissertation, University of Michigan.
Fellin, Philip and Eugene Litwak.
1963 "Neighborhood cohesion under conditions of mobility," *American Sociological Review* 28: 364–376.
Fellin, Philip and Eugene Litwak.
1968 "The neighborhood in urban American society," Social Work 13: 72–80.
Festinger, Leon.
1951 "Architecture and group membership," *Journal of Social Issues*, Number 7: 152–163.
Form, William H. and Sigmund Nosow.
1958 *Community in Disaster*. New York: Harper and Brothers.
Goode, William J.
1963 *World Revolution and Family Patterns*. London: The Free Press of Glencoe.
Gutkind, Peter C. W.
1962 "La famille Africaine et son adaptation á la vie urbaine," *Diogène* 37: 93–112.
Kadushin, Charles.
1966 "The friends and supporters of psychotherapy: on social circles in urban life," *American Sociological Review* 31: 786–802.
Kobrin, Salomon.
1958 "The conflict of values in delinquency areas," in Herman D. Stein and Richard A. Cloward, editors, *Social Perspectives on Behavior*, New York: Free Press of Glencoe.
Landy, D.
1960 "Problems of the person seeking help in our culture," *Social Welfare Forum*. New York University Press.
Lansing, J. B. and E. Mueller.
1967 *The Geographic Mobility of Labor*. Ann Arbor: University of Michigan Survey Research Center.
Litwak, Eugene.
1960a "Occupational mobility and extended family cohesion," *American Sociological Review* 25: 9–21.
1960b "Geographic mobility and extended family cohesion," *American Sociological Review* 25: 385–394.
1960c "Reference group theory, bureaucratic career, and neighborhood primary group cohesion," *Sociometry* 23: 72–84.
1961 "Voluntary associations and neighborhood cohesion," *American Sociological Review* 26: 258–271.
Litwak, Eugene and J. Figueira.
1968 "Technological innovation and theoretical functions of primary groups and bureaucratic structures," *American Journal of Sociology* 73: 468–481.
Maccoby, Eleanor E., Joseph P. Johnson, and Russell M. Church.
1958 "Community integration and the social control of delinquency," *Journal of Social Issues* 14: 38–51.
Merton, Robert K. and P. F. Lazarsfeld.
1954 "Friendship as a social process," in Morroe Berger, T. Abel and C. Page, editors, *Freedom and Control in a Modern Society*, New York: Van Nostrand: 18–66.

Parsons, Talcott.
1949 "The social structure of the family," in Ruth N. Anshen, editor, The Family: Its Function and Destiny. New York: Harper and Row.
Reiss, Albert J., Jr., and Albert L. Rhodes.
1961 "The distribution of juvenile delinquency in social class structure," *American Sociological Review* 26: 720–732.
Rosow, Irving.
1967 Social Integration of the Aged. New York: The Free Press.
Sewell, William H. and J. Michael Armer.
1966 "Neighborhood context and college plans," *American Sociological Review* 31: 159–168.
Simmel, Georg.
1957 "The metropolis and mental life," in Paul K. Hatt and Albert J. Reiss, Jr., editors, Cities and Society: The Revised Reader in Urban Sociology. New York: Free Press of Glencoe.
Streib, Gordon F.
1968 "Family patterns in retirement," in Marvin Sussman, editor, Sourcebook in Marriage and the Family. New York: Houghton, Mifflin and Company, 3rd edition.
Sussman, Marvin B. and Lee Burchinal.
1968 "Kin family network: unheralded structure in current conceptualizations of family functioning," in Marvin B. Sussman, editor, Sourcebook in Marriage and the Family. New York: Houghton, Mifflin and Company.
Tönnies, Ferdinand.
1940 Fundamental Concepts of Sociology. C. P. Loomis, trans. New York: American Book Company.
Turner, Ralph H.
1964 The Social Context of Ambition. A study of high-school seniors in Los Angeles. San Francisco: Chandler Publishing Company.
Whyte, W. H., Jr.
1956 The Organization Man. New York: Simon and Schuster.
Wilensky, Harold L.
1961 "Orderly careers and social participation," *American Sociological Review* 26:521–539.
Williams, Robin M., Jr.
1964 Strangers Next Door: ethnic relations in American Communities. Englewood Cliffs, New Jersey: Prentice-Hall.
Wilson, Alan B.
1964 "Social stratification and academic achievement," in A. Harry Passow, editor, Education in Depressed Areas. New York: Teachers College Press, Columbia University.
Wirth, Louis.
1957 "Urbanism as a way of life," in Paul K. Hatt and Albert J. Reiss, Jr., editors, Cities and Society: The Revised Reader in Urban Sociology. Glencoe: Free Press of Glencoe.

I.2 Social Inequalities in State Socialist Redistributive Economies

Dilemmas for Social Policy in Contemporary Socialist Societies of Eastern Europe

Iván Szelényi

In this paper, I will argue that in state socialist societies social inequalities are basically created and structured by redistributive mechanisms. The East European experience seems to differ sharply from the experiences of the market economies where the socio-economic inequalities are basically emerging from market situations and they might be restructured, or moderated by the redistributive intervention of the State.

In Eastern Europe the expansion of the dominating redistributive sphere of the economy adds to the privileges of the already privileged and powerful and, curiously enough, the interests of the powerless and disprivileged can be best served with increasingly transactive (and consequently *market-like)* relationships in the economic system.

I decided to put this argument forward since I am convinced that there are widespread and far-reaching misunderstandings concerning the social implications of economic processes and, more specifically, of economic reforms intending to replace gradually redistributive mechanisms with self-regulating ones, of the East European countries, both in Western and East European social science literature. The Western left-wing critics of East European socialism usually believe that socio-economic conflicts and social inequalities in Eastern Europe are the consequences of the surviving or re-emerging market forces, economic reforms by increasing the role of self-regulating economic mechanisms are attempts to restore "capitalism", and increase social inequalities. At this point the non-authoritarian and anti-bureaucratic Western left finds itself in a surprising alliance with East European conservative bureaucrats who also fight their reform-minded economists and sociologists in accusing them of "selling out the most precious achievements of socialism" (namely, equal accessibility of basic goods and services). Even those who argue the case for economic reform usually subscribe to the sociological assumption that the limitation of redistributive mechanisms is necessary for increased efficiency, but it works against social justice; increased inequalities are the price we have to pay for a more affluent economy.

In all these propositions it is assumed that the social implications of market and redistributive mechanisms are similar or the same under socialist conditions as in a capitalist society; the socio-economic laws, discovered in capitalist market economies, can be projected into the State socialist societies of Eastern Europe. I challenge this position both on empirical and theoretical grounds. There is ample empirical evidence that in State socialist societies the administrative allocation of scarce goods and services favours the more well-to-do and the introduction of market regulated prices of certain goods by economic reforms, in all cases I know of, served the interests of the working class. It is also theoretically and methodologically unacceptable to project socio-economic laws of one socio-economic formation into another one. If we want to understand the real nature of redistributive mechanisms in a socialist society, we have to start with a substantive analysis of the basic economic institution of these societies to understand the role played by redistribution in the social reproduction process and, more specifically, in the production, appropriation and allocation of surplus.

Inequalities emerging from socialist redistributive mechanisms

First I found myself confronted with the problem of inequalities emerging from redistributive mechanisms when I conducted surveys on the housing economy, and specifically on housing allocation in Hungary during the late sixties.

The housing economy I was studying was obviously a mixed one, it was composed of a redistributive and a market sector. In the redistributive sector, the owner was the State, rents were, in principle, not related to the value of the flats or houses and the allocation was administrative. It also comprised a market sector – namely, privately owned family houses and flats, with market regulated prices, but ownership was legally limited, one family could own only one house or flat, consequently a private rental market was technically impossible. (When we use the term "market sector", we apply a broad definition of the term since chances to gain profit out of privately owned houses were extremely limited).

From the early fifties the government made efforts to transform the nature of the housing economy. On the ideological level it was stated that under socialism housing is not a commodity, it should not be allocated on the market, the income of the families should not affect the type, standard and size of housing these families get. To attain these ideological goals, all housing which could be used for profit-making purposes (second flats or houses of families, or even large flats or houses with six rooms or more) were nationalized and the rents were fixed at a level at which the lowest income families could afford the best housing. During the early fifties, practically all new housing, at least in cities, was built, owned and administratively allocated by the State, consequently, in two or three years the State-owned housing became a dominating feature of the urban housing economy. (The question of rural housing is a rather complex one, so at this point I have to abstract from it.)

These changes had far-reaching consequences on the labour economy as well. The soaring inflation of the early fifties enabled the East European governments to introduce structural changes in the wage policy, wage increases falling behind inflation rate extracted housing costs from wages and salaries and accumulated them in the State budget. Housing economy became a redistributive one since the surplus which was used for the construction of new and maintenance of old housing did not appear in personal incomes, was in the first instance concentrated in the "central hand" and redistributed accordingly to central considerations. In principle, all housing could have been nationalized and rents abolished altogether (as it was attempted in the Soviet Union in the 1920's).

This co-ordinated transformation of the housing and labour economy is the main differentiating feature of the socialist development of Eastern Europe. In some of the capitalist market economies (for example in the U.K. and especially in Scotland) State or council ownership of housing also increased radically (probably in similar proportions to Eastern Europe), but it did not lead to the direct concentration of surplus used for housing purposes into a "central hand". In modern capitalist societies with the most advanced council housing system, housing costs are basically accumulated in personal incomes, council housing is the intervention of the State into a market situation to provide adequate housing to those who, for one reason or another, are unable to find high enough incomes on the labour market to cover housing costs. The State is covering these costs by taxing higher income groups, by redistributing real income, generated on a labour *market.* I am inclined to agree with those marxist urban sociologists who propose that the purpose of this state intervention is to save the market economy in the stage of monopoly capitalism, when the labour market controlled by monopoly interests is unable to guarantee the reproduction of housing for an increasing proportion of the labour force. Consequently the housing economy in correspondence with the labour economy remains basically a market one, using redistributive mechanisms when and where market does not guarantee the reproduction of housing and the reproduction of labour. The more well-to-do still buys or rents on the market; to build and rent out housing is still a profitable business for private enterprise. This State intervention helps capitalist market economy answer the challenges it is facing nowadays, it is serving through market ways, the interests of the monopoly capital and the more well-to-do (by keeping prices of labour down for business and by providing capital gain to above the average income home owners through inflation, from which low income groups forced into council housing are excluded).

Consequently I do propose that the changes occurring in Eastern Europe during the early fifties were qualitatively different, they transformed housing economy from a market economy into a redistributive one, through housing, the State not merely reallocated market generated income as in the case of Welfare capitalist societies, but redistributed surplus. From the mid-fifties the East European governments had to solve problems inherent to a redistributive economy and propose that later changes in housing policy could be understood as compromises whose purpose was to save the very redistributive nature of housing in the socialist societies.

By the mid-fifties it became clear for planners that the level of new housing construction is inadequate, housing construction was approaching a low which would not allow, in the long run, the simple reproduction of the housing stock in the period of rapid population increase. Pragmatist planners without asking for the theoretical reasons, realized that the State at least momentarily cannot accept responsibility to provide housing free for all and they proposed that those who can afford to build their own homes should be allowed to do so. In most of the East European countries "dogmatists" who wanted to preserve the "socialist" nature of housing by not allowing private constructions were defeated, and pragmatist planners allowed, later through mortgages and even slight subsidies encouraged family-home building activities. On the other hand, these measures were only compromises, aiming to increase housing construction, and the basic redistributive nature of the housing economy was maintained. (We have to exclude Yugoslavia from this analysis as a very special case which deserves special attention.) First of all, the State maintained a dominating role in housing construction, majority of new housing and an overwhelming majority of new urban housing was built by the State. The State did not regard housing construction as a business enterprise and the claim of radical reformists to introduce a State-owned rental market was always rejected, with the solemn declaration that a socialist state cannot make profit on housing. Rents were consequently kept at a low level, much below value and housing was, and is, administratively allocated. Furthermore, as already mentioned, the private or market sector was also kept under control, families could own only one flat and they were not supposed to rent it out for profit. (From time to time even the size of privately built houses was statutorily limited.) Central planning allowed certain market forces to operate where the redistributive mechanisms did not seem to work. Like the capitalist state used redistribution of income in defence of the market, the socialist state allowed market to operate to save the basic redistributive institutions.

It is not surprising, then, if we find the sources of inequalities in the major institution of the housing economy. Indeed, in my surveys on housing allocation in Hungary – and these findings were corroborated by the results of other surveys in Hungary, Poland and Czechoslovakia – I found that higher status groups, the better qualified with higher than average income, were heavily over-represented in the redistributive sector of the urban housing system and correspondingly a negative correlation was found between income and home ownership, qualification of the head of the household and home ownership. During the last three decades in Hungary, the better qualified – the professionals, white collars, and highly qualified workers – received State built and State owned flats; the working class, especially the semi-skilled and unskilled workers, had to build their own homes.[1] This trend is even more striking if we take the rural housing system into account. About half the working class in Hungary – and figures are comparable in other East European countries, specially again in Poland and Czechoslovakia – never had a chance to move to cities, not being able to buy a house there and not having a chance to get council housing, so they stayed in villages in privately owned, inherited or built homes. As in a capitalist Welfare society the poor is housed by the council and the rich buy or rent on the market (monopolising the advantages of home ownership), in State socialism professionals and the "middle class" (clerical workers and workers aristocracy) has the privilege to rent the heavily subsidized State housing and the working class has to buy or build on the market. Consequently, through the redistributive sector

1 See Appendix A, p. 76f.

of the housing economy, the State reallocates surplus in favour of higher income groups, by forcing those with less income to pay the total costs of their housing from wages or salaries in which, in principle, housing costs are not accumulated, and allocating all centralized surplus for housing to the better qualified. Consequently, in Hungary, but probably everywhere in Eastern Europe, social inequalities *after housing* are greater than before housing; if we want to measure the real extent of inequalities, we have to take into account the subsidies in better housing allocated systematically to the more well-to-do. This is a very significant factor, since the subsidy in the monthly rent of a newly built State flat is very close to, if not equal with, a monthly average wage in industry.

Consequently, the redistributive institutions in the housing economy are creating inequalities, shaping the structure of inequalities. (Someone could argue, of course – and a few economists who were willing to face the hard facts of state socialist housing policy in fact did so – that housing only compensates for the lack of inequality in the labour economy, since wages are not differentiated enough, the differentiation has to take place in housing and in the allocation of other goods and services. Such an explanation, on the other hand, would pre-suppose a functionalist explanation of social inequalities, the existence of "functional" or necessary inequalities, which is questionable enough in a market economy, but would make even less sense in a socialist non-market economy where central planning and not material reward allocates labour, especially across qualification levels.) Furthermore, in terms of social policy, it is quite obvious then that reforms which aim to ease the situation of those who require housing on the market do basically serve working class interests. If interest rates on mortgages are lowered, if administrative limitations on private housing construction are lifted, if construction materials bought by private constructors are subsidised, then we can be sure that inequalities in housing are decreasing; the strengthening of administrative control, more and more rigid redistribution will increase these inequalities.

But housing is only one – even if the most important – example of inequalities emerging from redistribution. In a recent study, J. Ladanyi (1975a+b) investigated the effect of state regulation of the prices of consumer goods in Hungary. Part of consumer prices (for example, vegetables or fruits) is determined on the market and these prices express the production costs, the prices of the most important consumer goods, on the other hand, are administratively regulated; they contain subsidies or are taxed, they are "deviated" from their actual value.

The regulation of consumer prices, the deviation of prices from values or production costs is supposedly motivated, or at least ideologically justified by social consideration. As the main authority of price policy in Hungary stated: "As a general rule those products have a low price (are subsidised) which play an important role in the consumption of lower income groups... " (Csikós-Nagy, 1971, 130p.) Consequently, the regulation of consumer prices is supposed to reallocate value from higher income groups to lower ones. In a most carefully carried out study, J. Ladanyi tested this proposition and measured the social effects of redistribution through the regulation of consumer prices. From official statistics on family budgets, he could determine the structure of consumption of different social strata and income groups. Surprisingly enough he found that the most heavily subsidised consumer goods did play a larger role in the consumption structure of higher status groups. He measured the *real value of the units of expenditure,* what he defined as:

$$\frac{\sum \text{expenditure} + \sum \text{Price-deviation (+subsidy or -tax)}}{\sum \text{expenditure}}$$

(Consequently, if the value of this indicator is above 1.0 it shows gain, if it is below 1.0 it shows loss from redistribution). He found this indicator as 1.049 for white collars, 1.043 for blue collars and 0.989 for agricultural workers. In fact, the real value of the units of expenditure underestimates the inequalities of redistribution, since absolute expenditures in higher income groups are significantly higher.[2] After taking the absolute level of expenditure into account, it was found that the white collars received about 50% more subsidy than the blue collars, but the same logic applied all along the social hierarchy, not only the white collars were more privileged than the blue collars, but the skilled workers were better off than the unskilled workers, leaving the agricultural labourers at the bottom with an absolute loss due to the deviation of prices from values (agricultural labourers consume more taxed and less subsidised goods). In fact, these gains and losses do not affect significantly the living standards, according to the cited investigation, the total gain of the most privileged group (high management and professionals) is just slightly more in a year than a two week average income in industry; the maximum loss is equivalent to two-three day average industrial income. On the other hand, it is still interesting that the deviation of consumer prices from production costs is increasing inequalities. Inequalities measured after taking price-deviations into account are greater – even if only slightly, by about 5% – than inequalities expressed by income distributions only.

Consequently, the redistributive mechanisms in the sphere of allocation of consumer good function in a similar manner as in the allocation of housing. They create on both occasions the inequalities, if consumer prices would correspond to production costs and the state would not intervene in a redistributive manner into the price structure, there would be less discrepancy between the real income level of white collars and those immediately active in the production process (industrial workers and agricultural labourers).

I would like to refer to a third research[3] as the final empirical illustration of the point I am trying to make. In 1967, the Central Statistical Office in Hungary conducted an investigation on personal incomes in the country. For the first time, beside wages and salaries, an attempt was made to take into consideration both cash and non-cash allowances (family allowances are examples for the first case and medical and educational benefits for the second). These data do not cover the two previously studied areas, since subsidies into the housing system and the deviation of consumer prices from production cost were not taken into account, but both for cash and especially for non-cash allowances, our previous findings are corroborated.

2 See Appendix B, p. 78.
3 See Appendix C, p. 78f.

Already, in the case of cash allowances, a significant discrepancy can be observed among different social strata; in white collar families, per capita allowances were about 20% higher than in families of industrial workers; agricultural labourers received less than half as much cash allowances as the white collars. The economically inactive population was an exception to this rule, they received almost four times as much cash allowances than the most privileged occupational group, but for them, in many instances, these cash allowances represented their total revenue. (In the case of those who did not have pensions and lived from welfare payments.)

Data on the correlation of income and cash allowances seems to contradict our previous evidence. It was found that per capita cash allowances are smaller in higher income groups; people in the lowest per capita income category received about 60% more cash allowances than those in the highest one. On the other hand, this is far from surprising, since the main component of cash allowance is family allowance. It is not necessarily the poorer families who receive more cash-allowance (this is clear from the data on the distribution of allowances among occupational strata) but those with more children.

The figures on the distribution of non-cash benefits confirm even more strongly our hypothesis, (the two main components of these being medical and educational benefits). White collars received almost 50% more per capita non cash benefits than industrial workers, high managers and professional more than twice as much as agricultural labourers. A strong positive correlation is found with income distribution as well, non-cash allowances being more than 20% higher in the highest per capita income group than in the lowest one. These figures basically indicate that higher social strata use medical services and facilities more frequently, and their children stay longer in the educational system. In fact, these indicators are very rough and they do not express adequately the qualitative differences which the different social strata have in using the health and educational systems. High bureaucrats and professional people not only use the medical services provided free by the state more often than blue collar workers, but the services they get are also systematically better (they have better access to highly qualified specialists or scarce medical facilities, e.g., to private rooms in hospitals, etc.). The same is true for the educational system. Not only are there greater opportunities for children of higher social strata to enter institutions of tertiary education, but it is also more probable that during their primary or secondary education they will have attended institutions which are more heavily subsidised (urban vs. rural schools, schools specialising in languages, mathematics or in other highly valued skills vs. schools with general curriculum, etc.). It is still the unaccomplished task of medical sociology or sociology of education in Eastern Europe to discover and document precisely these hidden inequalities, which naturally cannot be taken into account in such a general statistical data-collection as the one we were using above.

It is important finally to note that the cash and non-cash allowances taken into account by the study of the Central Statistical Office are very significant as components of real incomes; families of high bureaucrats and professionals receive monthly through these channels benefits which are equal to about a two week average industrial wage (more than twice the amount of that received by agricultural labourers).

In a recent paper Susan Ferge (S. Ferge, 1975, 718) emphasised that the inequality of the distribution of cash and non-cash allowances was smaller than the inequality of distribution of wages and salaries. She calculated an indicator, called „measure of inequality". She divided the average income of those who have higher than average incomes by the average incomes of those with lower than average incomes and this indicator was 2.32 in 1967 for Hungary. She also calculated the same indicator for cash and non-cash allowances and found that its value was only 1.92.

On the other hand, it is quite obvious that this does not indicate an equalising effect due to the system of cash and non-cash allowances. Any positive correlation between the allowances and incomes or social status will be to prove that redistribution increased inequalities. Hence, if such a positive correlation exists, then the absolute level of inequalities will be larger *after* the allowances are taken into account.

These three studies indicate that in Eastern Europe we might mislead ourselves if we try to measure inequalities by the distribution of wages and salaries. In fact, we can expect that the inequalities of living standards will be greater than those of wages, since in all of the above analysed cases, the redistributive mechanisms favoured those with better qualifications and already higher incomes. Through rents, cash and non-cash benefits and deviation of consumer prices from production costs, those with higher social status received more subsidy, people at the bottom of the social hierarchy less, or none.

Consequently, if by some miracle tomorrow rents would be raised so that they covered housing costs, the state stopped taxing and subsidising consumer goods and granting cash and non-cash benefits, and instead equally divided the sums used for these purposes up to now among wage earners; then these measures would lead to a more equal society, they would benefit the immediate producers, especially the agricultural labourers and the commuting "new working class", but also most industrial workers, probably with the exception of the most qualified "workers aristocracy".

Surprisingly then, the most extreme economic reformists in Eastern Europe who want to get rid of state subsidies and fringe benefits altogether, who do propose prices and rents covering costs and who, in fact, want to decrease state budgets radically by accumulating all costs of living in wages and abolishing redistributive intervention are articulating the interests of those who are directly involved in the process of production of material goods, they are articulating the interest of the working class.

I suggest on the basis of the presented empirical evidence, that in the State socialist societies of Eastern Europe a new system of inequalities is emerging. These inequalities cannot be explained as "inherited" from the capitalist past, or as the results of the survival or re-emergence of market relations. On the contrary, they are products of the basic economic institution which guarantees the expropriation of surplus from the immediate producer in State socialism, namely redistribution, they are inherent inequalities of State socialism.

Redistribution of real income in capitalist welfare society and the State socialist redistributive economic systems

But are those phenomena specifically State socialist? Redistribution of real income has similar side-effects in modern Western societies? Are Western Welfare capitalist societies significantly different from East European State socialism with regard to the role and nature of redistribution? Is there a socialist alternative to fight inequalities inherent in state socialist redistributive economies? Is a general theory of State capitalism, including both contemporary Western and East European societies, not an adequate tool to explain these inequalities? In an attempt to answer these highly justified questions on the following pages, I will try to elaborate upon the ideal type of State socialist redistributive economy or, if you like, to draw up a sketch of a possible political economy of State socialism. I propose that State socialism is qualitatively different from modern Western Welfare capitalism, it is based on historically new institutions of economic integration, socialist redistributive economy is crucially different from the redistribution of real income in welfare capitalist societies. I will attempt to apply Polanyi's (1957a) theory of models of economic integration, and especially of redistribution, to State socialism and to distinguish State socialism as a modern, rational redistributive economy from contemporary capitalist market or "post-market" economies.

But does this distinction make sense at all in an epoch when the State everywhere controls an increasing proportion of national income, and reallocates it through the national budgets? Isn't it more adequate to say that both in the West and in the East we deal with mixed economies, both combine elements of market and redistribution, the difference is only a slight – and possibly disappearing – quantitative one.

No one can question that economic politicians and planners, especially in allocating resources from the national budget, are involved in technically the same exercise and will face very similar problems in the United Kingdom or in West Germany as in Poland or Hungary. On the other hand, if we succeed in constructing the ideal types of socio-economic systems they operate in, if we succeed in showing the logic which integrates these systems, the contrast will be sharper. True enough, Western societies use redistributive mechanisms, but only when and if the market does not function and only if these mechanisms are necessary to defend the major socio-economic institution, private property. Similarly in State socialism, planners will introduce market mechanism, but only when and if redistribution does not work, the compromise with the market is only a compromise in defence of the redistributive power of the State.

Let us start this analysis with the most obvious, but probably also the most superficial difference – namely, the difference in ownership relations. It is well known that in modern Western societies the role of private ownership changed (with the increasing importance of absentee ownership, increased role of management, State control, etc.), but these changes left the system of legitimation of economic power basically unaltered, they did not challenge the right to private ownership of means of the production. In all contemporary Western societies – the private ownership of the means of the production is a good enough reason to expropriate surplus and dispose of it. The state, the trade unions, etc., might intervene, control, limit the extent of expropriation or influence the way the surplus is used, but they will not question the right of private owners to expropriate solely on the basis of ownership. Other principles of legitimation are also operating, but private property is an obvious one. In State socialism, private ownership does not legitimate expropriation (if such expropriation exists – and in many instances it does – it is "illegitimate"). The dominating principle which legitimates expropriation and disposal of surplus in State socialism is that of the redistributor who claims to have a "scientific" knowledge of how to use such surplus in an economically efficient and socially just way. Consequently, beyond the differences in ownership relation, we can discover two different dominating principles of legitimation – that of the private owner and the "scientific" or "technological" knowledge of the redistributor.

But not only the principle which legitimates the expropriation of surplus is different in the two systems, even the surplus itself is defined differently. Already Pearson (1957) has pointed out that it is not possible to find a formal distinction of surplus which would apply in all economic systems, the meaning of surplus is different in a market and in a redistributive economy. In fact, someone could argue that the surplus has a pure economic definition only under market conditions where the surplus is simply the difference between the costs of production and the market defined price of the product. Such a pure economic definition of the surplus is only possible in the non-embedded civil society, where economy has its autonomy and politics is a separate sphere of social activity. (Collective bargaining, trade unionism, etc., is a limitation of this autonomy in modern capitalist societies, but these very institutions function in the framework of the civil society, pluralistic, bourgeois democratic politics.) Societies based on redistributive economies are, on the other hand, embedded societies and Pearson has a strong point when he is proposing that in redistributive economies surplus is defined by power.

Under the conditions of this peculiar type of redistributive economy we are talking about, namely under the conditions of State socialist rational redistribution, the surplus as such is basically defined by political power. (Obviously, it would be necessary to distinguish between different types of redistributive economies. Economic anthropologists like Polanyi, Pearson or Dalton, when writing about redistribution basically referred to societies of the "Asiatic mode of production", and they never developed a substantive analysis of Soviet type of redistribution. The Soviet type of economic systems are as different from the Asiatic mode of production as they are from the capitalist mode of production and I propose to call this system rational redistribution vs. the traditional redistribution of classical Asiatic societies, by referring to the differences as to how redistributive power is legitimated. At this point, it is not possible to elaborate this question in detail, but with George Konrad we attempted to offer a systematic comparison of market, rational and traditional redistribution, in our forthcoming book, *Towards the class power of intelligentsia.)* The political rather than "economic" definition of the surplus means that wage levels and the extent of inequality among different categories of the labour force express first of all political considerations. The price of the labour in principle is not related to the value or surplus the labour will produce – the redistributive power will expropriate as much surplus as politically possible. The limit of expropriation is revolt. 1956 in Hungary or 1970 in Poland was a clear enough indication that there is an absolute limit of expropriation in State socialist societies – if the living standard starts to decline or if it remains stagnant on the long run, it might lead to a spontaneous revolt of the workers and the level and dynamics of wages are regulated by these political forces.

On an abstract theoretical level, this means that in State socialist societies the labour is not a market-commodity in a precise definition of the term, a labour market does not operate. Probably it is the commodity or non-commodity nature of the labour that draws the clearest contrast between State socialist and modern capitalist Welfare economies. Labour power is also bought and sold in State socialism, more than in any other society. (The proportion of self employed is less than in any capitalist society, a higher proportion of the labour force has to sell its labour.)

At this point I would like to refer to Polanyi's notion of "non-market trade." In analysing trade in Hammurabbi's *Babylon* he pointed out that the widespread use of money and the existence of a developed system of trade does not necessarily mean the existence of a market economy. Polanyi (1957b) argues that the prices of products are not regulated by the market, but they are fixed by royal authority. Under such circumstances, the income of the tradesmen is not the difference between the purchase price and the selling price of the product, but it is limited and guaranteed by the King. In principle, the King could fix the selling price of a product below the purchase price, and in this case, the tradesman would have more income by losing more – a not very probable case in Hammurabi's time but a more frequent one in State socialism. Anyway, sociologically the crucial characteristics of this trade is that the actors involved in the circulation process of goods (buyers, sellers, royal authority) are not transacting with each other, the relationship of the tradesmen to the royal authority is of dispositive nature. Trade can exist without market – to sum up Polanyi's argument, and in this marketless trade, the actors' position is dispositive; in market trade, transactive. Generally speaking, we can identify redistribution with dispositive, market with transactive relationships.

Quite obviously in State socialist societies those who sell their labour do have a dispositive relationship to those who buy labour. This means that the price of their labour is, in principle, not subject of bargaining, it is administratively fixed, it does not express potential value or surplus produced by the labour. It is also of crucial importance that the owners of labour do not have the right to decide to sell or not to sell their labour, they are under statutory obligation to do so. I propose that this system contrasts sharply with all capitalist welfare societies, where an element of bargaining (collective or individual) is always present. Furthermore, the owner of the labour has the right to withhold his labour from the market, to try to sell the products of his labour rather than his labour power, to try to withhold his labour until prices improve and to live from savings or starve, and he also might find it impossible to sell his labour since no one wants to buy it. In a capitalist welfare economy, the worker has the right not to sell his labour, but he is also threatened by unemployment – none of these options are open to the workers in State socialism.

At this point I have to make a few specifications. Certainly in all empirically known State socialist economies, the price of the labour does express to some extent the value or surplus produced by the labour and, in certain instances, it reflects also the changes in supply and demand. Wages in mining, for example, are higher, or those who were prepared to settle the "virgin lands" of Siberia under Krushtchev's scheme, were also entitled to higher income. But these are instances, I would argue, when planning is making compromises to market forces, if labour cannot be recruited otherwise, they are willing to obey the laws of supply and demand. The sad irony of the history is that labour camps were quite functional during the early development of State socialism, they furnished very cheap labour for areas where market would set a relatively high price for it. Nowadays, largely as a result of political rather than economic processes, forced labour is replaced with the more gallant compromise of planners to the market. But these measures are clearly compromises, they are in conflict with the ethos of rational redistribution and its reward system. Ideally, in rational redistribution rewards are allocated according to levels of qualification. The so-called socialist principle of allocation is the allocation according to work, but labour, according to principles of orthodox political economy, is divided into "simple" and "complex" (or skilled) and with the quite questionable and certainly unsustained assumption that skilled labour is producing more value than simple and is therefore better rewarded. This principle is embodied in the wage-nomenclatures, where wage levels are systematically increasing with the level of formal qualification. An unskilled worker is supposed to earn less than a skilled one, professionals should earn more than workers, and when the miner or the settler on the virgin lands of Siberia breaks this rule, he commits a sin, even if only a venial one. To be smart, to move quickly into the fields where demand is great and supply is low, to make a lot of money quickly just by recognising the opportunity, is not a socialist virtue. I am convinced that this ethos is deeply socialised in East European societies; the few with low qualification and high earnings suffer from guilt-feelings, they are momentarily fortunate pariahs, but well aware of their deviant nature. But even if someone would not internalise the dominating labour ethos of the State socialist societies, the statutory obligation to sell the labour would basically limit his chances for transaction in selling his labour. Everyone is obliged by law to sell his/her labour to bureaucratic labour-organisations; if someone is without a job he can, and frequently is, prosecuted. (The personal identification card contains information about jobs and if at an identity check a police officer notices that someone is out of a job for a given – fairly short – time, he has to take action against the person concerned.) People have to work, they have to do so usually in bureaucratic labour organisations and for administratively fixed wages. If Weber is correct – and I think he is – and the central institution of any capitalist society is the labour market, then the core institution of State socialist redistributive economy is the non-market trade of labour. An economy becomes a redistributive one only when the labour market is abolished and replaced with the non-market trade of labour.

It was necessary to show first how differently surplus is defined in market and redistributive economies, and to draw the contrast between labour market and non-market trade of labour to show the significant and qualitative difference between redistribution of real income in welfare societies under state monopoly capitalism and redistributive economic systems under State socialism. *The welfare state* in state monopoly capitalism *attempts to redistribute real income* but this income is first defined on a labour market. This labour market is not identical with the market of *laissez faire* capitalism due to State and trade union intervention, but it is still a market, where in principle the actors can transact with each other, can bargain for the price of labour, the owner of the labour power is legally entitled not to sell his labour and labour also might remain unsold. *Under State socialism the State redistributes surplus,* surplus which was never accumulated in personal incomes, but which was directly centralized in the State budget and reallocated according to centrally defined goals and values. Technically speaking, the difference lies in the sources of national budgets; capitalist welfare states rely heavily on different forms of taxes; socialist states derive revenues directly from the production organizations. Let us again take the example of housing to show the far-reaching consequences of these technical differences. In a capitalist Welfare state the total amount of housing cost is accumulated in the total amount of personal incomes. The distribution of these incomes is, on the other hand, highly unequal. A growing proportion of the working class is unable to sell its labour on the labour market which is manipulated by monopoly capital interests for a price which would include costs of housing. Under these circumstances, due to the deficiencies of the functioning of the labour market, the social reproduction process would break down, unless the State intervenes and reallocates income from higher to lower income groups by taxing the higher income groups and using these revenues for financing and subsidising housing for the poor. Under State socialism, housing costs are not accumulated in the total amount of personal incomes but they flow directly into the State budget and the State will provide housing for all, not only for the poor. By redistributing real income, the welfare state strengthens the nature of the socio-economic system. The principle of allocation when redistributing real income contradicts the principle which regulates the labour market and income formation (social justice or, more specifically, decent housing for all vs. competition, bargaining, transaction). This new principle will not override the old one, it remains dominant (since it is expressing the interest of the dominating class) but it is being challenged and, to some extent, it is limited. (In a simplified marxist analysis, one might say that the "Profithunger" of the ruling class is limited to help the survival of the system of capitalist exploitation.") Under State socialism, the same principle rules the non-market trade of labour as rules state housing or the state regulation of consumer prices, or the allocation of cash or non-cash benefits, etc. All these spheres are redistributive and all are based on the same reward system. Consequently, if the better qualified "deserves" higher income, it "deserves" also better housing, better medical services and better chances for his children to get a good education. Therefore, it is not surprising at all that under state monopoly capitalism, the scissor of social inequality is opened on the labour market and it is largest in terms of income, and is slightly diminishing due to the redistribution of real income, but under State socialism the inequalities of incomes are further increased by all redistributive measures of the State, all inequalities (in income, housing, etc.) being equally defined according to the logic of State socialist redistribution.

Up to now we have been talking about the structure of social inequalities and the mechanisms which bring them about in the two different systems. The question of the *extent of social inequalities* is another one. By proposing that there are inherent social inequalities under socialism, and that these inequalities are products of mechanisms which do serve equalizing functions under capitalism, I do not suggest that State socialist societies are more unequal than societies under State monopoly capitalism. It is extremely difficult to compare the general level of social inequalities between different socio-economic formations, and I have not seen any reliable study which has successfully mastered this task. If I were to design a study to compare State socialist and monopoly capitalist societies, my working hypothesis would be that, concerning the access to material goods, the overall level of social inequalities is still lower in the contemporary East European societies that in Western Europe, in North America or in Australia.

True enough, the "redistributors" are "selfish", they favour "their own kind" (or more sociologically speaking: the class which is organized around the monopoly of redistributive power), when they allocate scarce resources. High bureaucrats, their "executives" and ideologues will have better access to State-built new housing than the working class, but this privilege is quite a modest one in "natural terms". A department head in the Central Committee or Central Planning office – a major power figure in the redistributive power hierarchy – who makes daily decisions affecting hundreds of millions of Forints, Zlotys or Leva will be satisfied with a two-bedroom flat on 55 m^2 on a crowded and ugly new housing development. It is true that you will find few workers in high season in the heavily subsidised trade union or party vacation homes, but most of the "bosses" there have to share bathrooms, they will eat quite inferior food and might not be able to afford a double Scotch each evening before dinner. I am inclined to believe that even if we can speak about a new ruling class in East European state socialism then it is the most miserable privileged class in the history of mankind.

But the main point of my argument is not about the extent of inequalities, but about their nature and structure. The crucial point is that the type of inequalities I described above are rooted in relations of production which are specific to state socialist redistributive economics. They are expressions of the basic conflict of State socialist societies, the conflict between the "immediate producer" and the "redistributor". In a way the inequalities in the access to scarce material goods are only side products. If we can say that there is a new dominating class under State socialism then its main purpose is the maximization of redistributive power and better access to material goods is just a kind of "fringe-benefit" to its members. Especially in the early stages of development of capitalism, the level of consumption of the owners of capital was not necessarily very high (remember those who took seriously the teachings of Benjamin Franklin). What antagonizes the relationship between the owner of capital and the owner of the labour power is not the differences of their living standard, but the vested interest of the former in the maximization of profit, his interest in the capitalist system of exploitation. Similarly under State socialism the real antagonism between the immediate producers and those with redistributive power is emerging from the attempts of the "redistributors" to expropriate as much surplus as possible from those who are directly involved in the production process of material goods, to increase the amount of surplus which is available for redistribution, sociologically speaking to maximize redistributive power. It is only the individual interest of the department head of the Central Planning Office to get a free state built and owned flat which would add a half million Forints subsidy to his real income (the equivalent of a twenty-year income of an average industrial worker!), but his class interest is to increase the budget of his department with a few billion Forints next year, or more generally speaking to increase the proportion of national income which is reallocated through the State budget. Redistributive mechanisms under State socialism are the tools of the already powerful to increase their power, they do not challenge the inherent logic of inequalities, they are based on the values which justify these inequalities so how could we expect an equalising effect from them. To use Gerschenkron's terminology redistribution under State socialism is the historical „substitute“ of the exploitative mechanisms of capitalist societies, as it is a qualitatively different phenomena than the redistribution of real income in welfare societies which is after all a countervailing mechanism, challenging more or less successfully, inside the limits set by the capitalist nature of reproduction process, inequalities inherent to societies with private ownership of the means of production.

Towards policies expressing working class interests under State socialism

Is such a countervailing mechanism possible at all under State socialism? After all, it also took quite some time before capitalism developed into the fairly articulated conflict system with a relative powerful expression of the countervailing working class interests. The more recent the lords in the house of the power are, the more emphasis they will give to the ideologies of concensus. First they have to consolidate their power before they let anyone challenge it.

The consensus ideology, surrounding State socialist redistribution is a very powerful one – principles like the scientific allocation of social resources, the need to defend the societal interests against the individualistic ones, the necessity of long term planning, the preference of long term interests against short term interests, etc. are very appealing especially to the large masses of intellectuals who at least pretend that they have knowledge – technical or ideological – useful for the fulfilment of these tasks.

A quite unconscious search for a counter-ideology of socialist rational redistribution was on the other hand always present in socialist thinking, but illusions about the expected effects of the abolishment of private ownership of the means of production prevented the development of a coherent alternative theory. True, already Engels in his essay „Socialism; utopian and scientific“ attempts to shift emphasis from ownership relations in defining socialism as a system where the producers have direct control upon the conditions and products of their labour but he even did not contemplate about the possible conflict between the „direct control by the producer“ and „public control by the State“ (or any other public body). But the idea of the „direct power“ or „direct control“ survived – as a pure apologetical ideology in Soviet type of societies by pretending that the proletariat has direct power (for example in the so called „soviets“) when it obviously does not have it or more powerfully as the criticism of Soviet State socialism, the belief in non-bureaucratic, or „self managing“ socialism, or socialism with a human face.

It is not the purpose of this paper – which is descriptive-analytic and not ideological by intention – to take sides in this debate and to offer a description of a good, "better" or "real" socialism. It is probably enough if at this point we ascertain that the abolishment of private ownership of the means of production still leaves us with the unresolved dilemma: who will dispose with the products of labour, which are the principles which legitimate the right to dispose with surplus. In the State socialist societies of Eastern Europe the dominating principle which legitimates expropriation is the supposedly superior knowledge of the redistributor about the economically efficient and socially just allocation of social resources. But this principle can, and probably is more and more often challenged with the claim of producers to have the right to control the products of their labour – State socialist redistributive economy is challenged by economic mechanisms based on self regulation, self management.

This alternative principle of legitimation which corresponds to the immediate interests of the producers is on the other hand highly unarticulated. The East European societies are among the socially least conscious ones. But probably the working class of Eastern Europe is more aware of their antagonism with the "redistributors" than the ideologues, even if its "class-consciousness" is at the level of the consciousness of the Luddites. The riots in Gdansk during 1970 and further workers' strikes and riots elsewhere in Poland during the summer of 1976 are dramatic indications that the class character of opposition movements in Eastern Europe might change. Most of the political dissent up to now was largely the internal affair of intellectuals, political struggle was the struggle between different groups of intellectuals for power. In 1956 in Hungary – as Bill Lomax demonstrated very convincingly in his book "Hungary, 1956" – the political upheaval of intellectuals in fact lead to a revolutionary movement of the working class, but it was only a by-product of an originally intellectual movement, so Poland is probably the first historical example where the industrial workers initiated change and not without success. But organised, declared strikes and riots are only extreme examples – quite desperate moves in societies where the police control is so strict as in Eastern Europe today. Workers' attempts to challenge the redistributive economic system and to try to articulate their conflicting interests are much more widespread, but obviously quite unconscious or "spontaneous".

Hethy and Makó (1969; 1970) in analysing labour-management relations in one of the main heavy industrial centres of Hungary could identify a quite deliberate strategy of the workers to slow down production process and withhold production as a powerful weapon against exploitative wage systems, a kind of "functional equivalent" of strikes. Hethy and Makó with good theoretical instinct went as far as suggesting that the workers in fact attempted to establish transactive relationships with management and they felt that their success to do so is the precondition of long term industrial peace between labour and management.

We might add that there are numerous other instances when the "working people" in fact strive for transactive relationships and try to get out of the "disposition" forced upon them by the logic of rational redistribution. The most elementary interest of the immediate producer is to replace disposition with transaction on the non-market trade of labour, to increase his independence from the bureaucratic labour organisation. From the point of view of a class analysis peasant-workers are typical products of this struggle. The industrial worker who maintained his rural residence, to be able to establish a very intensive family mini-farm, producing goods for the urban market, providing income and covering the food needs of the family is more independent from the industrial employer than the established urban proletariat who does not have any income resource besides his wage. People with alternative income resources, people who do not have to worry about food and shelter might not be willing to work for exploitative wages, might give up their jobs if wages are too low and wait until another one comes. They are even in a better situation to manipulate the law about "vagrancy" not being before the eyes of the urban police. One of the unexpected consequences of the economic reform of 1968 in Hungary was the inflation of unskilled labour. Before the reform experts expected that wage differentials will increase if the labour movements and wage system is less administratively regulated, the price of qualified labour will increase more rapidly. Contrary to these expectations, wage differentials shrank, it turned out to be unskilled labour which found itself in a more powerful bargaining situation. But these unskilled workers were mainly peasant-workers who immediately exploited the more transactive relationships of the economic reform, if industrial wages were not high enough they fluctuated back to agricultural co-operatives and quite few of them using the less administrative regulation of urban fruit and vegetable market developed their family mini-farm into productive, efficient enterprises. A few of them even started to buy the old, scrapped tractors of agricultural cooperatives, fixed them and increased productivity of their mini-farms. Commodity producing peasant-workers started to purchase small vans to transport quickly their products to the cities. Quite a few agricultural co-operatives followed the pattern set by family mini-farming, not being bound by so strict wage regulations as the industry the increased wages attracted workers back from urban industry and set up industrial side branches. This industrial side branches were under-capitalised and badly equipped, still they could compete with the large scale industry organised according to the logic of redistributive economy since they turned out to be more transactive.

Many critics of the economic reforms both inside Eastern Europe and in the West would identify the process I just described as signs of the capitalist restoration, but I would see in them signs of the class struggle of the immediate producer to challenge the redistributive system of economy, to replace their dispositive situation in the labour-trade with a transactive one. After all the described process did not lead to the accumulation of capital, the peasant-workers did not use hired labour, all that they attempted to do to sell the products of their own labour and to withhold actually only temporarily – their labour power from bureaucratic labour organisation and to force redistributive power to appropriate less surplus and give more scope to the autonomy of consumers. The abolishment of the private ownership of the means of the production was not questioned, it was not private property which emerged from the economic reforms, but more self-regulating economic system, offering more chance of bargaining for the owners of the labour and more autonomy of the consumer. On the other hand this development obviously threatened redistributive power and when from the early seventies step by step the concessions of the reforms were taken back then it was a movement to restore redistributive power, to discipline the working class. Laws prohibiting the „private purchase“ of tractors and vans, the industrial side branches of agricultural co-operatives were introduced during the early seventies in Hungary and their purpose was clearly to make peasant-workers more dependent from bureaucratic labour organizations. As a significant step in taking back the concessions of the Hungarian reforms of 1968 from the early seventies, those who wanted to change employer for the second time in a year were obliged to use the services of a state employment agency, the right to choose an employer was suspended. This measure hit again the working class, especially the unskilled labour, who used high labour turnover as a weapon to increase wages. In turning back now to the introductory remarks and hypothesis of this paper, I would like to emphasize again that in evaluating the social consequences of policy measures in State socialist societies we have to re-evaluate our conceptual tools since the social meaning and consequences of superficially similar mechanisms can be strikingly different in State socialist redistributive economies than in capitalist societies. In State socialist societies those policies will express the immediate interests of the working class which challenge redistributive power, increase the bargaining power – collective or individual – of the workers.

If the political system would allow the establishment of a genuine workers party, dedicated to the articulation of working class interest, then this party could challenge the „conservatives“, the bolsheviks, the representatives of redistributive power by elaborating and alternative strategy based on the principles of self-management, self-regulation, and the autonomy of employees and consumers. The most important goals in the programme of such a party would be to guarantee the legal and economic conditions of free employment, to allow the producers to decide if they want to sell their labour power or rather the product of their labour, to allow them to withhold their labour when they find the price of the labours disadvantageous. (Curiously enough such a party might even fight for the „freedom to become unemployed“.) Such a party probably would fight for the „free association of producers“, namely for the right to establish alternative production organisations, which are not directly controlled by State redistributive power, in which producers can decide themselves how much they want to accumulate and how much they want to pay out to themselves in forms of wages. An equally important issue would be to increase the autonomy of the consumer, to question that the redistributor „knows better“ what people need and should consume, to accumulate a larger proportion of means in personal incomes and consequently to decrease the financial means which are allocated by the redistributors in forms of „collective consumption". To sum up, such a party would fight for more equality by limiting redistributive power and challenging it from the standpoint of "self-determination of the immediate producer".

I used the programme of this imaginary "workers party" just as a didactic tool to bring my points through and I am not suggesting that we could or should expect the emergence of such an opposition party in Eastern Europe. History is more imaginative than we are and can produce new institutions and mechanisms, can create structures and I am not prepared to predict the possible political system of a developed socialist society.

On the other hand I am quite sure that the developed stage of socialism will differ from the present early stage by offering more scope to the articulation of working class interests and to the development of an alternative "ethos" which would challenge the principles of legitimation of redistributive power. At present the handling of inequalities and conflict inherent to the functioning of State socialist redistributive economics is basically a "philanthropical" one and compares quite well with late nineteenth century anglo-saxon "charity" – there are always "good redistributors" who are ready to "help the poor" if they "deserve it", like the "good capitalist" of the last century. But probably with the consolidation of redistributive power we might expect the institutionalisation of the articulation of oppressed interest as the pre-condition for the development of real social policy.

The argument of this paper remains largely in a reformist framework, the sketched "party programme" is that of a reformist and not a revolutionary party. Probably only due to the highly underdeveloped nature of an alternative theory of "self-managing socialism" it is difficult to imagine how a society where the dominating principle of legitimation is the "self-determination of immediate producers" would function. Probably Yugoslavia is the closest approximation, at least it is a country with a confessed ideology of "self management" but socialist critics of the Yugoslav model who are more familiar with the empirical fact of this society are quite doubtful about the genuine nature of self management – Yugoslavia might be just the most humanised version of East European State socialism. Anyway with my present knowledge about actual socio-economic processes in societies which abolished the private ownership of the means of production it is hardly possible to imagine a socialist society without a strong redistributive power and it is highly probable that in a more developed stage the dominating principle of legitimation remains that one of the rational redistribution. Consequently the more developed stage of socialism in Eastern Europe might just be a reformed version of the present system and not a revolutionary negation of it. The novelty of the next stage is probably only an institutionalised articulation of interests and of an ethos in structural conflict with those of the redistributive economy, but without questioning the primacy of redistributive power.

Let us illustrate this point again with the previous "didactic example". If a "workers party" would ever succeed to defeat the "conservatives" and would gain power, it would have to accept the "realities of redistribution". The "new party in power" would take over the old bureaucracies which expropriate surplus and would maintain a large – probably just slightly smaller than under the "conservatives" – sphere of redistribution.

Like reformist social democrats learned to live with private property if they want to be in government, the "party of workers self determination" would probably similarly compromise with the institution of redistribution. What realistically can be expected is not more and not less than the institutionalisation of oppressed interests, in a way the transformation of State socialist societies into more articulate conflict systems.

I wanted to present a diagnosis and not an ideological dream even when I attempted to predict the possible lines of socio-economic and political change. But I think these changes are necessary not only desirable. At present majority interest in East European State socialism is highly inarticulated which builds the element of instability into these societies, relatively minor political upheavals can threaten the basic social structure, consequently the ruling elite will be ruthless in oppressing any kind of opposition. In fact during the last two decades the ruling elite became less ruthless, more tolerant, allowed the demystification of certain ideologies and in the long run this might lead to the conscious development of policies expressing interests of the working class even if these are in structural conflict with dominating redistributive interests.

APPENDIX A

There are no systematic, nationally representative data as far as I know concerning the correlation of social status or income with housing allocation, but all data from Hungary, Poland and Czechoslovakia I could find indicate that the better qualified and consequently higher income groups have better access to State owned housing, the less qualified and lower income groups will more probably depend on the market, they will own their homes.

For Hungary the most systematic data are available from the survey I carried out with George Konrad in 1968 on a representative and fairly large sample in two cities (Pecs and Szeged). The different social strata rented, owned or shared their housing in the following proportions.

	Rent	*Own housing (in %)*	*Share*	*Respondents all together N*	*%*
High bureaucrats and leading professionals	*58.9*	*34.4*	*6.6*	*90*	*100.0*
Other professionals	*59.4*	*31.2*	*9.4*	*128*	*100.0*
Technicians	*46.9*	*44.5*	*8.6*	*254*	*100.0*
Clerical workers	*53.6*	*34.6*	*11.7*	*112*	*100.0*
Employed in services	*50.6*	*34.8*	*15.0*	*73*	*100.0*
Skilled workers	*40.1*	*48.7*	*11.2*	*474*	*100.0*
Semi-skilled workers	*40.6*	*46.8*	*12.6*	*271*	*100.0*
Unskilled workers	*35.9*	*52.1*	*12.1*	*217*	*100.0*
Agricultural labourers	*8.4*	*91.7*	*0.0*	*36*	*100.0*
Former white collars in pension	*58.5*	*32.3*	*9.1*	*99*	*100.0*
Former blue collars in pension	*44.4*	*48.3*	*6.7*	*387*	*100.0*

The best data I could find for Poland are from the survey carried out by Wesolowski et al. in 1964–65 on the social stratification of three Polish cities (Lodz, Szczecin and Koszalin; see Slomczynski/Wesolowski, in: Wesolowski (ed.) 1970.) They found that in the cities they investigated the different social strata lived in the following proportions in newly built, state owned flats: (in %)

Professionals	40.6
Technicians	22.8
Clerical workers	22.8
Employed in services	15.7
Workers in supervisory positions	17.4
Skilled workers	12.6

Semi and unskilled workers	8.8

Families in different income groups lived in newly built, state owned housing in the following proportions (in %, income in Zloty per month)

2000 zl	10.6
2001–3000	18.2
3001–4000	34.4
4001 and more	37.3

(source: Slomczynski, K. and Wesolowski, W., 1970, pp. 108 and 111)

Data from Czechoslovakia are even less systematic, but they also point into the same direction. L. Mackova in 1967 carried out a survey among those who lived in the most frequently built standard apartment house type (these standard houses were the TO-6B and TO-8B houses. Unfortunately I do not know precisely what proportion of new State housing was built in these two standard house types, but there is no reason to believe that in other house types social stratification might be different.) Her survey was representative for all cities in Bohemia. She found that the tenants in the new flats she surveyed were distributed among the different occupational groups the following way: (in %)

Unskilled workers employed in services	8.2
Unskilled industrial workers	0.6
Skilled workers	32.7
Clerical workers	6.5
High bureaucrats and leading professionals	29.4
Other professionals	21.0
Inactives	1.6
	100.0% (N = 510)

(source: L. Mackova, 1970, p. 10)

In another survey in 1970 representative for cities in Bohemia L. Mackova found that families living in housing newly built by the State were distributed the following way among occupational groups:

Workers	35.7
White collars	39.7
High bureaucrats and leading professionals	11.6
Inactives	6.5
Fatherless families	6.4
	100.0% (N = 930)

(source: L. Mackova, 1971)

APPENDIX B

The figures expressing the social consequences of redistribution through the deviation of prices of consumer goods from production costs (by taxation or subsidies) are the following (data are calculated for one year):

	Real value of the unit of expenditure	Total amount of expenditures	Total expenditures + taxes or subsidies in Forints	Redistribution
High bureaucrats and professionals	1,048	24.084	25,232.4	1,148.4
Other white collar	1,049	21.174	22,208.0	1,034.0
Skilled and semi-skilled workers	1,044	16.534	17,266.8	732.8
Unskilled workers	1,038	14,076	14,604.9	528.9
White collars all together	1,049	21,770	22,827.4	1,057.4
Industrial workers all together	1,043	16,133	16,832.5	699.5
Families with industrial and agricultural income	0,981	14,035	13,789.6	-245.4
Agricultural labourers	0,989	12,694	12,560.5	-133.5

(source: J. Ladanyi, 1975/a, p. 23)

APPENDIX C

The monthly cash allowances were the following by occupational and income groups in 1967 in Hungary:

Occupational groups	Monthly per capita cash allowances (in Forints)	Income groups by per capita monthly income (in Forints)	Monthly per capita cash allowances (in Forints)
High bureaucrats and professionals	107	–600	147
Middle management	97	601–800	150
Other white collar	110	801–1000	138
White collars all together	102	1001–1200	126
Skilled workers	90	1201–1400	113
Semi- skilled workers	87	1401–1600	105

Occupational groups	Monthly per capita cash allowances (in Forints)	Income groups by per capita monthly income (in Forints)	Monthly per capita cash allowances (in Forints)
Unskilled workers	86	1601–1800	105
Industrial workers all together	88	1801–2000	89
Agricultural labourers	48	2001–2400	97
Inactives	398	2401–	88

(source: S. Ferge, 1975, p. 719 and Hungarian Central Statistical Office, 1972, pp. 183 and 188)

The distribution of *non-cash* allowances by occupational and income groups were the following:

Occupational groups	Monthly per capita non-cash allowances (in Forints)	Income groups by per capita monthly income (in Forints)	Monthly per capita non-cash allowances (in Forints)
High bureaucrats and professionals	260	–600	156
Middle management	221	601–800	167
Other white collar	220	801–1000	171
White collars all together	235	1001–1200	167
Skilled workers	163	1201–1400	161
Semi-skilled workers	153	1401–1600	163
Unskilled workers	149	1601–1800	163
Industrial workers all together	157	1801–2000	157
Agricultural labourers	114	2001–2400	161
Inactives	185	2401–	193

(source: S. Ferge, 1975, p. 724 and Hungarian Central Statistical Office, 1972, pp. 229–233)

Bibliography

BERÉNYI, József

1974 *Életszinvonal és szociálpolitika.* (Living standard and social policy). Budapest: Kossuth Kiadó.

CSIKÓS-NAGY, Béla

1971 *Magyar gazdaságpolitika.* (Hungarian economic policy). Budapest: Kossuth Könyvkiadó.

FERGE, Zsuzsa

1976 "A szocialista társadalmi struktura dinamikája." (Dynamics of socialist social structure). *Valóság,* No. 11, pp. 13–25.

1975 "Társadalompolitika, szociálpolitika és a központositott újraelosztás típusai." (Social policy and types of redistribution). *Közgazdasági Szemle,* No. 6, pp. 709–724.

HARASZTI, Miklós

1975 "Piece work in Hungary. I have heard the iron cry." *New Lift Review,* May-June, pp. 9–24.

HÉTHY, Lajos, MAKÓ, Csaba

1970 A teljesitményelv érvényesitése és az üzemi érdek és hatalmi viszonyok. (Differential incentives and the structure of interests and powers. Labour-management and intra-labour conflicts in a business organization of a centrally planned economy). Budapest: Magyar Tudományos Akadémia Szociológiai Kutató Csorportjának Közleményei.

1969' "Work performance, interests, powers and environment." (The case of cyclical slowdowns in a Hungarian factory). *The Sociological Review Monograph,* No. 17, February, pp. 123–150.

HUNGARIAN CENTRAL STATISTICAL OFFICE

1972 *A lakóssági jövedelmek szinvonala és szóródása.* (The level and distribution of personal incomes) Budapest: Központi Statisztikai Hivatal

LADANYI, Janos

1975a "Fogyasztói árak és szociálpolitika" (Consumer prices and social policy). *Valóság,* No. 12, pp. 16–29.

1975b "A fogyasztói áreltéritések hatása az egyes rétegek jövedelmére és fogyasztására." (The effect of price-regulations on the income and consumption of different social strata). Budapest: Szövetkezeti Kutató lntézet Közlemények, No. 102.

LENGYEL, László

1975 Életszinvonal és szociálpolitika" (Living standard and social policy). *Közgazdasági Szemle,* 1975, No. 1.

MACKOVA, Libuse

1970 *Byty a obyvatele v typove vystavbe TO-8B.* Praha: Vyzkumny Ustav Vystavby a Architektury.

1971 *Vyvoj domacnosti ve statni a druzstevni vystave.* Praha: Vyzkumny Ustav Vystavby a Architektury.

POLANYI, Karl

1957a "The economy as instituted process." In K. Polanyi et al (eds): *Trade and Market in the Early Empires.* Glencoe, Ill.: The Free Press, 1957, pp. 243–270.

1957b "Marketless trading in Hammurabi's time." In K. Polanyi et al (eds): *Trade and Market in the Early Empires.* Glencoe, Ill.: The Free Press, pp. 12–26.

PEARSON, Harry W.

1957 "The economy has no surplus – a critique of a theory of development." In K. Polanyi et al (eds.): *Trade and Market in the Early Empires.* Glencoe, Ill.: The Free Press, pp. 320–341.

SŁOMCZYNSKI, K., WESOLOWSKI, W.

1970 "Zróżnicowanie spoleczne: praca zbiorowa." In W. Wesolowski (ed), *Zrożnicowanie spoleczne (Social differentation: basic results).* Wroclaw: Ossolineum, pp. 93–146.

II. Social Structure of Socialist and Capitalist Societies

II.1 The Intelligentsia in the Class Structure of State Socialist Societies[1]

Iván Szelényi

The paper describes the class structure of East European state-socialist societies, positing the existence of a class dichotomy between the working class and the intelligentsia. This thesis challenges those theories which claim that the importance of class conflicts declined under state socialism and that therefore such societies should be described as containing nonantagonistic classes or strata. It also challenges the critical theories which acknowledge the existence of a new dominant class in Eastern Europe, but which describe that class as the bureaucracy or technobureaucracy. This paper attempts to base its class analysis on the exploration of the mechanisms and institutions of expropriation of surplus under state socialism. It is suggested that in contemporary Eastern Europe private ownership and market mechanisms of expropriation have been replaced by central planning and redistribution of the economic surplus. All those who have vested interests in the maximization of redistributive power are members of a new dominating class. If we define the new class this way it will include more than just the bureaucracy; potentially, it includes the whole intelligentsia. The paper describes the new dominant class of intelligentsia as a class *in statu nascendi.* The formation of this class takes a whole historical epoch. In the first stage of state-socialist development the Djilas thesis is basically accurate: under Stalinism and in the early post-Stalinist years the bureaucracy had the monopoly of power. During the last two decades, on the other hand, the social base of power holders has broadened, especially in those countries which experimented with economic and political reforms. The formation of a new dominant class which incorporates the whole of the intelligentsia is now under way.

In this paper I will describe the class structure of the East European state-socialist societies, positing the existence of a class dichotomy between the working class and the intelligentsia. It will be argued that the power to which intellectuals aspire in a state-socialist redistributive economy derives from the basic institutions of social reproduction and, more specifically, from the institutions which guarantee the expropriation of surplus from the direct producers; consequently, that power is of a class nature.

The thesis is a highly provocative one, challenging all academically respectable theories of East European social structure and of the structural position of the intelligentsia. Those schools of thought which acknowledge the existence of class relations in contemporary Eastern Europe posit class dichotomies radically different from the one I suggest.

---

1 This paper has been substantially revised from my article which appeared in Critique, nos. 10–11 (Winter-Spring 1978–79), pp. 51–76.

Official Soviet Marxism distinguishes between two "nonantagonistic" classes, the working class and the peasantry[2] those who build their arguments directly or indirectly on Trotsky's critical analysis of Soviet society suggest that a class antagonism exists between the working class and the bureaucracy or technobureaucracy (Kuron, Modzelewski, and Djilas are the best-known examples).[3] Most East European sociologists since Ossowski have tended to disagree both with the official Soviet Marxist position and with the Trotskyist position.[4] During the last two decades empirical sociologists have questioned whether class analysis indeed has any relevance to the study of East European societies, and they have tried to describe the East European social structure in terms of social stratification (e.g., Wesolowski, Ferge, and Hegedus).[5] All these schools of thought would object to defining the intelligentsia as a class; there would even be some disagreement whether intellectuals form a homogeneous stratum. Finally, those who have looked on the East European intelligentsia as a class have rarely used the term „class"; more frequently, they have simply described how the East European radical intelligentsia

---

2 The so-called two-class, one stratum model of social stratification under socialism is usually attributed to J. V. Stalin (1972).

3 Milovan Djilas developed the concept of the bureaucracy as a new ownership class under socialism. According to Djilas, „The bureaucrats in a non-Communist state are officials in modern capitalist economy, while the Communists are something different and new: a new class" (1957, p. 44). Djilas does acknowledge that the intellectual roots of his criticism of socialism can be found in the work of Trotsky, but he also correctly notes that Trotsky did not acknowledge the class character of the bureaucracy. „Attacking the party bureaucracy in the name of the revolution, he attacked the cult of the party and, although he was not conscious of it, the new class" (p. 50). In fact, the Trotskyist analysis – contrary to the intentions of Leon Trotsky himself – was always very close to different versions of a bureaucratic class theory; the writings of Shachtman and Burnham are well-known examples of an extension of the theories of Trotsky into a new class theory (Shachtman 1962; Burnham 1962). The strength of Djilas's analysis is that it ties his concept of the new class to the political and historical realities of Eastern Europe; he is not venturing into a general theory of a new managerial or bureaucratic class. Another influential application of the Trotskyist critique of the bureaucracy in Eastern Europe is the „open letter" by Kuron and Modzelewski (1966). Kuron and Modzelewski in this article are rather orthodox Trotskyists; they do not develop a bureaucratic class theory, but their analysis points in that direction. Kuron has since moved significantly from this orthodox Trotskyist position, but even in his recent work he did not develop a bureaucratic class theory (Kuron 1978).

4 Stanislaw Ossowski presented the first comprehensive and devastating criticism of the Soviet Marxist class theory from Eastern Europe (1963, pp. 110–13).

5 Hegedus (1977) and Ferge (1973) build on the theories of Ossowski. Both Hegedus and Ferge want to replace the Soviet Marxist theory of class under socialism with an analysis of the social structure in which the division of labor is of central importance (Hegedus 1977, pp. 47–57; Ferge 1973, pp. 77–116). They actually replace class analysis with stratification analysis, but while doing so they avoid the theoretical question of whether socialist societies are class societies. (The terminological shift from the concept of „class" to the concept of „social structure" is significant.) The main value of that kind of work in Eastern Europe was empirical – it prepared the ground to make empirical research on social stratification and social inequality legitimate in Eastern Europe. The task which was performed by Hegedus and Ferge in Hungary was done by Wesolowski in Poland (1970). Even Soviet sociologists conducted researches of this kind, describing stratificational inequalities, but they did not use their results to confront the official class theory (Shkaratan 1970).

strives for a power monopoly (e.g., Berdyaev and Machajski)[6] or for what probably can be called „class power." They have not attempted to define the economic foundations of this class or penetrated beyond a description of its ideology.

When I started my work 15 years ago I, like most empirical sociologists in Eastern Europe, was highly critical of official Soviet Marxist theory. Following the example of Ossowski and Hegedus, I spent about 10 years in empirical work, describing different aspects of the East European stratification system, measuring and explaining the extent and nature of social inequalities; in fact, my empirical findings were further proof of the purely apologetic nature and scientific inadequacy of official Soviet Marxism. Thus I had to look for alternative theoretical tools. The Trotskyist frame of reference was obviously more relevant to the study of East European social structure than official Soviet Marxism or stratification theory, but I was not convinced of the theoretical accuracy of the definition of the bureaucracy as an ownership class, and even less so of the empirical validity of the crucial distinction made between bureaucrats and the rest of the intelligentsia (or the "intelligentsia proper").

I found that it might be necessary to go beyond the fairly rigid and orthodox official Soviet or Trotskyist interpretation of the Marxist notion of class, but not by accepting the superficial critique of Marxist class analysis contained within bourgeois stratification theory – which, despite the obligatory Marxist jargon of East European sociology, had had a major impact on the methodology and way of thinking of my fellow East European empirical sociologists. I became convinced that Marxist class analysis could be a powerful tool for understanding structural conflicts under state socialism, but only if we tried to adapt it to the radically changed socioeconomic conditions which now prevail: that is, to the conditions of industrial societies which operate without the institution of private ownership and which consequently, at least according to this crucial criterion, should be accepted as socialist. If a society no longer legitimates the expropriation of surplus through private property, then we should move toward a substantive analysis of the mechanisms and institutions of expropriation of surplus which *are* characteristic of this society. If we can define antagonistic interests focusing on these institutions, we can explain them as class interests and remain within the framework of Marxist class analysis, broadly defined, even if we do not base our definition of class on ownership relations as Marx did. It will be suggested in this paper that redistribution is the main mechanism which guarantees expropriation in state-socialist societies. All those who have a vested interest in the maximization of redistributive power are members of a new

6 Nicolas Berdyaev, a former Marxist, in exile in the West after the October Revolution, suggests in an impressive study that in order to „understand the sources of Russian communism ... one must understand that singular phenomenon which is called ‚intelligentsia'" (1972, p. 19). He reconstructs the intellectual history of the Russian intelligentsia and argues that the „whole history of the Russian intelligentsia was a preparation for communism" (p. 122). Berdyaev does not develop anything like a class theory of the intelligentsia; he only suggests that the agent in Russia which was ready to absorb the Russian version of communism was not the proletariat but the intelligentsia. As Gouldner points out, the Polish-born Russian revolutionary Waclaw Machajski also claimed that socialism was an ideology of the intelligentsia (Gouldner 1975–76, 1979, p. 99).

dominating class, since their interests are antagonistic to those of the direct producers. If we define the new class this way it obviously includes more than just the bureaucracy or even the technobureaucracy. It potentially includes the whole intelligentsia.

Finally, I would like to make clear in this introduction that the class I am talking about is still *in statu nascendi*. I am describing a process, not a static situation. The intelligentsia as a group, from the priests and monks of the Middle Ages to the anarchist and Bolshevik revolutionaries of the 19th and early 20th centuries and to the scholar-planner-technocrats of the late 20th century, has no doubt always had aspirations toward power monopoly, but this claim became realistic only with the institution of state-socialist redistributive economics. The East European intelligentsia still has a long way to go before it becomes an integrated class with its own class consciousness – the state-socialist societies are still at a very early stage of their development. All that I am suggesting is that there is a historical tendency for the power exercised in Eastern Europe to be increasingly the class power of the intelligentsia.

In *The Intellectuals on the Road to Class Power* (Konrad and Szelényi [1979]; the book was written in 1974 and published in English in 1979), George Konrad and I attempted to document more fully the signs of the formation of the class power of the intelligentsia. In this paper I can do no more than describe the inadequacies of alternative theories of socialist social structure; analyze briefly the institutions of social reproduction and expropriation found under state socialism to show what kind of antagonism of interest is built upon them; and, finally, document some of the limitations of the definition of the intelligentsia as a class and define more precisely the intelligentsia as a class *in statu nascendi*.

Notes On Different Theories Of East European Class Structure

The official Soviet Marxist theory of socialist social structure dominated East European social science literature for three decades, from the early thirties until the late fifties. It is no doubt superfluous to mention that this domination was not purely a product of the intellectual strength of the argument; those with scholarly doubts were constantly reminded of the necessity of ideological discipline by other than purely academic methods. Even today this theory is officially unchallenged in the ideologically more conservative countries like East Germany and the Soviet Union. To see this, it is sufficient to look at any recent edition of a Soviet textbook on historical materialism. Granted, German and Soviet ideologues no longer object when in empirical research sociologists "absent-mindedly" forget about official class distinctions and use occupation as a variable in explaining the distribution of their data, as long as they do not draw theoretical conclusions. In the more liberal countries of Eastern Europe, like Hungary and Poland, no one with any academic prestige seriously pretends to accept the old Soviet Marxist dogma, but few people openly challenge it. One is simply no longer supposed to talk about class.

Official Soviet Marxist class theory has pretensions to rigid orthodoxy. It is argued that, because Marx defined classes on the basis of ownership, the same methodology should be applied in contemporary socialist societies; thus, because there are two forms of ownership – state and cooperative – there are two classes as well, the working class and the peasantry.

It should be clear from the beginning to everybody familiar with the logic of Marxist class analysis that, despite the formal orthodoxy, this is quite a flexible interpretation of Marx. Marx did not define his basic class dichotomy in terms of forms of ownership. The basic class antagonism in Marx's formulation exists between those who own the means of the production and those who are deprived of ownership. It is not the form of ownership, but ownership as such (or lack of ownership), which constitutes the class. On the other hand, it is possible to argue that Marx himself attributed class-forming force to forms of ownership. In *Capital* (1974, vol. 3, chap. 52) he defines landowners as a separate class simply because they own something other than "capital," and in the "Eighteenth Brumaire" he uses forms of ownership as the basis for further differentiation between classes, especially differentiation inside the ruling class.[7] What I want to show is simply that the official Soviet Marxist dogma is not such a rigorous interpretation of Marx as it claims; in fact, it shifts from the main thrust of Marxist class analysis into a fairly marginal area (as we will see, the Trotskyists' claim to be rigorously Marxist is more justified).

There is another methodological trick built into this theory: namely, on the formal level it operates only with forms of ownership, but when the empirical relevance of the theory is tested we are referred to a distinction between industry and agriculture. It obviously appeals to our common sense that there are workers and peasants in contemporary East European societies, and a distinction between them sounds like a meaningful one. But if it is really the form of ownership that matters, then classes cannot be defined this way; it is not the peasantry which is the other class, but those industrial and agricultural laborers who are employed by cooperatives, and all agricultural laborers who work in the state-owned agricultural categories belong to the working class. Consequently, the industrial worker should belong to the same class as the industrial manager, or even the minister of heavy industry; but the peasant who works in a cooperative should belong to a different class than his neighbor, who is also an agricultural laborer doing the same

7 In *Capital*, 1974, vol. 3, chap. 52, Marx adds a third class, the class of landowners, to bis basic class dichotomy between owners of capital and owners of labor power. By adding this third class to his scheme he changes the criteria which supposedly constitute classes. In this text he considers that it is probably not ownership or nonownership which generates classes, but the identity of revenues and sources of revenues. Unfortunately, as he enters this discussion the manuscript breaks off (Marx 1974, pp. 885–86). In „The Eighteenth Brumaire of Louis Bonaparte," where Marx offers his most complex map of class relations, he also makes a class or classlike distinction between „capital" and „landed property," but this time not on the grounds of source of income but on the basis of the difference in the „kind of property" the two classes respectively own (1970, p. 117). In this later essay Marx seems to work with many classes. The petty bourgeoisie as a potential ally of the workers is regarded as a class (p. 119); Marx also spends quite some time analyzing the lumpen proletariat (pp. 136, 144), and he explicitly considers the possibility of the development of the peasants into a class (pp. 170–71). It is quite possible to find textual evidence from this essay for a five- or possibly seven-class model.

type of work, having roughly the same income, education, and so forth, merely because he is employed on a state farm. This is obvious nonsense. Thus, what makes sense in the official Soviet Marxist class dichotomy is not the distinction between two ownership classes, but a stratificational distinction between people employed in the main sectors of the economy.

This official Soviet Marxist class theory has very little to do with Marxism; it has even less to do with the empirical realities of contemporary Eastern Europe. In fact, the unknown soldiers of the first silent revolution against this theory were the statisticians who were expected to use "Marxist class theory" in analyzing official statistics, especially population censuses. By 1960, at least in countries where statisticians and demographers had some self-respect, as in Hungary, they silently forgot their *histomat* seminars: in the population census volumes "class" no longer appeared, and statisticians used occupation as a variable to explain the distribution of data. In fact they had to do so, since "classes" as defined by the official dogma explained nothing, from the distribution of income to the allocation of housing. The significant difference was to be found between the major occupational groups, especially between white- and blue-collar workers. In a way we might argue that sociologists have undeservedly claimed the honor of being the champions in the struggle against the *histomat class* dogma. It was already practically destroyed by unknown civil servants in Central Statistical Offices. Ossowski and others only offered an ideological justification for an already existing statistical practice. Stratification theory has had a very different history in Eastern Europe and in the West. Critiques of stratification analysis from very early times emphasized its inbuilt conservative character. In the West stratification theory was a conservative weapon against "subversive" class analysis. But in Eastern Europe during the late fifties and early sixties, the discovery of social stratification was quite a subversive activity, subversion against an apologetic and conservative class theory. Those who nowadays criticize people like Ossowski from the ideological Left do not appreciate the intellectual and political courage he needed to challenge Soviet Marxism. The *histomat class* dichotomy served only one purpose: to justify the existing monopoly of power.

By defining the state and Party bureaucracy as the "working class," the official theory offered a convenient solution to the delicate question of the "dictatorship of the proletariat." Stratification analysis, however, at least proved that social inequalities did indeed exist and that the "physical workers" (probably not identical with the ideologically defined working class) were systematically the negatively privileged group in the East European "people's democracies." As time passed, the inherent limitations of stratification analysis came to the fore in Eastern Europe as they had in the West. Stratification analysis, by distinguishing between white-collar and blue-collar workers, between physical workers, clerical workers, professionals, and "professionals in leading positions" (using this polite term for highly placed Party and state bureaucrats), could statistically demonstrate the separation of white-collar workers, and especially the power elite, from the actual workers. But it could not offer any theory to explain the statistically observed differences. Most empirical sociologists used the term "working class" to describe manual workers, those directly involved in the production process, but they carefully avoided using any structural term for the upper half of the social hierarchy. We called them "people higher up in the social hierarchy," the higher-income group, higher social groups or strata – and no one seemed to pay much attention to the theoretical significance of this terminology.

Ossowski, the main theorist of social stratification, proposed that, since ownership had lost its explanatory importance with the elimination of private ownership, position in the social division of labor explained social structure and social inequalities.[8] But it was unclear what the theoretical significance of this thesis was: did it suggest that class relations no longer existed and that socialist social structure could only be explained by inequalities between different occupational groups, or did it mean that we should define classes in terms of the division of labor? Marx himself obviously flirted with the idea of basing class analysis on the division of labor as far back as the "German Ideology"[9] and Ossowski, a well trained Marxist, could claim still to be a Marxist while rejecting ownership classes and using division of Labor as the main variable for structural analysis. But as stratification research developed, it became clearer that East European empirical sociologists, by emphasizing the importance of the division of labor, wanted to replace class analysis with stratification analysis and were not interested in developing a new class definition. For East European empirical sociology, contemporary socialist society

8 In Ossowski's view, the importance of the ownership relationship radically declined in societies in which the means of production have been nationalized (1963, p. 182); he also mentions the importance of the emergence of a new class, or „stratum," of non manual white-collar workers (p. 183). This new class or stratum (interestingly, he does not seem to attach much importance to the terminological distinction) is, on the other hand, constituted by the nature of its work and not according to ownership relations. Ossowski also suggested that Marx himself cannot be interpreted as a theorist who worked only with a single class dichotomy based on ownership. In Ossowski's view, Marx combined at least three dichotomies to develop a complex map of class relations (Ossowski 1969, p. 82). Hegedus agrees with this, and he adds the „position in the division of labour" and the „sector of the economy" to „property relations" as the „independent variables in the mathematical model of the structure of socialist societies" (Hegedus 1977, p. 70).

9 Those East European sociologists who attempt to replace or at least combine ownership with „division of labor" frequently quote the „German Ideology." Indeed, in the „German Ideology" Marx and Engels still seemed to assume that the historical development of class relations directly corresponds to the evolution of the division of labor (1972, pp. 18–21). Marx and Engels go so far as to suggest that „the existing stage in the division of labour determines also the relations of individuals to one another with reference to the material, instrument and product of labour" (p. 19). But probably already while writing the „German Ideology" Marx and Engels began to see problems with this proposition. In particular, when they attempt to describe the transition to feudalism, it becomes clear that quantitative indicators of the division of labor are not sufficient to explain the differences in class relations between a slave and a feudal mode of production. It might not be accidental that the manuscript breaks off at this point and that the authors do not even attempt to continue the analysis and to describe the transition from feudalism to capitalism (p. 21). I would suggest that Marx should have developed the concept of „relations of production" first, which would have provided more sophisticated instruments for discussing the issues of transition of modes of production and transformation of class relations. It is interesting, however, that neither Hegedus nor Ferge seem to notice that from the point of view of class theory the „German Ideology" is still an early work – and indeed without the concept of relations of production it cannot be regarded as a mature statement of Marxist class theory (see Ferge 1973, pp. 77–78).

was a classless society, a thesis which did not bother the official ideological censors much and which also pleased Western anti-Marxists, who found it amusing that the first accomplishment of "Marxist sociology" was to get rid of the concept of class. The most consequential stratification theorist in Poland, Wesolowski, was even to question whether a working class existed at all in Eastern Europe, and he proposed that theoretically it might be more accurate to call workers a "stratum."[10] Suddenly we find the originally subversive stratification analysis turning out to be even more apologetic than Soviet Marxism. At least Soviet Marxists acknowledged that contemporary socialist societies were class societies (although composed of nonantagonistic classes – quite a squaring of the circle) and that classless "communist society" was still to come.

But this question of "classlessness" is not a purely ideological one. Wesolowski and the stratification school of sociology in Eastern Europe, by rejecting the applicability of class analysis to socialist societies, were in fact suggesting that it was impossible to define structural economic conflicts in these societies. Consequently, it was also impossible to explain existing social inequalities from structural economic conflicts. This has far-reaching consequences for empirical research and for the interpretation of empirical facts. If contemporary socialist societies are classless – that is, free from structural economic conflicts – then the inequalities we can observe and measure are not inherent characteristics of these societies. They are inherited from the capitalist past or, alternatively, are consequences of nonsocial factors (e.g., the ideologues of stratification theory would argue that inequalities will be overcome under socialism by the gradual development of productive forces or technology). If this theory stands, then the structure of inequalities could not reflect the socioeconomic laws of these societies and, historically, inequalities should decline. In my empirical work I found none of these assumptions to be true. The main inequalities which I observed in the fields of housing and urban structure or in the regional system were not inherited. They were emerging from the East European socialist strategy of economic growth. They were structured by the redistributive mechanisms of the socialist economy and not by surviving market forces. And, finally, there was little evidence that inequalities were declining. (It is not the purpose of this paper to elaborate this point, which was documented in my earlier publications on housing and urbanization in Eastern Europe.) Since I found the inequalities I observed to be inherent in East European societies and to be structured by basic state-socialist economic institutions, it was logical to assume that class antagonism lay behind these inequalities.

It was Leon Trotsky who first suggested the existence of antagonistic interests in the Soviet Union, when he analyzed the nature of conflict between the bureaucracy

10 In Wesolowski's formulation: „The proletarian revolution abolishes the class structure thus conceived. Deprived of their ‚opposed role,' the workers cease to be a class in the traditional sense of the term.... In the Marxian sense, they are no longer a ‚true class', but rather an ‚ex-class' we continue to call them ‚workers,' but not the working class in the Marxian sense of the term. Perhaps it would be convenient to call them ‚the Stratum of workers'" (1974, p. 123).

and the working class.[11] Trotsky himself never went so far as to call the bureaucracy a class. Sociologically speaking, he defined the bureaucrats as a ruling elite alien from the working class. The theory that Trotsky developed concerning the Soviet social structure is a curious one. It is basically a class theory since it assumes a class antagonism, but it operates with a one-class model. The oppressed class is opposed only by a political elite. But this contradiction is quite understandable. Trotsky as a scholar was more a political scientist than a sociologist. He did not show a great deal of interest in the critical examination of the economic institutions of the Soviet system. *He* in fact assumed that the economic revolution was accomplished and that the Soviet system needed only a new political infrastructure. Later theorists were less restrained than Trotsky himself, and those trying to elaborate the sociological nature of the antagonism discovered by Trotsky became interested in the definition of the other class, the new dominating or ruling class of Soviet-type societies. All those who either followed Trotsky directly or were influenced by him described the bureaucracy as the new class. These theorists – Djilas is the most influential among them – used the classical Marxist tools of class analysis and defined the bureaucracy as an ownership class, arguing that under state socialism the bureaucrats monopolized the disposition of the means of production.[12]

Undoubtedly we can learn more from Trotsky or from Djilas about the real nature of social structure under state socialism than from the official Soviet Marxists or from the stratification theorists, but I have serious doubts – both theoretical and empirical – that the dominating class of state-socialist societies can be identified with the bureaucracy. The fundamental theoretical dilemma is whether the bureaucracy can be defined as

11 Trotsky explicitly rejects attempts to define the Soviet bureaucracy as an ownership class. „The attempt to represent the Soviet bureaucracy as a class of ‚state capitalists‘ will obviously not withstand criticism. The bureaucracy has neither stocks, nor bonds… The individual bureaucrat cannot transmit to his heirs his rights in the exploitation of state apparatus“ (1972, pp. 249–50). But Trotsky very clearly sees that the bureaucracy which emerged in Stalinist Russia is a historically new phenomenon. „In its intermediary and regulating function, its concern to maintain social ranks, and its exploitation of the state apparatus for personal goals, the Soviet bureaucracy is similar to every bureaucracy, especially the fascist. But it is also in a vast way different. In no other regime has a bureaucracy achieved such a degree of independence from the dominating class. The Soviet bureaucracy has risen above a class which is hardly emerging from destitution and darkness.... Whereas the fascists, when they find themselves in power, are united with the big bourgeoisie ... the Soviet bureaucracy takes on bourgeois customs without having beside it a national bourgeoisie. In this sense it is something more than a bureaucracy“ (pp. 248–49). He defines the bureaucracy as a „stratum“ (p. 249), but this term certainly would not suit his aim of describing the parasitism (p. 250) of the bureaucracy, its bourgeoisie customs, etc.; therefore, he will often refer to a ruling Soviet caste (p. 253). In fact, in Trotsky the terms „ruling stratum“ and „ruling caste“ are used interchangeably. The Trotskyist concept of bureaucratic caste is a very insightful one, since it (unlike the concept of stratum) does emphasize the qualitatively new feature of the Soviet bureaucracy. However, the application of the concept to the Soviet bureaucracy does not seem to be very fortunate. Max Weber is very precise when he defines caste as a special case of „status groups“ or „estates,“ as a position in traditional social structures. Weber is also persuasive when he suggests that caste differs from ordinary status order because caste is oriented religiously and ritually (1958, p. 44). None of these criteria seems to apply to the Soviet bureaucracy.

12 Djilas states: „The specific characteristic of this new class is its collective ownership“ (1957, p. 54).

an ownership class. Such a definition equates the right of disposition with ownership, which is more than questionable. It hardly requires textual proof that Marx himself clearly distinguished between ownership and disposition, and without this distinction it would be impossible to understand the bureaucratic and technocratic phenomena of capitalist society. If we define the socialist bureaucrat as a member of an ownership class because he has the right to dispose of the means of production, why not apply the same logic to modern capitalism and call the technobureaucracy found in the latter a new dominating class? In my understanding, the strength of Marxist class analysis is its emphasis on mediations. It is a powerful theory because it explains why those who formally exercise power act in the interest of a ruling class which may itself be less visible. If we equate ownership with the right of disposal, then we make the concept of ownership so abstract and general that it loses all its theoretical strength.

Furthermore, if we define the dominating class as those who dispose of the means of production, then we make an empirically unjustified distinction between the technobureaucracy and the rest of the intelligentsia. I do not want to repeat here the well-known arguments as to how difficult it is to determine accurately who in fact has the right to dispose of the means of production in a state-socialist society. It is well known how limited the rights of a factory manager are. Strictly speaking, any ownership class which could be defined in terms of a real monopoly of the right of disposal might be as exclusive as the Politburo, which would mean restricting the membership of the new class to 10–20 individuals – an obvious nonsense. But even if we treat these problems of operationalization generously, we would still have to explain why a minor bureaucrat in an economic ministry or in the Central Planning Office is a member of the dominating class and why an influential professor of economics is not.

One empirical difficulty connected with this crucial distinction between the bureaucracy and the intellectuals is created by the relatively fast circulation of the intellectual elite in Eastern Europe. The present director of one of the comedy theaters in Budapest is a former high ranking officer of the political police. His former boss in the Hungarian equivalent of the KGB is today the manager of a big salami factory. Today one may be an officer in the political police, but tomorrow one might be the only person licensed to produce political jokes, or one might supervise salami production or sociological research, as a manager or an academic. The line between intellectuals and bureaucrats is a very shaky one in terms of personal career patterns. Many university graduates with academic ambitions enter the Party bureaucracy immediately after graduation, since they know that a few years in the Party bureaucracy is the most powerful recommendation to university chairs and other high academic positions. The intellectual elite circulates rapidly. It is stratified according to the levels of power rather than segmented into a bureaucrats/intellectuals dichotomy. It may well be more difficult to jump from the local level into the national power elite than to shift from the Academy of Science into the Central Committee of the Party or vice versa.

I would also argue that the bureaucratic class theory overemphasizes the power of bureaucrats and underestimates the impact of nonbureaucratic intellectuals on societal decision making. The bureaucrat in the Central Planning Office who allocates a few hundred million zloty or levas may not exercise a great deal of power, since the rules of the game are strictly set. However, those who have an impact on the formation of these rules, from the expert economics professor to the ideologically influential movie director or poet, may in fact have more power than the bureaucrat without having any right of disposal. Finally, I would like to add that from the point of view of material privilege it is practically impossible to distinguish between the technobureaucracy and the intelligentsia. Their living standards are practically identical. It is the level of power which stratifies them, not the bureaucracy/intellectuals dichotomy.

The Economic Foundations Of Class Antagonisms Under State Socialism

I found that existing class and stratification theories do not explain the nature and dynamism of social conflicts and inequalities in state-socialist societies. Despite their diverging political and ideological overtones, they all espouse "formal Marxism." They define class relations as ownership relations. I will propose first that in state-socialist societies, which by definition have abolished the institution of private ownership, we have to go beyond this formal Marxism and beyond the analysis of ownership if we want to find the economic foundation of class antagonisms.

Marx himself undoubtedly explained class relations from facts about ownership, but Marxist theory was a reaction to capitalist society, and even Marxist methodology may need crucial modifications when applied to the substantive analysis of noncapitalist socioeconomic formations. Marx himself became increasingly aware of the limitations of his own methodology, whereby the structure of different modes of production was derived from ownership relations. Already in the *Grundrisse* he proved to be highly flexible when analyzing non-Western societies. He seriously considered the possibility that the institutions of the village community were as important for the understanding of Asiatic societies as the forms of relations of ownership, and it is clear from his later correspondence that he understood the significance of the *obshchina* in the Russian model of development.[13] He started to differentiate between socioeconomic formations on the basis of criteria other than ownership. Generally speaking, I would argue that ownership played the crucial role it did in Marxist theory only because Marx developed his methodology in the course of his study of Western societies, where – already in the precapitalist stage of development – private ownership was the major socioeconomic

13 As Perry Anderson points out, in his early correspondence with Engels, Marx around 1853 assumed that a separate „Asiatic mode of production" should be identified (Anderson 1974, pp. 476–83) due to the domination of state ownership of the land under Asiatic feudalism. Later he changed his mind, and in the *Grundrisse* the „self-sustaining village community" seems to be the major variable which explains the existence of a separate „Asiatic mode of production" (Marx 1975b, pp. 66–70). In the light of Marx's early correspondence with Engels and the analysis of the *Grundrisse*, it seems clear that Marx could not decide what sort of ownership existed in the East, and from this we might safely conclude that therefore ownership cannot be all that important to identify „modes of production."

institution around which social conflicts were structured. But this methodology will not explain much about the functioning of societies where private ownership does not exist and where we cannot find inherent forces which would lead to the development of private ownership. When Marx inclined to accept Vera Zasulich's proposition that in Russia socialism might emerge directly from the village community, he had to give serious thought to the possibility that societies might bypass the development of private ownership.[14] Consequently, the history of mankind could not be explained simply in terms of how private ownership developed and why this institution would in the future cease to exist.

If this is true for non-European precapitalist formations, then the emphasis on ownership relations in the analysis of socialist societies is even more misleading. A formally applied orthodox Marxist methodology which assumes that socioeconomic antagonisms can emerge only from ownership relations loses all scientific strength and may well become pure apologetics when applied to state-socialist societies – societies which consciously abolished private ownership in the belief that this single historical act would generate the establishment of a nonantagonistic society. This may well explain how the most revolutionary theory of all time came to be a conservative state religion in all those countries which accept the ideological papacy of Moscow. Most contemporary Marxists try to solve this paradox by questioning whether Soviet Marxism is "real" Marxism, but not even the most sophisticated talmudic argument could explain why orthodox Soviet ideologues claim to be Marxist, even though when they are weighed on the scales of real Marxism they are found wanting.

I would argue that Soviet ideologues chose and cling to Marxism because they found something in its orthodox teaching that suited them in their effort to build an apologetic ideology of state socialism, and this is precisely the assumption that class antagonism can emerge only from conflicts related to ownership. Consequently, if we want to develop a critical theory of any of the phenomena of state-socialist societies, we have first to fight the myth of the all-importance of ownership and develop a substantive understanding of the economic institutions and mechanisms of such societies. The last half-century has proved that Marx let himself be misled by his own methodology. He attached exaggerated hopes to the abolition of private ownership, and he failed to foresee that the new society would create its own mechanisms of economic exploitation and political oppression, that the abolition of the class power of the bourgeoisie would lead to the emergence of a new, similarly alienated, and politically – at least for the time being – even more oppressive class power. But if this is indeed a new class power and not merely the political totalitarianism of a ruling elite, then we should be able to find its roots in

14 In 1881, in letters drafted to Zasulich, Marx goes so far as to suggest that „Russia is capable of developing and transforming the archaic form of its village community, instead of destroying it.“ In these letters he clearly hesitates to decide whether the development of private ownership is an absolute necessity and if it would not be possible to maintain the „collective element“ that he finds so attractive in the Russian communes. At the end he explicitly rejects a deterministic position and describes an alternative: „either the property element in it will overcome the collective element or the other way around“ (1975b, pp. 142–45).

specific state-socialist economic institutions, and obviously in something other than the state ownership of the means of production. In this way we might be able to go beyond the formal analysis of ownership relations but still stay within the general framework of a historical materialist perspective.

In attempting to broaden the frame of reference of class analysis sufficiently to make it applicable to state-socialist societies, I would suggest that the purpose of class analysis is to explain rationalized forms of economic exploitation and the forms of political and social oppression built on these. When Marx and Engels developed their theory of the class dichotomy of capitalist society, they were first of all interested in the capitalist system of economic exploitation to be found in the institutions and mechanisms which guaranteed the expropriation of surplus from the direct producer by the owner of capital. The crucial task of class analysis is, then, to understand the institutions of expropriation of surplus; and if around these institutions an antagonism of interests is to be found, then one may be justified in talking about class relations. Furthermore, I would argue that Marx defined his classes on the basis of ownership relations because in a capitalist market economy it was the private ownership of the means of production which legitimated expropriation. Following this logic, I suggest that to test whether class analysis is applicable to state-socialist societies at all, we first have to understand the state-socialist institutions of expropriation of surplus and define the principles which legitimate expropriation under state socialism.

Then we need to find out whether the direct producer is in a position to challenge this system of legitimation and whether his interests are systematically in conflict with those who expropriate or who legitimate the state socialist form of expropriation.

State-socialist societies developed and legitimated institutions of expropriation which are specifically state socialist, which are not known in other socioeconomic formations – and these are the institutions of state-socialist rational redistribution. In a recently published paper on the social inequalities engendered by state-socialist redistributive economies (Szelényi 1978), I tried to contrast the redistributive institutions of state-socialist societies with mechanisms of redistribution of real income in welfare capitalism. I do not want to, and due to the limitations of space I cannot, repeat the arguments developed there. Here I merely want to emphasize that, despite the increasing role of redistributive mechanisms in contemporary welfare capitalism, modern capitalist economies can still be distinguished as "late market economies" from "state-socialist redistributive economies." The redistributive intervention of the welfare state did not overrule the market logic of the economy in any of the contemporary Western capitalist societies. In all these societies the state only redistributes incomes. The incomes themselves are defined on the market. Furthermore, the economic surplus that can be used for extended reproduction is not allocated by the welfare redistributors; the key investment decisions are made according to the logic of profit maximization by the owners of capital or their representatives. Under welfare capitalism the basic class division is still, therefore, the division between the capitalist (who disposes of the surplus available for investments) and the wage laborer or direct producer. The welfare redistributor plays only a mediating role in this basic class dichotomy. In state-socialist societies redistribution is not limited to the reallocation of incomes: under state socialism it is the very surplus which is redistributed. If the main task of the redistributor is to allocate surplus, then this redistributor does not mediate between the owner of capital and the seller of labor power; he replaces the owner of capital. While contemporary welfare capitalism is a market economy modified by welfare-oriented income redistribution, state socialism is a redistributive economy. It is a new type of economy. While contemporary capitalism still can be characterized by the class dichotomy between capital owners and wage laborers, contemporary state socialism might be characterized by the antagonism between redistributors and direct producers. I claim that this analysis is a quite consistent adaptation of the Marxian methodology: the basic class distinction is established around the processes of production and expropriation and the allocation of surplus, around the key relations of production.[15]

If we define a new dominant class according to its relation to the institutions of redistribution in a state-socialist society, don't we necessarily agree with Djilas or with Dahrendorf? If the new dominant class is constituted by the institution of redistribution of surplus, is it not identical with the bureaucracy which makes the actual planning decisions? If the new class is constituted on redistributive power, don't we agree with Dahrendorf that in modern economies economic class is replaced by political power?[16]

It is central to my analysis that the new dominant class is neither bureaucratic in the precise Weberian sense of the term nor based on political power, as Dahrendorf suggested. The class which is organized around redistributive power is far from being bureaucratic, at least if we use the *term* "bureaucratic" in a precise Weberian sense.

15 „My distinction between „contemporary welfare capitalism“ and „state-socialist redistributive economies“ is a distinction between two ideal types. I am aware that empirically identifiable systems – say, the Swedish economy in 1980, or the Polish or Hungarian economy in any given year – might be to a degree mixtures of these ideal types. One might find examples in Sweden when the state does not limit itself to income redistribution, but might significantly affect investment decision, or one might be able to observe certain market mechanisms to be at work even in the crucial spheres of investments or trading of labor power in East European socialist societies. But these empirical „mixtures“ do not make the construction of ideal types unnecessary or invalid: it can still be claimed that Sweden is predominantly ruled by the ideal type of „welfare capitalism,“ Poland by „state-socialist redistributive economy.“

16 According to Dahrendorf, „From the point of view of social structure of industrial enterprises, this means a significant change in the basis of legitimacy of entrepreneurial authority... The old style capitalist exercised authority because he owned the instruments of production. By contrast to this legitimation by property, the authority of the manager resembles in many ways that of the heads of political institutions... The right of the manager to command and expect obedience accrues in part from the property rights delegated to him... But besides these... the manager... has to seek a second, and often more important, basis of legitimacy for his authority, namely, some kind of consensus among those who are bound to obey his commands... The manager, unlike the ‚full capitalist,‘ can ill afford to exercise his authority in direct and deliberate contravention to the wishes and interests of his subordinates“ (1959, pp. 44 45). Dahrendorf here suggests that even in the case of the industrial manager it is political power which constitutes class position – economic power based on ownership is replaced by political power based on Consensus. My analysis is rather different. I suggest that economic power based on ownership is replaced by economic power based on the teleological knowledge of the redistributor.

Both Weber and Marx[17] would agree that bureaucracy – at least in its pure form – is the product of civil society. Civil society is integrated by formal rationality; it is the first societal formation which separates ends and means, the telos and techne, and subordinates telos to techne.[18] Civil society emerged when the rationality of goal setting, or teleological thinking, was questioned, and rationality was more narrowly defined as the "optimal choice of means leading to a given end." Marx with critical and Weber with apologetic overtones state that in civil society goal setting is referred to the "irrational," to the sphere of beliefs, to bourgeois politics. In civil society a separate sphere of politics exists, where goal setting is ideally done in a pluralistic political system and executive functions are reserved for bureaucratic organizations. When Weber defined bureaucratic power he identified it with executive tasks, and he believed that it was rooted in the expert knowledge of the bureaucrat. Weber strongly believed that experts are unable to

---

17 Despite the fundamental differences in the Marxian and Weberian theories of bureaucracy, Marx and Weber both emphasize the executive nature of bureaucratic power and its dependence on modern capitalism and civil society. Probably the fullest and most interesting discussion of the bureaucracy by Marx can be found in his „Contribution to the Critique of Hegel's Philosophy of Law." Here Marx attempts to prove that Hegel is wrong in assuming that the bureaucracy is a „universal class." For Marx the basic classes are formed within civil society and the political state. The state bureaucracy is far from being the universal class; the state is not above civil society. In the light of this analysis the state bureaucracy rather appears as the executive arm of the bourgeoisie (Marx 1975a). From this analysis of Marx it follows that it is in fact quite problematic for Marxists whether a bureaucracy can exist under socialism, when civil society and, more specifically, the class antagonism of the bourgeoisie and proletariat have been abolished. For Weber bureaucratic domination is the purest type of legal authority. Of course, Weber does not think that the bureaucracy is an executive arm of the bourgeoisie, but he finds formalism or formal rationality the most crucial criterion of rational bureaucracy. The bureaucracy for Weber is efficient as long as it operates within formal rationality, as long as it uses technical knowledge, as long as it does not have to set goals but can execute goals set by a separate political mechanism. Weber is quite aware that the socialist project intends to transcend bourgeois formal rationality, and he very clearly sees the explosive contradiction between the substantive rationality socialism represents and the formal rationality of legal authority and bureaucratic domination. „For socialism would require a still higher degree of formal bureaucratization than capitalism. If this should prove not to be possible, it would demonstrate the existence of another of those fundamental elements of irrationality – a conflict between formal and substantive rationality of the sort which sociology so often encounters" (Weber 1978, pp. 217–26, esp. p. 225). See also, about Marx's theory of the bureaucracy, Perez-Diaz (1978, esp. pp. 10–11).

18 In the work of Marx the critique of bourgeois rationality, the critique of capitalism as the system in which techne dominates telos, is implicit. Marx did not develop any systematic theory of rationality, and this is only implied in his critique of political economy. The problematic of the relationship between telos and techne, teleological and technical rationality, will mostly appear only as the subordination of use value to exchange value, as the subordination of human need to profit interests, as the problem of production for profit rather than for the satisfaction of human needs. It is the Frankfurt School which develops the Marxist critique of capitalism as a critique of technical or instrumental rationality, as a critique of rationality which accepts the domination of telos by techne. This type of critical Marxism finds its roots in the early works of Horkheimer and Adorno (Horkheimer 1978; see also Connerton 1976, esp. pp. 27–28; Arato and Gebhardt 1978, esp. pp. 8–12) and is later more fully developed in Habermas (see esp. Habermas 1974, pp. 195–252, 268–76; also see Habermas 1970).

tell people what they ought to do, that they can only tell them how to reach goals they have selected for themselves according to criteria not susceptible to judgment in terms of "rationality." For societal analysis this means that bureaucracy only executes goals set by a separate political mechanism. Bureaucrats will always try to extend their power. They will claim that goal-setting functions are basically technicalities; that the only possible course of action is the one that they predict with their "scientific methods"; and that, since no alternatives are open, no political decision is required or possible. But even the most power-hungry bureaucrat operates within the framework set by the civil society. He can claim power only on the basis of his expert knowledge. He cannot claim to have the scientific, rational knowledge to set goals. I would argue that redistributive power under state socialism is basically of a different nature. It is not based on "expert knowledge." It is not based on the assumption that goal setting is something irrational and that only the choice of means can be considered as, properly speaking, rational activity. The bureaucrat of civil society has to operate in the sphere of "formal rationality." The redistributor of state socialism claims to operate within the framework of "substantive rationality" (to use again Weber's terminology).[19] He claims a monopoly of rational choice among goals. He claims a monopoly of technical knowledge. Thus the orthodox Soviet Marxist view that under socialism bureaucracy does not exist makes sense in a way. The teleological redistributor is of a different social nature from Weber's bureaucrat. The Weberian bureaucrat's claim to power does not challenge the fundamental power structure of civil society based on private ownership; the bureaucrat may have certain particularistic interests, but he cannot strive for his own class power.[20] Bureaucratic power, properly defined, can exist only in a world where techne dominates telos, in a world which is split into economy and politics, means and ends, subject and object; and this is the world of market capitalism, the world of private ownership, which is basically structured into a class dichotomy between owners and nonowners. Under these circum-

19 It is interesting to note that Weber does not develop his distinction between formal and substantive rationality in his general theory of types of rationalities, but only in his sociology of economic systems (1978, pp. 85–113). The need to develop the concept of substantive rationality arises for Weber when he begins to analyze the problems of planning and especially planning under socialist economies. When I am using the term „substantive rationality" to describe the specific nature of knowledge of the „teleological redistributors" I follow closely Weber's own logic. As Weber states, „Where a planned economy is radically carried out, it must further accept the inevitable reduction in formal, calculatory rationality... Substantive and formal ... rationality are ... after all largely distinct problems. This fundamental and, in the last analysis, unavoidable element of irrationality in economic systems is one of the important sources of all ‚social' problems, and above all, of the problems of socialism" (p. 111). This quotation, together with the one from n. 17 above, allows us to conclude that, since formal rationality is the rationality of the bureaucracy, the teleological redistributor and planning guided by substantive rationality do not fit the Weberian ideal type of bureaucracy.

20 For Marx it is obvious that the bureaucracy does not represent such a separate set of interests which would allow us to define the bureaucracy as a class. The bureaucracy only expresses as general interests the particularistic interests of the dominant class, of the bourgeoisie. What is peculiarly bureaucratic interest is nothing more than the transformation of the particular interests into universal ones (1975a, pp. 44–48, esp. p. 46; see also Perez-Diaz 1978, pp. 28–32)

stances the bureaucrat of civil society will mediate conflicts between the basic classes, but his main interest is in the maintenance of the status quo of class relations, since by challenging it he would undermine the very basis of his existence.

The Marxist ideal of socialism is an attack not only on capitalism narrowly defined but also on the very principles on which civil society is built. All previous critical theorists criticized capitalism from the standpoint and values of civil society. Marx and Engels were the first to claim that the radical revolutionary transformation of the capitalist mode of production is impossible without the rejection of civil society and its values, without the rejection of bourgeois humanism and bourgeois democracy.[21] The ideal society they proposed would reunite ·a world split into separate, alienated spheres of existence. It would be a society in which telos again dominated techne, a society ruled by substantive rationality. When I suggest that the intelligentsia is a class *in statu nascendi* in contemporary state socialism, what I am saying is that in this new society, which is the negation of civil society, the intellectuals attempt to monopolize this substantive rationality. And if they succeed in doing so the power they claim will be of a class nature, since it is based on the dominant principle of legitimation.

It would be wrong, on the other hand, to believe that this new class (and the new society) is the product of the Marxist ideal. On the contrary, it would be more realistic to say that intellectuals have used Marxist ideals in order to grasp class power. They had been unable to do this successfully in previous socioeconomic formations. Marx believed that his teachings would become a material force through the revolutionary praxis of the proletariat, but things happened otherwise. It was the Russian intelligentsia which realized the potential of Marxist ideology and transformed it into a powerful weapon of class struggle.[22]

Neither was it accidental that this happened in Russia and that Russia's example was followed first by other East European countries. The new society in which telos dominates techne emerged from societies where there existed an "intelligentsia" properly speaking, where intellectuals consciously articulated their aspirations to occupy a dominant position in the social structure.

---

21 Marx formulates clearly that the purpose of his materialism is to transcend civil society in thesis 10 on Feuerbach: „The standpoint of the old materialism is ‚civil' society; the standpoint of the new is human society or socialised humanity" (1972, p. 13). When Marx emphasizes that the standpoint of his new historical materialism is socialized humanity, he rejects the individualism of civil society, which is a clear indication that he does not limit his project to the critique of capitalism and its political economy but intends more: to develop a comprehensive critique of civil society too.

22 Gouldner does not believe that the proletariat came to power in the so-called socialist revolutions, or that it is likely for the proletariat ever to come to power: „The Communist Manifesto had held that the history of all hitherto existing society was the history of class struggles: freeman and slave, patrician and plebian, lord and serf, guildmaster and journeyman, and, then, bourgeoisie and proletariat. In this series, however, there was one unspoken regularity: the slaves did not succeed the masters, the plebians did not vanquish the patricians, the serfs did not overthrow the lords, and the journeymen did not triumph over the guildmasters. The lowliest class never came to power. Nor does it seem likely to now" (1979, p. 93).

In other words, state socialism and its new dominant class emerged in Eastern Europe because two sets of conditions met there. On the one hand, a redistributive economic system was created, and this system served as an objective base for class power rooted in the teleological knowledge of planners and redistributors. On the other hand, in this part of the world a new type of intellectual, the intelligentsia, developed prior to the socialist revolutionary transformation. This East European intelligentsia was distinguished from other types of intellectuals precisely by the importance it attached to the teleological component of its knowledge. In 1917 in Russia and following the Second World War in Eastern Europe, when the objective position of a new class was created with the abolition of private ownership and the creation of a centrally, "scientifically" planned economy, the "agents" to fill these positions – the intelligentsia – were also ready for their new historical task.

The central hypothesis of my analysis, therefore, is that the new class in Eastern European state socialism is broader than the bureaucracy: it is composed of all those who have a vested interest in the production and reproduction of a certain type of intellectual knowledge – teleological knowledge – which is legitimating redistributive power under socialist redistributive economies. The new dominant class is composed, therefore, of a type of intellectual, the intelligentsia.

In this paper I use the concept of intellectuals as a generic concept. Unlike Gouldner,[23] I do not claim that all intellectuals in all modern societies are on the road to class power. My hypothesis is a more modest one. All that I suggest is that one type of intellectual, the intelligentsia, gains class power under state-socialist redistributive economies. I disagree with Gouldner concerning the possibilities of class formation of the other major modern type of intellectuals, the professionals. While Gouldner maintains that professionalism leads intellectuals into the new dominant class position,[24] I propose that professionalism integrates intellectuals into the basic class structure of market capitalism. As long as intellectuals accept their definition as professionals – what market capitalism offers them – they cannot claim class power of their own. They will remain only a semi-

23 Gouldner, unlike most left-wing theorists of the new class (e.g., Djilas, Burnham, or Shachtman), does not exclude from the new class the „proper intellectuals": ideologues, social scientists, etc. While left-wing theories mostly limit the new class to managers and/or technocrats and bureaucrats, Gouldner uses a broad concept which includes all intellectuals: „In all countries ... in the twentieth century ... a New Class composed of intellectuals and the technical intelligentsia ... enter into contention with the groups already in control of the society's economy, whether these are businessmen or party leaders" (1979, p. 1). I want to note here that Gouldner is using the concept „intelligentsia" rather differently than I do in this paper. I think my usage is closer to the conventional one (see Gella 1976, esp. pp. 9–27) It is also interesting that Gouldner, while using a broad definition of „intellectuals," still excludes from this the Party leaders, but he never explains why he does that.

24 Gouldner believes that the vehicle by which the new class replaces the rule of money capital with the rule of „cultural capital" is professionalism: „Professionalism in effect devalues the authority of the old class" (1979, p. 19). I think Gouldner is wrong: professionalism, by emphasizing the significance of technical knowledge, does not represent any challenge to the ideological and cultural hegemony of the bourgeoisie.

autonomous stratum – or, to use Erik Olin Wright's more precise terminology, they will remain in a contradictory class location.[25]

At this stage I have to offer at least a working definition of the concepts of "intellectuals," "professionals," and "intelligentsia."

I will follow Gouldner in defining intellectuals as those who are bound together by the "culture of critical discourse" (CCD).[26] The CCD, according to Gouldner's definition, is a "speech community"[27] which has been developed since the Enlightenment by the modern "men of idea." These modern men of idea, whom I will call intellectuals, within the CCD do gain monopoly of a kind of knowledge which has two main characteristics: it is secular (in Gouldner's definition, it does not accept any authority but reason) and it is theoretical. The theoreticity of the knowledge intellectuals monopolize is sometimes also linked by Gouldner to its "context-variability."[28] The CCD is common to all modern intellectuals, under both market capitalism and state socialism. But in its historical evolution the CCD takes two different forms. Where modernization coincides with the development of market capitalism, the CCD leads to professionalization. Professionalism is the form of knowledge within the CCD in which the technical component, the know-how, dominates the teleological component. In those social-historical contexts where attempts to modernize do not coincide with market capitalism – already in prerevolutionary Eastern Europe and more so in this area after the socialist transformation – the teleological component of intellectual knowledge is not subordinated to technical know-how; intellectuals are not defined as professionals but, rather, as intelligentsia.

25 Erik Olin Wright introduced the concept of "contradictory class locations" to describe positions in the class structure that more conventional orthodox Marxists would call "strata." According to Wright, "An alternative way of dealing with ... ambiguities in the class structure is to regard some positions as occupying objectively contradictory locations within class relations ... (In a sense, of course, all class positions are 'contradictory locations' in that class relations are intrinsically antagonistic, contradictory social relations. The point is that certain positions in the class structure constitute doubly contradictory locations: they represent positions which are torn between the basic contradictory class relations of capitalist society. I will for convenience simply refer to them as 'contradictory class locations'.)" (1978, pp. 61–62).

26 Gouldner defines the culture of critical discourse this way: "The culture of critical discourse (CCDJ is an historically evolved set of rules, a grammar of discourse, which (1) is concerned to justify its assertions, but (2) whose mode of justification does not proceed by invoking authorities, and (3) prefers to elicit the voluntary consent of those addressed solely on the basis of arguments adduced" (1979, p. 28).

27 Gouldner calls the CCD a "grammar of discourse" and therefore the new class of intellectuals is a "speech community" (1979, p. 28).

28 Gouldner uses the concept of context-variability to describe the CCD. "Here, good speech is speech that can make its own principles explicit and is oriented to conforming with them, rather than stressing context-sensitivity and context-variability. Good speech here thus has theoreticity" (1979, p. 28).

My basic typology therefore is the following:

Intellectuals
= those modern men of idea who are bound together by the CCD

Professionals
= intellectuals under market capitalism in whose knowledge technical know-how dominates the teleological component.

Intelligentsia
= intellectuals who maintain the domination of the teleological component of knowledge above technical know-how, intellectuals in pre- and postrevolutionary Eastern Europe, in societies where modernization does not coincide with the development of civil society and market capitalism.

It is not accidental that most of the sociological and philosophical literature on intellectuals concerns Eastern Europe (publications on the Russian and Polish intelligentsia, particularly, dominate the field).[29] I would attribute a symbolic importance to the fact that the very term "intelligentsia" is of Russian origin. Anglo-Saxon authors, when they had to go beyond the notion of "professionals," needed to transliterate a Russian expression into English. Capitalism in England produced professionals. Eastern Europe, fluctuating between Asiatic and European feudalism, between feudalism and Western capitalism, between East European absolutism and civil society, gave birth to an intelligentsia. For a genuine empiricist (who is by definition a product of a "pure" civil society), trained in Anglo-Saxon pragmatism and positivism, the notion of an intelligentsia is an obscure, prescientific (or nonscientific) one. The scientific category is "professionals," which includes a group of occupations: people with certain qualifications performing social and economic functions for which these qualifications are necessary. Professionals are people who have a monopoly of knowledge of how to choose means to reach already selected goals. They are experts whose services are bought by those who set the goals. Professionals are the product of civil society and of market capitalism. The very basis of their existence – like the basis of the existence of the bureaucracy – is the definition

29 Aleksander Gella emphasizes the uniqueness of the concept of intelligentsia for Eastern Europe: "While all other classes and Strata of Eastern Europe have had their Counterparts in the West, the intelligentsia, strictly speaking, did not" (1976, p. 10). He suggests that one should make a clear distinction between the concepts of intellectuals and intelligentsia (p. 11) and should locate the intelligentsia in the mid-19th-century East European context. Interestingly, he notes that the use of the term "intelligentsia" first occurs at almost the same time in Germany, Russia, and Poland (in 1849, 1846, and 1844, respectively) (p. 12).

of "expert knowledge" as knowledge relating to means and a market demand for this knowledge from those who set goals.

The history of Western intellectuals is a continuous struggle against this definition. The best Western intellects never accepted this subordinate social role. They reserved their right to make judgments about the goals they were hired to execute. Among left-wing theorists, the belief prevailed that genuine intellectuals were more than professionals: they were social critics.[30] But despite such reservations, most of those with rare intellectual skills were continuously "corrupted" by Western capitalism. High wages were offered for their executive skills, and they were increasingly allowed to wield bureaucratic power in compensation for their intellectual frustration.

This mass transformation of intellectuals into professionals simply did not occur in Eastern Europe. The numerical expansion of intellectuals from the 18th century onward was not followed by a similar increase in market demand for professionals. For many decades – in the late 18th and early 19th centuries – the intellectuals were in the vanguard of the fight for the Westernization of Eastern Europe, but by the mid-19th century, especially in Russia, Western professionalization looked less and less attractive to many of them. East European intellectuals increasingly realized the advantages of not being professionals. They defined themselves as intelligentsia, people with not only executive skills but also moral commitment and historical vision. This late 19th-century East European intelligentsia was open to ideologies which projected new "teleological societies," societies ruled by substantive rationality. The East European intelligentsia was ready to bypass Western professionalization, which had proved a historical dead end for intellectuals in their long march to power. It was ready for the Bolshevik call to form a historical vanguard to lead the revolutionary transformation of society and create a new rational order based on the principles of scientific socialism. The Leninist emphasis on superrationality in organization, the fight against any form of anarchism and spontaneity, the skepticism concerning bourgeois electoralism as a legitimate way to choose among alternatives, appealed not only to those who shared Bolshevik values but to all intellectuals who believed they knew how a rational society should be organized. Lenin argued on the eve of the October Revolution that the Bolsheviks were ready to take power, not because they could count on the support of the majority of the population, but because they had enough cadres to fill all major decision-making positions.[31] What the new society needed first of all was cadres armed with the tools of scientific socialism,

30 Paul Baran (1961) makes a crucial distinction between "mental workers" and "intellectuals" which is typical of most left-wing ideologues. For Baran, to be an intellectual means to be a "social critic." Those who fall short on this criterion – however competent they might be in their professions – can only be defined as "mental workers."

31 Lenin, in September 1917, when he tried to convince his fellow Bolsheviks that the Party was ready to take state power, clearly indicated that for such a move the Party does not need the vote of the majority of the population, or even that of the working class. The Party will be ready to govern as soon as it can produce enough cadres to rule. In Lenin's own words, "The proletariat, we are told, will not be able to set the state apparatus in motion. Since the 1905 revolution, Russia has been governed by 130,000 landowners. Yet we are told that the 240,000 members of the Bolshevik Party will not be able to govern Russia.... These 240,000 are already backed by no less than a million

cadres with teleological knowledge, to lead society and to run the state-socialist redistributive economy.

It should be clear from this short and necessarily superficial argument that the class which is organized around the position of teleological redistributor stretches beyond those who make the immediate redistributive decisions. It is integrated by the ethos of state-socialist rational redistribution, and it includes all those who claim power – not only economic power but, for example, cultural or administrative power – on the basis of their monopoly of teleological knowledge. It potentially integrates the whole intelligentsia into a dominating class. The main thrust of this analysis is the rejection of the bureaucratic class concept, but without the acceptance of Dahrendorf's proposition that in modern societies economic class power is being replaced by political class power. The intelligentsia's claims under state socialism are legitimated in the same way as is the expropriation of surplus. The class power of the intelligentsia stretches beyond the economic sphere, but its foundations are in the basic institutions which guarantee social reproduction in state-socialist societies. Critics of Dahrendorf[32] rightly point out that he is basically rejecting class analysis. He calls the political elite a class and argues that classes proper – that is, classes emerging from economic antagonisms – no longer exist. When I suggest that the intelligentsia is in the process of becoming a class, I am not describing the political or bureaucratic elite of state socialism; I am using a broad, economically based category.

Here I have to acknowledge one major theoretical problem all attempts – including mine – which try to offer a class analysis of state socialism are confronted with. When I suggest that those who rule in Eastern Europe are not members of an elite constituted by political power, but that they form a class which is based in the system of economic reproduction, I have to justify why the concept of class is applicable to socioeconomic systems like state socialism where the separation of political and economic instances is much more limited than under market capitalism. Most class theorists would agree that the concept of class is applicable only in social-historical contexts where the political and economic instances are separated.[33]

---

votes.... We therefore already have a 'state apparatus' of one million people devoted to the socialist state. " (1970, p. 413).

32 Giddens claims that Dahrendorf does not actually reformulate the concept of class, but replaces class with authority. "Indeed, Dahrendorf might be accused of escaping from the issues involved by the same sort of terminological speciousness of which he accuses Marx: 'for while private property may disappear (empirical hypothesis), this can have no possible bearing upon the existence or disappearance of classes (trick of definition).' In attempting to reformulate the concept of class, Dahrendorf throws out the baby with the bath water by substituting 'authority' for 'class.' We already possess in sociology a reasonably adequate conceptual framework with which to analyse systems of authority, and there is little purpose served in confusing this with the terminology of 'class'" (1973, pp. 74–75).

33 Bauman, in the most original analysis, suggested that state socialiasm produced a new system of authority which he, with a sense of humor, calls "partynominal authority" (1974, p. 136). He suggested that this partynominal authority is different from legal authority since it is "intimately attached to *Wertrationalität*" (p. 136). From this it follows that under partynominal authority

I would try to defend my position and the applicability of the concept of class for contemporary Eastern Europe by claiming that under state socialism at least a relative separation of the "economic" from the "political" can be observed. Historically speaking, with the consolidation of the new socialist economic and social system this separation in fact increased. Following the revolutions the "political instance" seems to have a "primacy." This will later be criticized as "Stalinist voluntarism" in economic policy. With post-Stalinist "liberalization" this primacy of the political is reduced, and the need for scientific planning is emphasized. The "making of the new dominant class" of state socialism can be understood only in the historical process of this relative separation of the economic from the political. In the very first stage of state socialism those who rule do not yet appear as a class. The ruling Party and state apparatus appear to be constituted outside the economic system, constituted simply by coercive political power. (In this perspective the concept of "caste" of Trotsky is imprecise, but insightful.) We can understand only in the light of the later development that the main historic function of this Party and state apparatus is to facilitate the emergence of the new dominant class of intelligentsia as soon as the old social system is defeated politically and a relative separation of the economic instance becomes possible again. In this perspective the Party and state apparatus, which in the early stages of socialist development appears as a bureaucratic elite, caste, or – to put it probably more precisely – estate, is actually a sort of vanguard of the new dominant class, the intelligentsia. This function of the early Party and state apparatus is obscured by the fact that the political history of state socialism can be described in terms of political struggles between the Party and state apparatus, which is constituted by the primacy of the political instance, and the technocratic and liberal and ideological intelligentsia, which represents the interest of the relative separation of the economic from the political.

The making of the new dominant class of intelligentsia is therefore identical with the historical process of relative separation of the economic from the political, the relative decline of the primacy of the political. From this proposition it follows that what Dahrendorf supposed to happen namely, the replacement of "economic class power" by "political class power" – did not occur even under state socialism. A new dominant class emerged under state socialism only to the extent to which economic power can be conceived as relatively autonomous. The economic class was not replaced by a political

neither the concept of "class" nor the notion of "bureaucracy" is applicable; both class and bureaucratic relations assume legal authority and *"Zweckrationalität."* Bauman proposes the concept of "officialdom" to describe the distribution of power under partynominal authority. The notion of officialdom is a very insightful one and an interesting candidate to replace class for the analysis of the social structure in state-socialist societies. Balint Balla offered an analysis similar in many respects to that of Bauman. Balla documented in great detail why the Weberian concept of bureaucracy is inapplicable to Soviet type societies, and he proposed the notion of *"Kaderverwaltung"* (administration by cadres) to describe the system of domination of state socialism (1972, esp. pp. 47–62, 173–204). One ought to consider the need, following the analyses of Bauman and Balla, to try to develop a completely new terminology to describe structural positions under state socialism. For some sociologists this might be a more attractive attempt than my analysis which, more modestly, tries only to reinterpret the concept of class for state-socialist conditions.

class. However, Dahrendorf's analysis still offers insights for the understanding of social structures under state socialism. It is true that the separation of the economic and political instances declines with the transition from capitalism into state socialism. In this sense I would like to acknowledge that "class" under state socialism is a somewhat different concept than under market capitalism. While under capitalism class appears as economic class, under state socialism the classes which are formed probably should be called political-economic classes to acknowledge that, besides economic factors, political forces also play a role in constituting them.

The empirical and historical analysis of the complex interplay of political and economic forces in constituting the new class is important to explain the internal differentiation and dynamics of the new dominant class of the intelligentsia. It ought to be clear from the above analysis that I do not try to describe the new dominant class as a homogeneous one. The main fractions within the new class probably could be defined by the relative importance of political power in constituting them. The Party apparatus, more clearly constituted by political power, is a distinct fraction of the new class. The Party apparatus is in conflict – both historically and in contemporary struggles – with the planning-technocratic intelligentsia, which is more clearly constituted by the economic system. Most of political history is the struggle of the planning-technocratic intelligentsia (often articulated by their ideologues, the "liberal intellectuals") for economic reforms. On the surface it appears that the history of state socialism can be described as the struggle of liberal intellectuals against the Party apparatus. These conflicts between Party apparatus and rational planners and their liberal ideologues are real but not basic. The liberal, planning-technocratic intelligentsia gradually shares power with the Party apparatchik intelligentsia. The major economic antagonism is not between liberal intellectuals and the Party bureaucrats, but between the two classes, between the intelligentsia and the working class.

As was suggested earlier, if a class dichotomy exists in society, it must be rooted in the antagonism of interests with respect to the institutions which guarantee expropriation in the economic system. This antagonism under state socialism can be described in terms of conflicts between redistributive power and the interests of the direct producers – the antagonism on which the class dichotomy between the intelligentsia and the working class is based.

But does such an antagonism in fact exist? Is there a structural conflict of interest between the direct producer and the teleological redistributor? I would argue that such an antagonism does in fact exist and that the working class has an alternative system of legitimation. The dominating power under state socialism is challenged in a de facto way from time to time by attempts at self-determination by the working class, by the steadily re-emerging vision of self-managing socialism as an alternative to state-socialist redistributive economy. Yugoslavia, with her highly questionable claim to be the only country which has realized "self-managing socialism," is only one instance, but it can be shown that in political crises spontaneous working class movements emerge unexpectedly, attempting to bring the economy more directly under workers' control. (Probably the classic example is the workers' councils formed in 1956 in Hungary without intellectuals or ideologues, on the initiative of the workers and under workers' control, but similar developments occurred in Czechoslovakia around 1968 and in Poland more recently.) These two alternative conceptions of socialism are already present in the classical theories.

Marx and Engels originally emphasized only that socialism would be that form of social organization which abolished the institution of private ownership, without specifying what the economic institutions of socialist society would look like. But later Engels, in particular, tried to define the *differentia specifica* of socialism as the self-determination of direct producers.[34] The Bolshevik fixation on discipline and order subsequently omitted all content from this concept and transformed it into a pure slogan, a pure ideology of state-socialist redistribution which served to deprive the working class of all power and to make workers far more powerless than workers in a capitalist factory or in a capitalist economy at large.

A socialist counterethos based on the principle of self-determination of the direct producer is highly underdeveloped and unarticulated and in fact is more evident in spontaneous opposition movements by the workers of Eastern Europe than in codified ideologies. I would argue that one reason for the underdeveloped nature of this alternative vision of socialism is the class nature of the intelligentsia under state socialism.

The emergence of "organic intellectuals" of the working class, intellectuals who articulate working-class interests from within the ranks of a class *in statu nascendi,* is far less likely here than it is under capitalist conditions where intellectuals, after all, do not occupy a major position of their own in the class structure, but are by definition between classes. Furthermore, I am inclined to believe that the counterethos of self-determination will remain in the long run only an opposition ideology in Eastern Europe. It cannot replace the ethos of rational redistribution, only continuously challenge it, at most limiting redistributive power slightly and forcing redistributors to consider more seriously the interests of the direct producer. It is difficult to imagine a modern noncapitalist industrial society without strong redistributive mechanisms. A certain degree of expropriation

34 Even the classics of Marxism seem to operate with different "models of socialism"; they seem to present different views of what constitutes the essence of a revolutionary socialist transformation of capitalism. In the "Communist Manifesto," Marx and Engels seem to assume that the socialist transformation is identical with the abolition of private ownership and the introduction of state ownership of the means of production or, in more contemporary terminology, they see the essence of socialism in "nationalization of the means of production." Marx and Engels clearly state in the "Communist Manifesto": "The theory of Communists may be summed up in a single sentence: abolition of private property" (Marx and Engels 1970, p. 47). Then they add, "The proletariat will use its political supremacy to centralise all instruments of production in the hands of the State ..." (p. 52). But in other works the emphasis is on the socialization rather than simply on the nationalization of the means of production. Engels, in "Socialism: Utopian and Scientific," written more than four decades after the manifesto, strongly argues that "state ownership does not do away with the capitalistic nature of the productive forces" (1970, p. 422). Here Engels emphasized that the criterion of socialist transformation is the replacement of the capitalist mode of appropriation with a "direct social appropriation" (p. 423). This is more than a terminological difference. Two different visions of socialism (one based on state ownership, the other based on the principle of direct power of the immediate producer) find their roots here.

from the direct producer may be unavoidable, and I have little doubt that if an opposition movement based on the ideology of self-management succeeded in coming to power its leaders would still have to exercise a certain degree of redistributive power. When in August 1980 the Polish working class won major concessions, Lech Wałesa, the chief negotiator of Solidarity, summed up the working-class victory this way: From now on we are co-owners. This is possibly the most realistic formulation of the challenge which the direct producer can pose to the teleological redistributor. What Wałesa put forward was not a program to "abolish" teleological redistribution or central planning. In a sense, Wałesa proposed a sharing of powers between two "owners," the acceptance of two principles of legitimation, the establishment of a dual power system. Realistically, it might be very difficult to go much beyond this; it might not be possible to imagine a society based only on the "immediate power of the direct producer" in an anarchosyndicalist fashion. Nonetheless, spontaneous working-class movements toward self-determination and workers' control and intellectual attempts to develop a counterideology based on the principles of self-management are highly important; they challenge the dominating ethos, and they represent forces which might transform contemporary socialist societies into articulated conflict systems. If we understand working-class interest in terms of a class hostility to redistributive power, then it becomes clear that self-determination is something qualitatively different from decentralization of administration, an easily acceptable concept for any teleological redistributor. The requirements of decentralization of administration, a central theme in most socioeconomic reforms in Eastern Europe during the last two decades, correspond to the spirit of redistributive power. Struggles between decentralization and centralization reflect conflicts between different levels of redistributive power. Real movement toward self-determination can only occur with the development of the countervailing power of the direct producer, a power which could force redistributive power into compromises. Decentralization in itself is only the delegation of power to lower echelons of the power structure and does not affect the relationship between the powerful and the powerless. (Probably Yugoslavia – at least if we can believe its internal left-wing critics – is merely a more decentralized version of the state socialism found in other East European countries.)

The purpose of the arguments above is to show that it may be meaningful to assume that a crucial structural antagonism exists within state-socialist redistributive economies between the class which is organized around the redistributor and the class which is to be found in the position of direct producer. It is to be hoped that any existing lack of theoretical sophistication and empirical documentation will only serve to stimulate both theoretical and empirical work in this direction, which may well be of crucial importance for the further development of socialist theory.

The Dominant Class Of State Socialism *In Statu Nascendi*

The intelligentsia is on its way to becoming the dominant class of East European state-socialist societies, but we are still only at the beginning of an obviously long historical process. Consequently, if we call the intelligentsia a class, we should be aware of a number of limitations in the use of this concept for the analysis of contemporary East European societies. The intelligentsia in many respects forms a different kind of class from the bourgeoisie, and it is not clear that all the connotations attached to the notion of a dominant class will ever be applicable to the intellectuals. First of all, the intelligentsia is not only an ownership class; it is not an inheritance class either. Despite the laborite reform of inheritance laws which has taken place in countries ruled by social democratic parties for decades, the bourgeoisie is still an inheritance class: bourgeois wealth and, to a large extent, power are passed from one generation to the next. No doubt from a purely political economic point of view this does not make a great deal of difference: the class power of the bourgeoisie is based on its right to expropriate surplus. With the legitimation of private ownership of the means of production, the roots of class conflict lie in the antagonism between capital and labor. In other words, if a social democratic party ever succeeded in abolishing inheritance of the means of the production, this ideal capitalism would still be capitalism as long as private ownership entitled anyone to expropriate surplus. What really matters is the nature of exploitation. On the other hand, it would be foolish to deny that inheritance is very important when it comes to judgments about the morality of capitalism. Societies which limit the inheritance of wealth and power are perceived to be "better" than those which do not do so. The East European intelligentsia, at least at present, is a noninheritance class. The intellectuals are unable to pass their power position to their children. This is especially true at the highest echelons of power. At these highest echelons of power "socialist nepotism" is not unheard of, but it is relatively infrequent. (Interesting exceptions are Romania and North Korea.) The intelligentsia is also a fairly open class. It receives new members from the "dominated class." You do not have to be the son or daughter of an intellectual to enter the class. It is possible to argue, on the other hand, that the intelligentsia is slowly losing its open character. A significant proportion of university graduates in Eastern Europe are still from nonintellectual backgrounds, but the proportion is steadily declining.[35] It is also possible to argue that this open character was always a relative one. The intelligentsia received new members, but only very rarely did these intellectuals let their own sons or daughters leave the dominant class. In other words, upward mobility into the intelligentsia is high, but downward mobility is quite insignificant, and even if crucial positions are not transferred along family lines, those who are born into the

35 According to Zsuzsa Ferge, the proportion of children of whom at least one parent is a manual worker in institutions of tertiary education increased dramatically with the socialist transformation. This proportion increased in Hungary from 3.5 % in 1938 to 48.5% in 1950. Over the next 20 years this proportion declined, to 37.1% by 1970 (1979, p. 145). Hungary does not seem to be atypical of Eastern Europe; see Walter D. Conner's quite similar data on the USSR and Poland (1979, pp. 177–214, esp. p. 206).

families of the powerful are significantly privileged. They usually start their careers in higher positions, and they climb the ladders of power faster. As state socialism matures, the inheritance of wealth also plays a more important role than formerly. Even if it is incomparable with inheritance in capitalist society, the inheritance of flats, dachas, cars, and so forth is clearly and increasingly a privilege. Finally, *one* could argue that the open character of the dominant class was only a temporary phenomenon and that any new and numerically expanding dominant class is "open." There are simply not enough sons and daughters to occupy the new positions.

In fact, even if the *numerus clausus* had not operated and all children of the intelligentsia had been admitted straight into the university, enough places would still have remained for the children of blue-collar families simply because the university population expanded so rapidly. (I think few children of the intelligentsia were kept out in the long run. The *numerus clausus* guaranteeing a certain proportion of non-white collar children at the universities usually placed children of intellectuals on a waiting list. After one or two years all who really wanted to enter the university could do so). But despite all this evidence we should acknowledge that the intelligentsia, compared with the bourgeoisie, is basically a noninheritance class and that this may be significant for those who wish to make moral judgments concerning its rise to power.

Furthermore, the intelligentsia is not a "selfish" class. It does not expropriate surplus in order to consume it. The selfishness of the bourgeoisie, the conspicuous consumption of the leisure class, the extent of inequality in terms of consumed and personally possessed material goods, are important criteria in moral judgments of capitalism. Theoretically, selfishness is not a crucial criterion; the dominant class can be ascetic – and in fact, if we can believe Benjamin Franklin, the bourgeoisie has been highly ascetic in the past. It is also important to remind ourselves that in modern capitalism, with progressive taxation, absentee ownership, and so forth, most of the surplus is not consumed by the owners of capital. It is reinvested or allocated through the state budget. We could imagine an egalitarian capitalism, with ascetic capitalists who only expropriate in order to reinvest, which would not be less capitalistic as long as the exploitation was of a capitalist nature. We also should not overemphasize the unselfishness of the East European intelligentsia. There is a significant degree of inequality between the intellectuals and the working class. Wage differentials in Eastern Europe between a university professor and a plumber or taxi driver are frighteningly similar to those in a Western welfare society.[36] Eastern Europe is only more equal in terms of the extremes – it does not know the extreme rich and does not allow the existence of the extreme poor – but the gap of inequality for the

36 Reliable data from Eastern Europe are not easily available. To the best of my knowledge, Zsuzsa Ferge offers the most reliable and comprehensive data for Hungary. According to her figures (based on investigations carried out in the mid 1960s), in Hungary the top 20% of the income earners earned 36.2% of the total income, the top 5% earned 11.8%. Comparable figures for a group of countries composed of the United States, Sweden, and Denmark were, according to Ferge, 42.7% and 16.4% (1979, p. 169).

overwhelming majority is nonetheless significant, and it follows in direction the class distinction between intellectuals and workers.[37]

The intelligentsia, furthermore, is privileged not only in terms of income distribution. For example, the intellectuals have a better chance of getting a highly subsidized state flat; they fill trade union vacation homes during peak seasons; they are the only people who have access to the well-equipped Party hospitals and who can shop in the tax-free hard currency shops. Wherever the analyst looks in the East European redistributive economy he will find the intellectuals in a privileged situation, even in those spheres where, in a capitalist welfare state, socialist policy counteracts inequalities.[38]

But it is still true that intellectuals not only cannot pass on to their children the surplus which is expropriated under their power, but they are by and large unable to use it for their personal purposes. A capitalist, despite trade union and state control, even today can commit economic suicide, can overconsume and underinvest, but the redistributor of state socialism does not own the surplus which flows through his hands. He only administers it. However, it is crucial to emphasize that this unselfishness of the intelligentsia is only true in terms of material goods, not in terms of power. The chances for the redistributor to increase his personal wealth are very limited, but he is not only permitted but also structurally motivated to maximize his redistributive power. If the law of capitalism consists in the striving for more profit, the law of state socialism consists in the striving for the maximization of redistributive power, and from this point of view the teleological redistributor – with, of course, evangelistic zeal – will be as ruthless as any capitalist could ever be.

Furthermore, the East European intelligentsia, at least at present, is only a "class in itself" – it has not developed a class consciousness.

One could argue that, at least according to orthodox Marxist class theory, "class" does not have a sociological meaning without class consciousness. Class, properly speaking, is always "class for itself." The East European intelligentsia is obviously not a class in this sense. Not only does it not recognize the class nature of its own power, but it promotes the ideology of classlessness and consensus and, even more paradoxically, claims that the power exercised by the intellectuals is in fact the power of the proletariat. The revolutionary intelligentsia interprets itself as the tool of the dictatorship of the proletariat. Dominating classes are not usually very keen on promoting the development of class consciousness. Dominating classes always promote ideologies of consensus, while dominated classes have a vested interest in becoming classes for themselves and in emphasizing the conflictual nature of social relations. However, I am ready to acknowledge that class consciousness or even, more generally speaking, social consciousness in contempo-

37 According to Ferge, in Hungarian state-owned firms in 1975 the ratio of total monthly income of top management to the income of workers was 2.5:1. The same ratio for middle-level management was 1.5:1. She also claims that the ratio is steadily declining. For the top management the above ratio in 1968 was 3.0:1; in other words, she reports a decline of almost 20% over less than 10 years (1979, p. 180).

38 For inequalities in administrative and redistributive allocation, see Szelényi (1978) and Ferge (1979, pp. 233–73).

rary Eastern Europe exists at a very low level. Social consciousness is less articulated than that in bourgeois society at a very early stage of its development. On the level of political analysis one can see this in the vulnerability of state-socialist societies when confronted with significant changes. The events of 1956 were totally unexpected in Hungary. No one was able to predict the rapid rise and fall of the "Prague Spring" or the more recent working-class opposition movements in Poland. The East European societies know less about themselves, despite fairly well developed sociological and public opinion research, than bourgeois societies did even in times when the terms "sociology" and "opinion poll" did not exist. I would argue that the inarticulate nature of social consciousness is one of the main social and political problems East European societies are faced with today. It produces political and economic instability. It is partially responsible for the repressive political infrastructure, since the dominating class overestimates the forces which threaten its power monopoly and may feel it necessary to eliminate by administrative measure critics who in bourgeois political systems would be peacefully coopted by means of sheer "repressive tolerance." On the other hand, the inarticulate nature of social consciousness is the direct product of the class formation of the intelligentsia. The fact that the intelligentsia for the first time in the history of mankind is becoming a dominating social class prevents the development of opposing class ideologies, prevents the emergence of organic intellectuals of oppressed classes. Bourgeois society was able to produce conflicting class ideologies because intellectuals, the potential ideologues, occupied an intermediary position between two basic classes and could become organic intellectuals of one or the other of them. The fact that the intelligentsia is not a class in capitalist society, but only a stratum (and this means that intellectuals do not have a system of interests antagonistic to other major components of the social structure), is the precondition for the development of class consciousness. It is a precondition of the development of the proletariat as a class for itself. As the principle which legitimates the claim of the intellectuals to power becomes the main principle of legitimation of social and economic power in society, the intelligentsia loses its potential to produce organic intellectuals of the dominated classes. It only promotes ideologies which are in its own basic class interest, the most important being the ideology of classlessness.

The state-socialist redistributive economy represents a new system of economic exploitation. Under this economic system the immediate producer has no more control over the product of his labor than the worker in a capitalist economy. But in state-socialist societies the cultural deprivation of the working class is probably more serious than the economic – the worker is deprived not only of the products of his labor, but also of his social identity. Curiously enough, one of the first measures of the so-called dictatorship of the proletariat was the abolition of all working-class organizations.

The authorities outlawed not only political organizations such as parties, trade unions, and youth groups, but even workers' choirs and hiking clubs. Since the working class has ultimate power in society – argued the official ideologues of state socialism – there is no longer any need for specifically worker organizations. The trade unions were transformed into worker management corporations (in all East European societies managerial and engineering staff belong to the same union as workers), and the same logic was applied to "innocent" cultural and sporting organizations or clubs.

Not only are the workers deprived of the opportunity to associate with their fellow workers, but their quest for identity as workers is also continuously questioned. The worker is replaced with an ideological notion, that of the proletariat – the worker who is aware of his historical mission. The worker finds himself labeled as "petty bourgeois" or "lumpen proletariat" if he tries to live up to his immediate values and aspirations, and he is accused of lacking proletarian consciousness. The empirically identifiable values, aspirations, and ways of life of the actual physical workers are confronted with the ideals of "socialist man," who socially and in class terms is a faceless creature devised by Soviet Marxist ideologues. If someone were to analyze carefully the ideal type of socialist man – a test still to be done he would find striking similarities with the values and tastes of the highbrow upper middle class of any advanced industrial society. Socialist man should read books, listen to music, be dressed like, and behave with his children as doctrinaire left-wing academics do. If a semiskilled factory laborer in Prague does not match this ideal, then he should be ashamed of himself. State-socialist society does not permit self-identification in terms of position in the social structure. One cannot be proud of being a worker or peasant: the cultural image is a homogeneous one, and conflicting or competing values simply do not exist. There is only a single hierarchy of values. The ideology of classlessness of state socialism could not suppress all expressions of working-class consciousness. Haraszti's powerful book *A Worker in a Worker's State* (1977) offers convincing evidence of the existence of a significant degree of "class identity" and "conflict consciousness," to use Michael Mann's terminology,[39] among workers. The workers Haraszti worked with in the Red Star Tractor Factory in Budapest could draw as clear a distinction between a "we" and a "they" as any "traditional worker" can under capitalism.[40] Haraszti found that a strong identity among blue-collar workers on

---

39 Michael Mann distinguishes among four elements of consciousness-identity, opposition, totality, and alternative. According to Mann, these four elements are separate in reality and any can occur without the others. However, he claims that revolutionary class consciousness can develop only if all four elements are present in the consciousness of the working class (1973, pp. 68–73).

40 The development of workers' consciousness of class identity and even of some perception of opposition and totality is powerfully argued by Haraszti in his discussion of how workers distinguish between "we" and "they": "They, them theirs I don't believe that anyone who has ever worked in a factory ... can be in any doubt about what these words mean. In every place of work them means the same thing: the management, those who give orders and take the decisions, employ labour and pay wages, the men and their agents who are in charge. The word lumps together those whom one knows and those whom one does not know, those whom one likes and those whom one hates, the foreman with whom one is on friendly terms, the design engineer whom one addresses formally, the manager whom one approaches with obsequious respect, the secretaries, the timekeepers, the inspectors, the factory journal and the guards. Although we mainly talk about factory matters, them transcends the walls of the factory and encompasses everything which is above, far away, outside the power of whoever is speaking. I have also worked in offices in which, just like here, they had directors and subordinates, some of whom were privileged and others on low salaries. But nowhere, except among factory workers, have I heard this absolute them, peremptory, exact, and crystal clear. This usage not only differentiates industrial workers from others, even within the

the production line was reinforced by a perception of an antagonism between workers and all those who work in the office rather than on the shop floor. "They" were the enemy. It is worth noting that for the workers Haraszti described, this "enemy" was not only high-level management but included the lowest echelons of salaried supervisory personnel: the night guard who searched the workers at the factory gate after their shifts was one of "them," was also an enemy. Haraszti empirically identified a perception by the workers of a dichotomic class structure in the Red Star Tractor Factory, a strong feeling of identity among blue-collar workers and an ability to perceive the conflictual nature of class relations. What Haraszti could not document, in Michael Mann's terminology, was a sense of class totality; the vision of an "alternative" was rather naive. From the Haraszti study we can establish the existence of a conflict consciousness, but we still do not have proofs of the existence of a class consciousness.

The recent events in Poland, especially since August 1980, are of major importance for the understanding of class dynamics under state socialism.[41] Since August 1980 one can find signs of development of a consciousness among the Polish working class which may point beyond a simple class identity and conflict consciousness. In orthodox Marxist language, one can suggest the transition from a "trade union consciousness" to "class consciousness" among the Polish working class during August 1980. It would be premature even to attempt to offer a full analysis of the present Polish struggles; without aspiring to draw far-reaching conclusions, I would like to point to a few interesting new elements in the development of class consciousness of the Polish working class.

It is of theoretical importance that the first six of the 21 demands formulated by the Solidarity movement on August 24, 1980 *(L' Alternative* 1980, pp. 14–15), are political, and only the rest can be called "normal" trade union demands. It is probably even more important that the very first demand is for unions which are independent from management, which are genuine organizations of workers rather than worker-management corporations. The striking workers of the Gdansk shipyard put the "question of organization" first in this list of demands, before the trade union issues. In fact, in the agreements later reached with the government, Solidarity compromised on many trade union-type demands but was unwilling to compromise on the question of organization. Under some government pressure, Solidarity accepted that the unions are not political in nature *(L' Alternative* 1980, p. 44) and agreed that the movement would not play the role of a political party. But this concession was significantly less than the acceptance of a "proper trade union" role for Solidarity. The intention of the Polish Communist Party and government was to limit the activities of Solidarity to "bread and butter" issues, but

factory it traces a subtle demarcation line between the majority and those whose posts and qualifications are such that they lost sight of the distance which divides the common destiny; dropping them is the first sign that someone really wanted to start climbing the ladder" (Haraszti 1977, pp. 71–72).

41 For rich documentation of the Polish events see the special issue of *L'Alternative* (no. 7), November-December 1980. This special issue published the full text of the "Information Bulletin" of the Solidarity movement from August 23, 1980, until August 31, 1980 *(L' Alternative* 1980) For an interesting theoretical analysis see Arato (1981).

– as Kania, the first secretary of the Polish CP, noted with disquiet – with the establishment of Solidarity Poland moved rather toward a "dual power" system (Arato 1981). It is probably true that, in the early stages at least, when Solidarity was virtually identical with the striking shipbuilders of Gdansk and had not become an occupationally highly heterogeneous body, the movement's main aim was not to challenge the existence of the Party and/or the government. Even the issue of the composition of the Party and government appears to be secondary. The main objective was to establish the "countervailing power" of workers. The editors of the "Information Bulletin" of Solidarity expressed this in the following way in their declaration dated August 28, 1980: "Malheureusement certaines pertes dues à la mauvaise gestion ... ne pourront être récupérées ... Nous ne cherchons pas de coupables ... Il s'agit avant tout de créer les conditions qui garantiront la non-reproduction de ces pertes. Cela sera possible quand le monopole du pouvoir ne sera plus transformé par ce pouvoir en monopole de l'intelligence, du savoir et de la rationalité. On ne pourra y parvenir sans décentraliser le pouvoir, sans créer les conditions qui permettront l'utilisation du savoir professionnel des savants et l'intelligence collective de la classe ouvrière» (*L'Alternative* 1980, p. 29).

What the movement is seeking to achieve, therefore, is not a change of personnel in the existing power structure, but a new system of power in which the "collective intelligence of the working class" can be utilized side by side with the professional knowledge of scholars. According to the authors of the declaration, the decentralization of power, the reform of the planning system (and a "better utilization of the professional knowledge of scholars"), is necessary, but not sufficient. In addition to decentralization of the planning system, they insist that the right of the producers to dispose of the products of their labor be respected. In the wording of the declaration: «Nous faisons confiance aux militants sociaux et aux spécialistes qui insistent sur la nécessité de réformes fondamentales dans le système de planification et de gestion de l'économie... Cela n'est certes pas facile... mais il faut entamer le processus de changement... en créant les conditions d'une authentique participation de tous ceux qui travaillent et qui ont le droit d'attendre des effets de leur activité, à l'élaboration du destin de notre pays» *(L'Alternalive* 1980, p. 29). Unlike Hungary in 1956 and Czechoslovakia in 1968, where the opposition was initiated and led by sections of the intelligentsia, in Poland in 1980 the movement emerged from the working class directly. Unlike 1970 and 1976, in 1980 the Polish workers were no longer willing to restrict their struggles to bread-and-butter issues; they moved beyond conflict consciousness, and one can identify elements of class consciousness in their actions. In this sense Poland in 1980–81 represents an important further stage in the unfolding of the new class structure of state socialism.

But even in the light of the Polish events of 1980–81 the analyst can identify only elements of this new class structure: the new class regulations and the new dominant class of state socialism are still in the making, still *in statu nascendi.*

As I proposed above, the new relations between the rulers and ruled will appear in class relations only after the political and economic instance becomes relatively separated, after civil society gains a significant autonomy from the political state.

As long as the civil society is penetrated by the totalitarian political state, all political movements in Eastern Europe will aim first at the establishment of basic civil liberties. The Polish working class – and the workers of other East European nations – obviously cannot articulate successfully the interests of workers' self-determination as long as basic civil liberties are not guaranteed to all, as long as at least a relative autonomy of civil society from the political state is not achieved. Both the rationalization of the central planning and management of the economic (and cultural-political) system and the aspiration to workers' self-determination require the relative autonomy of civil society, guarantees of civil liberties. At this stage it appears that the only conflict is the one between the state and civil society, between the "powers" and "society." The central thesis of this essay is that, as the relative autonomy of civil society is achieved, this ideologically constructed facade of consensus of the whole society against the powers disappears, and the new and now class type of conflict between intelligentsia and the working class becomes obvious.

In a sense this paper does not therefore reject Djilas. Djilas offered a theory that probably accurately described the agents who first held power under state socialism, under the conditions of total penetration of civil society by a totalitarian state. Under these circumstances – under Stalinism-state socialism indeed is dominated by the party and state apparatus. Unlike Djilas, I would not call this apparatus a class, since I could not locate it in an identifiable economic structure. My main claim is that during the last 20 years, since the publication of Djilas's work, profound changes have taken place under state socialism. Stalinist economic voluntarism is gradually replaced with a more rationalized system of planning whose claim to be "scientific" must be taken more seriously, and there has been some tendency toward an increase in the autonomy of civil society. As these processes continue the circle of the power holders gradually opens up, the power monopoly of the party and state apparatus declines. The apparatchiks gradually begin to share power with the intellectuals, and the power of apparatchiks is gradually replaced with the class power of the intelligentsia. My claim is that, while Djilas accurately identified the power holders prior to the 1960s, since then analysts have noted the emergence of a genuinely new class of intelligentsia. This intelligentsia is broader than the "new class" of Djilas, and it is also more clearly of a class nature. As one can see from the example of Poland in 1980–81, and especially from the events following the imposition of martial law on December 13, 1981, these apparatchiks still hold on to their power. But in this later stage of development of state-socialist societies we can already see what Djilas could not notice in the late 1950s: the replacement of a conflict between the apparatchiks and the society by conflicts between a new dominant class of intelligentsia and the working class as the most likely outcome of political and economic developments in contemporary Eastern Europe.

References

L'Alternative: Special Issue on Poland. 1980. (November-December.)

Anderson, Perry. 1974. *Lineages of the Absolutist State.* London: New Left Books.

Arato, Andrew. 1981. "Civil Society against the State." *Telos,* no. 47 (Spring), pp. 23–47.

Arato, Andrew, and Eike Gebhardt, eds. 1978. *The Essential Frankfurt School Reader.* Oxford: Basil Blackwell.

Balla, Balint. 1972. *Kaderverwaltung. Versuch zur Idealtypisierung der 'Bürokratie' sowjetisch-volksdemokratischen Typs.* Stuttgart: Ferdinand Enke.

Baran, Paul. 1961. "The Commitment of the Intellectuals." *Monthly Review* 13 (May), pp. 8–18.

Bauman, Zygmunt. 1974. "Officialdom and Class – Bases of Inequality in Socialist Society." Pp. 129–48 in *The Social Analysis of Class Structure,* edited by Frank Parkin. London: Tavistock.

Berdyaev, Nicolas. 1972. *The Origin of Russian Communism.* Ann Arbor: University of Michigan Press.

Burnham, James W. 1962. *The Managerial Revolution.* Bloomington: Indiana University Press.

Connerton, Paul, ed. 1976. *Critical Sociology: selected Readings.* Harmondsworth: Penguin.

Connor, Walter D. 1979. *Socialism, Politics and Equality: Hierarchy and Change in Eastern Europe and the USSR.* New York: Columbia University Press.

Dahrendorf, Ralf. 1959. *Class and Class Conflict in Industrial Society.* London: Routledge & Kegan Paul.

Dijalas, Milovan. 1957. *The New Class: an Analysis of the Communist System.* New York: Holt, Rinehart & Winston.

Engels, Frederick. 1970. "Socialism Utopian and Scientific." Pp. 375–428 in *Karl Marx and Frederick Engels: Selected Works.* Moscow: Progress Publishers.

Ferge, Zsuzsa. 1973. *Társadalmunk Rétegzodése.* Budapest: Kozgazdasagi & Jogi Konyvkiado,

---. 1979. *Revival: Society in the Making: Hungarian Social and Societal Policy 1945–75.* New York: Sharpe.

Gella, Aleksander, ed. 1976. *The Intelligentsia and the lntellectuals; Theory, Method and Case Study.* London: Sage.

Giddens, Anthony. 1973. *The Class Structure of the Advanced Societies.* London: Hutchinson University Library.

Gouldner, A. W. 1975–76. "Prologue to a Theory of Revolutionary Intellectuals." *Telos,* no. 26 (Winter), pp. 3–36.

---. 1979. *The Future of Intellectuals and the Rise of the New Class.* New York: Seabury.

Habermas, Jürgen. 1970. *Toward a Rational Society: Student Protest, Science, and Politics,* translated by Jeremy J. Shapiro. Boston: Beacon.

---. 1974. *Theory and Practice,* translated by John Viertel. London: Heinemann.

Haraszti, Miklos. 1977. *A Worker in a Worker's State: Piece-Rates in Hungary.* Harmondsworth: Penguin.

Hegedus, András. 1977. *The Structure* of *Socialist Society* London: Constable.

Horkheimer, Max. 1978. "The End of Reason." Pp. 26–48, in A. Arato/E. Gebhardt (eds.), *The Essential Frankfurt School Reader.* Oxford: Basil Blackwell.

Konrad, George, and Iván Szelényi. 1979. *The Intellectuals on the Road to Class Power.* New York: Harcourt Brace Jovanovich.

Kuron, J. 1978. «Pour une platform unique de l'opposition.» In *La Pologne: Une société en dissidence,* edited by Z. Erard and G. M. Zygier. Paris.

Kuron, J., and K. Modzelewski. 1966. "An Open Letter to the Party." *New Politics* 5 (2): 5–46.

Lenin, V. I. 1970. "Can the Bolsheviks Retain State Power?" Pp. 393–434 in *Selected Works,* vol. 2. Moscow: Progress Publishers.

Mann, Michael. 1973. *Consciousness and Action among the Western Working Class.* London: Macmillan

Marx, Karl. 1970. "The Eighteenth Brumaire of Louis Bonaparte." Pp. 96–179 in *Karl Marx and Frederick Engels: Selected Works.* Moscow: Progress Publishers.

---. 1972. "Theses on Feuerbach." Pp. 11–13 in *On Historical Materialism,* by K. Marx, F. Engels, and V. I. Lenin. Moscow: Progress Publishers.

---. 1974. *Capital.* Vol. 3 Moscow: Progress Publishers.

---. 1975a. "Contribution to the Critique of Hegel's Philosophy of Law." Pp. 5–129 in *Karl Marx and Frederick Engels: Collected Works,* vol. 3. New York International Publishers.

---. 1975b. *Precapitalist Economic Formations.* New York: International Publishers.

Marx, Karl, and Frederick Engels 1970. "Manifeste of the Communist Party." Pp. 31–63 in *Karl Marx and Frederick Engels: Selected Works.* Moscow: Progress Publishers.

---. 1972. "The German Ideology." Pp. 14–76 in *On Historical Materialism,* by K. Marx, F. Engels, and V. I. Lenin. Moscow: Progress Publishers.

Ossowski, Stanislaw. 1963. *Class Structure in the Social Consciousness.* London: Routledge & Kegan Paul.

---. 1969. "Old Notions and New Problems – Interpretations of Social Structure in Modem Society." Pp. 79–89 in *Social Inequality,* edited by André Beteille. London: Penguin.

Perez-Diaz, Victor M. 1978. *State, Bureaucracy and Civil Society: A critical discussion of the political theory of Karl Marx.* London: Macmillan.

Shachtman, M. 1962. *The Bureaucratic Revolution.* New York: Donald.

Shkaratan, O. I. 1970. *Problemy sotsial'noi struktury rabochego klassa SSSR.* Moscow: Mysl.

Stalin, J. V. 1972. *Economic Problems of Socialism in the USSR.* Peking: FLP.

Szelényi, Iván. 1978. "Social Inequalities in State Socialist Redistributive Economies." *International Journal of Comparative Sociology* 10: 63–87.

Trotsky, Leon. 1972. *The Revolution Betrayed.* New York: Pathfinder.

Weber, Max. 1958. *The Religion of India: the Sociology of Hinduism and Buddhism.* New York: Free Press.

---. 1978. *Economy and Society: An Outline of Interpretive Sociology,* edited by G. Roth and C. Wittich. Berkeley, Los Angeles, London: University of California Press, 2 Volumes.

Wesolowski, Wlodzimierz, ed. 1970. *Zróżnicowanie spoleczne.* Warsaw: Wydownictwo Polskiej Akademii Nauk.

Wesolowksi, Wlodzimierz. 1974. "The Notion of Strata and Class in Socialist Society." Pp. 122–148 in *Social Inequality,* edited by André Beteille. London: Penguin.

Wright, Erik O. 1978. *Class, Crisis and the State.* London: New Left Books.

II.2 Circulation or Reproduction of Elites during the Post-Communist Transformation of Eastern Europe

Iván Szelényi and Szonja Szelényi*

Introduction

This special issue of *Theory and Society* reports the results of a crossnational comparative study of elite recruitment in postcommunist Eastern Europe. An international team of social scientists (composed of scholars from the United States and several Eastern European countries) conducted a large-scale survey under the title *Social Stratification in Eastern Europe After 1989*. These surveys were conducted in Russia and in five Eastern European countries (Bulgaria, the Czech Republic, Hungary, Poland, and Slovakia).

The authors of the articles that are contained in this special issue met in Erdötarcsa (Hungary) in December 1993 for an intensive workshop. The purpose of the workshop was to analyze the first results of the study from Hungary, Poland, and Russia. The articles that follow are products of this meeting. In this introduction we: (a) explain why the study of postcommunist elite recruitment is of theoretical and political interest; (b) describe the common conceptual framework that orients the articles in this special issue, (c) outline the nature of the survey research that we conducted in Eastern Europe, and (d) summarize our findings from Hungary, Poland, and Russia.

The research puzzle: Theoretical and political controversies

Circulation versus reproduction

In this special issue, we focus our attention on a topical theoretical controversy in Eastern Europe and the successor states of the former Soviet Union: what happened to socialist elites with the transition to postcommunism? Who were the people who held command positions under socialism, and how were these people affected by the postcommunist transformation? If there *was* a change in the composition of Eastern European elites, what happened to the old cadres and where did the new elites come from?

* University of California, Stanford University.

Two competing answers have been offered to these questions so far. The first (the elite reproduction theory) suggests that revolutionary changes in Eastern Europe did not affect the social composition of elites. This is because the old nomenklatura elite has managed to survive at the top of the class structure and is now becoming the new propertied bourgeoisie. The second argument (the elite circulation theory) claims that the transition to postcommunism resulted in a structural change at the top of the class hierarchy: new people are recruited for command positions on the basis of new principles.

The question of elite recruitment is not merely of academic interest; polemics around the subject also inform political struggles that are currently underway in Eastern Europe. The political Right, for example, generally advocates the reproduction of elite theory: it claims that there was insufficient change in elite personnel with the transition to postcommunism, and calls for another (i.e., political) revolution. By contrast, the political Left argues that the circulation of elites has been far too excessive in the last several years, and calls for a much slower pace of change for the future.

To illustrate the political significance of these seemingly academic debates, recall Lech Walesa's presidential campaign against Mazowiecki in the fall of 1991. He accused the former Prime Minister of Poland of being "too soft" on Communists because he had allowed them to become proprietors after 1989. Following Walesa's example, the emergent East European New Right often focuses its attack on former Communists who have supposedly converted their old political privileges into new economic ones. Thus, ideologues of the Hungarian and Polish New Right call for a second revolution in Eastern Europe, arguing that the ruling conservative parties have "betrayed" the revolution and, because of this, the so-called "velvet revolution" has not led to radical enough social change. The political Left takes the opposite position. Former orthodox Communists, reform Communists, and contemporary liberals warn against too rapid changes in elite personnel. They worry about political witch-hunts; a new wave of "counterselection" in which anticommunists openly refuse to hire competent people for important positions in the class structure if they were members of the Communist Party before 1989.

Both the New Right and the Old (or Reformed) Left touch on sympathetic chords in certain circles of the citizenry. During the fall of 1993, the Polish electorate responded to the calmer voice of the former reform Communists and gave an absolute majority to parties on the political Left in parliamentary elections. Along similar lines, the May 1994 elections in Hungary produced a victory for the reform-minded successors of the old Communists. In Russia, however, the December 1993 elections have shown that both programs can mobilize people: the ultra Right-wing Zhirinovsky did extremely well in the elections, but so did the former Communists.

In the articles presented in this volume, we distinguish between two theories of elite recruitment: the reproduction of elites theory and the circulation of elites theory.[1] The dominant view of elites in Eastern Europe is one of "reproduction." The Hungarian

1 See Iván Szelényi and Szonja Szelényi, "Az elit cirkulációja?" [Circulation of Elites?], *Kritika,* No. 9 (1990): 8–10.

Elemér Hankiss and the Polish Jadwiga Staniszkis have offered similar versions of this approach. As early as 1989, Hankiss suggested that the old nomenklatura elite would become the new "grande bourgeoisie" with the marketization of the economy.[2] Around the same time, Staniszkis began to write about the emergent "political capitalism" of postcommunist Eastern Europe.[3] In her view, the former nomenklatura uses its political power to gain private wealth. Staniszkis and Hankiss both agreed that the process of privatization would benefit the Communist political class, which could retain its position at the top of the class structure without many constraints.

Likewise, the Hungarian Erzsébet Szalai offered a similar analysis of Eastern Europe. In her research on large Hungarian firms, she noticed that a new technocratic stratum was emerging in the early 1980s, and that it gradually began to appropriate some key property rights.[4] Szalai explained the dynamics of political change in Hungary during the 1980s in terms of increasing struggle between the "old elite" and the "new technocracy." According to her, the "old elite" was composed of members of the nomenklatura who assumed political power after the 1956 revolution: they were not typically highly educated, but most had a firm ideological commitment to the cause of Communism. By contrast, the "new elite" was younger, better educated, and specifically technocratic in its skills and orientation. Not surprisingly, given its education and social background, the new elite increasingly disliked the way the old guard ran the country, and was, therefore, attracted to the idea that the institutions of state socialism must be radically transformed. Surely, but gradually, the "new technocracy" lost faith in socialism and began to support the project of market transformation. In this process, they slowly appropriated property rights and set themselves up as the new private entrepreneurs of the new regime.[5] But, as Szalai points out, members of the "new technocracy" were not successful politically. Their political victory over the old guard was short-lived, and they were soon replaced in political power by a "new ruling estate" whose members came from noncommunist circles.[6]

As should be clear from the above three stories, Hankiss, Staniszkis, and Szalai offer a similar diagnosis for Eastern Europe: while the socioeconomic system changes radically, those at the top of the class structure remain the same. In other words, the personnel

2 Elemér Hankiss, "Reform and conversion of power," Paper presented at the conference "Mittel-Europa: Herausforderungen der Reformen," organized by the Konrad Adenauer Stiftung, 29–31 May 1989; Elemér Hankiss, *East European Alternatives* (Oxford: Oxford University Press, 1990).

3 Jadwiga Staniszkis, *The Dynamics of Breakthrough in Eastern Europe* (Berkeley: University of California Press, 1991).

4 Erzsébet Szalai, "Az új elít" [The New Elite], pages 169–177 in *Gazdaság és Hatalom [Economy and Power]*, ed. Erzsébet Szalai (Budapest: Aula Kiadó, 1990). For more on the concept of the "new technocracy," see Erzsébet Szalai, "A Hatalom Metamorfózisa" [the Transformation of Power], pages 61–114 in Útelágazás *[Cross-Roads]*, ed. Erzsébet Szalai (Budapest: Pesti Szalon Könyvkiadó).

5 Erzsébet Szalai, „A Hatalom Metamorfózisa," 84–85.

6 Erzsébet Szalai calls this social group "the new elite." See Szalai, "Ismét az Új Elíról" [The New Elite Revisited], 181–186 in *Gazdagság és Hatalom [Economy and Power]*. In "A Hatalom Metamorfózisa," she introduces the more appealing term: "new ruling estate." Here we use the term "new ruling estate" and "new political elite" interchangeably.

do not change, only the principles by which they legitimate their authority, power, and privilege are altered.

Unlike the other two authors, however, Szalai draws an important distinction between the "new technocracy" and the "old elite": the latter can be downwardly mobile with the transformation of the economy. She also points to the struggle between the excommunist "new technocracy" and the anticommunist "new political elite." By extending Szalai's argument, we proposed a "circulation of elites" hypothesis that posited that the former elite will be able to maintain its privileged position at the top of the class structure, but there will be political limits determining the extent to which they will be successful at this. Some members of the old elite will be downwardly mobile, some will stay in the social space they occupied before, and some will be upwardly mobile into the ranks of the old elite.[7]

With the conceptual apparatus of Pierre Bourdieu, one may interpret Hankiss and Staniszkis as offering a theory that assumes no or few limits to the convertibility of political capital into economic capital.[8] Szalai's hypothesis is more complex, however. Following her, we suggest that those who relied exclusively or overwhelmingly on political capital for their power and privilege (i.e., the "old elite") are likely to be downwardly mobile, while those who combined cultural and political capital (i.e., the "new technocracy") are better positioned to achieve positive privileges in terms of economic capital today. The "new political elite" is likely to come from the ranks of people who were low in political capital in the past, but high in cultural capital. It remains to be seen if the "new political elite" will occupy positions of mere political authority or if they will be successful in achieving economic privileges as well.

7 There is an analogous discussion concerning the social implications of market reform in China, known as "the market transition debate." This was initiated by Victor Nee in 'The Theory of Market Transition," *American Sociological Review* 54 (1989): 663–681. There, as in two subsequent papers ["Social inequality in reforming state socialism," *American Sociological Review* 56 (1991): 267–282, and "The emergence of market society," *American Journal of Sociology 101* (1996): 908–949], Nee offers a radical circulation of elites hypothesis, arguing that market reform benefits new economic actors and former cadres lose out. This position has been challenged by several China specialists, in particular by Andrew Walder, "Career Mobility and Communist Political Order." *American Sociological Review 60 (1995): 309*–328. There, Walder takes a position similar to Szalai's, claiming that the technocratic fraction of the old elite benefits from market transformation.

8 Pierre Bourdieu, "The forms of capital," in J. G. Richardson, editor, *Handbook of Theory and Research of Education* (New York: Greenwood Press, 1986). Bourdieu offers a multi-dimensional analysis of social structure. In his view, social spaces in which social actors are located are shaped by three types of capital: economic, cultural, and social. In this and other articles of this special issue, we use the terms economic and cultural capital in a way similar to Bourdieu's. But, we frequently substitute the term "political capital" for his concept of "social capital." By "political capital," we mean a highly institutionalized sub-type of social capital that can be measured by membership in the Communist Party.

Cross-national variations in elite reproduction

We expect different trends in elite reproduction in the three countries (Hungary, Poland, and Russia) that are included in this special issue. Since the economic and political reforms have been more successful in Hungary than in Russia (or in Poland) over the last two decades, we think that the old elites are most likely to reproduce themselves here. This is so, in part, because of the existence of at least a partially meritocratic system of elite recruitment under the Kádár regime; this system meant that many of those in possession of cultural capital already occupied positions concomitant with their skills in 1989.

By contrast, we expect a greater amount of elite circulation in Poland because attempts to copy the Kádár regime – by trying to reach some compromise with the technical intelligentsia or to coopt the technocrats at least – were fundamentally unsuccessful. The Polish bureaucracy tried to bring the technocracy into positions of authority during the so-called "second industrialization of Poland" and, again, during the Jaruzelski regime. The response that the Polish regime received was not favorable: the Polish intelligentsia stayed out of power and organized into a counter-elite.

Russia may be more similar to Hungary, but for very different reasons. Common wisdom suggests (although data have yet to bear this out) that Russia may not have allowed the technical intelligentsia into positions of power to the same degree that Hungary did. Therefore, the Russian nomenklatura may have been more similar (in 1989 and in 1990) to the Polish nomenklatura than to the Hungarian one. Still, there is at least *prima facie* evidence of a high degree of elite reproduction in Russia. In part, this can be attributed to the fact that, as of the fall of 1993 when our fieldwork took place, Russia had changed last in the postcommunist direction; thus its elites have not yet begun to "circulate."

To explain this three-way comparison, we introduce another idea: the strength of counter-elites. While the nomenklatura may have had similar characteristics in Poland and Russia, we think the circulation of the elites was facilitated in Poland by the existence of a large, well established counter-elite. In Russia, the counter-elite was less well developed, and in the absence of alternative cadres, the old nomenklatura was able to hold onto the country's command positions. The continued domination of elite positions by former cadres is also helped by general social instability that is particularly evident in Russia. Since the character of the emergent society is still unclear, and because the new democratic institutions do not work in a predictable way, there are fewer "political entrepreneurs" ready to try the new game in Russia. For these reasons, the old cadres are likely to remain unchallenged.

In general terms, then, our theory suggests that one may expect a high degree of elite reproduction in countries where the technocracy was co-opted by the nomenklatura, as well as in countries in which there was no counter-elite. By contrast, we expect a high degree of elite circulation in countries where the co-optation of the technocracy did not take place, or in countries with a well-formed counter-elite. These hypotheses are summarized in Table 1.[9]

9 We are grateful to Tamás Kolosi; these hypotheses were developed in the course of several conversations with him.

To test the empirical validity of these hypotheses, we initiated a cross-national comparative study of elites in 1990.[10] By mid-1994, surveys were completed in six countries: Bulgaria, the Czech Republic, Hungary, Poland, Russia, and Slovakia.[11] During 1993–1994, we conducted personal interviews with about 40,000 respondents in these countries. We worked out a complex research design; interviewing respondents from different random samples. In each country, we interviewed 2,000 elite members: 1,000 of these were in nomenklatura positions in 1988, 600 were members of the new economic elite, and 400 were part of the 1993 political or cultural elites. In addition, in each country we interviewed 5,000 randomly selected members of the general population in order to obtain a base-line against which to compare our models of elite reproduction. We conducted life-history interviews with all of our respondents: we asked them to provide us with a full account of their activity history, educational career, and party memberships. We also asked them about their parents and grandparents, and found out relevant information about their friends.

By the end of 1993, data on the elite part of the study were available in three of the six countries: Hungary, Poland, and Russia. A group of us from the United States and from the three countries met and wrote the first draft of the articles that are presented this special issue.

Table 1. Hypotheses regarding circulation/reproduction

Country	Cooptation	Counter-elite	Circulation or reproduction
Hungary	yes	some	some reproduction
Poland	some	yes	some circulation
Russia	none	none	reproduction

Empirical results: Elite reproduction in Hungary, Poland, and Russia

The distinction between "circulation" and "reproduction" is a relative one. Five years are long enough for one to expect some change in the personnel occupying key command positions under any circumstance; a complete turnover of personnel is, however, unimaginable even under the most revolutionary conditions. When we assess "how much" circulation or reproduction took place in a country, therefore, we always have to think about this question in relative terms.

In the following analyses we examine a number of issues: (a) we explore the destinations of the old nomenklatura elite and the origins of the new elite, (b) we analyze

10 At the 1990 World Congress of Sociology, a group of scholars from the United States and from several Eastern European countries met to initiate such a survey. The project team was headed by Iván Szelényi and Donald Treiman.

11 A similar survey is being carried out in China in 1995, under the direction of Iván Szelényi, Donald Treiman, and Andrew Walder.

cross-national variations in elite reproduction, and (c) we look at differences among economic, cultural, and political elites. Our main conclusions are as follows:

a. There is limited outflow from the old nomenklatura. Many of those who were in nomenklatura positions in 1988 were found in top elite positions five years later. Those who were downwardly mobile usually just "slipped" a single step down in the status hierarchy, or the worst that happened to the old nomenklatura elite is that they went into early retirement. In other words, the 1988 nomenklatura did not fare badly with the transition to postcommunism: it had a good chance to reproduce itself in positions of authority. However, we also find substantial inflow into the new elites; in this sense, therefore, there is substantial circulation in elite personnel in Eastern Europe. There are many new faces among those who were at the top of the social hierarchy in 1993. Most of those who were upwardly mobile did not come from the bottom of the class structure, but typically arrived at the top from upper- or from middle class backgrounds.
b. In terms of our cross-national analyses, our results show that the old nomenklatura elites in Russia were better able to survive at the top of the class structure than elites in Poland or Hungary. Contrary to our expectations, however, the circulation of elites in Hungary was greater (and faster) than in Poland.
c. We find that the circulation of elites in Hungary was particularly strong among the old and the new economic elites. The relatively high degree of elite circulation in Hungary may be attributed to (what we call) "administered social mobility" right after the transition to postcommunism. The victory of the Socialist Party in 1994 can thus be interpreted as a vote against such "administered mobility"; it was a vote favoring a more gradual transformation of the stratification order.
d. Our overall conclusion is that changes during the postcommunist era were (and continue to be) path-dependent[12] and involutionary,[13] rather than revolutionary. Where greater turbulances took place (i.e., in the political sphere), a "trajectory correction" seems to be taking place. The 1993–94 elections support this claim. As a result of these political changes – while Communism is far from being restored – social structure is most likely to shift further backward toward an even more involutionary path of transformation.

12 For the concept of "path-dependent development," see David Stark, "Path dependence and privatization strategies in East Central Europe," *East European Politics and Societies* 6 (1992): 17–51; and David Stark, "Recombinant property and East European capitalism," *American Journal of Sociology 91,* (1998): 481–510.

13 Philip Huang adopted this term to explain socioeconomic change in China. See Huang, *The Peasant Family and Rural Development in the Yangzi Delta – 1350 to 1988* (Stanford: Stanford University Press, 1990).

The destinations of the old nomenklatura elite and the origins of the new elite

If we assess the extent of circulation/reproduction of elites by contrasting the destinations of the old nomenklatura elite (see Table 2) with the origins of the new elites (see Table 3), we obtain two somewhat different stories about what happened with the transition to postcommunism in Eastern Europe.

The first one of these stories suggests that the marketization of the socialist economy has generated a considerable degree of elite reproduction: those in elite positions in 1988 were more likely to remain in positions of authority than to leave such positions by 1993. The "old guard," in this sense, is rarely in trouble in Eastern Europe. In fact, if anything it seems to be doing quite well. Doing well, however, does not necessarily mean that they were completely unharmed by the economic transformation of 1989. Many were demoted from their nationally-important command posts, although most survived this type of downward mobility reasonably well. In Hungary and in Poland, a significant percentage of the 1988 nomenklatura retired by 1993: some took early retirement, and only a few have had to accept lowerstatus jobs.

The second story that emerges from these tables suggests that we may have witnessed a significant amount of elite circulation with the transition to postcommunism: the majority of those who were in elite positions in 1993 were not members of the nomenklatura in 1988. These new faces at the top of the class structure, however, are not necessarily

Table 2. Destinations of the old-nomenklatura elite

Class position in 1993	Russia in %	Poland in %	Hungary in %
Elite	64.2	38.2	20.0
Non-elite with subordinates	15.5	18.4	31.5
Non-elite without subordinates	10.6	16.6	15.7
Retired	9.7	26.8	32.8
	(N = 854)	(N = 888)	(N = 662)

Note. Entries are percentages. Columns may not sum correctly because of rounding error.

Table 3. The class origins ofthe new (1993) elites

Class position in 1988	Russia in %	Poland in %	Hungary in %
Nomenklatura member	51.0	40.7	32.7
Other official	33.4	37.9	47.5
Non-elite	15.6	21.4	19.8
	(N = 958)	(N = 960)	(N = 783)

Note. Entries are percentages. Columns may not sum correctly because of rounding error.

all that new: they often come from positions that were "next in line," and so these individuals would probably have been promoted to an elite position within a year or so, even without a regime change.

Given the seemingly contradictory nature of these results, it might be useful to elaborate on these findings in greater detail. Table 2 shows the class position of the old nomenklatura elite at the time of our survey (that is, in 1993). Although the dominant theme that emerges from this table is one of reproduction, there are significant cross-national differences in this pattern. If we employ a generous definition of elites (for example, by combining what may be called "true" elite positions with those that were not strictly speaking elite positions, but were supervisory roles), we find that the rate of reproduction is 80 percent in Russia, 57 percent in Poland, and 50 percent in Hungary. A narrower definition (one that omits supervisors from its definition of elites) supports the reproduction argument only in Russia: this definition produces 64 percent reproduction in Russia, but only 38 percent in Poland, and 20 percent in Hungary. The real degree of reproduction is presumably somewhere between these two (i.e., broad and narrow) definitions of elites. The broad definition is likely to err by ignoring those downwardly mobile elites who lost some status with the transition to postcommunism by moving from a nationally important command post in 1988 to a less-powerful supervisory position in 1993. The narrower definition is likely to err in the opposite direction.

Beyond doubt, the relatively high degree of elite reproduction that we observe in Table 2 was generated by the fact that outflow from 1988 nomenklatura positions is more likely to be of a "sideways" rather than a "downward" type: those who left elite positions in Poland and Hungary were more likely to be retired by 1993 than working in rank-and-file jobs."[14] About one third of the old cadres retired (i.e., moved "sideways" in the class structure) and one-sixth were "demoted" to rank-and-file jobs (i.e., were "downwardly" mobile). In and of itself, retirement in the postcommunist era does not necessarily mean that the old cadres have experienced a significant loss of status. On the contrary, former members of the economic nomenklatura frequently work as consultants for (domestic or foreign) firms even in retirement. In Hungary, for example, where our narrow definition of 1993 elites produced only 20 percent reproduction, many of those who appear to have lost ground are, in fact, still in positions of authority in the postcommunist era (as demonstrated by our broader definition of elites). Although we thus find considerable reproduction of elites in all three countries, without doubt, our results show that there has been much greater turbulence at the top of the social hierarchy in Poland and in Hungary.

In examining the social origins of the new elites, we find fewer crossnational differences: Table 3 reveals a striking similarity in the degree of elite circulation across the three countries. To be sure, there appears to be somewhat less circulation in Russia, where we find that 51 percent of the 1993 elites were in a nomenklatura position in 1988. Moreover, Poland seems to display somewhat less evidence of circulation than Hungary: the propor-

14 This is consistent with Szalai's observation that "members of the 'old ruling class' mainly opted for retirement." See E. Szalai, "A Hatalom Metamorfózisa," 98.

tion of new elites coming from the old nomenklatura is 41 percent in Poland, but only 33 percent in Hungary. Nevertheless, the main story that emerges from these results is that there has been a relatively modest inflow of rank-and-file officials into the new elites: less than one-fifth of the new powerholders were nonelites in 1988. The real pool from which the new incumbents of command posts were recruited is mid-management; that is, the new bosses are those who were already in positions of some authority in 1988.[15]

Overall, the process of upward mobility during the postcommunist transition seems to be quite orderly. Long-range jumps in the social hierarchy appear to be rare, and the most common way to secure a position of authority in the postcommunist world is by slowly climbing the social ladder. In looking at the rate of inflow into the new elite, one cannot ignore the impressive amount of circulation at the top of the class structure. But, it is equally important not to overemphasize the significance of this circulation. This is because our results clearly show that the new ruling elite in Eastern Europe does not come from the bottom of the class structure, but from middle layers of management.

Our two stories (reproduction in terms of outflow rates and circulation in terms of inflow rates) do not necessarily contradict one another. After all, it is conceivable that most former nomenklatura members can stay in positions of authority even when most new elite members were not nomenklatura members in 1988. This is not a zero-sum game. The political and economic institutions of postcommunist societies changed dramatically between 1988 and 1993: while some fractions of the elite shrunk (e.g., the political elite), others increased (e.g., the economic elite). This is particularly so for the economic elite. In 1988, the economic elite constituted the top managers of the largest 200 firms, but in 1993, they were the CEOs[16] of the 3,000 largest enterprises. Some of the circulation that we observe in our sample, therefore, was generated by this type of structural change in the economy.

Our more general conclusion, therefore, is that the first five years of postcommunist transformation can be characterized by relative stability in personnel and a rather significant change in institutional structure. The dominant trend in the transformation of political and, in particular, economic institutions points toward a decentralization of decision-making power. Consequently, this results in the growth of the number of elite positions. Continuity in personnel and path-dependent transformation in economic and political institutions describe the realities of postcommunist societies.

Cross-national differences and differences across economic, cultural, and political elites

Although, in general we find that there are considerable similarities across nations in terms of their degree of elite reproduction, we also find enough differences between them to conclude that our hypothesis concerning Russia and Eastern Europe is support-

15 This suggests that Szalai was correct in observing that "among those new technocrats who retained their power position, an important group comes from the 'former deputy department heads.'" See "A Hatalom Metamorfózisa," 102.

16 CEO = Chief Executive Officer = Geschäftsführer bzw. geschäftsführendes Vorstandsmitglied eines Unternehmens.

ed by empirical evidence. In other words, it appears that the former nomenklatura in Russia was more successful at retaining its position of power and privilege than members of the nomenklatura in Eastern Europe.

The comparison of Poland and Hungary, however, offers us counterintuitive and unexpected findings. Indeed, our results on this comparison are so different from what we initially expected that they force us to re-think some of our earlier theoretical assumptions about elite reproduction. While we expected to see greater circulation in Poland and reproduction in Hungary, our results show that the opposite is, in fact, true: 57 percent of those who were in Polish nomenklatura positions in 1988 survived at the top of the class structure five years later, while only 51 percent survived in Hungary.

It is particularly interesting to see how much higher the proportion of retirees are in Hungary than in the other two countries: 33 percent of those in nomenklatura positions had retired by 1993 in Hungary, compared with the 27 percent in Poland, and the 10 percent in Russia. These differences in retirement cannot be attributed to the age composition of the nomenklatura elites in the three countries because the average age of the old Hungarian cadres was the same as that in Poland and Russia. What, then, explains this difference? Following 1989, many more people in elite positions either took or were sent into early retirement in Hungary. One quarter of those who held nomenklatura positions in Hungary but retired by 1993 were less than 60 years old, and 80 percent of them were less than 70 years old. Since our survey targeted respondents in the uppermost reaches of the social hierarchy, it is surprising that such a large percentage of our respondents retired before age 60. Thus, at least some of the circulation in personnel in Hungary was generated by these early retirements.

A more detailed comparison of the different strata of nomenklatura elites in Poland and Hungary offers further interesting and unanticipated results. Differences in the outflow rates within the economic nomenklatura in Hungary and Poland are particularly counter-intuitive.

Table 4. Destinations of the old nomenklatura elite (economic elite only)

Class position in 1993	Russia in %	Poland in %	Hungary in %
Elite	81.1	56.6	29.2
Non-elite with subordinates	13.2	12.6	18.3
Non-elite without subordinates	1.7	7.2	4.9
Retired	3.3	23.6	47.6
	(N = 60)	(N = 263)	(N = 82)

Note. Entries are percentages. Columns may not sum correctly because of rounding error.

As Table 4 shows, only 48 percent of those who were in old economic command posts in Hungary remained in positions of authority after 1993. By contrast, almost 70 percent of the old Polish economic leaders were still in positions of authority five years later. The better survival capacity of the former economic leaders in Poland is also supported by data on the social origins of the new elites. According to Table 5 exactly half of the new Polish economic elite were members of the nomenklatura in 1988, while only one-third of the Hungarian CEOs came from a similar class position. These results are particularly surprising given that during the later stages of state socialism, it was generally assumed that the Hungarian economic management was better trained, more competent, and less politically-motivated than their Polish counterpart. But it is equally surprising that the Polish economy (in which the old economic elites survived longer) produced better results in the postcommunist era than the Hungarian one.[17]

Cross-national differences in the reproduction of elites, however, were not restricted to the economic sphere. Our data show, for example, that there was much greater circulation of cultural elites in Hungary than in Poland: only 56 percent of the 1988 cultural elites remained in an elite position in Hungary, while 61 percent survived in Poland (see Table 6). This is an unanticipated result. By 1988, it was generally believed that

Table 5. Origins of the new (1993) elites (economic elites only)

Class position in 1988	Russia in %	Poland in %	Hungary in %
Nomenklatura member	52.6	50.7	34.9
Other official	33.4	38.8	54.7
Non-elite	14.0	10.5	10.4
	(N = 565)	(N = 588)	(N = 489)

Note. Entries are percentages. Columns may not sum correctly because of rounding error.

Table 6. Destinations of the old nomenklatura elite (cultural elite only)

Class position in 1993	Russia in %	Poland in %	Hungary in %
Elite	49.4	43.9	9.0
Non-elite with subordinates	20.8	17.1	47.5
Non-elite without subordinates	21.8	10.5	14.3
Retired	8.0	28.5	29.2
	(N = 212)	(N = 123)	(N = 154)

Note. Entries are percentages. Columns may not sum correctly because of rounding error.

17 We have to note that the differential survival rates of economic elites in Poland and Hungary may be an artifact of methodological differences in our surveys. In the Polish case, a larger number of economic managers were interviewed and it is likely, therefore, that there were fewer CEOs in the 1988 economic nomenclature in the sample. Non-CEOs may have a better chance for survival, thus this may explain the greater survival rate of the Polish economic nomenklatura.

Hungary was ruled by ideologically liberal policies in science, tertiary education, and the media. Hungarian Radio and Television and the printed media impressed observers with their (relatively) free and objective character, and their tertiary-educated (rather than politically-motivated) administrators. Along similar lines, by the late 1980s, the Hungarian National Academy of Sciences was noted for its selection of members on the basis of academic merit, rather than political credentials. By contrast, the Polish media were less free, a sizable Polish *samizdat* (underground publications) blossomed on the censorship of the legal press, and the so-called "flying universities" profited from the political conservativism of official academic institutions (see Table 7).

In spite of these basic differences, Hungary and Poland are quite similar in terms of the fate of their political nomenklatura and the origins of their new political elites. In Table 8, for example, we find that the political nomenklatura in both countries was more likely to be downwardly mobile than either the economic or the cultural elites. This is understandable, of course, since the changes in 1989 were principally geared toward a transformation of the political system in these countries. We also find (in Table 9) that the new political elites in both Hungary and Poland are the only fraction of the new elite that recruited a large number of its members from non-elite positions: in both countries about 40 percent of the new political elite held non-elite jobs prior to the transition to postcommunism.

Table 7. Origins of the new (1993) elites (cultural elites only)

Class position in 1988	Russia in %	Poland in %	Hungary in %
Nomenklatura member	44.9	29.9	27.1
Other official	14.4	45.5	47.4
Non-elite	14.4	24.4	25.5
	(N = 138)	(N = 90)	(N = 133)

Note. Entries are percentages. Columns may not sum correctly because of rounding error.

Table 8. Destinations of the old nomenklatura elite (political elites only)

Class position in 1993	Russia in %	Poland in %	Hungary in %
Elite	67.7	27.5	21.9
Non-elite with subordinates	13.7	15.1	23.0
Non-elite without subordinates	7.6	29.3	23.9
Retired	11.0	28.1	31.2
	(N = 582)	(N = 502)	(N = 426)

Note. Entries are percentages. Columns may not sum correctly because of rounding error.

Table 9. Origins of the new (1993) elites (political elites only)

Class position in 1988	Russia in %	Poland in %	Hungary in %
Nomenklatura member	51.0	23.7	30.4
Other official	29.4	33.3	26.1
Non-elite	19.6	43.0	43.5
	(N = 255)	(N = 282)	(N = 161)

Note. Entries are percentages. Columns may not sum correctly because of rounding error.

"Administered mobility" in postcommunist Hungary?

The faster circulation of Hungarian economic and cultural elites suggests that our hypotheses concerning the effects of the existence of a counter-elite may not stand up to critical scrutiny. Initially, we hypothesized that the larger and the better-organized Polish counter-elite will be more inclined to take over positions of decision-making power because, in the course of many years of underground activities, it was able to obtain political expertise and thus was better prepared to step into the vacuum that was created at the top of the class structure in 1989. In light of the data that we present here, one wonders whether this is not a naive assumption. Those who aspire to elite positions and will fill power vacuums at times of system breakdown do not necessarily have to be particularly competent; it is enough for them to be ambitious. In retrospect, we are inclined to believe that the greater circulation of elites in Hungary can thus be explained by the relative administrative and political inexperience of the new political elite that came to power in 1990. The less experience the new political officeholders had, the more likely it was that they did not trust those subordinates who carried over from the Communist regime. They thus wanted to work with people they could trust. Under these circumstances, postcommunist elites (particularly in Hungary) were tempted to think about Communist conspiracies and to suspect that survivors of the *ancien regime* would try to sabotage the reform policies of the new era. Ironically, not unlike their Communist predecessors during the late 1940s, these postcommunist political elites were inclined to cast doubt on what some of them believed to be the mythology of competence. It was argued that anticommunists did not have a chance to gain appropriate expertise during the Communist epoch, and that it is unfair to discriminate against them only because (on paper) they are less qualified for the job. Furthermore, they argued, that excessive emphasis on experience only serves the reproduction of the old Communist elite and is likely to block the revolutionary transformation of society. While during the late 1940s the old Communist elites opted for "reds" over the "experts;' the 1989 elites in Hungary were similarly inclined to choose their political allies (although now the old patriots were the anticommunists). Guided by such ideological considerations, the new political elite occasionally tried to eliminate subordinates (even if they had the appropriate credentials) and replace them with their "own" clients; that is, people they knew personally and people they felt they could trust. Relatives, schoolmates, and neighbors were thus promoted to jobs primarily on the basis of their personal loyalty.

The greater degree of circulation of the Hungarian cultural elite is particularly instructive. We are inclined to explain this in terms of the social characteristics of the new Hungarian political elite. The new political elite in Hungary is quite different from the Russian and the Polish elite in terms of its social background, education, and occupational history.

In Russia, there was a clear trend toward the creation of a *bureaucratic caste,* which was likely to reproduce itself across generations. Children of the nomenklatura were more likely to become nomenklatura themselves in Russia than in either Poland or Hungary; and this pattern of reproduction seems to continue in the postcommunist world. To a significant degree, the new elites also come from the former caste of the cadre or the nomenklatura. In socialist Russia, a much smaller percentage of the nomenklatura elite had working-class or peasant origins. By contrast, the Polish and the Hungarian nomenklatura were more open to members of the lower classes; this was particularly true for the first period of socialism. In Hungary, for example, it was only after 1970 that children from professional families began to enter the nomenklatura in larger numbers, and in the last few decades of socialism (probably because of the financial opportunities that have emerged for entrepreneurs in the second economy), cadre children were not particularly attracted to the occupational careers of their parents. In Poland, the elite continued to draw heavily on the working class for its members until the very end of the socialist period.

In 1989, there was an abrupt change in the social origins of the new political elite. In both Hungary and Poland, the proportion of children from professional backgrounds who are entering elite positions is on the increase. In Poland, children from working-class background continue to play an important role in the formation of the new political elite; this is probably due to the important role that the Solidarity movement played in the Polish transformation in 1989–90. In Hungary, however, the new political elite is recruited almost exclusively from professional families. This was particularly true in 1990–94 for the parliamentary representatives of the Center-right parties. The political cadres of the ruling Hungarian Christian-Nationalist party typically came from multi-generational professional families and, hence, were direct descendants of the so-called Hungarian genteel middle class *(magyar keresztény úri középosztály).* The new Hungarian political elite and, in particular, the members of the first ruling Hungarian coalition were humanistic intellectuals (e.g., historians, novelists, poets), while the old nomenklatura was dominated by the technical intelligentsia. The greater degree of circulation within the Hungarian cultural elite, therefore, was probably due to the fact that this new political elite was especially likely to believe in the importance of culture because they were humanistic intellectuals themselves. As a result, they were likely to have clients and former colleagues who aspired to command positions in the area of culture, science, and media.

Between 1988 and 1993 therefore, Hungary has experienced what one might call *administered* mobility or circulation. The new Hungarian political elite – being insecure in its own competence – pushed for a faster than functional change in personnel. This change was implemented in an administered fashion; in other words, dismissals and appointments were guided by considerations of personal or political loyalty rather than meritocratic criteria. This has triggered off a specifically postcommunist process of counter-selection that placed greater value on patronage than individual competence.

The dynamics of electoral campaigns in 1993–94 and the eventual outcomes of parliamentary elections in both Poland and Hungary are consistent with our administered mobility hypothesis. In May 1994, the Hungarian electorate gave the absolute majority of parliamentary seats to the reconstituted party of the old Communists. It is notable that the key slogan of these elections was "competence." The socialists won the confidence of the electorate by presenting themselves as more competent experts, who are knowledgeable about politics and who know how to run the country. In so doing, they discredited the former ruling party (i.e., the Christian-Nationalist coalition) as a group of arrogant amateurs. In an indirect way, during these elections the Hungarian electorate also cast a vote about the question of circulation versus reproduction of elites. If we think that people took campaign rhetoric seriously, then the results can be interpreted as a vote against the administered circulation of elite personnel. The September 1993 Polish elections can be interpreted in a similar way. These elections were also won by the two successor parties of the former Communist Party. Although the question of "competence" was not raised as an explicit issue during these elections, the election results suggest that – in an indirect fashion at least – this was important in Poland as well.

It is one thing to say, of course, that these reconstituted Communists won on the basis of "competence;' yet it is quite another to assess just how competent they really are. In Hungary, for example, the newly formed government can hardly be called a "government of experts." Most new ministers and their deputies are people who were rewarded for their political loyalty either to the Socialist or the Liberal parties. The new government did not waste much time in firing people who were placed in their positions of authority by the former government: it quickly dismissed them so that the new government could begin to build its own clientele. It is thus possible that only the colors of the government changed, but the old logic of patronage remains the same.

We completed our data collection in the three countries by the summer of 1993. The second round of the elections in Hungary (May 1994), Poland (September 1993), and Russia (December 1993) represented an important change in all three countries. It is reasonable to hypothesize that our data from the summer of 1993 overestimate how much circulation of elites actually took place. In Hungary and Poland, in particular, these elections appear to have "corrected" the administered circulation of the immediate postcommunist regime and moved back into positions of authority people who were temporarily on *"parking orbits"* between 1989 and 1994. This is particularly likely to be the case with the political elite. During the summer of 1993, the new political elite was the only stratum into which there was a substantial upward mobility from 1988 rank-and-file positions.

Meta-theoretical implications

After the fall of the Berlin Wall, most commentators argued that a revolutionary break within the old Communist regime was taking place in Eastern Europe. It did not take much time, however, before one began to notice continuities at least in the workings of economic institutions. As early as 1992, in fact, David Stark wrote about path-dependent change of economic institutions as distinct from transition from redistribution to market economies – emphasizing the strong involutionary trends both in economic management and in property relations. As Stark put it: the change was from "plan" to "clan": what was presented as "privatization" may be more accurately described as a more gradual reshuffling of property rights within public ownership;[18] what was presented as transition of redistribution to market may be more an involution of redistributed institutions, often probably just a decentralization of redistribution.[19]

When we began to formulate the hypotheses for our elite study, we kept in mind the idea that the post-1989 developments in Eastern Europe may have been uneven: economic change is possibly path-dependent and involutionary, while political transformation is more likely to be revolutionary. The difference between the transition from capitalism to socialism (in 1949) and the transition from socialism to capitalism (in 1989) is that while in the former case the smashing of the capitalist economy required the smashing of the capitalist state, in the latter case the smashing of the socialist state and its replacement with democratic institutions prevents the possibility of a revolutionary break in the economy. One could have argued that such a path-dependent readjustment in the economy is necessary within a democratic polity. The shock therapy approach to reform, even if it were economically rational, is politically suicidal because it does not take into consideration the brief nature of political cycles and, thus, it miscalculates the amount of time needed to implement radical economic reform. Political elites that attempt to implement shock therapy in the economy are unlikely to have sufficient time to complete the process: before the policy could possibly produce results, new elections are held and the elites are invariably voted out of office. In this way, democratic polities necessarily slow down the pace of economic change in Eastern Europe.

The political events since the summer of 1993 and the unanticipated results of the Hungarian survey are leading us to the conclusion that, even in politics, the revolution was more apparent than real. With only one cycle of political change, we already see a

18 See David Stark, "Path dependence and privatization strategies in East Central Europe," 1992, also David Stark, "Privatization in Hungary – From plan to market or from plan to clan?" *East European Politics and Societies* 4 (Fall, 1990): 351–392.

19 This point was made by Jean C. Oi, "Fiscal reform and the economic foundation of local state corporatism in China," *World Politics* 45 (1992): 99–126 and Nan Lin, "Local market socialism – Local corporatism in action in rural China," *Theory and Society,* 24/3 (1995): 301–354 for China. The survival of redistributive mechanisms in a new guise may be true for Eastern Europe as well. See Erzsébet Szalai, "Perpetuum mobile," (1992) in Útelágazás, 115–169. See also Éva Voszka, *Privatizáció és Szervezeti Decentralizáció* [Privatization and Organizational Decentralization], (Budapest: Pénzügykutató Intézet, 1991), and Éva Voszka, *Tulajdonreform* [Property Reform], (Budapest: Pénzügykutató Intézet, 1991).

major correction in the political trajectory of postcommunist societies. The events of 1989 may be more radical and more revolutionary in the rhetoric of the new political elites that came to power with the disintegration of state socialism. This new political elite had a vested interest in presenting the changes in a revolutionary light. Public opinion probably never accepted much of this radicalism and even if it accepted it for a while, it did not take too long for it to correct itself.

The discrepancy in the rhetoric of the new political elite and the value system of the society became apparent early in the game. Public opinion polls showed as early as 1990 that there was strong public support for egalitarian values and for a strong welfare state. The new political elite – which incidentally was more "reformist" than "revolutionary" while in opposition during the 1970s and 1980s – was radicalized fast. It began to push hard for a free market, individual responsibility, privatization, and elimination of the welfare state only in recent years. For a while, this new elite assumed that public opinion was merely "lagging behind" the times and that it would eventually "catch up" with the leading views of the political elite. But the opposite turned out to be the case: as the public saw the disintegration of the welfare state, it began to turn against privatization. Instead of learning from the new elite, the Polish and the Hungarian electorate gave an instruction to its new political leaders in 1993–94: it ejected them from their position of power for their non-prudent radicalism.

During 1989–90, modernization theory returned to Eastern Europe with a vengeance.[20] At first it appeared as if the fall of Communism brought with it the end of history and that all societies were converging around models of liberal capitalism. With the events of 1994, however, the direction that these societies are taking is becoming less clear.

Postcommunist societies, even under the leadership of socialist governments, are undoubtedly in the process of capitalist transformation. The victory of socialist parties in Poland and in Hungary did not bring a return to state socialism. As the first socialist prime minister of postcommunist Hungary (Gyula Horn) claimed shortly after his party's victory: Hungary is now in the process of "building capitalism." The socialist parties are fundamentally different from the old Communists and, in terms of western politics, they tend to be on the right wing of social-democratic movements. Still, the path-dependent nature or involuntary character of change is apparent. What the character of the new societies will be after the transformation was consolidated is less clear today than it appeared in 1989–90. Arguably, strong forces operate that point in the direction of continuity both within the Communist and even with the precommunist past. Where does this path-dependent, involuntary character of postcommunist transformation leave us?

In assessing the prospects of postcommunism and the value of modernization theory, Michael Burawoy arrives at the somewhat bleak prognosis that the laws of postcommunist societies "will not be the laws of modern capitalism, but more likely, of a merchant capitalism or some might say of a feudal capitalism – plowing a third road to the Third

20 See Michael Burawoy, "The end of Sovietology and the renaissance of modernization theory," *Contemporary Sociology* (1992): 774–785.

World.... Modernization theory conspires in obscuring the ever widening gap between ideology and reality. It fosters a false optimism about the future."[21]

One does not have to share the gloom of Burawoy's diagnosis in order to appreciate his theoretical insights. Burawoy's desperation is motivated by his disappointment that Eastern Europe abandoned the socialist path, and by his desire to sustain hope in the possibility of democratic socialism.[22] In light of what we have learned about social change of the past five years of postcommunism, one does not have to share Burawoy's political agenda in order to share his doubts about the inevitability of historical convergence around the model of "First World" liberal capitalism and appreciate how powerful those forces are that keep societies on developmental trajectories both in terms of the economic institutions or logic of stratification systems.

Burawoy is undoubtedly right: there is no guarantee that Eastern Europe or the post-Soviet states are sailing smoothly toward modern capitalism; they can just as easily move into the Third World instead. Nor is there a guarantee that their social structure is being "modernized": instead of socialist counter-selection being replaced by a meritocratic system of selection, one sees the functioning of postcommunist patronage or counter-selection, be it of the patriotic-Christian type or the postcommunist socialist version.

Conclusions

What, then, have we learned so far about the reproduction and the circulation of elites during the postcommunist transformation? First, it is clear that our data do not support a simple elite reproduction or power conversion theory. The changes of political and economic institutions under postcommunism are consequential: some of the old elites are pushed out of their positions of power and privilege, and so there is substantial change at the top of the class structure.

Second, it is equally inaccurate to think about these changes as if they represent some revolutionary break. What we can report on is path-dependent transformation both of political, economic, and cultural institutions and in the composition of incumbents of command positions in those institutions. The dominant trend was a somewhat accelerated move from the "middle" to the "top." Occasionally, the new political elites may have taken their own revolutionary rhetoric too seriously (this could have been the case in Hungary during the 1990 and 1994 elections) – but this backfired because as soon as some administered mobility into/out of elite positions was attempted, it was quickly "corrected."

These analyses offer substantial support for Erzsébet Szalai's sober "elite circulation" theory: the bureaucratic fraction of the old communist elites were shifting out from top power positions. Many taking early retirement or taking minor but decent jobs; the

21 Ibid., 784.
22 Ibid., 788.

technocratic fraction of late state socialist elites, in particular economic managers and middle managers, on the whole retained or even improved their positions. And, finally, some new space was created for those who were (usually noncommunist party members) rank-and-file professionals mainly in politics, but also in culture and in the economy.

Acknowledgments

An earlier version of this article was presented at the annual meeting of the American Sociological Association in Miami in August 1993. This research was supported by grants from the American Council of Learned Societies, the Social Science Research Council, the National Science Foundation, the National Council for Soviet and East European Research, the Dutch National Science Foundation, the Hungarian National Science Foundation, and the Polish National Science Foundation. We are grateful for the productive comments of Richard Anderson, Jozsef Böröcz, Gil Eyal, Éva Fodor, Eric Hanley, Ákos Róna-Tas, W. Richard Scott, Andrew Walder, Jacek Wasilewski, Edmund Wnuk-Lipiński, and Natasha Yershova. The opinions expressed in this article are those of the authors.

III. Transition from Socialism to Capitalism

III.1 On Irony: An Invitation to Neoclassical Sociology

Gil Eyal, Iván Szelényi and Eleanor Townsley

Abstract

This article proffers an invitation to neoclassical sociology. This is understood as a Habermasian reconstruction of the fundamental vision of the discipline as conceptualized by classical theorists, particularly Weber. Taking the cases of Eastern and Central Europe as a laboratory, we argue against the idea of a single, homogenizing globalizing logic. Currently and historically what we see instead is a remarkable diversity of capitalist forms and destinations. Neither sociological theories of networks and embeddedness nor economic models of rational action adequately comprehend this diversity. A neoclassical approach enjoins an empirical research agenda comparing capitalisms, and an ironic, historical approach to analysis to inform an immanent critique of capitalist possibilities.

Keywords capitalism, class, cultural capital, post-socialist, status

I. Social Theory After The Fall Of Socialism: Rethinking 'The Crisis Of Western Sociology'

The collapse of state socialism presents a challenge to sociology, and in particular, to sociology's tradition of critical social analysis. Sociology and socialism were twin-born in the massive social changes of the 19th century, and their original visions shared premises and presuppositions. In particular, both were critical of the anarchy of markets and, as an alternative, both advocated the collective rational ordering of society, aided and informed by social science. The affinity between sociology and socialism was most evident in the work of Saint-Simon and Comte who wanted to build an intellectually and spiritually superior social order, but it was also apparent in the work of Marx and Durkheim. For these latter thinkers, sociological theory formed an alternative to liberal political economy just as socialism offered an alternative to capitalism. The other branch of classical sociology, represented by Weber, was not as sanguine about the possibility of socialism. Weber subjected the ideals of collectivism to critical scrutiny from the perspective of individual liberty (as did later thinkers like Mill and Popper). Despite disagreement about the desirability of socialism, however, Weber shared a common critical vantage point with Marx and Durkheim, i.e. one informed by an awareness of the *possibility* of a socialist alternative to capitalism.

In his *The Coming Crisis of Western Sociology* (1970), Alvin Gouldner bequeathed to us an analysis of sociology that showed how the problematic relation between socialism and sociology continued into the 20th century, long after the classical social thinkers. True, the brutality and bleakness of actually existing socialism tarnished the socialist vantage point for many intellectuals, but Gouldner's analysis demonstrated nonetheless that the 20th-century split between positivism and critical social science was precisely a division over the issue of how socialist realities and possibilities were to be weighed against each other. On one side, 20th-century positivists tended to translate their horror of the 'dark side' of actually existing socialism into an uncritical acceptance and apologia for capitalism. The very meaning of positivism changed. Where for Comte 'positivism' was a rejection of 'negativism' – a call to be brave and to dare to think about a world that could be better – for 20th-century positivists, positivism became a description and justification of the existing world as the only possible one. On the other side, critical social science criticized 'actually existing socialism', not from the point of view of the existing order of things, but on the basis of a vision of true socialism. Theorists like the 'Western Marxists' argued that the societies of Eastern and Central Europe simply did not measure up to the ideal; they were not sufficiently 'socialistic' or worse, they were a version of 'state capitalism'. In this context, Gouldner argued that what was once a productive tension between actuality and possibility had now bifurcated into a one-sided emphasis on either inert actuality (positivism) or abstract possibility (critical social science), *both* of which had lost any critical dimension.

We think Gouldner's search for a way to rescue sociology from the impasse between positivism and critical social science is relevant once again. Our reasons are somewhat different than Gouldner's however. In 1970, Gouldner, like many other social scientists, believed that he was witnessing the merging of capitalism and socialism – what Daniel Bell (1973) called 'post-industrial society'. It was in this merger, he argued, that the critical imagination of sociology was lost. Positivism and marxism mirrored each other from across the divide, because both were ideological reflections of the rise of a new class of intellectuals that would eventually replace the dominant classes of *both* capitalism *and* state socialism.[1] This was the 'coming crisis of Western sociology': not only had sociolo-

1 Gouldner argued that the power of the new class derived from its monopoly on specialized professional knowledges, as well as from its control over the means of cultural legitimation, what he called the 'culture of critical discourse' (CCD). This he defined as 'an historically evolved set of rules, a grammar of discourse, which (1) is concerned to *justify* its assertions, but (2) whose *mode* of justification does not proceed by invoking authorities, and (3) prefers to elicit the *voluntary* consent of those addressed solely on the basis of arguments adduced' [italics in original] (1979: 28). Gouldner argued that the CCD was the basis of intellectual class identity and that it was often arraigned against traditional authority and social institutions. In the West, where the CCD was objectified as 'cultural capital' in the form of credentials and was justified by the highly successful ideology of professionalism, the New Class carried increasing weight in social affairs. New Class personnel were crucial components in the functioning of modern states, economies, and universities in which knowledge had become indispensable and the power of the old bourgeoisie was waning. Hence, New Class members were in a position to press their claims to disrupt, subvert, and cause trouble for the old moneyed class – with little fear of retribution (Gouldner, 1979: 19–20).

gy lost the critical vantage point it once possessed in socialism, it had also lost the agent that could occupy this vantage point, namely the Mannheimian socially unattached intellectual.

Gouldner argued nonetheless, that the critical potential of the sociological tradition could be reconstructed. Drawing a parallel with the Young Hegelians and their reradicalization of Hegelian philosophy, he suggested that sociology's radical potential lay in its commitment to *reflexivity* i.e. in using the values and weapons of the intellectual's own 'culture of critical discourse' against intellectuals themselves. If he or she is committed to reflexivity as a first principle, even the self-interested social scientist can arrive at a radical vision of a better society because reflexivity means exposing his or her own interests and modes of reasoning to self-critical scrutiny.

We think there is much to be learned from Gouldner. The crisis of sociology he predicted has arrived, although not exactly in the way he expected. Instead of meeting socialism halfway, which seemed likely in the heyday of social democracy, the capitalist world of 21st-century Western Europe and North America is further away from socialism than it has been in the last 50 years. And instead of meeting capitalism halfway, which seemed likely in the years of reform communism in Eastern Europe, postcommunist societies pursue a wide range of new strategies to *make capitalism*. Indeed, rather than a convergence of the two main social systems of the 20th century, the 21st century presents us with a dazzling variety of *capitalisms* all over the globe. The only exceptions are the two tiny, moribund islands of actually existing communism: Cuba and North Korea. So, world history has not followed the trajectory predicted by Gouldner (and so many others). With that stipulated however, it *is* true that the world is no longer divided between two competing social systems, and that in the postcommunist context, sociology is showing signs of 'crisis'.

The dominant ideology of 21st-century capitalism is globalization: a worldview that asserts the existence of a single global capitalist logic. Sociology has lost its critical vantage point, then, not because of the convergence of marxism and positivism, which Gouldner predicted, but because the perception of a monolithic globalization obviates the idea of a critical vantage point. And this is a dual crisis because it was precisely this critical vantage point that distinguished sociology from the other social sciences, and in particular from economics.

In a world seemingly dominated by the globalizing logic of capitalist markets and liberal culture, sociology struggles to distinguish its object, methods, and social role. Indeed, many contemporary strands of sociology are formulated as a conscious alternative to the dominance of neoclassical economics. This is the case for economic sociology with its emphasis on embeddedness, of network analysts who purport to demonstrate how markets are composed of networks of social relations, and also for neoinstitutionalist sociologists who emphasize the conventionalized and organizational substratum of economic relations. But we would argue that even the most positivist sociology of the past, and even those theorists thought to be the most antisocialist or the most non-political, distinguished themselves from economics by an explicit or implicit criticism of a social order based purely on markets. For example, Parsons emphasized socialization and culture over economic expedience, and liberal thinkers were always suspicious of the elements of collectivism and constructive rationality in his vision of the 'social system' (Wagner, 1994). Ironically, then, even the positivist sociological 'escape route' away from socialism partook in the discipline's critical heritage. It defined social reality as distinct and more fundamental than the operation of markets, and on this basis it could point to an alternative beyond the status quo. With the fall of socialism, however, even the positivist 'escape route' is in danger of being overtaken by the socialist joke, i.e. that socialism is merely a long detour from capitalism to capitalism, or, in this case, that sociology is nothing but a long detour from liberal political economy to neoclassical economics.

Nothing symbolizes this dire possibility better than the ascendancy of 'rational choice' theory which threatens to erase the distinctions between economics and sociology, merging them both into a systematic 'economic description of the social' (Gordon, 1991). Rational choice theory accommodates and marginalizes all the defenses erected against it – embeddedness, networks, institutions – all are assimilable into the maximizing calculus of rational actors. In a world without 'actually existing socialism', it appears that the neoliberal version of capitalism reigns supreme across the globe. Economic actors are disembedded, institutions are consciously designed, and a price tag is put on traditions, path dependencies, and network ties so all can fit within its maximizing calculus. In such a world, the escape route of sociological positivism seems pointless as it circles back and ends at the same place. The imperialism of capital is matched by the theoretical imperialism of 'rational choice', and both point towards a single capitalist destination – the end of history

Should sociology accept this vision of triumphant capitalism? Must postsocialist sociology lose its object of analysis and its critical perspective? We think not. Instead, we argue that the postsocialist crisis in sociology offers opportunities for renewing the critical vision of the discipline. It offers sociology the chance to take stock and reconstruct its classical heritage, this time outside the polarity of capitalism versus socialism, and armed with the critical powers of ironic self-reflection. Just as economics returned to its classical roots to reconstitute the discipline in the face of massive global market failure in the 1970s, so we think sociology might profitably return to its classical roots to reconstitute itself in the shadow of the fall of socialism. In economics, such a return implied a return to the notion of the self-interested individual. In sharp contrast, however, in sociology such a return implies the question: what are the origins of modernity, or of capitalism? Thus, we are not suggesting a return to the classical tradition conceived superficially as a theoretical 'toolbox' from which to draw concepts and insights at whim. Rather, we propose a reconstruction (in the Habermasian sense of the term) of the fundamental critical vision of the classical sociological thinkers (Habermas, 1990).

In marked contrast to neoclassical economics, which posits a single capitalist logic and a single mode of rational human action, what we call 'neoclassical sociology' is a field of critical social analysis in which the method of inquiry is *ironic*.[2] Taking

2 Neoclassical economics is serious and anti-ironic. There is only one truth and there is only one system. There is one capitalist logic and one set of rules for acting in a rational economic manner.

Gouldner's analysis as our point of departure, we observe that irony – as long as it is rooted in self-irony – is always undertaken in the *reflexive* mode. The researcher who engages in irony begins his or her analysis by suspending his or her own values, judgments, and knowledge about the world, and accepting as valid the point of view of 'the other'. This is done in the understanding that his or her own values and those of the other are relational, i.e. they only exist and take meaning in relationship to each other, or to put it another way, in conversation with each other. This is the reflexive premise of the ironic method, or to put it with Mannheim ([1936] 1985), this is *relational* analysis. The purpose of ironic analysis is to show the temporary nature of both positions and their determination by the relations that describe and constitute them.[3] Thus irony begins with reflexivity but does not end there. A better world is still a goal of ironic analysis, a goal pursued in the conversation between subject and object, between alter and ego. Indeed, this is the radical promise of irony for critical social analysis. Precisely because he or she does not need a 'critical vantage point', the ironic analyst does not have to formulate a positive statement about the most desirable or the best solution. Ironic analysis only has to persuade the other that there is a range of possible solutions and there are multiple ways to perceive and rank those solutions as desirable. Being ironic, then, is the opposite of being serious or earnest. Seriousness assumes faith in the supremacy of a position. The ironic analyst does not occupy such moral high ground, and wants to convince others that they do not occupy such high ground either. It is for this reason that humor or jokes are important instruments in ironic analysis.[4] Irony is also distinct from cynicism. To invoke Mannheim again, we would say that a cynical position is relativist while an ironic analysis is relationist, by which we mean that ironic analysis accepts the possibility of multiple truths, with each truth still distinguishable from untruth.

This article is an 'invitation to neoclassical sociology' and therefore to ironic analysis. While we coin the term 'neoclassical sociology', we do not think we have invented a new field of inquiry.[5] Rather, we present an examination and critique of sociology's response

---

Those who do not follow the rules are 'irrational'. Ironically – precisely in the sense of the term we use in this article – marxism converges with neoclassical economics in the common assumption of a single global capitalist logic. The only difference between the two schools of thought is that one thinks it a desirable development and the other, an undesirable one. In contrast, neoclassical sociology operates with the assumption of capitalism as *multiple destinations*. Whether or not the capitalism that is now emerging in Russia will converge with capitalism as we know it from the United States or Western Europe must be explored *empirically* rather than assumed by *theoretical fiat*.

3 This is where our understanding converges with postmodern analyses of irony. See for example Hutcheon (1992, 1995) and in particular the discussion of the differences between premodernist, modernist, and postmodernist irony.

4 The typical form of a joke is a question to which the listener assumes an obvious answer. A good joke provides an unexpected answer which is as plausible as the one the listener had in mind. We say someone lacks a sense of humor when he or she fails to understand jokes. A person without a sense of humor is serious and insists that his or her own beliefs cannot be made the subject of jokes; that his or her position cannot be questioned in this manner. This is why we cannot conceptualize irony without self-irony. If one loses humor about oneself and one's own position then there is no irony or reflexivity.

5 Indeed, we acknowledge and thank Victor Nee for the term 'neoclassical sociology'.

to a world without socialism and, in particular, to the ever-powerful challenge of economics. In this effort, we seek to discover a way to balance the duality of affirmative and critical perspectives that has characterized the discipline from its inception. To this end, the remainder of the article addresses three interrelated questions posed by socialism's demise, each of which suggests directions for a reconstructed, neoclassical sociology.

First, how should sociologists think about capitalism in the postsocialist era? How can we avoid reifying capitalism as a single homogenous globalizing logic? We think the answer is a reconstruction of the Weberian concept of capitalism, a comparative approach that conceptualizes capitalism as a *plurality* of forms and destinations.

Second, does the end of actually existing socialism mean the end of class analysis? Should we accept the claim that classes are disappearing or dead (Inglehart and Rabier, 1986; Pakulski and Waters, 1996)? We do not think so. Rather, we argue that the transition to capitalism in Eastern Europe provides exciting new materials for a reconstructed class analysis, raising important questions about the 'classness' of collective actors and the role of intellectuals in social change.

Third, is a critical social science possible in the absence of a socialist alternative? Does the repudiation of socialism necessarily mean the repudiation of the role of the intellectual as social critic? Again, we think not. Rather than retreating to the position of a sociological technician, or collapsing sociology into moral critique, we propose that the sobering experience of the demise of the teleological intellectual be used to formulate a new mode of critical intellectual engagement, namely, irony.

II. How Should Sociologists Think About Capitalism In The Postsocialist Era?

The basic premise of neoclassical sociology is that since the possibility of a socialist alternative can no longer be detected with the instruments of social science, the task before us is the comparative analysis of capitalist forms and destinations. This is a central argument in our book *Making Capitalism Without Capitalists* (1998), which analyzes transitions from socialism to capitalism in Hungary, Poland, and the Czech Republic. Before turning to our framework for the study of comparative capitalisms, however, we revisit the question of how to think about socialism and capitalism in the postsocialist world.

The absence of a socialist alternative and the nature of capitalism

We argue that the possibility of a socialist alternative can no longer serve as the basis for a critical social science because we cannot currently detect such an alternative *empirically*. Our premise is that critical social science should be based on the detection of 'real alternatives', and a social alternative can be thought of as real only if there are social actors (other than the social scientist) who are engaged in empirically observable collective action of an 'emergent' nature (Williams, 1980: 32–49), i.e. collective action that points toward an alternative social order. This position is empirical without being positivist since reality is indeed praxis, and we (and our analyses) are involved in it. We only add the weak empirical caveat that socially transformative praxis must have an identifiable social agent.

In the current historical moment, we find no collective actor that is willing to take on the project of building socialism. Not only is it the case that workers no longer constitute a class agent mobilized for socialism,[6] even the intelligentsia is no longer interested in building socialism.[7] Indeed, as an empirical matter we observe that the consciousness of the leading fractions of the intellectual class in Western capitalism as well as the former socialist countries of Eastern Europe are marked precisely by the experience of disillusionment with socialism. Although they were historically identified with building socialism, disillusionment now permeates intellectual identities and worldviews so profoundly that we think it is unlikely that these class fractions will become carriers of a socialist project in the foreseeable future.

To be clear: we are not arguing that the absence of a *proximate* socialist alternative means socialism is impossible in principle, or that socialism will not be built in some future we are unable to see. We have no crystal ball and social science has a bad track record of prediction. Nor do we think that the absence of a socialist alternative means that marxism is dead or irrelevant. On the contrary: in a world dominated by capitalist financial markets, where the livelihoods of millions are contingent on the mysterious movement of stocks and currencies, marxism has much to contribute to the ethical critique of capitalism. No longer required to justify the practicalities of building socialism, whether in the form of the Gulag or the inefficiencies of socialist planning, marxism may experience a renaissance. Our point is simply that the probability of finding collective actors mobilized to build a socialist society in the near future are extremely slim, especially in Eastern Europe.

If we are correct that there is no proximate socialist alternative in the new world order, then does it follow that capitalism – defined as a single, homogeneous, global logic – is 'the only game in town'? We do not think so. To accept such a proposition is both ahistorical and naive. Instead, following Weber ([1904–5]1958: 13–31), we suggest that

6 We do not deny the realities of capitalist exploitation or suggest that the working class does not exist or that it is disappearing. In contemporary Eastern Europe, however, we do observe that the working class is demobilized, with little capacity for collective action. Elsewhere in the world, when the working class does act collectively, it engages in trade union struggles rather than building revolutionary class consciousness. On this, see our response to Michael Burawoy in the review symposium in the *American Journal of Sociology [106 (2001): 1099–1120]* which included our book: Eyal et al., 2001.

7 We think that by now the historical record demonstrates beyond doubt that a socialist project is impossible without the collective action of the intelligentsia, or at least a sizable fraction thereof. There are no historical cases where the working class has been able to carry and implement a socialist project without the support of radical intellectuals, but there is, on the other hand, a wealth of evidence to indicate that a radical intelligentsia is a class actor capable of carrying and implementing a socialist alternative even where a working class does not exist (e.g. China). Here we rely on the rich tradition of analyzing socialism as the creation of a 'new class' of intellectuals (Bakunin, 1966; Djilas, 1957; Gouldner, 1979; Konrád and Szelényi, 1979; Machajski, 1937; Nomad, 1937, 1959).

capitalism comes in many forms, and that a comparative analysis of multiple 'capitalisms' and their consequences is the critical task facing sociologists today.

Weber offers a generic definition of capitalist economic action as the building block for a comparative analysis of capitalisms: action is capitalist if it is oriented towards profit through peaceful means, and if it applies rational criteria to measure inputs expended against benefits accrued. No other more concrete criteria of capitalism are required by this definition. Whether or not an economic system is 'capitalist' then, is a matter of degree; it is more capitalist to the extent that it is organized to render the calculation of costs and benefits rational. Of course, since calculation is a social practice, capitalist rationalization implies a host of social institutions and a corresponding set of productive relations that reproduce them. Among these one would usually include individual private property in the means of production, the separation of direct producers from the means of production, and price-regulating markets (Weber, [1915–21]1978: 915, 1393–95; [1927]1981: 276–8; Callon, 1998). But capitalist economic action can also take place under conditions where property is not fully private, where labor is not separated from the means of production, or outside of price-regulating markets (Weber, [1904–5]1958: 13–31; [1915–21]1978: 635–40, 1393–95; [1927]1981: 335–6; Polanyi, [1944]1957; 1957). Thus, it is possible to think about multiple forms of capitalism as historically specific assemblages of various elements differing in the type and in the extent to which they enable rational economic calculation.

This understanding is in tension with Weber's other argument that modern Western capitalism is the most rational or powerful combination of these various social institutions and productive relations. There is, after all, his famous proposition that modern Western capitalism is an 'iron cage' of individual private property and self-regulating markets into which agents are locked because these arrangements provide for the most rational profitseeking behavior. Here, Weber suggests strongly that modern Western capitalism functions as the *terminus* of history, and thus, this is precisely where we part ways with Weber's analysis. Indeed, we think Weber was empirically wrong and that capitalism did not develop in a unilinear way as the 'iron cage' metaphor suggests. Shortly after Weber's death, some of the elements he considered to be essential characteristics of the highest form of capitalist development – for example, self-regulating markets – were replaced, or at least marginalized, by massive regulatory state intervention (Polanyi, [1944]1957). Fifty years later, self-regulating markets became dominant once again, due to attacks on the welfare state and the influence of neoclassical economics. But this happened in a context thoroughly different from the one Weber imagined – a context of massively transformed property relations, large corporations, shareholding, institutional ownership, and mutual funds or pension funds capital (Bell, 1973; Gates, 1998). So, although we follow his interpretive, historical approach to the analysis of capitalism, we argue that Weber's generic concept of capitalism must be reconstructed against the grain of his 'iron cage' metaphor.[8]

8 This theoretical choice is precisely what distinguishes our position as neo-classical sociologists from Weber's position as a classical sociologist. Weber's slippage from multiple rationalities and

This is what we do in our book, comparing transitions to capitalism in Eastern and Central Europe to explore how various elements are combined in different cases. Specifically, we describe and analyze the interrelations between property relations, the means and degree of state regulation and planning, the degree of development of capital and labor markets, the nature of welfare state institutions and the disposition of surplus labor, the availability of intellectual technologies of calculation, the nature of interorganizational relationships, the type of capitalist actors and their degree of classness, and the modes of justification of profit-seeking behavior.[9] In this, we adopt Weber's ([1903–17]1949: 33–9) assumption of multiple rationalities rather than a single unifying capitalist rationality, and we follow his methodological commitment to a developmentalist rather than an evolutionary mode of explanation ([1903–17]1949: 50–112). It is on this basis that we propose a comparative framework for analyzing the diversity of capitalist forms and relations, and we argue such a framework is absolutely necessary if we seek to pursue a critical sociology in the face of triumphalist claims of the end of history.

The globalization-convergence thesis

Since 1989, a new orthodoxy of neoliberal popularizers and neoclassical economists has interpreted the term 'globalization' to mean a process of convergence on a single homogenous world capitalist system. This system is understood to be governed by the unified systemic logic of competitive global markets, bolstered by international economic agencies such as the IMF (International Monetary Fund / Internationaler Währungsfonds) and the World Bank. This systemic logic, which approximates the neoliberal doctrine, weakens states and dilutes the significance of differences between national economies,

---

trajectories to a single capitalist destination of history was symptomatically historically constrained: first, it reflected his sense of western superiority, and thus the condition of European hegemony over the rest of the world; second, it was an ideological reflection of the political choice between capitalism and socialism that he believed he faced. Weber was no simple-minded ideologue of liberal capitalism. He is better characterized as a 'liberal in despair', fully aware of the price that would have to be paid for liberal capitalism (Mommsen, 1984). But faced with the choice between capitalism and socialism, he opted for the former. This was clear in his late essays about socialism in Russia (Weber [1905–6, 1917]1995), but we also think this political dilemma found its way into his description of capitalism, urging him to depict it as more formidable and inescapable than it appeared on the basis of his empirical analyses. Since we write at a time when the opposition between socialism and capitalism no longer has the same urgency, we think sociology should no longer be constrained by the extortionist logic of the choice between them.

9 The conceptual status of such assemblages is not very different from what an earlier generation of marxists termed 'social formations', and what the 'regulation school' today calls 'modes of regulation' (Harvey, 1989: 121–2). It strikes us, however, that Weber's methodology offers a more flexible analytical framework for comparison. Concepts like 'regimes of accumulation' tend to assume a systemic principle operating behind the backs of actors, totalizing their various responses, because they attempt to distinguish economic types according to the mode in which they handle the endemic crisis tendencies of capitalism. Methodologically this means that actual cases must correspond to types. In the weberian scheme in contrast, one compares actual cases with an analytical typology in order to evaluate the likely consequences of conditions in each case, asking how they affect the rationality of economic actors (Roth, 1971).

pushing them inexorably towards convergence (Ohmae, 1995; Reich, 1992; Schmidt, 1995).[10] We think that this globalization-as-convergence thesis has several conceptual and empirical shortcomings.

First, the argument's plausibility rests heavily on an implicit sense of the 'end of history'; on the idea that the process of globalization is unique to the postmodern era, that it is driven by factors that have not existed before, and that it is irreversible. This is false. Even a cursory glance at the historical record reveals that what we are witnessing today is, at best, a second round of globalization, if not a more cyclical phenomenon (Hirst and Thompson, 1996; Schumpeter, [1942]1976; Wallerstein, 2000; Weiss, 1998). Processes of globalization operated in full force from the late 19th century to the First World War, a period that witnessed a dramatic increase in the volume of foreign trade, the rise of international currency markets, and mass movements of immigrant labor between continents. Even more importantly, we observe that shortly thereafter, these processes were reversed, blocked, or at least slowed by the growth of protectionism, restrictions on immigration, and state intervention (Polanyi, [1944]1957). There is no reason to think that this could not happen again; indeed, there are some indications that it is already occurring. Powerful antiglobal movements are countering the current round of globalization. For example, the last decade has witnessed the creation of more new nation states than in any single previous decade (Mann, 1997). In addition, there has been an increase in national conflicts, and arguably, a strengthening of national consciousness everywhere. Strong regional trends also work against unfettered global capitalism. With respect to commodities trading, for example, there is evidence that what we are witnessing is not globalization at all, but rather the formation of regional blocks (NAFTA (=North American Free Trade Agreement/Nordamerikanisches Freihandelsabkommen), EU, Southeast Asia), between which there is only minimal trade (Fligstein, 1997; Hirst and Thompson, 1996; Weiss, 1998).

To give the globalization thesis its due, it is probably most accurate when applied to international currency markets and the movement of financial capital. These have become truly global and, more importantly, instantaneous, i.e. shrinking the time–space horizon of economic action (Giddens, 1998; Harvey, 1989: 160–72, 284–307). But even here, we do not see evidence that convergence is propelled by the impersonal economic logic of capitalism per se. Rather, the recent round of convergence was orchestrated by international economic agencies in the aftermath of the Asian financial crisis. And, while global financial markets brought formidable pressure to bear on the Southeast

10 On the left side of the ideological divide, the reception of the 'globalization-as-convergence' thesis has been more complex, and we cannot do it justice here. Some, notably world-system theorists and international political economists, have articulated a similar, though darker, version, in which the unified systemic logic of global capitalism is conquering the globe and finally confirms Marx's prediction. This version is particularly suited to utopian socialism, which gains strength from being contrasted with the distopic view of capitalism, and has arguably served to inspire the recent attacks on the IMF and WTO (=World Trade Organizsation/Welthandelsorganisation) in Seattle and elsewhere. But many other marxists have been much more suspicious of the convergence thesis, and in fact supply us with ammunition against it. For a brief presentation of the internal debate, see Hirst and Thompson (1996).

Asian states, the direction of this pressure towards the greater homogeneity of financial institutions was shaped by concrete actors, by theories of the essence of the crisis, and by the rhetoric of 'transparency' deployed by the Fed (=Federal Reserve System) and the IMF to delegitimate these countries' existing policies (Stiglitz, 1999). In this context, it is impossible to verify the globalization-as-convergence thesis *empirically*, since the theory itself has played a central role in defining the situation it purports to explain, shaping the very outcomes it predicts.

In short, although we claim no special expertise on the points reviewed above, we note that they cast doubt on the thesis of globalization-as-convergence. Moreover, where we do profess some detailed knowledge, that is, in our analysis of the transitions from socialism to capitalism in post-1989 Eastern and Central Europe, we find that the evidence weighs quite strongly against the unitary view of global capitalism.

Eastern Europe: the historical laboratory

In a very real sense, the countries of Eastern and Central Europe served as the laboratory of global capitalism in the 1990s. Western neoclassical economists were given free rein to impose their capitalist blueprint, and they did so with alacrity. Far from producing a single, homogenous result, however, the laboratory has produced capitalist systems that vary widely. For example, former socialist societies in Eastern and Central Europe vary in the extent to which they receive foreign investment and engage in foreign trade, thus they vary precisely in the degree to which they can be considered 'global'. Instead of homogenization and convergence, then, we observe that the transition to capitalism in the former socialist world is marked by divergence.[11]

In our book, we try to explain this diversity, arguing that the pivotal causal mechanism that distinguished transitions in different countries was intraclass conflict within the late communist dominant class. The outcomes of these intraclass conflicts were decisive for the subsequent course of transition and capitalist development in different Eastern and Central European countries, since they explain in each case who the agents were who led the transition, and what kind of capitalism they tried to create.

In Russia, and also to a large extent in Rumania, Bulgaria, Serbia, Ukraine, and Belarus, the victorious fraction of the late communist dominant class was composed of party bureaucrats. During the transition to capitalism, these actors converted their political offices into private property. They were less interested and, arguably, less capable of building capitalist institutions such as free markets in labor and capital. So, in these countries we find *capitalists without capitalism*: former communist officials amassed private fortunes in the course of the transition but now operate in the context of weak or non-functioning market institutions. The most spectacular case is Russia where one finds a strong propertied bourgeoisie operating in a context marked by the failure of monetary consolidation, the replacement of market by barter, and the enserfment of

11 For explanations of the diversity of transition paths see Fish (1998) and King (2001). Note however, we do not think the diversity of transitions to capitalism in Eastern and Central Europe reflects a 'return' to presocialist differences, as has been suggested by some authors (e.g. Rothschild, 1989).

workers (Bonnell, 1999; Burawoy and Krotov, 1992; Woodruff, 1999). The resulting situation is what Burawoy (1996) calls 'involution', i.e. a form of adaptation to the imposition of capitalism from above, in which precapitalist actors and institutions use barter, household production, and client–patron relations to either insulate themselves from the logic of the market or defensively adjust to its pressure. To use Polanyi's ([1944]1957) terminology, the failure or weakness of market institutions is corrected by institutions of reciprocity, which embed economic relations in a movement contrary to the disembedding logic of markets and money.

In contrast, the countries of Central Europe experienced a different transition process, and they appear to be headed in a different direction than Eastern European involution. In Hungary, Poland, the Czech Republic, and to a lesser extent in Slovakia, and the Baltic states, the bureaucratic fraction of the dominant class did not emerge victorious in the intraclass struggles of late communism. Instead, bureaucrats were defeated by a coalition of technocrats, former dissident intellectuals, and members of the educated middle management of socialist enterprises. By its very nature, this coalition was incapable of engaging in mass conversions of political offices into private property. That is, many of its members never held political office under communism, and those who did were constrained by the fact of the coalition and, in particular, the scrutiny of a free press and democratically elected parliaments. At the same time, the ideological bonds uniting this intellectual coalition were grounded in the idea of building market institutions as an ethical mission – as a means of purging society of the evils of communism. Thus, transitional societies in Central Europe saw the early development of labor and capital markets, a strong emphasis on monetary consolidation and on price liberalization. The transformation of property rights, by contrast, was comparatively slow. Early in the transition, this created diffuse ownership rights, giving managers wide latitude to control firms, with the state still functioning as the final support, particularly in terms of bailouts of 'privatized' firms.[12] Later, these countries saw the coalition of managers and technocrats strike profitable deals with foreign business partners, who took over the newly privatized firms and gave the managers and technocrats well-paid managerial positions in what were now foreign-owned firms. During both of these changes in ownership relations, however, we emphasize the absence of a domestic bourgeoisie. This is a particularly glaring feature of the Central European transitions, especially when they are compared to the development of predatory capitalist classes in countries like Russia. There *is* an absentee capitalist class in Central Europe, in the form of foreign ownership by multinational corporations, but its alliance is with domestic technocrats and managers who also control the state. Thus, we argue that the Central European transition produced *capitalism without capitalists*, since these countries developed market institutions quickly but no domestic propertied bourgeoisie. The resulting developmental trajectory is not one of 'involution', but one of 'dependent development' (Evans, 1979);

12 David Stark (1996) called this 'recombinant property', and we have analyzed it elsewhere (Eyal et al., 1997) as 'managerialism'. In retrospect it seems to have been a temporary snapshot of a particular strategy of transition. On this point see Hanley et al., 2002.

most economic growth is taking place in export-oriented foreign-owned firms with the encouragement of state actors. While domestic markets remain modest, these countries are undergoing an export-led industrialization, typically in high technology sectors.[13]

The conclusion we draw from this most privileged historical laboratory of Central and Eastern Europe then, is that origins, trajectories, and above all, class actors, matter a great deal in shaping the type of capitalism produced in the transition from socialism. We conclude further that this evidence casts doubt on the argument of a single, homogenous, global capitalism. To be clear: we do not deny the possibility that at some point in the future these societies may converge on the neoliberal vision of capitalism, but to engage in such speculation is futurology, not sociology. The epistemological status of the globalization-as-convergence argument, to our mind, is identical to that of the marxist insistence on the existence of a socialist alternative: there is no empirical evidence for it in the present. Indeed, all empirical evidence points to the contrary, with Central Europe, Eastern Europe and even China *more* different now than they were 20 or 50 years ago.[14]

Sociological responses: network analysis, embeddedness, and the new institutionalism

This complex historical diversity of capitalist forms is precisely what is not apprehended in the mainstream sociological response to the crisis caused by the fall of socialism; namely, the response offered by neo-institutionalist sociology and network analysis. This perspective contends that there is a more concrete, and more fundamental level of social

13 This describes the Hungarian case particularly well; no other country of comparable size has such massive foreign ownership, which seems to be responsible for substantial levels of economic growth. Poland and the Czech Republic are the closest to Hungary in this respect, with Slovenia, Slovakia, and the Baltic Republics following somewhat behind.

14 The cases of the Chinese and Vietnamese transitions to capitalism further support our argument about the diversity of capitalist forms. These countries have approached transition in a wholly different way than Central and Eastern Europe, and they have done so with remarkable success. Simply put, the distinction here is between 'capitalism from above' and 'capitalism from below'. In the first case, the Central and Eastern European countries embarked on a strategy of transition that prioritized the privatization or reorganization of the huge state sector, and this priority meant that the process was controlled by the victorious fraction of the dominant class. In China and Vietnam, on the other hand, the emphasis was not on transforming the state sector, but on encouraging the emergence of entrepreneurship 'from below' in specially designated 'developmental zones', which also enjoy foreign investment. Note, however, that this highly successful strategy, which creates 'socialist entrepreneurs' (Szelényi, 1988), depends on political conditions in which the communist party still maintains the state sector and shields the emerging private sector. The other precipitating condition is the influx of foreign capital, in particular, that from relatively small sources in Hong Kong and Taiwan. Capitalist development in mainland China then, seems (ironically) to follow the pattern that characterized post-Second World War Taiwan: authoritarian government stimulating growth in the small businesses sector in the context of a tightly controlled influx of foreign investment. It bears little resemblance to capitalism in post-1989 Eastern or Central Europe. And, none of the three types of capitalism correspond to the version of neoliberal capitalism that is held out as the global norm today – as the model towards which all systems are converging.

reality in which the abstract market mechanisms theorized by neoclassical economics are 'embedded'; a level of reality composed of networks, conventions, imitation, and habits, rather than the rational maximizing action of individuals or the forces of supply and demand (see for example, Granovetter, 1985; Meyer and Rowan, 1977; White, 1992). As we intimated earlier, however, we consider the response of neo-institutionalist sociology and network analysis to be the contemporary 'escape route' of sociological positivism and, as such, limited. These approaches are positivist because their response to the crisis of postsocialist sociology consists in defining the sociological enterprise as the study of certain *timeless* social mechanisms, such as networks and interaction. This strategy avoids what we argue to be the main task of a critical sociology – to produce an analysis that responds to the historical specificity of our times. Just as earlier sociological positivism drew implicit and unacknowledged vigor from the existence of the socialist alternative, we think that neo-institutionalist sociology and network analysis are marked by an implicit and unacknowledged concession that such an alternative no longer exists. Gone are the grand social systems of a thinker like Parsons. Instead, neo-institutionalist sociology and network analysis strike a retreat to the level of the concrete, everyday, interpersonal, and habitual. Thus, instead of contesting the meaning of rationality, they deny its significance and emphasize blind imitation (Meyer and Rowan, 1977). Instead of contesting the notion of a single capitalist logic, they evade the issue altogether and emphasize embeddedness (Granovetter, 1985). Instead of responding to proclamations that classes are disappearing, they collapse the notion of social structure into the methodological individualism of 'networks'. We contend that all of these intellectual choices involve an implicit concession to 'rational choice' theory and neoclassical economics: imitation is rational under the assumption of bounded rationality (Simon, 1982); networks are assets manipulated by the maximizing individual; and embeddedness simply denotes the brackets around the rational choice calculus, the assumption of 'all else being equal ...'.

The transition to capitalism in Eastern Europe provides an empirical laboratory to assess the utility and critical potential of these positivist approaches, just as it does for the globalization-as-convergence thesis. So, for example, if we apply neo-institutionalist sociology and network analysis to a case like Russia, where there are capitalists but no fully-fledged capitalism, we find economic integration is occurring through networks, embeddedness, and reciprocity, i.e. precisely through those mechanisms highlighted in neo-institutionalist and network-analytic approaches. We do not think this is a vindication of these approaches, however. On the contrary, it reveals their lack of critical historical relevance. Such positivist analyses fall to observe the socio-historical consequences of embeddedness and networks in the context of the postsocialist transition to capitalism. Such analyses are unlikely to observe that Russia's economic system is on a path of involutionary economic development toward political capitalism (of the type Weber identified in 19th century Prussia) and, in this context, the political culture is likely to be authoritarian and work against the development of liberal democratic institutions (Schluchter, 1985). Our point is that while it is possible at a certain level of abstraction to treat embeddedness and networks as invariant conditions of economic action, this approach is unlikely to offer historical insight. It is unlikely to support the kind of historical comparisons between different types of capitalism and their consequences that are the order of the day if sociology is to continue its critical mission.

Put another way, we argue that sociological theories of embeddedness and networks tend to take the nature of social actors as given or unproblematic. In this, these theories are like neoclassical economics. Neither perspective closely examines the role of social actors, particularly collective actors, in the transition from socialism to capitalism in Eastern and Central Europe. On the one hand, neoclassical economists (and many sociologists) think the crucial issue of the transition is 'institution building'. They think that if they design the correct set of institutions, preferably copied from the West, this guarantees a smooth transition to market capitalism. To this day, neoclassical economists engage in endless justifications explaining why their transition programs have not worked (Aslund, 1995). On the other hand, the crucial issue for network analysts is 'path dependency'. Here the focus is on how the survival of institutions and network ties from the communist period limits the development of 'pure' market relations (Stark, 1992). In the absence of an analysis of actors, however, 'path dependency' remains an inert notion, incapable of accounting for the contrast between the dynamism of the Central European economies and the stagnation of the Eastern European ones. It is against both of these perspectives then, that our approach to the analysis of comparative capitalism focuses on *actors*. We argue that the social positions, trajectories, worldviews, identities, and alliances of the actors who envisaged and implemented the capitalist project in Eastern and Central Europe have been absolutely decisive for the types of capitalism that have emerged in these countries.

Comparative capitalisms

Our analysis of comparative capitalism in *contemporary* Eastern and Central Europe also suggests that we aim our new critical lens at the *history* of capitalism, rereading what we thought we knew about Western capitalism from the historically novel angle of postsocialism. We are not arguing that capitalism has become more diverse since the demise of socialism, but rather that we are more capable of seeing and appreciating its diversity. Previously, the existence of a socialist alternative obscured the importance of capitalist diversity. So, although a wealth of scholarship existed documenting divergent and unique trajectories of capitalist development in the past, for example in Japan or Southeast Asia (e.g. Dore, 1973), these differences have been undertheorized. The dominance of marxist world system theories and neoliberal globalization theories has meant that these rich historical accounts were never used to inform a sustained comparison of the divergent routes of capitalist development, nor were they theoretically integrated back into the concept of capitalism. Indeed, in contrast to the theoretical development in the field of comparative democratic and authoritarian political regimes (e.g. O'Donnell and Schmitter, 1986), we would observe that the theoretical development of the field of comparative capitalism is dismal (for an exception see Fligstein, 1996).

With the demise of socialism, however, we think the field of comparative capitalism will inform a new critical social science. Instead of being drawn into the extortionist logic of choice that dictates that one *either* stands for capitalism *or* for socialism, no matter what their varieties and costs, with the fall of socialism we are released from this false polarity. Now we recognize the critical value of distinguishing types of societies and processes of social developments, and mapping their likely consequences. In this we follow Weber, who compared different capitalist formations around the world and throughout history in an effort to address a pressing political choice facing the society in which he lived. Specifically, Weber wanted to show that political capitalism, in both its ancient form and the Prussian version that marked German society in his day, imposed severe costs on social development, blocking industrialization and political liberalism. We tend to share the harshness of Weber's judgment with respect to the contemporary form of political capitalism in Russia. Like Weber we think the social costs of political capitalism are heavy. This is the sort of calculus we believe critical social theory can and should provide, using the tools of empirical social science so that social actors can assess the costs and benefits of different social arrangements and courses of action for themselves. We return to a discussion of the social role of critical sociology in the final section of the article.

III. Does The End Of Actually Existing Socialism Mean The End Of Class Analysis?

Another casualty of the 'end of history' proposition has been class analysis. We hear everywhere that classes are declining or dead, and that the East European transition to capitalism proves it. And it is accurate to say that the demise of socialism poses a challenge not only to marxism but also to sociology's rich tradition of class analysis. The main reason is that the postcommunist transition is the first time in history that capitalism has developed in a society that had formerly abolished private property, and which did not have even an embryonic class of private proprietors. This is the central puzzle of our book and why we entitled it *Making Capitalism Without Capitalists*. This label best describes the Central European case, but it also identifies the universal circumstance in which the initial stages of the transition from socialism to capitalism occurred following 1989. Previous theories of the transition to capitalism provide little insight into this unique circumstance because they invariably assume that a propertied class always exists *before* there is a capitalist system. For example, the debate on the transition from feudalism to capitalism revolved around whether this agent was an urban commercial bourgeoisie or an entrepreneurial landed nobility (Ashton and Philpin, 1985; Dobb, 1946; Holton, 1985; Sweezy, 1942). Such an agent was everywhere absent at the outset of the postcommunist transition, and indeed, until much later in Central Europe. In the postcommunist context then, class analysis might seem to be irrelevant to the emergence of capitalism. Into this analytical lacuna the 'end of history' argument rushes once again. It proclaims the end of classes, positing the main question of the transition to be: how do we *design* the correct capitalist institutions to foster entrepreneurship and civil society?

Instead of this, we propose the empirical question: who are the agents and forces that shape the transition?

We contend that the question of agents is crucial; indeed, the central claim of our book is that the transition to capitalism in Central Europe was a *class project of the intelligentsia*.[15] While some intellectuals and technocrats have presented their role in the transition to capitalism as that of a proxy for a propertied bourgeoisie which had not yet emerged, we argue that these intellectuals are far better characterized as a cultural bourgeoisie, or *Bildungsbürgertum* (Kocka, 1993). By this, we mean that these fractions of the intelligentsia were class agents defined by the structural characteristic of possessing cultural capital rather than economic capital, and by the historical project of building a bourgeois civilization, i.e. of building capitalist market institutions, liberal democracy, the rule of law, and civil society.

This concept of a 'cultural bourgeoisie' requires us to break with traditional class analysis in two ways. First, intellectuals have typically been analyzed as a 'new class' when they exhibit anticapitalist or postcapitalist characteristics. The concept of the 'new class' has been applied either to the role of intellectuals in socialist systems (Djilas, 1957; Konrád and Szelényi, 1979; Machajski, 1937) or to situations where they emerged as a subversive force within capitalism (Bell, 1973; Burnham, 1941; Gouldner, 1979). In cases where intellectuals do not stand in opposition to the capitalist project, or where they advocate capitalism, this is taken as evidence that intellectuals do not constitute a class, since they do not act in their own interests (e.g. Brint, 1984). In a second sociological tradition, classes are defined as collective actors whose interests are rooted in the economic system; their positions are defined either in terms of property relations or market position. In this perspective, cultural markers of distinction play a secondary role, at best, in class structuration (Giddens, 1973: 99–117). The notion of a cultural bourgeoisie breaks with both these traditions of class analysis and points toward a reformulation. First, we argue that thinking about cultural capital as a basis of class position implies a more general concept of 'classness' which has application far beyond the analysis of the transition in Eastern and Central Europe. Second, we suggest that thinking about intellectuals as a capitalist agent means paying attention to the specific power that intellectuals wield, namely discourse, and on this basis, rethinking the role of intellectuals in social change more generally.

Classness

We trace the idea of 'classness' to Weber (again!), taking as our point of departure his distinction between 'class' and 'rank' as alternative concepts describing social structure. 'Rank' refers to a society composed of estates, understood as hierarchies in which

15 We focus on Central Europe here to the exclusion of the East European and Russian cases (i.e. of 'capitalists without capitalism') because the latter pose less of a puzzle. The role played by nomenklatura members who turned themselves into private capitalists allows us to think of them as a capitalist class in-the-making. For those familiar with discussions of the transition from feudalism to capitalism, the analogy to tax-farming nobles and officials who utilize their position in the old regime to become *rentier* capitalists will be obvious (Staniszkis, 1991).

personal ties of loyalty and obedience connect members, and in which one's station in life is relatively fixed by law and tradition. 'Class society', in contrast, is composed of classes, defined as categories of actors who do not form a community (in Weber's sense of the term), and whose members are not bound to each other by personal ties or fixed in place by law and tradition. Rather, in class societies, actors display probabilities to act on the basis of shared market position. This analytical distinction can be described as a continuum. To the extent that very clear and binding rules of inclusion and exclusion define individual membership in a community, one is closer to the 'rank' pole of the continuum. To the extent that such rules do not exist but individuals still act in a concerted manner on the basis of shared interests, one is closer to the 'class' pole of the continuum. In specific empirical circumstances, social actors may be characterized by their different positions along the continuum; that is, by their different degrees of 'classness' or 'rankness'.

Building on this idea, we suggest that Weber's analytical distinction between rank and class is usefully elaborated by Bourdieu's theory of the different types of capital (Bourdieu, [1983]1986; Eyal et al., 1998: 66–70). Thus, rank society can be understood as a stratification order where social capital is dominant. Estates, after all, are hierarchical networks composed of patron–client relations, in which individuals operate according to ascribed social characteristics. Class society, in contrast, defines a stratification order in which economic capital is dominant, and money rather than nobility acquires symbolic power and sets the rate of conversion for all other types of capital.

What of cultural capital? Our argument is that cultural capital occupies a middle position on the rank–class continuum. On the one hand, a stratification order where cultural capital is dominant typically gives rise to groupings that resemble estates. Such groups usually practice professional closure through some form of credentialing, and they cultivate elaborate internal hierarchies. From the moment they are achieved, credentials function ascriptively to entitle their bearers to goods and privileges (Collins, 1979). Of course, the credential must first be achieved in competition and legitimated by the ideology of meritocracy, and with respect to this ideology – what Gouldner called the Culture of Critical Discourse (CCD) – intellectuals resemble a class. That is, they are a collective actor brought together not by concrete ties, but by abstract relations and probable shared interests. We contend, therefore, that because the intelligentsia is a category defined by the possession of cultural capital, it should be seen as a class actor, albeit a class actor characterized by a relatively low degree of classness.

It is precisely this social location between rank and class that describes the contradictory, hybrid nature of the intelligentsia, and that makes it a collective actor with great transformative potential. This can be seen clearly in late communist societies where the intelligentsia was probably the only actor capable of, or interested in, effecting a transition from socialism to capitalism; that is, a transition from a rank order where possessing social capital in the form of party membership and party network ties conferred the most advantage, to a class society (albeit with a low degree of classness) in which cultural capital is dominant, and economic capital is ascendant.

Intellectuals in the capitalist transition

How have Central European intellectuals become capitalist agents, and in what sense is capitalism an *intellectual* class project? This is a counterintuitive puzzle, particularly when we recall that many of Central Europe's liberal intellectuals were just as enthusiastic about socialism earlier in their careers as they are about capitalism now. Many of them were once committed to the goal of reforming socialism, as 'new left' intellectuals, as technocrats interested in efficiency and scientific planning, or as reformers working inside the communist party. Thus, the temptation might be to see the current zeal for capitalism among Central European intellectuals as a case of 'bad faith'; one might argue they are no more than ideologues-for-hire providing services to capitalism in exchange for economic security. We think this temptation should be resisted for three reasons. First, as we argue in our book, there was no dominant capitalist class to command the services of the intellectuals during the postcommunist transformation. Moreover, Central European intellectuals were probably the strongest they had ever been, holding more official positions and wielding more social power than ever before. Second, there is no intrinsic reason why capitalism would require the sort of ethical justification these Central European intellectuals articulated. Capitalism is a self-legitimating system. It 'works' without requiring that workers or entrepreneurs believe in its superior moral nature. Therefore, the moral zeal and faith in the superiority of capitalism that marked the postcommunist transition must be traced to the biographies and worldviews of Central European intellectuals themselves. And this is our third point: an analysis of these biographies and worldviews reveals not just a few scattered intellectuals in high positions who embrace capitalism, but shows instead that capitalism is a class project of the intelligentsia, i.e. a collective action to build a new social order.

Central European intellectuals are no strangers to transformative social projects. Three decades ago, the socialist intelligentsia undertook a collective project to reform and humanize socialism. They sought to become the new dominant class of a rationalized socialism, exercising power as teleological redistributors (Konrád and Szelényi, 1979). Slowly, they turned away from this project as they came to realize that the bureaucratic character of socialism made such rationalization impossible. It is only in the long path out of this failed class project, after a decades-long process of negotiation, conflict, and struggle, that the Central European intelligentsia has come to embrace the project of building civil society and capitalism. Analyzing this process, we argue that the current capitalist project of the intelligentsia has been adopted for the same reasons that the socialist one was. That is, the project of building capitalism was undertaken, not on behalf of other classes, but precisely because the Central European intelligentsia was searching for a new social role and a new way of valorizing cultural capital (Eyal et al., 1998: 46–85, 135–42).

To elaborate this proposition fully, we argue, we need to think about the class power of intellectuals in a new way. Previous class analysis of intellectuals has tended to think of the valorization of cultural capital narrowly, associating it with social closure based in the monopoly of relatively esoteric discourse. This understanding of intellectual power and intellectual class capacities indicated a permanent conflict between the quest for professional autonomy, on the one hand, and the commodification of professional services in market capitalism, on the other (Gouldner, 1979: 18–27). Consequently, socialism seemed much more conducive to intellectual class formation, because the mechanism of economic exploitation, redistribution, also created a position that intellectuals could occupy as central planners with a monopoly over esoteric, teleological discourse (Djilas, 1957; Konrád and Szelényi, 1979). In both cases, however, we think the analysis of the valorization of cultural capital was limited. Cultural capital is, after all, *discourse.* For discourse to operate as capital, i.e. to be converted and accumulated, *monopoly* – limiting access to non-certified members – is only one condition. The other condition is a certain degree of *generosity.* That is, for discourse to work as capital it must be able to persuade the largest number of speakers to adopt its rules, to speak its language, to employ the perspective it offers, and to pose problems and justify assertions in the way it does (Foucault, 1982; Gouldner, 1979; Rose, 1992). From this perspective, we argue that the Central European intelligentsia became a 'cultural bourgeoisie' and undertook the project of making capitalism and civil society, because they discovered in such a project the possibility of articulating a new and powerfully rational discourse. In the process of transition, the Central European intelligentsia imposed new standards of rationality, and persuaded all other actors to speak the new language that they had invented. It is precisely in this way, that the intelligentsia as a class actor took center-stage in the Central European transition to capitalism (Eyal, 2000).

Marxist and Weberian theories of social change

This understanding of discourse as the basis of intellectual class power has implications for classical Marxist and Weberian theories of social change. Marxist theory explains social change in terms of struggles between antagonistic classes over economic interests, while weberian theory is notoriously vague, offering the nebulous notion of 'charisma' as the revolutionary force in history. In our book, we propose a synthesis and revision of these theories: social change is indeed made by classes in conflict, as Marx argues, but the carrier of social change is usually an intellectual class actor; specifically, intellectuals broach change using cultural capital, which functions in the same way that Weber argues charisma does.

How is cultural capital like charisma? First, because cultural capital occupies a middle position between rank and class, groups defined by the possession of cultural capital may develop collective interests in *either* a stratification order based on rank *or* one based on class. Put another way, intellectuals in any given stratification system always have an interest in the contrary principle of stratification. So, for example, intellectual critiques of socialist rank order were often based on appeals to merit and talent, while intellectual critiques in class societies are often based in ideologies of social closure, such as professional autonomy or academic freedom. Note, however, that in both kinds of stratification order, where intellectuals function as a collective actor, they are marked by a low degree of classness (or 'rankness'). This suggests an explanation of the fundamental yet ephemeral nature of intellectual class power in revolutionary transformation;

because the possessors of cultural capital constitute a weakly formed collective actor, betterformed actors always eventually take their place.[16]

Second, the transformative, charismatic capacity of cultural capital is fundamental to its nature as discourse. Inventing a new kind of discourse tends to have revolutionary consequences because it imposes a new mode of speaking and of perceiving the world; it has the power of 'world-making' (Bourdieu, 1987a; Goodman, 1978) and 'world-destroying'. At the same time that discourse imposes a certain vision of the world as true, it also classifies, names, and invokes new social actors, classes among them. In this way, discourse divides the world into the true and the false, the harbingers of the future and the relics of the past. Those who speak in the old ways suddenly find themselves impugned as immoral and irrational. It is not simply that they articulate a different opinion; they are incompetent in the most profound sense of the term since they do not speak the new discourse – they do not understand the real 'truth'.[17] From this perspective, it becomes clear how cultural capital as discourse can produce radical change, similar to the burst of charisma that Weber described. It is even possible to account for Weber's ambiguous insistence on the importance of the charismatic individual in social change. Discourse, although it is a collective product, tends to consecrate certain spokespersons, virtuosi who embody its charismatic qualities.

Thus, as Weber perceived, a charismatic individual very often triggers the making of intellectual classes and the formulation of transformative discourse; it is difficult to deny the importance of a Mao Tze Tung.

However, just as the role of charisma is temporary – as change is quickly institutionalized and the revolution betrays its sons – so too, the rule of cultural capital is ephemeral. The power of cultural capital is the power of discourse, and discourse, as Foucault explains, cannot be possessed. The power of truth is such that the truthful are also subject to it, and sooner or later, new truths, new versions, and new reflexive twists come to challenge the one Truth. The more it is proclaimed, repeated, and consecrated, the less convincing it is to those conversant with the rules of the Culture of Critical Discourse.

---

16 The possessors of cultural capital are truly Marx's 'universal class' then, since they tend to abolish themselves and their own class rule after the revolution. They might also be understood as Weber's historical 'switchmen', operators who switch civilizations from one form of social structure and principle of stratification to another, but who, when the train has jumped tracks, stay behind. Their class power never lasts. Thus Gouldner was correct when he argued that intellectuals were a 'flawed universal class' but he was wrong about why: he thought they were flawed because they were self-interested and would set up their own class domination; we suggest that they are flawed precisely for the opposite reason, because they are weakly formed as a class and cannot sustain their class rule in the long run (Gouldner, 1979: 83–5).

17 Bourdieu calls this 'symbolic violence' and it appears self-evident that it would characterize the assumption of power by fascists or communists. We would observe, however, that the liberal intellectuals who took power in Central Europe after the fall of communism also tended to be illiberal toward those who disagreed with them: they immediately castigated opponents as incompetent, as relics of the past, as sliding back into communism, or of totalitarianism (for a good example, see Klaus, [1991]1992). It is ironic to find this kind of symbolic violence when the new victorious discourse is a 'liberal' one.

Thus in the transition in Central Europe, as soon as intellectuals fulfill their historic mission and the new social structure is in place, the discursive power of the intellectuals who led the transition becomes less important. Intellectuals are slowly relegated back to their positions as members of a comparatively privileged estate. And as soon as this happens, space is opened up where intellectuals begin to disagree with each other again. They attach themselves to a variety of different classes as organic intellectuals, and a plurality of discourses emerges once again. The classness of intellectuals under these conditions is even lower than it was during the period of transition, and correspondingly their capacity for ethical nuance is greatly enhanced. It is also at this point that the ironic critique that we recommend becomes possible. All this describes the 'universal' nature of the intellectual class, whose rule is based in the enormous but temporary power of cultural capital, and which is therefore bound to abolish itself in the same moment that it becomes dominant.

This reinterpretation and synthesis of theories of social change high-lights Bourdieu's point that classes are first and foremost 'classes on paper'. One should not overemphasize structural conditions in the making of classes; the discursive power of intellectuals, what Bourdieu calls 'symbolic power', is no less important (Bourdieu, 1991). In the transition from socialist rank order to capitalist class society we see this: we find intellectuals playing a crucial role as they name, classify, and make new classes and class positions. While a marxist might argue that intellectuals only *seem* to make classes when in fact they are ideologues who speak for and about classes already formed in the womb of the previous society, we find this unconvincing. Such an analysis may well characterize the role of intellectuals in the French or other classical bourgeois revolutions, but it is manifestly inaccurate for the 1989 revolutions, or indeed for the Bolshevik revolution. No capitalist class preceded the collective action of intellectuals in the post-1989 Central European transitions to capitalism. On the contrary, a capitalist class was invented and called forth by these very intellectuals. We are not being postmodern. We are not arguing that classes simply come into being if you name them, without the necessary structural conditions, but strictly speaking such conditions need not include the existence of classes, even in their embryonic form. Socialist economic systems were in deep structural crisis by the 1980s, and this crisis was the material foundation on which the new critical discourse of the intellectuals was constructed. However, it would be naive and misleading to assume that the nomenklatura was already an embryonic propertied bourgeoisie, and that intellectuals were unwittingly articulating its future interests. It actually required immense imagination to invent the idea of a new bourgeoisie in the context of late communist society. Indeed, if anyone had suggested in 1980 that a transition from socialism to capitalism would occur within 10 years in Eastern Europe, they would have been laughed out of court, even by Western anticommunists and certainly by the finest minds in social science. So, to be very clear: to emphasize the role of discursive power in making classes does not mean that classes are unimportant, nor is it a sophisticated backhanded way of saying that classes are disappearing. Instead, we are proposing a renewal of class analysis that identifies discourse as a central moment in the process of making classes.

Another case: class analysis in 20th-century capitalism

Our rethinking of the class concept and the role of intellectuals in social change also suggests a historical reanalysis of the nature of intellectual class action in Western capitalism. Using our analytical framework, we can expand our analysis of intellectual class action not only as it manifests in bursts of anticapitalist agitation, but also in intellectual efforts to reform and rationalize capitalism.

A case in point is the rise of managerialism in the United States in the early 20th century. As for Burnham (1941), we think the significance of this case is not that managers were poised to take power away from capitalists and establish their own class domination, but rather, that managers aimed to rationalize capitalism by persuading all other class actors to speak the new managerialist discourse (Shenhav, 1999). From this perspective, Berle and Means' (1931) argument and the 60-year debate about ownership and control (Zeitlin, 1974) is beside the point. Managers' power did not rest solely on their ability to *limit* discourse, certainly not initially, and hence the fact of 'control' was not necessarily the most significant dimension of managerial power. Rather, the managerial revolution was about *propagating* and *generalizing* the discourse of managerialism; it was about persuading owners, trade unionists, and everyone else to speak the discourse of managerialism. In this way, managerialism altered the balance of class forces because it inserted managers between capital and labor, reducing the classness of both. The new center of negotiations between owners and workers became 'productivity', and as wage gains became linked to productivity increases (Block and Burns, 1986), managers emerged as 'professionals of productivity' – measuring it, fostering it, organizing in order to attain it, motivating workers to attain it, and so forth. In the same process, the class struggle was decomposed into two component struggles: a struggle between owners and managers over issues of rational management and efficiency, on the one hand, and a struggle between managers and workers over discipline, motivation, and knowledge, on the other. This is the way managers sought to rationalize capitalism, organizing the hegemony of capital in face of opposition by capitalists themselves.

It does not follow then, that simply because managers failed to wrest class power away from capitalists, managerialism is a failed new class project (Martin and Szelényi, 1988). We argue precisely the opposite. Just as the perspective of neoclassical sociology allows us to see the intellectual class as co-founder of capitalism, civil society, and modernity in contemporary Central Europe, so the managerialist movement in the early 20th-century United States can be seen as a successful class project because it effectively imposed its new discourse and altered the balance of class forces by transforming the classness of contending classes. In both cases, the absence of the socialist alternative permits us to think more broadly about the class power of intellectuals and their role in social change. The neoclassical perspective allows us to see that the collective action of intellectuals does not always necessarily point towards the *transcendence* of capitalism, but also towards its *transformation* and *rationalization* into a diversity of forms and destinations.

IV: Is Critical Social Science Possible In The Absence Of A Socialist Alternative?

Does it follow from our analysis that critical social science is impossible? Can we do without the socialist vantage point of classical theory, or do we need to fabricate 'real socialist utopias' to ground a new critical sociology? Our answer is that the disappearance of a socialist alternative is actually a great opportunity for critical social science. It means the disappearance of any obligation or temptation for sociologists (and critical intellectuals in general) to play the role of high priests in some emerging or actual social order. Indeed, we now have the opportunity to turn the postsocialist demotion of intellectual claims and aspirations into an intellectual strength – to embrace the critical power of irony.

This new form of critical imagination is not the whim of a few disgruntled intellectuals. It is an historically determined objective opportunity afforded by the same collective experiences we analyzed above; collective experiences which have transformed many formerly critical intellectuals into ideologues of capitalism, and many others into utopian socialists. We propose that this same experience of disillusionment with 'actually existing socialism' can also inspire a *new form of critical reflection*. This is particularly important at the current moment in which the strong polarities of the embattled, transformative discourse of the transition are dissipating and giving way to a plurality of more nuanced viewpoints. Now we should suspend the attitude of a convert and ask ourselves: If we believed in (democratic, self-managing, humane) socialism for so long but now think we were fundamentally wrong, *is it possible we could be wrong again?* Is the real lesson of the past that we should not take our intellectual infatuations or ourselves too seriously?

In 1961, after just enough time had passed so the polarities of communism's transformative discourse were weakening, Leszek Kolakowski wrote an essay that asked what the role of intellectuals should be in 'mature' communist society. We think his essay is timely again as we inquire into the possibilities for critical social science in the shadow of the fall of socialism.

Kolakowski distinguished three different roles that intellectuals could play: *priest*, *jester*, and *philosopher king*. The priest is usually critical, since he or she specializes in developing a utopian or transcendent vision of a more desirable, more rational, and morally superior society, which is then contrasted with existing society.[18] The priest's is not the only possible critical perspective, however. The jester produces ironic critique, but it differs from priestly ire in that it is oriented empirically rather than morally, and thus it offers immanent rather than transcendent critique.[19] As immanent critique, the jester's

18 As Kolakowski says: '[t]he priest is the guardian of the absolute; he sustains the cult of the final and the obvious as acknowledged by and contained in the tradition' ([1961]1968: 33).

19 As Kolakowski formulates it: '[t]he jester is he who moves in good society without belonging to it, and treats it with impertinence; he who doubts all that appears self-evident. The jester . . . observe[s] . . . from the sidelines in order to unveil the non-obvious behind the obvious, the non-final behind the final . . .' ([1961]1968: 33–4).

analysis never contrasts the present with a vision of a more rational or more just society. Rather, the jester exposes the arbitrariness of the present, emphasizing that what appears rational, inevitable, just, and pure is accidental, temporary, absurd, and hybrid (Jacobs and Smith, 1997). Different from both priest and jester, the philosopher king typifies the intellectual as a ruler who tries to impose on earth the perfect regime envisioned in thought. Like the priest then, the philosopher king offers transcendence, but unlike the priest the philosopher king does not perform a critical role. The jester presents an even sharper contrast with the philosopher king: not only is the jester critical but also empirical, and therefore non-transcendent.

A fourth intellectual role that can be added to Kolakowski's typology is that of an *engineer*, or better, Weber's idea of a *magician* (Weber, [1922]1964; Bourdieu, 1987b). We think this is how most social scientists in the United States see themselves. The magician/engineer is aligned with the jester, in the sense that the technical attitude is also empirical, and is thus opposed to the transcendental stance of the philosopher king and the priest. But the magician/engineer also differs from the jester in several respects. As Weber notes, the magician is strongly constrained by the demands of clients to fulfill specific requests. This is also the situation confronting the engineer. The jester, in contrast, is not answerable to the specific demands of particular clients, but to a *public*. The jester's task is to surprise the public, to formulate ideas they have not imagined, or to state out loud what they are not willing to admit. The only way for the magician or engineer to protect themselves from the demand constraints of clients is through the complexity and esoteric nature of their expertise, their complicated models and technology. Thus magicians/engineers must take themselves and their models very seriously, and this works against their capacity for self-irony. We think this is a fair description of most positivist social science, which although it is the ally of critical neoclassical sociology, has difficulty subjecting its own fundamental assumptions to scrutiny or ironic self-reflection.

Figure 1 is an attempt to systematically summarize our distinctions between different kinds of intellectual roles. Beginning with the typology of roles in Weber's *The Sociology of Religion* ([1922]1964), we follow Bourdieu's (1987b) analysis of the ideal types of priest, philosopher king, magician, and jester to characterize the contemporary field of social science inquiry. This field of cultural production is described by the intersection of two relations. The first relation that defines the field as we have represented it is the contradiction between *critical* and *affirmative* positions. This is the tension between those who are proximate to *temporal power* on the one hand, and by this we mean political power that is extra-intellectual; and those who lay claim to *pastoral power*, on the other hand, which is specifically understood to be intellectual power arising from the command of cultural capital, or as Gouldner might have it, power arising from a superior grasp of and commitment to the Culture of Critical Discourse. The philosopher king and the magician always dabble in temporal power either as dictators, technicians, or partisan advisors. In contrast, the priest and the jester do not aspire to temporal power but articulate a critique of the status quo, which attempts to influence others by sheer intellectual force of argument.

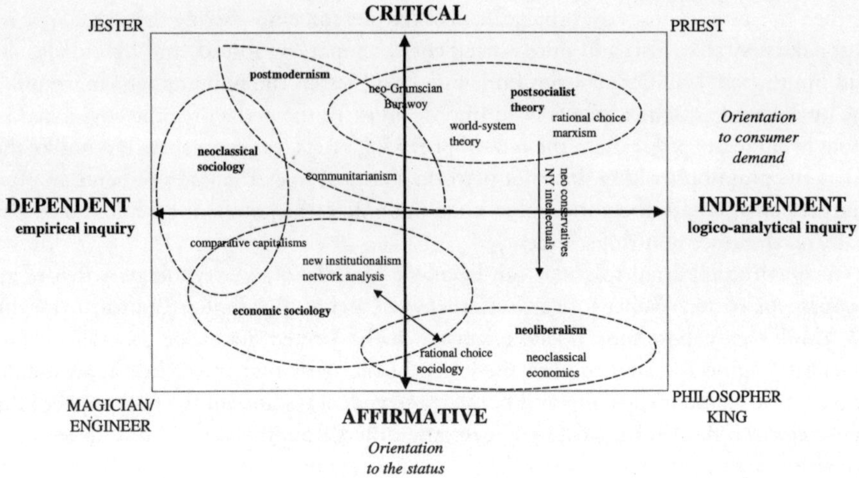

Figure 1. The field of social scientific inquiry in the shadow of the fall of socialism. The prophet does not appear in this figure. Prophecy describes the charisma of cultural capital in periods of social change during which time the social relations in the field of intellectual production are characteristically held in abeyance.

The second relation that structures the field of sociocultural inquiry is the contradictory interests of *suppliers* and *consumers* of cultural 'goods'. By cultural goods, we mean products of intellectual practice such as knowledge, salvation, professional services, technical expertise, or art. In general, suppliers of such goods are interested in *independence from demand*. Suppliers want to shape consumer tastes but they do not want to cater to the demands of specific clients. This is essentially what the priest and philosopher king do, they tell people what they should aspire to or they try to convert them to their vision of otherworldly salvation or pure aesthetic ideals. In contrast, consumers of cultural goods are interested in getting their needs and wishes satisfied. Consumers would like their tastes to shape intellectual production. This describes the context in which magicians (engineers) and jesters work: they cater to popular demand or specific clients by providing this-worldly salvation or entertainment. In contrast to priests and philosopher kings then, jesters and magicians are more *dependent* on client demands.

Once we have defined this field of intellectual production, we can use it to array the classification of various research agendas and academic projects that are at play in the analysis of the transition to capitalism in Central and Eastern Europe, and in the contemporary field of sociohistorical inquiry more generally. We borrow heavily here from Michael Burawoy's new classification of theoretical perspectives, amending it somewhat in light of our disagreements with him.[20] We identify four or five paradigms, acknowledging freely that the edges are blurry, which is why we have drawn them as fuzzy, extended, intersecting ellipses. Indeed, the term 'paradigm' is not really appropriate since each of these groupings refers simultaneously to research programs, concrete groups of intellectuals, and intellectual projects, and the historical trajectories of these programs, intellectuals, and projects, and the interactions of all of these with each other over time. Nonetheless, there is an understanding that these groupings constitute relatively well understood and continuous lines of inquiry, groups of intellectual biographies, and intellectual projects over time.

Beginning with *postsocialist* theory, we would observe that it is critical and utopian since it remains distant from political power and attempts to shape consumers' tastes. The trajectory it has charted in the last century is an upward one from a position closest to the philosopher king to a more priestly role. In its enduring critique of capitalism as well as in its struggles against stalinism and other abuses of actually existing socialism, postsocialist theory remains resolutely opposed to any affirmation of the status quo. At the same time, however, postsocialist theory may be becoming more dependent on consumers' tastes and therefore more empirical in its methods. It has neglected consumers to its own cost in the past, and it now needs to strike alliances with postcolonial and postmodern theories and practitioners who occupy a great deal of the critical space in the field of social scientific inquiry. In contrast to postsocialism, we characterize *neoliberalism* as the contemporary expression of the philosopher king. Thus neoliberal dissidents in Eastern Europe and neoconservative intellectuals in the United States commonly profess to know what is moral, while neoclassical economists and monetarists assert what is true and efficient. As social scientists, many of these intellectuals are not interested in dictating to the world, and this is particularly true as we move out of economics and into the rational choice movement in sociology. While these intellectuals remain relentlessly noncritical, they adopt 'methodological individualism' not because it helps them impose their vision on the world but because it produces empirical results. In this, they display their willingness to cater to consumers' tastes and distinguish themselves from their more theoretically inclined philosopher king-*like* colleagues in neoclassical economics.

Turning next to *neoclassical sociology*, where we locate ourselves, we note that there is wide variation in the orientation to the status quo and therefore a broad range of intellectuals included in this grouping. While some neoclassical analysts are jesters and very critical of the status quo, and here we think of a writer like Foucault, other neoclassical analysts are more affirmative, more willing to connect with temporal power and play the role of technicians. What unites these positions, however, is the rejection of any intellectual claim to represent others or to tell them what to do. Neoclassical sociology claims to provide tools for analysis that are useful for social actors, either because they dispel mystifications or because they allow social actors to measure, calculate, and explain their lives and social worlds.

---

20 These are taken from a course syllabus to be taught at Central European University this year, which Michael Burawoy has kindly shared with us. On our disagreements, see note 5.

Similar to critical neoclassical sociology, *postmodernism* at its best displays a commitment to immanent critique, without claiming to represent social actors or consumers. The danger of postmodern critique, however, is a collapse into cynicism. We understand the distinction between irony and cynicism to be that irony is dialogic, while cynicism is monologic. Cynicism does not think that there is anybody to talk to but irony wishes to dislodge the interlocutors from their received truths in order to converse further. That is why postmodernism is located between independence from and dependence upon consumers. On the one hand, postmodernism is not interested in shaping consumer taste, but on the other hand, it is also not willing to listen or cater to clients; this is particularly true of the more obscure side of cultural studies. Nonetheless, postmodernism is generally critical, although some of its 'everything goes' rhetoric is likely to descend into an affirmation of the status quo. Hence we have represented postmodernism diagonally in the social scientific field.

To these four 'paradigms' taken from Burawoy's recent classification, we add the fifth grouping of *economic sociology*. In many respects, we think this is a more important paradigm in the space of inquiry engaged by the fall of socialism than is 'postmodernism'. (Indeed, we include postmodernism with some misgivings, since in many respects in this particular representation 'postmodernism' is the critical side of economic sociology. After all, both share the attempt to avoid the antinomies of modernity and to find a 'third way' between market and plan, rationality and irrationality, etc.) We also include arrows on Figure 1 to convey a sense of dynamism, as individuals and concepts travel on certain trajectories. For example, the neoconservatives are shown as having descended from critical to affirmative space in the field as they traveled the road from Trotskyism to neoliberalism over the course of the 20th century. Arrows also denote certain transactions across boundaries; so for example, some of the concepts of economic sociology and rational choice theory are 'paired concepts', each mirroring the other and thus reinforcing both.

Reviewing the current possibilities in the field of sociocultural inquiry represented in Figure 1, we argue that in the shadow of the end of socialism neoclassical sociology and the ironic method offer the most compelling and fruitful vantage point for a critical social science. Importantly, we feel comfortable with irony because it disengages us from a universalistic moral stance. While the priest may argue that we are morally irresponsible, we respond that the position of the jester is more rigorous than that of the priest, since the jester follows a situated ethics of responsibility as distinct from the priest's overarching ethics of conviction (Weber, [1906]1958: 143). What the priest labels irresponsible is precisely what we understand to be the ironic capacity to appreciate one's mistakes. The jester's best jest is always aimed at him- or herself. The jester never takes him- or herself too seriously, so his or her critical position is therefore more flexible and open to nuance than the priest's can ever be. However noble the priest's intentions, he or she cannot escape the burden of persuading people that the ethical superiority of the utopian future is worth certain sacrifices. In contrast, the promise of neoclassical sociology as ironic critique is simply that the critical theorist will not turn his or her gaze away from the sacrifices being made at each step of the way. He or she will not push the flock ahead to the Promised Land, but will take pains to describe the social costs of each step and who will bear them. This means that the critical social scientist must attend to the openness of the present, to the multiple trajectories it contains – as in the framework of 'multiple capitalisms'.

To be clear: the task of the critical theorist is to describe and appraise the possible alternative trajectories of social development empirically; to show that what exists is not inevitable; that alternative forms of conduct are open to social actors; to elucidate the costs and consequences of these forms of conduct; and to do all this without positing which of them is correct or desirable. A critical scientific social theory leaves it to social actors themselves to weigh whether or not they are willing to pay the costs of particular courses of action. Put another way, ironic critique aims to expose the arbitrariness of the present, uncovering its hybrid and accidental origins (Foucault, 1977; Graham et al. 1991) without trying to dictate to social actors what to do. The purpose of such irony is to enrich public dialogue by casting doubt on what was taken for granted before the dialogue began; this is precisely the role of the jester. As Habermas (1972) contends, the human interest represented by social science is critical communication – a project of exchange and dialogue between social scientists and social actors that is meant to increase rationality, in part, by increasing the reflexive capacities of social actors. Irony serves the social scientist well in such an endeavor, since it requires him or her to engage in constant autocritique, not to take him- or herself too seriously, and to remain open to dialogic possibilities.

References

Ashton, T. H. and Philpin, C. H. E., eds. (1985) *The Brenner Debate: agrarian class structure and economic development in pre-industrial Europe.* Cambridge: Cambridge University Press.

Åslund, Anders (1995) *How Russia Became a Market Economy.* Washington, DC: Brookings Institution.

Bakunin, Nikolai (1966) 'Marx, the Bismarck of Socialism', in L. Krimmerman and L. Perry (eds) *Patterns of Anarchy.* New York: Anchor Books.

Bell, Daniel (1973) *The Coming of Post-Industrial Society. A venture in social forecasting.* New York: Basic Books.

Berle, Adolf and Means, Gardiner C. (1931) *The Modern Corporation and Private Property.* New York: Harcourt, Brace, Jovanovich.

Block, Fred and Burns, Gene A. (1986) 'Productivity as a Social Problem: The Uses and Misuses of Social Indicators', *American Sociological Review* 51(6): 757–80.

Bonnell, Vicky [Victoria E.] (1999) 'Russia's New Entrepreneurs', Paper presented at the Carnegie Project Workshop, October, University of California, Berkeley.

Bourdieu, Pierre ([1983]1986) 'The Forms of Capital', in John G. Richardson (ed.) *Handbook of Theory and Research for the Sociology of Education.* New York: Greenwood Press: 15–29.

Bourdieu, Pierre (1987a) *In Other Words – Essays Towards a Reflexive Sociology.* Cambridge: Polity Press.

Bourdieu, Pierre (1987b) 'Legitimation and Structured Interests in Weber's Sociology of Religion', in Scott Lash and S. Whimster (eds) *Max Weber, Rationality and Modernity*. London: Allen & Unwin: 119–139.

Bourdieu, Pierre (1991) "The Social Space and Genesis of Classes", in *Language and Symbolic Domination*. Cambridge, MA: Harvard University Press: 229–251.

Brint, Steven (1984) " 'New Class' and Cumulative Trend. Explanations of the Liberal Political Attitudes of Professionals", *American Journal of Sociology* 90(1): 30–71.

Burawoy, Michael (1996) 'The state and economic involution – Russia through a China lens', *World Development* 24(6): 1105–17.

Burawoy, Michael (2001) 'Neoclassical Sociology: From the End of Communism to the End of Classes, *American Journal of Sociology* 106: 1099–1120.

Burawoy, Michael and Krotov, Pavel (1992) 'The Soviet Transition from Socialism to Capitalism: Worker Control and Economic Bargaining in the Wood Industry', *American Sociological Review* 57(1): 16–38.

Burnham, James (1941) *The Managerial Revolution: What is happening in the world*. New York: Day.

Callon, Michel (1998) 'Introduction: The Embeddedness of Economic Markets in Economics', in *The Laws of the Markets*. Oxford: Blackwell: 1–57.

Collins, Randall (1979) *The Credential Society. An historical sociology of education and stratification*. New York: Academic Press.

Djilas, Milovan (1957) *The New Class – An Analysis of the Communist System*. New York: Holt, Rinehart & Winston.

Dobb, Maurice Herbert (1946) *Studies in the Development of Capitalism*. London: Routledge & Kegan Paul.

Dore, Ronald Philip (1973) *British Factory, Japanese Factory: the Origins of National Diversity in Industrial Relations*. London: Allen & Unwin.

Evans, Peter (1979) *Dependent Development: The Alliance of Multinational State, and Local Capital in Brazil*. Princeton, NJ: Princeton University Press.

Eyal, Gil (2000) 'Anti-politics and the Spirit of Capitalism: Dissidents, Monetarists, and the Czech Transition to Capitalism', *Theory and Society* 29(1): 49–92.

Eyal, Gil, Iván Szelényi and Eleanor Townsley (1997) 'Capitalism Without Capitalists: The Remaking of the Economic Institutions of State-Socialism', *New Left Review* 222 (March/April): 60–92.

Eyal, Gil, Iván Szelényi and Eleanor Townsley (1998) *Making Capitalism Without Capitalists. Class Formation and Elite Struggles in Post-communist Central Europe*. London etc: Verso.

Eyal, Gil, Iván Szelényi and Eleanor Townsley (2001) 'The utopia of post-socialist theory and the ironic view of history in neo-classical sociology', *American Journal of Sociology* 106(4): 1121–1128.

Fish, Steven M. (1998) 'The Determinants of Economic Reform in the Post-Communist World', *East European Politics and Societies* 12(1): 31–78.

Fligstein, Neil (1996) 'Markets as Politics – a Political-cultural Approach to Market Institutions', *American Sociological Review* 61(4): 656–73.

Fligstein, Neil (July 1997) 'Is Globalization the Cause of the Crises of Welfare States?', Sociology Departmental Colloquium, University of California, Berkeley.

Foucault, Michel (1977) "Nietzsche, Genealogy and History", in D. F. Bouchard (ed.) *Language, Counter-Memory, Practice. Selected Essays and Interviews.* Chicago Il.: University of Chicago Press: 139–164.

Foucault, Michel (1982) 'The Subject and Power', in Hubert L. Dreyfus and Paul Rabinow (eds) *Michel Foucault: Beyond Structuralism and Hermeneutics.* Chicago, IL: University of Chicago Press: 208–225.

Gates, Jeffrey R. (1998) *The Ownership Solution. Toward a shared capitalism for the twenty-first century.* London etc.: Allen Lane, Penguin.

Giddens, Anthony (1973) *The Class Structure of Advanced Societies.* London: Hutchinson University Library.

Giddens, Anthony (1998) *The Third Way.* Cambridge: Polity Press.

Goodman, Nelson (1978) *Ways of World-making.* Indianapolis, IN: Hackett.

Graham Burchell, Colin Gordon and Peter Miller eds. (1991) *The Foucault Effect: Studies in Governmentality.* With two lectures by and an Interview with Michael Focault. Chicago, IL: University of Chicago Press.

Gouldner, Alvin (1970) *The Coming Crisis of Western Sociology.* New York: Baric Books.

Gouldner, Alvin (1979) *The Future of the Intellectuals and the Rise of the New Class: A frame of reference, theses, conjectures, arguments and an historical perspective on the role of intellectuals and intelligentsia in the international class contest of the modern era.* London Macmillan.

Granovetter, Mark (1985) 'Economic Action and Social Structure: The Problem of Embeddedness', *American Journal of Sociology* 91(3): 481–510.

Habermas, Jürgen (1972) *Knowledge and Human Interests.* Boston, MA: Beacon Press.

Habermas, Jürgen (1990) *The Philosophical Discourse of Modernity: Twelve Lectures.* Cambridge, MA: MIT Press.

Hanley, Eric, King, Lawrence P. and Toth, István János (2002) 'The State, International Agencies, and Property Transformation in Postcommunist Hungary', *American Journal of Sociology* 108(1): 129–167.

Harvey, David (1989) *The Condition of Post-Modernity: An Enquiry into the Origins of Cultural Change.* Oxford: Blackwell.

Hirst, Paul and Thompson, Graham (1996) *Globalization in Question. The International Economy and the Possibilities of Governance.* Cambridge, Polity Press.

Holton, R. J. (1985) *The Transition from Feudalism to Capitalism.* London: Basingstoke.

Hutcheon, Linda (1992) 'The Power of Postmodern Irony', in *Genre Trope Gender. Essays by Northrop Frye, Linda Hutcheon, and Shirley Neuman.* Ottawa, Canada: Carleton University Press for the Department of English, Carleton University.

Hutcheon, Linda (1995) *Irony's Edge: The Theory and Politics of Irony.* London: Routledge

Inglehart, Ronald and Rabier, Jacques-René (1986) 'Political Realignment in Advanced Industrial Society: From Class-based Politics to Quality-of-Life Politics', *Government and Opposition* 21(4): 456–79.

Jacobs, Ronald N. and Smith, Philip (1997) 'Romance, Irony, and Solidarity', *Sociological Theory* 15(1): 60–80.

King, Lawrence P. (2001) *The Basic Features of Post-Communist Capitalism in Eastern Europe. Firms in Hungary, the Czech Republic and Slovakia.* Westport, CT: Praeger.

Klaus, Václav ([1991]1992) 'Challenges of the Transformation Process: Lessons to be Learned from the Czechoslovak Experience', Lecture given at the Institute for

Economic Affairs, London, March 1991, pp. 11–15 in his *Dismantling Socialism: A Preliminary Report (A Road to Market Economy II)*. Prague: Top Agency.
Kocka, Jürgen (1993) *Bourgeois Society in 19th Century Europe*. Oxford etc.: Berg.
Kolakowski, Leszek ([1961]1968) 'The Priest and the Jester', in *Toward a Marxist Humanism. Essays on the Left Today*. New York: Grove Press: 9–37.
Konrád, George and Szelényi, Iván (1979) *The Intellectuals on the Road to Class Power*. New York: Harcourt, Brace, Jovanovich.
Machajski, Waclaw (1937) 'On the Expropriation of the Capitalists', in V. F. Calverton (ed.) *The Making of Society. An Outline of Sociology*. New York: Modern Library: 427–436.
Mann, Michael (1997) 'Has Globalization Ended the Rise and Rise of the Nation-state?', *Review of International Political Economy* 4(3): 472–96.
Mannheim, Karl ([1936]1985) *Ideology and Utopia. An Introduction to the Sociology of Knowledge*. New York: Harcourt, Brace, Jovanovich.
Martin, Bill and Szelényi, Iván (1988) 'Three Waves of New Class Theory', *Theory and Society* 17: 645–67.
Meyer, John and Rowan, Brian (1977) 'Institutionalized Organizations: Formal Structure as Myth and Ceremony', *American Journal of Sociology* 83(2): 340–63.
Mommsen, Wolfgang (1984) *Max Weber and German Politics, 1890–1920*. Chicago, IL: Chicago University Press.
Nomad, Max (1937) 'Masters, old and new', in V. F. Calverton (ed.) *The Making of Society*. New York: Modern Library.
Nomad, Max (1959) *Aspects of Revolt*. New York: Bookman Associates.
O'Donnell, Guillermo A. and Schmitter, Philippe eds. (1986) *Transitions from Authoritarian Rule: Comparative Perspectives*. Baltimore, MD: Johns Hopkins University Press.
Ohmae, Kenichi (1995) *The End of the Nation State: The Rise of Regional Economies*. London: Harper Collins.
Pakulski, Jan and Waters, Malcolm (1996) *The Death of Class*. London: Sage.
Polanyi, Karl ([1944]1957) *The Great Transformation: The Political and Economic Origins of our Time*. Boston, MA: Beacon Press.
Polanyi, Karl (1957) 'The Economy as an Instituted Process', in Karl Polanyi, Conrad M. Arensberg and Harry W. Pearson (eds.) *Trade and Market in the Early Empires*. Glencoe, ILL: The Free Press.
Reich, Robert P. (1992) *The Work of Nations: Preparing ourselves for 21st-century capitalism*. New York: Vintage.
Rose, Nikolas (1992) 'Engineering the Human Soul: Analyzing Psychological Expertise', *Science in Context* 5(2): 351–69.
Roth, Guenther (1971) 'Max Weber's Comparative Approach and Historical Typology', in I. Vallier (ed.) *Comparative Methods in Sociology*. Berkeley: University of California Press: 75–93.
Rothschild, Joseph (1989) *Return to Diversity: a Political History of East Central Europe since World War II*. New York: Oxford University Press.
Schluchter, Wolfgang (1985) *The Rise of Western Rationalism: Max Weber's Developmental History*. Los Angeles: University of California Press.
Schmidt, Vivien A. (1995) 'The New World Order, Incorporated: The Rise of Business and the Decline of the Nation-State', *Daedalus* 124(2): 75–106.

Schumpeter, Joseph A. ([1942]1976) *Capitalism, Socialism and Democracy*. New York: Harper Perennial.
Shenhav, Yehouda A. (1999) *Manufacturing Rationality: The Engineering Foundations of the Managerial Revolution*. Oxford: Oxford University Press.
Simon, Herbert (1982) *Models of Bounded Rationality: 1. Economic Analysis and Public Policies*. Cambridge, MA: MIT Press.
Staniszkis, Jadwiga (1991) "Political Capitalism in Poland", *East European Politics and Societies* 5(1): 127–41.
Stark, David (1992) "Path Dependence and Privatization Strategies in East Central Europe", *East European Politics and Societies* 6(1): 17–54.
Stark, David (1996) 'Recombinant Property in East European Capitalism', *American Journal of Sociology* 101(4): 993–1027.
Stiglitz, Joseph E. (1999) *State Versus Market: Have Asian Currency Crises Affected The Reform Debate?* Dhaka: Bangladesh Economic Association.
Sweezy, Paul (1942) *The Theory of Capitalist Development: Principles of Marxian Political Economy*. New York: Oxford University Press.
Szelényi, Iván (1988) *Socialist Entrepreneurs. Embourgoisement in rural Hungary*. Madison: Wisconsin University Press.
Wagner, Peter (1994) *A Sociology of Modernity, Liberty and Discipline*. London: Routledge.
Wallerstein, Immanuel (2000) 'Globalization or the Age of Transition? A Long-Term View of the Trajectory of the World-System', *International Sociology* XV(2): 249–65.
Weber, Max ([1903–17]1949) *The Methodology of the Social Sciences*, ed. and trans. by Edward A. Shils and Henry A. Finch. New York: Free Press.
Weber, Max ([1904–5]1958) *The Protestant Ethic and the Spirit of Capitalism*, translated by Talcott Parsons. New York: Scribner.
Weber, Max ([1906]1958) 'Capitalism and Rural Society in Germany', 363–85 in H. H. Gerth and C. Wright Mills (eds) *From Max Weber*. New York: Oxford University Press.
Weber, Max ([1922]1978) *Economy and Society. An Outline of Interpretive Sociology*, edited by G. Roth and C. Wittich. Berkeley, Los Angeles, London: University of California Press 2 vols.
Weber, Max ([1922]1964) *The Sociology of Religion*. Boston, MA: Beacon Press.
Weber, Max ([1927]1981) *General Economic History*. New Brunswick, NJ: Transaction Books.
Weber, Max ([1905–6, 1917]1995) *The Russian Revolutions*, ed. and trans. Gordon C. Wells and Peter Baehr. Ithaca, NY: Cornell University Press.
Weiss, Linda (1998) *The Myth of the Powerless State*. Ithaca, NY: Cornell University Press.
White, Harrison C. (1992) *Identity and Control: A Structural Theory of Social Action*. Princeton, NJ: Princeton University Press.
Williams, Raymond (1980) *Problems of Materialism and Culture. Selected Essays*. London: Verso.
Woodruff, David (1999) *Money Unmade: Barter and the Fate of Russian Capitalism*. Ithaca, NY: Cornell University Press.
Zeitlin, Maurice (1974) 'Corporate Ownership and Control: the Large Corporation and the Capitalist Class', *American Journal of Sociology* 79(5): 1073–1119.

III.2 The New Capitalism in Eastern Europe: Towards a Comparative Political Economy of Post-Communism

Lawrence P. King and Iván Szelényi

Introduction

In the first edition of Smelser-Swedberg's Handbook (1994) we wrote a chapter under the title "The Socialist Economic System." This paper can be read as a follow up, or a new section of the previous one since our aim now is to describe the economic systems which have emerged with the sudden collapse (as happened in Eastern Europe) or gradual erosion (as is currently the case in East Asia) of the socialist economic system. The chapter in the first edition was about the emergence of a distinctive social structure and economy that accompanied development under the Soviet model of total state ownership and "rational- redistribution," whereby party bureaucrats setting a plan move resources (especially capital and labor) around the economy (Kornai 1980). This produced a tendency towards a shortage economy, and the formation of a privileged class of intellectuals (composed of bureaucrats, technocrats, and humanistic intellectuals) that disproportionately benefited from state redistribution relative to workers (Konrad and Szelényi 1979). The chapter in this second edition describes the new systems that have emerged in the postcommunist world and the reform communist systems of East Asia, which all have developed increasingly capitalist social structures based on the growing dominance of private property and market-integration, above all in capital and labor markets.

Our analysis demonstrates the overwhelming conditioning power of social structures – including intra-elite structures – in processes of economic change. The emergent post-communist systems have several features that distinguish them from capitalists systems we know from East Asia, from the North-Atlantic region, or from the old periphery of the capitalist system before the fall of communism. Whether the unique features identified below are only transition phenomena, and eventually postcommunist capitalisms will merge with the rest of the capitalist world into one unified system, remains to be seen. A growing literature has detailed the persistent differences between capitalist systems, most typically the differences between East Asian "state-led" capitalism, Anglo-Saxon "market-led" forms, and Northern European "negotiated or consensual" capitalisms (see Thurow 1992; Hart 1992, Marquand 1997; Coates 2000). It is reasonable to assume, therefore, that the rather different trajectories former communist societies take during the process of transition may be consequential for the structure of their socio-economic systems once they are consolidated.

Whether the postcommunist world is converging toward a single form of capitalism under the impact of strong forces of globalization, or the future is a multiplicity of capitalist socio-economic organizations, is in itself an intriguing question. Some of us (Fligstein 1996; Stark and Bruszt, 1998, 2001; Nee 1998; Eyal, Szelényi and Townsley 1998, 2001; King 2001a, 2001b, 2002) suggested in earlier publications that the core of the classical concern of comparative macro-sociology, namely the cross systemic comparison between capitalism and socialism, should be substituted by a "neo-classical"[1] research program, which focuses on "comparative capitalisms." Michael Burawoy (2001a) challenged this position, seeing capitalism as a unitary system. Indeed, both from the prespective of world system theory and that of neo-classical economics the multiplicity of capitalisms makes little sense (ironically these otherwise so different approaches seem to converge when it comes to the characteristics of contemporary capitalism). From this perspective, there is a single logic of capitalism, since, as Burawoy puts it, capitalism "erases the past." From this perspective path-dependency in the transition to capitalism may be real, but it is relatively unimportant and will vanish with the consolidation of capitalism.

One also may wonder whether all former communist states can be simply called "capitalist," or whether some or even all constitute a new form of socio-economic organization somewhere between capitalism and socialism. Some scholars, most prominently David Stark (1992), insist that the term "transition" is inaccurate. From this perspective, the reality of postcommunism is not that capitalism is being built *on* the ruins of socialism. Rather, a new system is emerging built *with* the ruins of socialism, combining features of socialism and capitalism. Stark argued that individual private property has not been sufficiently formed in Central Europe, creating a system dominated by what he calls "recombinant property," which is neither private property nor state ownership, and which is integrated by networks as opposed to markets (Stark 1996; Stark and Bruszt 1998). While the evidence indicates that Stark was too hasty to pass judgement (see Hanley, King and Toth 2002). This implies that there are limitations to the extent that the new postcommunist economies are indeed capitalist. Many observers (including Burawoy and Krotov (1992)) have pointed out how poorly market institutions have developed in Russia, drawing attention to the pervasive role of barter in economic exchange. Andrew Walder (1995) criticized the market transition theory of Victor Nee (1989), for not realizing that in China, redistribution, rather than being replaced by markets, is decentralized to the local level. As a result, the continuity with communist economic system is much stronger than market transition theory implies. Victor Nee himself slightly revised his 1989 "market transition" thesis by pointing out the "hybrid"

1 It is "neo-classical" because it is concerned with the origin and functioning of capitalism, the questions that occupied the "founding fathers" of sociology (Marx, Weber and Durkheim) and is inspired by Weber's emphasis on the multiplicities of capitalist forms. In this respect neo-classical sociology is the polar opposite of neo-classical economics, which operates with the assumption of a unified capitalist system.

character of Chinese economy (Nee 1992), although he maintained that China was moving in the direction of full capitalism.

Some, however, argue that none of the postcommunist systems approximate the "ideal type" of modern rational capitalism (see Eyal, Szelényi, and Townsley 1998; King 2002). In Central Europe individual private property may not have been formed to the extent we know it from the West (Eyal and co-authors call it "capitalism without capitalists"). In Russia and some other post-Soviet states the market institutions may be rather underdeveloped (Eyal and co-authors labeled this "capitalists without capitalism"). In China, given the political monopoly of the Communist Party, and lack of progress made in privatizing state and collectively owned industries, it may be problematic to talk about capitalism at all. Rather, China may have a "socialist mixed economy," in which capitalism is primarily being built from "below."

In this paper we bracket these two issues. While none of the former communist systems offers a close approximation to the ideal type of capitalism, they certainly are on their way from socialist redistributive economies to market capitalist systems. In all countries (arguably with the exception of North Korea) we see clear trends of the formation of private property, the making of market institutions and the emergence of stratification system based on class. While we believe the postcommunist world can be analyzed as examples of capitalism, we do not accept Burawoy's critique. While the communist systems were undergoing convergence with each other, the postcommunist world is undergoing a clear divergence – both politically and economically (see EBRD[2] 1999). However, even if world system theory or neo-classical economics are right, and eventually capitalism will converge into one single system, the process of such convergence will last long enough to make the study of diverse trajectories or pathways from communism to capitalism of sufficient intellectual interest.

Instead of dealing with these two interesting, but meta-theoretical questions, this paper will focus on two sets of issues. First, we review what are the unique features of the transition from communism to capitalism; to what extent and in what ways is this transition different from previous historical instances of transitions to market economies? Second, we will offer an attempt to develop a comparative political economy of various forms of postcommunist capitalism.[3]

---

2 EBRD = European Bank for Reconstruction and Development.

3 The transition from communism to capitalism, from socialist-redistributive economies to market integrated systems, is largely uncharted territory. This chapter does not offer a review of every important piece of research in these areas, although it does make reference to many of the most influential works. This chapter can therefore be complimented by a review of the publications of the World Bank and the European Bank for Reconstruction and Development on the transition, most prominently the latter's additions of the *Transition Report*, as well as its newsletter (Transition Newsletter) put out jointly with The William Davidson Institute at the University of Michigan Business School. The latter also has hundreds of very useful working papers, almost all using original data (see http://www.wdi.bus.umich.edu). Of course, as social scientists we should keep in mind the basic facts of the sociology of knowledge, the EBRD is a bank which is both a member bank of the World Bank, and which is actually a fairly substantial investor in the transition economies. In the official publications of the World Bank and the EBRD, there is a clearly discernable

In this analysis, we describe three ideal-typical paths by which capitalism has emerged from communism. In some countries capitalism emerged "from below," by the creation of a new, market integrated private (and "hybrid") sector in the shadow of the old socialist redistributive economy. In this scenario, a new capitalist class emerges "from below" – from actors that emerged in the non-planned sector of the economy. China is the most obvious example. In other countries, capitalism is created with a revolution "from above," in a process where state elites try to transform the old socialist redistribute economy into a market capitalist system by following the neoliberal economist's "blueprint" (see Stark 1992). In this path, the new capitalist class emerges "from above" to the extent that neoliberal policy enables the nomenklatura (and its clients) to transform itself into a grand bourgeoisie. This is Russia's path. Finally, there have been attempts to make capitalism "from without." In these systems elites also try to follow the neoliberal blueprint with a major exception; rather than allowing the nomenklatura (or its clients) to privatize large State Owned Enterprises (SOEs), they rely on foreign ownership and cooperation with multinationals. Hungary is the exemplar of this path.

These pathways produce different outcomes. Those countries that followed "capitalism from without" have created an economy where market institutions are highly developed and economies are well integrated into the world economy. We call this system "liberal capitalism." "Capitalism from below" also creates market-integrated systems, but they rely more on relatively small domestic capitalist (or "hybrid") enterprises co-existing with a large state owned sector, which is increasingly market- dependent (and thus "state capitalist"). Because of the existence of non-capitalist property forms integrated by markets (hybrid and state capitalist), we call this "hybrid capitalism." "Capitalism from above" results in a "patrimonial" system. In such systems patron-client relationships pervade the economy: between the state and enterprises, as well as between management and labor. In patrimonial systems, the redistributive institutions are destroyed, to be replaced by economic activity deeply embedded in reciprocity and networks in addition

perspective from which much of the analysis is cast (it is from a financial investor's point of view [which, according to Nobel laureate Joseph E. Stiglitz (2002) among many others (e.g. Gowan 1995), has a bias in favor of preserving the value of money and the repayment of loans over other features of transition, such as the minimization of poverty or unemployment]. The excellent but far less numerous publications of the United Nations Development Program (especially the Human Development Reports on the FSU (= Florida State University) and East Europe) offers a very useful contrasting perspective in these regards. Similarly, social scientists should be even more careful than usual in using postcommunist official statistics (see the very useful paper by Filer and Hanousek [2001] for an extended discussion of reliability and validity issues, as well as a compilation of country websites and a list of firm-level data sets).

Finally, for those wishing to use this chapter as a reference to all of the economic sociology of postcommunist society, there is a good deal of economic sociology of postcommunist countries that we do not address, such as comparative welfare institutions (Haney 2002), gender and racial stratification and poverty (Kligman and Szelényi 2002, Fodor 2002), and patterns of consumption (Davis 2000). A more comprehensive typology of postcommunist capitalism might well incorporate these dimensions.

to market integration. Businesses cancel each other's debts, use local monies, and engage in barter.

We believe it is far from accidental why countries built capitalism in these different ways. The path taken can be explained by the divergent constellation of class forces and inter- and intra-class struggles (Eyal, Szelényi and Townsley 1998; King 2001a, 2001b, 2002). The pattern of class conflict and constellations are significantly affected by historical and cultural heritages, as well as differences in the level of economic development, the geographic proximity to the core capitalist economies, and especially the timing of industrialization and its articulation with the development of nationalism (see King 2001b). These factors can be thought of as creating the opportunity structure in which class formation, coalition building, and conflict take place.

1/ Unique features of the transition from communism to capitalism

Arguably, the transition from communism to capitalism is strikingly different from all previous transitions to capitalism in two ways. It is the first case in history when capitalism emerged from a system, which did not know the institution of private ownership and in which a class of private proprietors did not exist. It is also the first instance in history when capitalism emerges from a non-capitalist economy where capital accumulation already took place, and in which industrialization was more or less completed.

a/ Making capitalism without capitalists

Karl Marx was arguably quite correct when he suggested that "within the wombs" of a decaying mode of production, the "embryo" of the new mode of production is already formed. While it can be debated whether this proposition holds for all transitions[4], it certainly seems to be true – prior to the fall of communism – for all instances of transition to capitalism. Indeed, in the classical case of transition, the transition from feudalism to capitalism in Europe, private ownership emerges first.

Feudal lords often gradually transform themselves into private landlords, and a propertied bourgeois class emerges (in England, of capitalist tenant farmers) and market integration of the economy gradually gains ground. Even the French revisionist historians, who challenge the Marxian thesis that the French revolution can be accurately understood as the struggle of the bourgeoisie against the aristocracy, do not doubt that a propertied bourgeoisie and the institution of private ownership existed well before the revolution.

Socialism, however, was conceived as a negation of capitalism. Therefore actually existing socialist societies were great experiments in operating a socio-economic system without the basic institution of capitalism: private ownership. In all instances the tran-

4 Perry Anderson for instance – under some weberian influence – in *Passages from Antiquity to Feudalism* (1974) considers the possibility that feudalism may not have been born "within the wombs" of Antiquity, but rather can be best understood as some sort of merger of the "Germanic form" with "Antiquity").

sition to socialism occurred in societies which eliminated some time ago the institution of private property, and eliminated the class of the propertied grand bourgeoisie as well. All major – and often not only the major – means of production were nationalized. Former owners were sent into re-education camps, jailed, killed, sent into exile, or in the best case scenario tolerated at the very margins of the society, stripped of their private wealth. Even the middle and small bourgeoisie was usually eliminated, or at least greatly constrained. Few of the shopkeepers, merchants, and artisans could continue their individual businesses. They were forced to become state employees and work in government owned and managed large operations, or they were forced to join so called "producers cooperatives." In most countries the same thing happened even to the peasantry.

In terms of property and class relations actually existing socialism was indeed a radical negation of any form of known capitalism. Markets were less radically erased. After initial attempts to get rid of markets and monetary institutions most socialist economies did allow some room for the operation of market mechanisms. As socialism progressed from Stalinism to reform communism, market forces began to gain some ground. Market forces, however, were typically limited to the sphere of consumption and not the allocation of capital goods. Preciously little or no price regulating markets were allowed to operate. For example, the "non-market trade of labor" was a widely known phenomenon. Thus labor power did take the form of a commodity, but its price was administratively set and was sheltered in this way from the forces of supply and demand. With rare exceptions socialist economies were economies of "shortage" (Kornai, 1980). This was observable in the non-market trade for labor: unemployment was the exception and labor shortage was the rule.

Even in the most reform-oriented countries, Hungary and Poland, and even until the very fall of communism, private ownership was limited to consumer goods, and markets to the sphere of consumption. There was no capitalist class in the making, and there were no signs of accumulation of private capital. This is not to say that there were no differences in terms of wealth across groups or classes of the population. As reform progressed the bureaucratic estate, or "caste," began to "commodify" its bureaucratic privileges (Manchin and Szelényi, 1987). Real estate may have been the most important vehicle to accumulate some private wealth. Members of the nomenklatura began to build privately owned housing – usually of modest, but occasionally of high quality – with government subsidies for themselves and/or for their children. One also can find evidence of other instances of such proto-accumulation of private capital: the purchase of luxury cars, the collection of valuable artwork, the opening of secret bank accounts in Western countries. Some "proper" capital accumulation also took place in the "second economy" by the emergent new socialist petty bourgeoisie in some reform communist countries (more in Hungary, than elsewhere). Finally, during the terminal illness of state socialism some of the smartest members of the nomenklatura tried to find ways to transform their "right to control" into individual private property. In Hungary and Poland in 1988 a process of "spontaneous" privatization got under way (Vozka 1993; Hankiss 1990, Staniszkis 1991). In Russia, during the perestroika period, the nomenklatura attempted to accumulate wealth by funneling state resources to the newly legalized cooperative sectors, especially new banks [often established by Komsomol members (the future oligarchs) and older communist party aparatchiks (see Hoffman 2002)]. If the collapse of communism had not occurred in 1989, and the system would have continued functioning for a few more decades, the nomenklatura might have undergone a similar transformation to the one experienced by the feudal aristocracy in Western Europe.

But the fall of communism came far too fast. Most of the economy was not affected by spontaneous privatization. With very few exceptions the reform communist new petty bourgeoisie did not have enough time and opportunity to accumulate enough private ownership to become a major player after the fall of communism. The individual wealth accumulated in consumer goods (or smuggled into Western bank accounts) typically also remained rather trivial and hardly was enough to qualify its possessor as a new "grand bourgeois." Thus it is reasonable to claim that it was during the transition from communism to capitalism that capitalism was made on the ruins (or with the ruins) of a system which did not know the institution of private ownership and in which no propertied bourgeoisie existed.

But is this of any significance? Does it matter, what the pre-capitalist class relations were for the development of capitalism? Contra Burawoy and neo-classical economic accounts, we believe it has a major impact on the kinds of trajectories countries take after the fall of communism. Because of the exceptional weakness of the bourgeoisie during late state socialism, the early stages of postcommunist capitalism has to operate with some sort of "substitute bourgeoisie." We will argue in the second half of this paper that what kind of "substitute bourgeoisie" becomes hegemonic will have a major impact on which of the three trajectories to capitalism postcommunist countries will follow.

In countries that follow "capitalism from above" the former communist nomenklatura is likely to be such a "substitute bourgeoisie." This segment of the postcommunist power elite allies with elements of the technocracy (firm managers) and succeeds to a substantial degree to use its political office to convert public goods into its individual private ownership. In regimes that pursue "capitalism from without" the trend toward such political capitalism is weak. Civil society is relatively strong, and an alliance of technocrats and dissident intellectuals blocks the nomenklatura in its bid to gain possession of the "commanding heights" of the economy. Instead, the hegemonic role is played by foreign investors, who rely on domestic expert-managers to run their local operations. In regimes that build "capitalism from below," the technocracy remains hegemonic, but does not overthrow the political bureaucracy. Thus the nomenklatura remains in power. However, it must come to accommodate and eventually share power with a group of emerging domestic capitalists (such as has occurred in China, where the Communist Party recently welcomed capitalists into its ranks.) At any rate, the nomenklatura will eventually become "structurally dependent" on the rate of investment of this class of private capitalists.

Thus, path traveled will determine the nature of the emergent capitalist systems (liberal, patrimonial, or hybrid), and thus their propensity for economic growth (see King 2001a, 2001b, and 2002 for applications of this argument.) How long lasting this effect will be is difficult to predict, but after more than a decade after the transition process began it seems to be quite consequential for the way postcommunist capitalism operates.

B/ Making capitalism after industrialization

The "historic mission" of capitalism was to separate the producers from the means of production, accumulate capital, launch and complete industrialization. Since actually existing socialism was implemented only in countries that did not complete capitalist development, socialism performed the same historic functions. Socialism, as reinterpreted by Lenin, became an ideology of modernization (Lane 1981). The task was to "catch up and overtake" the capitalist world. As a result state socialism proved to be a strategy of accelerated industrialization and accumulation. At least in its "classical epoch", during the 1930s in Russia, the late 1940 and early 1950s in Eastern Europe and China, what distinguished socialism from capitalism most was its capacity to invest a larger proportion of GNP[5] into the productive sphere compared to consumption. In addition, there was a tendency to concentrate development more in the secondary and less in the tertiary sector, and to create monopolistic industrial structures, as these priorities tendencies maximized what was redistributed, thereby facilitating control by the bureaucracy (Kornai 1992).

This massive industrialization and capital accumulation was accomplished by an incomplete, contradictory separation of the producers from the means of subsistence and production. In one respect socialism went even further than capitalism. While there were country-by-country variations, it almost completely eliminated self-employment and universalized wage labor. At the same time, given the economics of shortage, socialism could only operate by allowing massive subsistence production (which occasionally resulted in massive starvation). There were other limits on the separation of producers from the means of production, also resulting from the economics of shortage. Workers could hardly be laid of, and, as a result, they had certain property rights in the means of production (because the full set of capitalist property rights – the right to residual income, the right to transferability, and the right to control – are limited by the de facto right that workers have to some income from the firm, since they can not practically be excluded from all benefits even if they don't do anything at all.) Therefore, the income of workers under socialism could be understood as composed of wages, which reflected the compensation for their wage labor, and "rent," which they collected as co-owners of the means of production.

The transition from communism to capitalism therefore does not lead to industrialization and capital accumulation. In fact, in some respects, exactly the opposite is happening: "capitalism from above" and "capitalism from without" results in a massive de-industrialization and substantial destruction of the previously accumulated capital, thus in de-accumulation. In the latter path, however, foreign direct investment (FDI[6]) leads to re-industrialization. None-the-less, during the process of transition the former

5 GNP = Gross National Product = Bruttosozialprodukt.

6 FDI = Foreign Direct Investment/Direktinvestitionen = grenzüberschreitende Vermögensanlagen.

communist economies are massively reconfigured as they are integrated into the world economy.

Socialism also led to "over-industrialization" – no capitalist country ever achieved as high a proportion of the labor force employed in manufacturing industry as typically found in socialist economies. Since socialism was a strategy of accelerated economic growth, in particular during the "classical epoch," "department one" (heavy industry) grew faster than it ever did under the conditions of a market economy. Socialism turned out to be "production for production sake" (Heller, Fehér and Márkus 1983), with excessive concentration of production in mining and heavy industry. The fact that socialism fell when world manufacturing already suffered from excess capacity contributed to the destruction of the productive capacities of former socialist economies.

This is much less the case in China and Vietnam, where the agrarian sector remained dominant through the whole socialist epoch, though China in particular also created a large heavy industrial capacity, which has proved to be dysfunctional as China is being integrated into the world economy. In East Asia, socialism did not finish the task of industrialization and accumulation, therefore the transition to capitalism follows the more traditional pattern. Anywhere from 150 to 100 million people are underemployed in the Chinese countryside.[7] As migrant workers they move first to rural industry, but also to urban industrial centers as a supply of cheap labor, not unlike the rise of rural proto-industrialization and then the massive rural-urban migration in early capitalist development. This is different from the European postcommunist transition, where the transition leads to a de-urbanization and in same cases re-ruralization and even re-peasantization.

---

7 The key to the surplus relationship between the peasantry and the rational redistributers in the past until this day is that they could not buy subsidized state grain but had to grow their own. The system still disadvantages the rural population by requiring them to pay higher taxes (the so called agricultural tax) and provides subsidized health and education systems to the urban. Some say that 150 million are underemployed. Others estimate its only 100 million. In terms of possession of the land, all rural people regardless of their jobs or degree of underemployment have life-long claim to village land. The exact size of their fields (and thus their expected grain deliveries and taxes) was set by the size of household 15 years ago. The state's policy is to have no redistributions for 30 years, in order to encourage residents to use the land wisely. However, many places redistribute every two to three years to keep up with changes in the household size of the villagers, while other places don't. Just last year they began to let rural residents sign long term leases with non-villagers for right to farm land (and take up tax and grain quotas); but even in this situation the ownership remains with the village, and the villager is entitled to the return of his land back after lease is up. We are not aware of any research indicating how widespread these arrangements are, but to the extent that it has caught on it is probably in the wealthiest areas. China is very clear they won't allow a landless rural mass to emerge. This is one of the impetuses for the VTE (= Village Township Enterprise) reforms, which served to diversify employment in rural areas; VTEs did this successfully from 1985–96, although since then the picture is less rosy. Thus, virtually every rural resident is guaranteed access to land, both as a place to build a house (which they own as private property) and as a place to till the soil. Because farming is often so poorly remunerated, most people want at least one member of the household in non-farm jobs and the route to high incomes, not to mention wealth, is outside farming. (Deborah Davis personal communication, Davis 2003).

Once the de-industrialization and de-accumulation cycle was completed – by the year 2000 this was achieved everywhere in Europe – the postcommunist capitalist economies have joined the global capitalist system in different ways. For those that followed "capitalism from without," a substantial re-industrialization, primarily through foreign direct investment (FDI), is under way. Given the high human capital resources, and low wage levels and transportation costs in the region, high tech industries often move in and create new industrial capacities oriented toward the international market (see King 2001a, 2001b, 2002). The second half of the 1990s for these regimes is an epoch of growth, which occasionally is rather dynamic. But much of this growth takes place in the sector which is owned by, or linked with, foreign capital, and which is primarily export-oriented.[8] It remains to be seen whether recession or weak recovery in the core countries will lead to an even sharper decline in these regimes, or whether they will now be able to develop their domestic markets and compensate for the declining demands for their products on foreign markets by a growth in domestic consumption.

While it is premature to describe the postcommunist "capitalism from without" as being trapped in the "dependent development," (Evans 1979) it is clear that these countries are more dependent on foreign investments than any of the "dependent" Third World countries during the 1960s, when dependency theory captured the socio-economic condition in Latin America or South-East Asian the most accurately. Nevertheless, the Czech Republic, Hungary or Poland is not the replay of Brazil, Columbia, Malaysia or Thailand during the 1960s. The postcommunist liberal regimes are not only human capital rich and in close geographic proximity to major capital and commodity markets

8 For an analysis of the developmental impact of FDI using firm-level data in Hungary, see Toth 2001; King 2000, King and Varadi 2002. For the Czech Republic see Djankov and Hoekman 2000; for Poland see Liberska 1997; Kaminski and Smarzýńska 2001; for China see Kinoshita 1999. While these studies describe foreign owned firms as more efficient and/or dynamic than domestically owned firms, they do point out that the spillover effects (the use of domestic suppliers) are less than anticipated. This means that the beneficial effects of FDI might not be truly long-lasting, for firms might stop investing once they establish themselves as monopolists or oligopolists, and began pumping surplus out of the domestic economy by repatriating profits. If they are not contributing to the domestic economy by making purchases from domestic firms, their developmental benefit will indeed be less than many anticipated. Furthermore, they contribute to trade deficits because of their very high level of imports. Finally, studies have found that in both Poland (Dyker and Kubielas 2000), and Hungary (Toth 2001) firms exporting to Western Europe have a low level of technological upgrading, thereby casting further doubt on the transformative power of FDI. Clearly, the empirical question on the role of FDI in the transition is far from resolved – despite the correlation between high levels of FDI and postcommunist performance. It is quite possible that the effects of FDI are different in the various environments in different countries. Only longitudinal cross-country firm level surveys will shed light on the question of origin of ownership and performance. Thus far, one of the thorniest issues in the literature on firm performance and property change is how to deal with endogeneity. That is, how do we know that foreign firms perform better because they are foreign owned, or they are foreign owned because they are better firms (the jewels of the industrial structure are privatized by foreigner, and the inefficient firms are left for domestic owners). It is by no means an easy task to fully control for this. Selection bias issues are equally relevant in evaluating other property forms as well, such as state ownership.

of the core of the capitalist system, but they are also about to join the European Union. It remains to be seen whether there will be convergence with the core in the long-run. It is not possible to tell whether the fate of postcommunist liberal capitalism will be similar to the kind of partial convergence with the capitalist core experienced by Southern Europe, but it wouldn't be surprising.

Regimes created by "capitalism from above," however, follow a rather different trajectory. In these countries foreign capital is far more modest, and their development shows a closer resemblance to what one would expect from "the development of underdevelopment" (Frank 1969). These countries also experienced substantial de-industrialization and de-accumulation, but so far there are no signs of a similar re-industrialization. There was a massive resurgence of the subsistence economy (in Russia or Romania for instance), and exports will tend to be limited to raw materials, which becomes the most important sector in the economy. Burawoy's notion of non-productive merchant capital (Burawoy and Krotov 1992) and "economic involution" (Burawoy 1996; 2001b) captures these processes.

In brief, "capitalism from without" means that postcommunist semi-peripheral regimes may be moving towards the core (though they may be locked in their semi-peripheral position – only the future can tell), while "capitalism from above" seems to be heading toward the periphery of the capitalist world system. Capitalism from below, because its most important cases were in primarily agrarian countries, has lead to a move up in the world-system, from the ranks of the super-poor to the poor, with the future an open book.[9]

2/Diverse destinations after the fall of communism

In the previous discussion we suggested that after the fall of communism postcommunist socio-economic systems were moving along different trajectories. These trajectories lead to three different destinations, or three big families of postcommunist capitalism. These are ideal types: concrete paths taken by various postcommunist countries always combine elements from all three to different extents, and thus the emergent capitalist systems will combine elements of all three types as well.

China and Vietnam are the best empirical examples of "capitalism from below" leading to hybrid capitalism. Arguably Hungary was also along that path between the mid 1970s and mid 1980s and there were signs of similar development in Poland, Estonia, and to a lesser extent in some other socialist countries of Europe. Capitalism from below occurred only in countries where the Communist Party was able to retain its political monopoly: the power of the apparatus and the force of socialist ideology remained strong enough to offer a lasting defense of the public sector against privatization. Under these circumstances capitalism is developing in "new spaces" created next to the planned pub-

9 Most agree that China's continued success hinges on the health of the banking sector, where state owned banks channel the very high savings rate of the population into the SOE (= State-owned enterprise) sector. If the Chinese population ever lost confidence in state owned banks it would create a major crisis for the SOE sector.

lic sector. At some point the privatization of the public sector inevitably comes on the agenda, as happened in China in 1994. But it will happen once a market integrated private sector is already quite established, and privatization will also likely be rather gradual and occur through fair auctions with the participation of many homegrown domestic capitalists. As a result, it will not result in massive unemployment and de-accumulation.

Capitalism from below most naturally begins in the agricultural sector. First collective farms are either dismantled – as in China – or they are loosened up sufficiently to allow private farming activity by individual peasants, initially part time, and eventually even full time, as happened in the later stages of reform communism in Hungary (Szelényi 1988). Capitalism from below may also coincide with an influx of foreign capital. However, since the public sector is defended this did not open the doors wide for giant multinationals, but rather attracted smaller investors in the Chinese case, or paved the road towards capitalism by creating a debt-trap as happened in Hungary or Poland.

To what extent capitalism from below coincides with "political capitalism" is debatable and it is one of the central contested issues in the so called "market transition debate." In his seminal article Victor Nee (1989) insisted that capitalism from below benefits the "direct producers" and undermines the power of redistributors, while others (like Walder [1995], Rona-Tas [1994], and Staniszkzis [1991][10]) insisted that cadres benefit from the transition. We do not have the definite data to adjudicate between the competing claims. However, in the context of capitalism from below, especially in comparison with the other trajectories, Nee had a good point. In China the central bureaucracy retains its political monopoly, and therefore has neither the motivation nor (in absence of mass privatization) the opportunity to convert public goods into their individual private wealth. In the case of capitalism from below, local apparatchiks may take advantage of new rural industries, camouflaged often as "collective" firms, but in practice operating as private enterprises (so called "red-cap" enterprises). Nevertheless, the space for non-cadre entrepreneurs to start business and be successful is there, which is far from the case in strategies of "capitalism from above."

It is also likely that China has experienced a rise in political capitalism as the private sector grew in importance. After the private economy becomes so large that its reversal seems impossible, then it becomes increasingly rational for the nomenklatura to hedge its bets and get involved in the private economy often through their children (thus the social category of HCC – high cadre children).

Capitalism from below resembles the "classical road" to capitalism, the road we are familiar with especially in the United States or in the other "white colonies." (This is very different of course from the European "classical" transition, where capitalism emerges both from below, but also "from above," by feudal relations turning into capitalist relations). In "capitalism from below" a propertied bourgeoisie is created rather gradually and market institutions are similarly established in a gradualist way (see Barry Naughton's analysis of "growing out of the plan" [1995]). Given the existence of a sizeable

10 Although Rona-Tas really speaks to another historical context, to what we call here "capitalism from without."

public sector and the political domination of the communist party with anti-capitalist ideology "capitalism from below" is still a unique postcommunist way of creating capitalism. This eventually creates a "hybrid" capitalist system where small and medium private (and mixed property) enterprises co-exist with state owned enterprises, which also begin to behave like capitalist firms. This is not just a socialist mixed economy, because the state owned enterprises represent a form of "state capitalism" as they are increasingly integrated by the market and are seeking to maximize profits.

Diametrically opposed to "capitalism from below" is "capitalism from above." This strategy opened up rather unexpectedly when in 1988–1991 European communist regimes "melted down." Until the mid 1980s no one seriously considered that this would be a possibility. During this time, no scenario was developed for a way to turn an economy based exclusively on public ownership into a system of private property. East European economists, speculating about ways to escape the deepening economic crisis of state socialism, threw their hands up and said jokingly: "we know how to make fish-soup out of fish (thus how to nationalize private property), but we do not have the faintest idea, how to make fish from a fish-soup (thus how to convert a socialist system into a liberal market economy.)" The recipe for this culinary miracle was discovered during the second half of the 1980s and it was called "shock therapy" and "mass privatization."[11] The key idea was that a modern capitalist economy could be created with one bold move in which the public sector is offered en masse for privatization. All firms will be transferred to identifiable private owners, without much worry about the price paid for these firms. This strategy represented a coalition of elements of the communist-era bureaucracy with elements of the technocracy, mostly enterprise directors.[12]

The creation of private property "from above" took the form either of "voucher" privatization schemes where property was distributed to all citizens, or firms were essentially given to their employees and managers. In practice most countries implemented a mass privatization based on both of these strategies (Liberman, Nestor and Desai 1997). This was of course only possible if the Communist Party was ready to give up its

---

11 See Lipton and Sachs 1990 for possibly the most influential statement of this position. See also Murrel 1993, Gowan 1995, King 2002, 2003 and Stiglitz 2002 for a discussion of this theory. See anthropologist Janine Wedel 2001 for an excellent discussion of the role of Western economic advisors in the postcommunist transition.

12 The only major exception is the Czech Republic, where the technocracy and dissident intellectuals implemented a substantial mass privatization program. But even this program covered a much smaller proportion of the economy than in Russia, since it included a much larger portion of firms were sold through direct sales to foreign investors (FDI per capita was almost an order of magnitude greater in the Czech Republic than in Russia). Mass privatization programs can also benefit enterprise managers (a fraction of the technocracy) because it can fragment outside owners, leaving control to enterprise insiders. In the Czech case, mass privatization was also used by Vaclav Klaus, a technocrat, to boost his political popularity (the citizen vouchers bore his name). While the implementation of this program boosted the Czech Republic's claim to be the most neoliberal postcommunist county in the first half of the 1990s, it ironically blocked substantial amounts of FDI (McDermott 2002), which only grew to very high levels (surpassing the early leader Hungary in the late 1990s).

power and the ideology of socialism could be de-legitimated. Until mid 1988 or early 1989 this sounded like an unrealistic scenario. However, as we know, socialism melted down during the fall of 1989. Either a new elite grabbed political power, or the old elite changed its ideological colors over night. In both cases they decided to "build capitalism" in exactly the same way that "socialism was built," by a blue-print, led from above, by modernizing elites. This transformation would again be led by a "vanguard" with privileged theoretical knowledge (this time neo-classical economics instead of Marxist-Leninism). Sachs, possibly the most influential neoliberal ideologue, even entitled a very influential article in the Economist "What is to be done" (1990), deliberately invoking Lenin's famous language. The message was clear, there is nothing inherently wrong with vanguardism, only the end of history changed.[13]

In capitalism "from above," the emergent socio-economic system will have a distinctive **patrimonial** character. In patrimonial regimes "political capitalism" reigns supreme. Communist apparatchiks manage to exchange their political capital into private property, frequently using management buy-outs to achieve these aims (see Earle and Estrin 2001; Freeland 2000; Klebnikov 2000). This creates a group of owners of giant corporations with no experience as "capitalists," typically without any international contacts, and with no capital for restructuring. This significantly contributed to causing a sharp drop in demand and the supply of key investment inputs, resulting in generalized economic stagnation(see King 2002, 2003b for the development of this argument linking mass privatization to enterprise failure).

Those regimes in which the technocracy and humanistic intellectuals form an alliance against the party bureaucrats pursue "capitalism from without," ultimately creating a **liberal capitalist** system, which relies on Western multinationals. It is "liberal" in the sense that it is dominated by legal-rational authority. In these regimes privatization is a reasonably transparent process. Public firms are auctioned off at public auctions, or ownership is transferred to workers or citizens via vouchers, which are traded on the market place. There is limited "political capitalism" – former communist apparatchiks are rarely able to manipulate the process sufficiently to acquire massive private wealth. It typically only happens in small or medium sized firms, and large corporation virtually never become the private property of individual communist apparatchiks or even groups of former communist apparatchiks.[14]

13 Of course, this time around the vanguard paid lip service to representative democracy. Sachs himself admitted that the "ideal" democratic system was one in which the executive was elected and then allowed to act without any constraints until the next election (see Rodrik 1996, 32, note 30). Sachs and other prominent neoliberals offered a political economy that emphasized the dangers of "losers" and "winners" in "partial" reform systems reversing the transition or locking in "incomplete" reforms. We believe this danger is overemphasized, as suggested by reforms in China, Poland (see King 2002), and elsewhere (see King 2003b for a 14 country comparison that covers the vast majority of the postcommunist population).

14 Elite survey data backs up this claim. According to I. Szelényi and S. Szelényi (1995), more than twice as many former members of nomenklatura made it into the new economic elite in Russia than in Poland (p. 629).

In the early stages of the transition the privatization of large enterprises creates a certain amount of "quasi-private property" or "recombinant property" (Stark 1996). Under these circumstances governments retain substantial indirect control, mainly through the banking system (as long as banks are not privatized and as long as they own substantial stocks in privatized firms). Evidence from Hungary indicates that recombinant property was never dominant (King 2001a: 32–34) and was a transitory phenomenon limited to the very largest enterprises in capital-intensive sectors (Hanley, King and Toth 2002).[15] Over a relatively brief period of time, by the mid to late 1990s, ownership tends to shift into the hands of foreign investors. Market institutions are created in these regimes fairly early in the game. Prices are deregulated, currency is made convertible, the banking system is modernized and eventually some or most of it privatized, capital imports are deregulated and so on. Under such circumstances even if corporate management is able to acquire controlling private ownership in their firms, they still have incentives to bring in foreign investors in order to attract capital for restructuring and secure access to export markets.

Table 1 summarizes the overall argument relating class coalitions to the development of three distinct types of capitalism. The remainder of this chapter will explain this table, with examples from Russia, China and Central Europe.

There are exogenous and endogenous factors, which may help us to explain why some countries followed a liberal or patrimonial path and why some managed to go a long way by "building capitalism" from below. In this chapter we will focus our attention to the "endogenous" factors, which are rooted in the class structure, the dynamics of struggles among different factions of elites.

It would be foolish, however, to deny that exogenous factors are not consequential. Most importantly the level of economic development countries achieved prior communism, and, to some degree, were able to retain under communism as well as the proximity of markets in core countries are likely to play an important role. It cannot be accidental that the only countries which are bordering the European Union, and which were traditionally more developed, created liberal capitalism. One possible argument is that the more developed countries were able to adopt the neoliberal policies, since they could afford to pay the rather high price of neoliberal shock therapy. Less developed countries, however, may have experimented with some shock but they had to suspend it before it could work since their population could not tolerate more pain [hence shock without therapy – see Gerber and Hout (1998); but see Murell (1993); and King (2002, 2003b) for a different interpretation of Russia's "neoliberalness."] Thus, the argument could be made that the better economic performance in Central Europe may have nothing to do with their economic policies, or the path their capitalist development took, but can be explained simply by the fact that they were stronger economies and closer to Western markets.

15 It seems more likely that what Stark labeled "recombinant property" in most cases was simply an attempt by the state to break up huge horizontally and vertically integrated industrial firms (such as steel and aluminum producers) so that there individual pieces could be more easily privatized.

Table 1: Varieties of postcommunist capitalism

Path to Capitalism	Capitalisms from Without	Capitalism from Above	Capitalism from Below
Transitional political strategy/ elite struggle/ class and intra-dominant class alliance	Technocracy defeats bureaucracy and struggles with former dissidents for hegemony	Bureaucracy retains power, uses office to acquire private property, allies with technocracy	Technocracy hegemonic, allies with domestic bourgeoisie, but bureaucracy retains political power
Type of Capitalism	Liberal systems (Czech Republic, Hungary, Poland)	Patrimonial systems (Russia, Ukraine, Rumania, Serbia under Milosevic)	Hybrid Systems (China, Vietnam)
Dominant Class Formation	Multinationals, Some Domestic Capitalists	Patron-Client Ownership Networks; Parasitic Financial-Industrial Groups	Domestic ownership class; Marketized hybrid property forms
Extent of Class formation	Under way, but dual structure, with patron-client relations	Dominant estate structure, mainly patron-client-relations	Some class formation, but great deal of patron-client relations
Foreign capital	Dominant	Very limited	Supplementary, smaller investors
Political capitalism	Little	Lot, dominant	Some
Domestic (petty, or middle) bourgeoisie	Some	Little	Lot
Firm Integration	Markets with low levels of non-market horizontal coordination (barter, debt-swaps, arrears)	Markets and high levels of non-market horizontal coordination (barter, debt-swaps, arrears)	Markets and central plan (and the barter associated with planning)
Economic dynamism	Some	Little-none	A great deal
Leading sector	Manufacturing exports	Raw materials export	Manufacturing exports
Dynamic of accumulation	FDI; importing capital; export driven, some technological upgrading; financial fragility	Political accumulation; capital flight; technological downgrading	State-led development of SOEs, technological upgrading; growth of new private sector
Size of the state	Medium	Large	Large
State capacity/ Formal bureaucracy	Modest/Very	Little/Almost none	Great/Very
State-Economy interaction	State provides adequate public goods (e.g. stock of human capital); some personalistic enforcement of laws; state implements an industrial policy; medium informal sector	State does not provide adequate public goods (e.g. stock of human capital); extensive personalistic enforcement of laws by patrons to benefit clients; huge informal sector	State provides public goods (e.g. infrastructure ; state implements industrial policy; small informal sector
Political institutions	Liberal democracy	Multi-party authoritarianism (unfree and unfair elections or "non-polyarchy")	selective and partial process of liberalization of totalitarian regime

This exogenous explanation is not without merit, but it has its limits. First of all, during the socialist epoch the gap in the level of economic development among the socialist countries narrowed and just began to grow again after the fall of communism. And there are also curious exceptions to such economic determinism. For instance, how can one explain the unusual success of the Baltic states, which were for half a century parts of the Soviet Union. Sure, they were relatively better developed regions of the USSR, nevertheless they were within the USSR and during the 1990s they comfortably outperformed the countries of the Balkans. And China is also an important exception to economic determinism. What made it possible in China to advance towards market institutions more effectively than some of the patrimonial regimes of Eastern Europe?

In addition to geography and prior-level of development, let us add a possible cultural explanation to the different routes various societies took. We do not know how far this analysis could be pushed, but it certainly deserves attention that the reconfiguration of postcommunist states occurred along religious lines. It may be just an artifact, or it may have something to do with elective affinities between religion and modernization, but the three types of capitalisms correspond to various great world religions. All liberal regimes are dominated by Western Christianity; patrimonial states are either Orthodox (or Islamic), while hybrid capitalism happened to be in the Confucian and Taoist part of the world. It is beyond our competence to assess how important this fact may be, we just have to note that such an affinity between religion and type of modernization might exist.

We argue that the pattern of class conflict and intra-class alliance (or inter-elite struggle) determines which path to capitalism is selected. This does not have to be thought of as an alternative explanation to geography, prior level of development, or culture. These factors affect the opportunity structure of the different segments of the class structure. For example, the fact that a country is closer to Western Europe and more culturally similar might make an alliance of technocrats and multinationals seem much more possible. At a micro-level, it is likely to result in networks linking socialist managers with foreign managers. This seems to have occurred in Hungary, which then translated into an early lead in FDI resulting from the formation of small Joint Ventures joining up former socialist era managers with often small and medium sized enterprise actors in the core (e.g. Germany, Austria) (see King and Varadi 2002; King 2001a: 55–58).

The fact that a county industrialized prior to the imposition of socialism means that its middle classes (its technocrats and cultural intellectuals) will have memories, and a different set of internalized myths about the "nation", that weakens their enthusiasm for Communism [King 2001b; see Darden's (2002) excellent study on nationalism in the Former Soviet Union (FSU)]. Thus, these exogenous factors are important most of all because they affect the pattern of intra- and inter-class conflict and alliance.

In the remainder of this chapter, we will discuss the different paths to, as well as different resulting types of, capitalism. It must be kept in mind that these three paths are only ideal types, and thus features of the three resultant styles of capitalism will be found in all postcommunist countries. There are some multinationals and modern capitalist markets in Russia, while in Hungary, the archetype of "capitalism from without," paternalism plays an important role not only in the political-cultural sphere, but even in the economy. Barter is not unknown in the Central European economies, and some degree of "capitalism from below" can be found in the Czech Republic and Hungary as well. Indeed, in Poland and Slovenia there were strong elements of this path, because they severely delayed the privatization of very large state owned enterprises. Thus, they created a space for more capitalism from the ground up, even as they pursued capitalism "from without" through strategic foreign investment.[16] Political capitalism (thus the use of political office to acquire private wealth), which is a central feature of patrimonial regimes, is far from non-existent in systems that build "capitalism from below" such as in China (as executions for corruption attest to). Similarly, China has seen a great deal of FDI (in fact, it has been the biggest recipient in the world since the late 1990s, but its levels are still modest on a per capita basis)

Capitalism From Above Leading to Patrimonial Capitalism

In those countries that wound up with patrimonial systems, a fraction of the communist political apparatus was able to retain its power and defend the privileges of its clients as well. While the momentum of technocratic reforms and intellectual challenges in Central Eastern Europe in the late sixties might have been able to radically transform the power structure if not for Soviet military might, the bureaucratic estate in Russia was never seriously challenged. Indeed, the collapse of communism cannot be seen as a defeat of the Communist Party bureaucracy by outside forces. While Russia had dissident intellectuals (such as Solzhenitsyn), who like in Central Europe had a role to play in delegitimizing the regime (see Shlapentokh 1990), they were not nearly as powerful relative to the nomenklatura. That is, the key players in this transition were members of the political bureaucracy itself (Linz and Stepan 1996; Garcelon 1997; and the authoritative Reddaway and Glinski 2001). The driving force of change was the party's growing recognition that it could not compete economically and militarily with Western capitalism (Szelényi, I. and B. Szelényi 1995). Gorbachev should be seen as a technocratic reformer who opened up to intellectuals as ammunition against the Brezhnev era hardliners that he viewed as standing in the way of necessary reforms (see Shlapentokh 1990; Flaherty 1990). At the same time, the perestroika reforms that legalized individual profitable activity and cooperatives (in 1986 and 1987) created vast opportunities for elites in managerial and ministerial positions to profit as middle-men – enabling them to accumulate personal wealth (the most outstanding journalistic account is Klebnikov's *The Godfather of the Kremlin* [2000]). This gave at least some partocrats the ability to see a future for themselves in a postcommunist world.

Gorbachev's move was initially successful, as he managed to replace much of the top Brezhnez era elite whom he saw as corrupt and inefficient bureaucratic obstacles to reform (Hanley et al. 1995: 647). However, these reforms started to get out of control as activists in the Baltics and Armenia used Glasnost to espouse anti-Russian nationalism.

16 In these countries "capitalism from above" was slowed down the resistance by workers and other political groups as well as the legacy of workers self-management (for Polish workers see Kramer 1995: 654; also see Ekiert 2001; for Slovenia see Mencinger 1996; Gligorov 1995).

Soon, the partocracy realized they could survive on the regional level, drawing their attention away from the center, and initiating the disintegration of the Soviet Union (Helf and Hahn 1992; Linz and Stepan 1996).

In the Russian Federation, 1988 saw the emergence of "civil society" in the form of Democratic Russia (DR). A full 80 percent of respondents in one survey of DR's Moscow activists were technocrats, or "specialists," holders of technical and professional degrees and skills (whereas 28 percent of those employed in the Russian Republic fit this definition). While this movement mobilized the real discontent and grievances of the intelligentsia, it was nonetheless "launched from within the highest echelons of the Soviet-Party state. This movement against the party's political monopoly was part of, and contributed to, a struggle of technocratic reformers against party conservatives. This essentially split the party internally, creating two warring factions (the Democratic Platform and the Russian Communist Party)" (Garcelon 1997: 39, 47, 49).

When Gorbachev tried to use limited elections against party conservatives, his strategy backfired. Yeltsin rose to prominence through his control over the Moscow Association of Voters, which provided leadership for the mass-based DR movement. The fact that this was a section of the Communist Party coming to power (and not a non-communist elite, as in Poland) is clear. A full 86 percent of DR's deputies were party members and Yeltsin himself had been a member of the Politburo (Garcelon 1997: 64).

In June the Russian Supreme Soviet declared its "sovereignty" from the USSR, and a dual-power structure emerged. After the failed coup of 1991, Yeltsin assumed full power over Russian territory. DR, having always been more of a top-down product of a section of the bureaucratic estate, soon withered into irrelevance. Yeltsin chose instead to align with enterprise managers and implemented shock therapy from above (Popov 2000). Indeed, a full 74 percent of Yeltsin's appointees were members of the nomenklatura (Garcelon 1997: 70).

In January 1992, the radical transformation of the Russian economy began. With the help of a team of Western economists headed by Jeffrey Sachs, "a radical reform package focusing on economic liberalization and privatization was adopted...". (EBRD[17] 1996: 169; see Wedel 2001). Six months of this shock therapy led to unprecedented hyperinflation and a fall in living standards. To shore up support, Yeltsin incorporated into his regime representatives of enterprise directors, such as Chernomyrdin, chairman of the board of Gazprom (Russia's giant natural gas monopoly), who was made vice premier of the fuel and energy sector, and later replaced Gaidar as Prime Minister when the public outcry against shock therapy forced his ouster (Reddaway and Glinski 2001). At the same time that Chernomyrdin joined the government, a privatization plan relying on a combination of citizen vouchers and giveaways to managers and employees was launched in June of 1992. This was easily the largest, most rapid transformation of ownership in world history. "By July of 1994, 15,052 medium- and large-scale enterprises, employing more than 80 per cent of the industrial workforce, had been privatized..." (EBRD 1996: 169). Thus, in Russia, a self-recreated bureaucratic estate, in coalition with

17 EBRD = European Bank for Reconstruction and Development.

elements of the technocracy in charge of large enterprises, unleashed "capitalism from above" via a full dose of shock therapy.

In these systems, communist ideology was of course instantly abandoned, but the former communist parties were not taken over by technocrats and transformed into centrist or even right wing social democratic movements as it happened in the liberal regimes. Instead the core of the political apparatus retained control over the successor parties and turned the communist ideology into nationalist, often xenophobic ideology. Iliescu in Romania (at least during the early 1990s – less so after his return to power) and Milosevic in Serbia are prime examples. The transformation was more complex in Russia, where the successor party lost political power, but Yeltsin followed policies which were quite similar to those of Iliescu and Milosevic. In those countries where working class resistance, political or economic, did not weaken the political apparatus, the technocratic and intellectual opposition could not smash the political bureaucracy. Instead, it adapted a nationalistic, xenophobic rhetoric and the practices of political capitalism).

The Economic Institutions of Postcommunist Patrimonial Capitalism

Because part of the "blueprint" for creating capitalism includes rapidly liberalizing prices, eliminating trade barriers, and drastically curtailing the money supply (by reducing monetary emissions, raising interest rates, and curtailing subsidies). As a result, postcommunist firms confront a harsh new environment. Rapid price deregulation, given the monopolistic structure of Soviet style economies, will lead to a jump in the price of inputs. The wholesale liberalization of imports creates an enormous drop in aggregate demand for domestic producers, as they must face global competition.[18] With monetary emissions severely limited, government subsidies drastically curtailed, and credit dramatically more expensive, most firms run into severe cash flow problems and a shortage of capital for restructuring and even day-to-day transactions. Similarly, there was also the devastation resulting from the political destruction of the old Warsaw pact Council for Mutual Economic Aid (Comecon, also called the Council of Mutual Economic Assistance or the CMEA) trading system. For many states, a vast majority of exports and imports were from the COMECON, accounting for a huge amount of economic activity. The breakdown of this trading system therefore disrupted supply chains and created a gigantic loss of markets.[19]

In addition to these shocks, many firms suffer shocks associated with mass privatization (King 2002, 2003). While the rapid privatization of small and some medium sized businesses is beneficial because it provides a superior incentive structure for those in control of these enterprises, large SOEs can not be rapidly privatized without unacceptable costs. Most importantly, mass privatization means that the resulting private corporation will not have an owner or owners with sufficient resources to restructure

18 Theoretically, firms should be able to import these inputs. However, firms can not instantly find these inputs, and may not be able to afford them.

19 For a discussion of these points see Stiglitz 2002; Amsden, Kochanowicz and Taylor 1994; Gowan 1995, 1999; Andor and Summers 1998; Chussodovsky 1997; and UNDP (= United Nations Development Program) 1999.

the company. Without any capital to carry out desperately needed restructuring, and without the injection of any new managerial talent, many firms found themselves in untenable positions. Mass privatization also frequently created outside owners with very poor arrangements to monitor firm managers or even to monitor other (typically inside) owners. This was virtually inevitable, as these economies lacked a developed business information infrastructure, and effective legal protection of shareholder rights, that help "make markets" in advanced capitalist systems.

The combination of these two conditions led to massive amounts of asset stripping in the postcommunist economy, wreaking havoc on the functioning of many firms.[20] This is a paradox from the neoliberal perspective – while involving the state in the economy is allegedly a recipe for rent seeking behavior – not involving the state in the transition creates an environment that encourages corruption (see King 2001a, 2001b).

Only those firms with privileged access to raw materials, or those that enjoy "natural protection" as a result of prohibitive shipping costs (like furniture) are likely to be able to successfully restructure (King 2002, 2003; for useful reviews of sectoral change in the Russian economy see Vorobyov and Zhukov [2000] and Schroeder [1998]). This creates what Gustofson (1999: 219) calls a "barbell economy" to indicate the hollowing out of the manufacturing sector, leaving only a significant raw materials sector and a financial services sector (the sphere of "merchant capital" (Krotov and Burawoy 1992) or financial clientelism (King 2001a).

These structural challenges are exacerbated by the "habitus" of former communist officials turned private owners. They are likely to be less entrepreneurial, and more inclined to be paternalistic towards their business partners and employees (one may also call this "corruption" if one wants to use value-burdened labels). Communist apparatchiks turned capitalists might ruin the emerging capitalist system just as much as they ruined socialism. In regimes "from without" the domestic expert-managers carry their habituses with themselves as well, and are not immune to paternalism either. Such actors are used to operating within the system of a paternalistic state and are likely to continue their state-dependent, deferential role. Paradoxically, multinational investors need these local experts exactly because they are well networked and have such local social and political know-how. Nevertheless, with "capitalism from without" foreign owners call the shots, and this, together with the existence of liberal press and democratic parliamentary institutions which guarantee some degree of transparency, limits paternalism (and corruption).

In regimes of "capitalism from above," the combination of massive structural challenges facing enterprises led by "inappropriate" agents typically results in economic disaster. Asset stripping typically becomes the most "rational" way to respond, further exacerbating the precarious position of most firms (see King 2003).

In this situation, firms frequently can not afford to pay wages. This contributes to labor markets remaining under-developed, and paternalism frequently characterizes the

20 In Russia, for example, capital flight in all its forms has averaged about $40 billion a year (Golovachev 2002).

relationship between workers and managers. This retreat from labor markets leads firms to aid workers in gaining access to the means of subsistence. Workers typically must resort to food grown on garden plots or collective potato farming to survive, and they are thus increasingly re-united with the means of their subsistence (Burawoy and Krotov 1992; Southworth 2001; King 2002) (the enterprise and the household become increasingly merged in the Weberian framework.) As vertical patron-client relations grow in importance, workers are separated from each other, and their "classness" decreases.

As firms entered into financial crisis and technical bankruptcy, they frequently could not pay taxes, which at any rate were drastically contracting along with the economy.[21] This loss of revenues, when combined with the anti-statist ideology of the neoliberals, quickly led to a lack of state support for the basic institutions that enable firms to successfully restructure by raising their quality and changing their product line to compete on the world market. An important instance of this occurs when the state stops supporting the educational institutions that turn out skilled manpower, leading to a crisis for many firms. Of particular importance is the production of experts with scientific credentials by local polytechnic institutes. While some of this is brain drain, case study data indicate that much is also the result of a shortage of new technicians (see McDermott 2002 for the Czech Republic, and King 2002 for Russia). Furthermore, because the crisis of education also affects primary educational institutions, the shortage of skilled manpower will only intensify in the future (UNDP 1999: 58).

As a result of widespread financial crises, firms up and down commodity chains are unable to get the money or credit the need to continue production. Rather than go out of business, however, managers reactivate old "horizontal" ties (or generate new ones) to managers at other firms that functioned to compensate for the scarcity of inputs in the shortage economy. These networks now function to aid in production given the absence of money and credit in the new capitalist economy. These network ties allow the firms to withdrawal from the market through inter-enterprise arrears, debt-swaps and barter (see David Woodruff (1999) for an outstanding account of these processes in Russia). Barter decreases the efficiency of transactions (because a middleman typically must be used), shields firms from market-pressures (because business partners are selected on network ties, not price considerations), and makes taxation highly problematic (because it makes it easy to conceal transactions from the state, and because in-kind taxes are easy to over-value when they are paid, which are difficult and expensive to collect anyway).

The loss of tax revenue from enterprise failure, exacerbated by the rise of hard-to-tax barter inevitably weakened the state. As the state was increasingly unable to meet its formal obligations, it began to break down. Poorly paid (or unpaid) state officials are easily corrupted, and the bureaucratic nature of the state decomposed. It became riddled by reactivated (as well as new) patron-client ties between government officials and businessmen. Private market success came to depend to a high degree on arbitrary political

21 In Russia, for example, receipts of the consolidated state budget declined from 41% of GDP in 1990 to only 26.8% in 1997, even though GDP was only about 50% of its prior level (Vorobyov and Zhukov 2000: 5).

decisions and the exercise of private force. As the state both gets weaker and loses its bureaucratic character, "mafias" rise to fulfill some of the functions of the state – such as contract enforcement (Varese 2001).

Over time, the politically constituted ownership groups will spread throughout the economy – swallowing up the shares of insider-dominated firms that can be stripped of their assets in one way or the other. Therefore, the compromise between the bureaucratic estate and enterprise managers will not result in equal gains for both segments of the former elite in the long run. In Russia, the eventual takeover of insider-owned firms by politically connected financial groups, who then typically fall to make any investment into restructuring the enterprise, is quite common.

Capitalism from above is also not conducive to the development of domestic small business. Since in both trajectories there was the massive privatization of the public sector, starting small and growing bigger was very difficult. The ensuing economic collapse and state disintegration (which includes an increase in the size of mafia groups to fill the void), and inability of banks to provide loans to new enterprises (banks funnel money out of the system, they do not turn savings into investments [see Popov 1999 for an insightful discussion of the specificity of the Russian banking system in comparative postcommunist perspective], means that new enterprises face incredible odds.

Finally, the economic changes that result from following the path of "capitalism from above" will have inevitable political consequences. Specifically, the existence of a large class of political capitalists who owe their very ownership of property to particular patrons in political office means that there will be enormous pressure to erode the institutions of democracy. For, unlike in Hungary or Poland, owners in Russia may lose their property rights if their patron loses office. Thus, what results are systems in which elections matter, but they are neither particularly free nor fair.[22]

Capitalism From Without Leading to Liberal Capitalism

On the whole classes were not particularly well formed under state socialism. Socialist society can be better described as a rank order, rather than a class stratified society. Nevertheless, classes were in formation and in particular the strength of the working class had far reaching consequences for how intra-class struggles among various factions of the ruling elites unfolded. Arguably, in Central Europe, in particular in Hungary and Poland, the power monopoly of the political apparatus had been challenged for quite some time by an emerging alliance between enlightened technocrats, usually operating within the communist party, and critical intellectuals (Kennedy 1992).

This alliance was based on common interest. Politically, both wanted freedom from the bureaucratic estate. Economically, both believed they could do just as well in a capitalist system by becoming professionals and selling their relatively scarce labor power on

22 The most infamous example of this was the "loans for shares" program, in which a handful of politically connected businessmen gained control of Russia's oil companies for a small fraction of what they were worth in exchange for ensuring Yeltsin's 1996 reelection (see Wolosky 2000; Klebnikov 2000; Freeland 2000; Hoffman 2002; and the authoritative account in Reddaway and Glinski 2000).

the market or by becoming entrepreneurs. A major factor in this was the possibility of working for some large multinational corporation.

The formation of the working class was the most advanced in Poland of course, where the collective action of workers in 1980 almost brought down the rule of the communist political apparatus, which was only saved by the military dictatorship of Jaruzelski. In the summer of 1981, sudden price hikes precipitated strikes throughout the country, but particularly in the Baltic cities. In August, general strikes in Gdansk and Szczecin spread through the country, ending with government recognition of the right to form independent unions (Kramer 1995: 673). The working class entered into an alliance with a group of dissident intellectuals that had defended worker strikes in 1976 (Kennedy 1987; Bernhard 1993). The workers and intellectuals picked up the support of the disaffected technocrats and professionals (Kubik 1994; Kennedy 1992; Kennedy 1987; Karabel 1993), culminating in the 10 million-strong Solidarity Union (which was four times larger than the Communist Party, and ten times greater than the official trade unions [Ost 1990: 139–140]). From this movement an anti-communist political counterelite was created, bent on abolishing the nomenclatura and wresting control from the bureaucratic estate (Wasilewski and Wnuk-Lipiński 1995: 674).

For the rest of 1981, Solidarity tried to negotiate the institutionalization of its power to determine and implement economic policy. Ultimately, the government would not agree to share its economic power. Massive strikes continued throughout the year, precipitating Jaruzelski's imposition of martial law, during which he outlawed Solidarity and arrested many of its leaders (Ost 1990: 113–148). The threat of Soviet intervention was crucial in this.

In an effort to restore some legitimacy, Jaruzelski sought to drive a wedge between intellectuals and workers, to make concessions to the Church, and even to open up to a small class of "socialist entrepreneurs" like in Hungary (Kennedy 1992: 55–56; Ost 1990: 155; Korbonski 1999: 146). While Solidarity was weakened by this, Jaruzelski never won any measure of legitimacy, and Poland continued to undergo serious economic problems and the build-up of international debt (partially to bolster consumption, and partially to try to invest its way out of the slump) (Korbonski 1999: 143). Unable to garner support for his 1987 economic plan, and with the additional blow of the new Polish Pope (John Paul II) calling for the re-legalization of Solidarity, the party teetered near collapse. As a result of declining living standards, a new round of strikes started in Gdansk and Krakow in April of 1988. In August, strikes started in Silesia, and began to spread northward. That same month, Jaruzelski initiated the Round Table meeting with the opposition, which would lead, in short order, to the decisive defeat of the government in semi-free elections, ending Communist rule.

Hungary followed a somewhat similar pattern. While the Hungarian working class never engaged in the kind of collective action taken by the Polish working class, it was sufficiently a threat to the communist apparatus that it had to try to buy political peace by opening up the second economy to workers and peasants. The resulting petty bourgeoisification in Hungary played a substantial role in eroding the ideological hegemony of the communist bureaucracy and laid the groundwork for the Hungarian technocratic-intellectual alliance to defeat the bureaucracy (Rona-Tas 1997). In both countries the political apparatus was wiped out in 1989. It lost political power altogether, and therefore had neither the will nor the capacity to carry out a project of political capitalism. The ideology of the victorious technocratic-intellectual elite by 1989 was neoliberalism (see Eyal, Szelényi and Townsley 1998; Eyal 2000). However, the technocratic-intellectual alliance did not last for too long (Szalai 2001). The intellectual elite turned against the technocracy, which was now seen as part of the former communist establishment.

In 1990, in both Poland and Hungary the newly formed Socialist Party suffered a humiliating defeat. The intellectual themselves were split into a liberal and patriotic-Christian wings and the last decade can be described as struggles among these various political forces. Nevertheless, despite the political differences all of these intellectual and technocratic elites, they favored neoliberal policies, and in particular, cooperation with foreign investors. Hungary and Poland are in many respects the "purest types," the alliance of classes or elites may have been somewhat different in the other liberal regimes, but our key hypothesis is that in all of these regimes the communist bureaucracy was unseated by an alliance between reform minded technocrats with liberal and patriotic-Christian intellectuals. This alliance received some initial support from the working class, though for the most part it was demobilized after the defeat of the communist bureaucracy.

In these regimes, neoliberalism served as the ideological cement to the alliance of the technocracy and the political dissidents (the humanistic intellectuals). Its chief appeal was its radical anti-statism. However, because these systems were functioning democracies, political elites abandoned strict adherence to neolibreal precepts (see Nuti and Kolodko 1997; Sznajder and King 2002; King 2003b) especially ideas favoring the quick "mass" privatization of the SOE sector. First, direct sales to foreigners were prevalent everywhere in Central Europe. The Hungarians privatized relatively rapidly via auctions, which frequently resulted in FDI. Slovakia, Slovenia and Poland delayed the privatization of many large SOEs, choosing to first restructure them and then privatize them later through competitive auctions (often to Mutlinationals [MNCs]).[23] Only the Czech Republic managed to implement a significant mass privatization program – which most analysts now acknowledge led to major problems in "governance." Only the Czech Republic's very high level of FDI has kept this country out of the patrimonial camp.[24]

The Economic Institutions of Postcommunist Liberal Capitalism

To the extent that the Central European cases pursued the neoliberal transition strategy, and to the extent that they were dependent on imports from and exports to the former COMECON system (the economic counterpart to the Warsaw Pact), they suffered

23 In 1995 a small program covering some small and medium enterprises was implemented. These firms constituted only about 10% of the productive capacity of the SOE sector (Baltowski and Mickanwicz 2000). MNC = Mulitnational Corporation.

24 And indeed, the Czech Republic has low state capacity and weak security of property rights compared to its liberal neighbors, despite its privileged starting point (King 2003a). There also seemed to be quite a bit of political capitalism around the Klaus administration.

de-industrialization just as in the FSU (= Florida State University). However, FDI partially compensates for the problems created by shock liberalization and stabilization, as it leads to re-industrialization. Multinationals provide capital and technology, expertise, and access to world markets. This allows more firms in non-resource-based manufacturing to restructure to enable their survival on the market – and to export to Western Europe without massive technological downgrading and occasionally with substantial upgrading (see case studies in King 2001a, 2001b; King and Varadi 2002; King 2002). Taxes from these restructuring privatized firms, as well as continued revenues from large SOEs and their domestic suppliers, allow the economy to avoid the vicious circle of declining state capacity and market withdrawal that follows from "capitalism from above." The presence of high levels of FDI also reduces the level of non-market firm survival strategies like barter and inter-enterprise arrears, as well as reducing wage arrears.

The new private economy will be strengthened, as large greenfields, as well as small joint ventures, emerge. Domestically owned small and medium-sized businesses, however, are likely to suffer in at least the short and medium term because of foreign competition in consumer markets, and the replacement of industrial input producers with the suppliers from elsewhere in the global empires of MNCs. Basically, there will be capitalist growth, but it will depend on the investment strategy of particular MNCs, the lending decisions of foreign owned banks, and the ability to import industrial inputs and capital from, and export manufactured goods to, the core of the capitalist world economy. Because there is capital account liberalization, and because these economies are so sensitive to the cost of currencies and external markets, they will be "fragile" – or prone to devaluation (which partially restores the market for some domestic companies, even as it results in much less consumption for those with savings or on fixed incomes).

Finally, democracy is consolidated because relatively little political capitalism exists, resulting in little pressure to manipulate elections.

Capitalism from Below leading to Hybrid Capitalism

Arguably, China followed most closely the script described by Konrad and Szelényi (1979). In 1978 the political bureaucracy formed an alliance with the technocratic intelligentsia, and in fact accepted the leadership of the technocratically minded faction of the party elite during the years of Deng Xiao Ping.[25]

The rise of the technocracy can be traced to the disastrous policies of the political/ideological hard-line faction of the Party during the Great Leap Forward and Cultural Revolution. On the one hand, these disastrous policy failures greatly undermined the legitimacy of the political bureaucracy and forced it to give the leadership to the technocratic faction. On the other hand, these disasters emboldened, if not empowered, the dominated class, who had no choice but to abandon central policies and experiment with reform on their own. Yang's (1996) historical study shows that in regions more

25 A study (Li 2001) of the "fourth generation" of Chinese leaders – those who will succeed the current leadership of Jiang Zemin – has confirmed the technocratic background of this elite group. Most of these leaders have an educational background in technology and started their career either as technocrats-managers in the state industrial sector or as professionals.

heavily affected by the Great Leap Forward calamity, spontaneous reforms started earlier and took more radical forms. Another study (Zhou 1996) also shows that many of the initial agricultural reform measures were actually spontaneously taken by local peasants, without the government's sanction. The central government only sanctioned it after it had become faits accompli. Deng Xiao Ping himself acknowledges that the success of VTE (= Village Township Enterprise) is completely unexpected (Chen 1989).

The bureaucracy and technocracy keep each other under control to the present day.[26] The technocracy did not allow the political apparatus to implement a political capitalist scenario (it had little incentive to do so anyway, since it was not deprived from its political power and many of its economic privileges). The communist bureaucracy, on the other hand, put strict limits on how far the technocracy could go in its attempts to ally with the intelligentsia and to pursue a liberal policy. This is seen most clearly in the events of Tiananmen square, where the intelligentsia and workers were repressed; the former much less severely than the latter (see Walder and Xiaoxia 1993).

Workers and peasants could take advantages of the resulting "balance of power." Thus, Nee is probably correct to a large extent when he sees the "direct producers" benefiting from transition in China, while they proved to be the losers in the two other systems.[27]

It is in this sense that the path to capitalism was "from below." Economists (Jiang 2001; Naughton 1992; Naughton 1994) have found that China's transition first started with the opening up the large domestic markets, giving small firms an enormous space to grow in the production of consumer products, an area where SOEs were less concentrated. While many markets remain regulated and the national consumer market largely segregated, small local-based firms, supported by local governments, often gain advantages over large state-owned firms (and foreign firms for that matter) in accessing local resources and materials.

The Economic Institutions of Hybrid Capitalism

Since Nee's agenda setting article in 1989, studies done by both sides of the "market transition" debate have consistently shown both substantial numbers of non-cadre entrepreneurs in rural China and substantial positive returns to household incomes produced by this (Nee 1989; Nee 1996; Walder 2002).

However, a recent study by Walder and Zhao (2002) of rural China shows that the emergence of capitalism in China can be divided into two periods. In the first, during the first full decade of economic reform (the 1980s), non-elites with non-agricultural jobs were most likely to become private entrepreneurs. In the second decade, however, when

26 Walder and associates have long studied the dual career paths and bifurcated elite structure in China (Li and Walder 2001; Walder 1995; Walder et al. 2000). Basically the findings are: 1/ there are two distinctive paths into the Chinese elite: prestigious administrative positions within the bureaucracy and professional positions; 2/ there is a considerable amount of circulation between the two (the study on the fourth-generation leader (Li 2001) attests to this too); and 3/ the dual career paths create a bifurcated elite structure.

27 For a useful review of the rather large body of stratification literature in China, see Bian (2002).

public enterprises begin to be privatized, public enterprise managers and relatives of cadres become the most likely to become new private entrepreneurs. Therefore, it seems plausible that there is a growing "political capitalism" problem.

Thus, China's hybrid capitalist system still has a good deal of patrimonial relationships that mirror processes observed in Eastern Europe and the former Soviet Union. Steinfeld's case study (1998) shows that among many Chinese SOEs the exchange of products is often not accompanied by monetary transaction, instead resulting in accumulation of unpaid inter-corporate debts – known as "triangular debts." Other elements of Russia's patrimonial system are present. Wank (1999) finds that patron-client relationship also survived the transition and became commodified – because private entrepreneurs still need to have resourceful patrons in the bureaucracy to get deals done.[28] Indeed, the worst inefficiencies of patrimonialism can be identified. Ding (2000) reports on how offshore businesses have become a major channel for the Chinese nomenklatura to turn state assets into private wealth. Lin and Zhang (1999) study how subsidiaries to urban SOEs have been used as a vehicle to transfer state assets into private or corporate wealth.

Even it is empirically true that cadres in China benefit more from the transition than non-cadres, the situation is still very different from the "political capitalism" in Eastern Europe, where the apparatchiks simply directly sell off state assets and accumulate private wealth that is then channeled out of the local economy. Thus far, cadres help their children, but refrain from becoming capitalists themselves. In China, because a thriving private economy exists, political capitalists are likely to reinvest the pilfered funds back into the domestic economy, where they know there political connections can help them get high returns. Moreover, private entrepreneurs thus far have not entered into cadre positions (Walder and Zhao 2002).

All these changes considered, we believe China and Vietnam's economic systems can best be described as hybrid capitalist systems. While China is moving in the direction of a full-fledged capitalist system, it is not there yet. Most crucially, there is not a clear dominance of private property. For although the state has decentralized, the most dynamic sector of the Chinese economy, the Village Township Enterprises (VTEs), are still not privately owned, although they are market dependent. These locally owned firms out-perform SOEs, and between 1985 and 1996 they increased from 14.6% of gross industrial output to 27.8%, while SOEs fell from 65% to 28.5% (see Peng 2001). Nan Lin (1995) proposes a "local market socialism" perspective to understand the hybrid nature of the Chinese political economy. He claims that the "local market socialism" perspective integrates socialism as the political axis, market-oriented reform as the economic axis, and locally embedded social networks as the social axis. Similar to Walder (1995) and Oi (1999), he also argues that decentralization does not mean abandoning the command

28 Wank argues that Chinese cadres, rich in networked social capital, play a crucial *functional* role as the broker between private firms and the state, between the coexisting market and redistributive systems, and provide the institutional infrastructure for market and reduce transaction costs.

system. Instead, the command system and newly emerged market mechanisms are both incorporated and embedded in local sociocultural networks.[29]

However, there is no doubt that China is moving in the direction of "capitalism." First, many VTEs are merely "red caps" – in which local state ownership is merely legal cover for what are really private businesses (see Liu 1992; Nee and Su 1996). Moreover, privatization has finally started to make headway in China, which up until the late 1990s mostly "grew out of the plan" without actively dismantling state ownership (Naughton 1995). The privatization of state and collectively owned industries has been greatly accelerated in recent years. Lin and Zhu (2001) use a 1998 national survey to show that by 1998 private ownership in SOEs is already quite substantial. Cao et al. (1999) study the accelerated privatization process since 1995 and argue that it is helped by the federalist structure of the Chinese political economy – and regions with larger private economies are more likely to privatize their SOEs (because the newly unemployed will be more likely to find jobs). On the other hand, many collectively-owned enterprises are also being aggressively privatized by their local governments. By 2002, the massive rural VTE sector, which had employed more than 80 million people at its zenith, underwent significant privatization, shrinking to half its former size (Walder and Zhao 2002: 5; Li and Rozelle [2000] also report empirical evidence of the privatization of VTEs).

Another factor pushing in the direction of capitalist property relations is the importance of foreign direct investment in China's economy. While per capita levels of FDI remain modest compared to Central Europe, as a percentage of total investment they are quite high and absolute levels are enormous. Of particular importance has been Taiwanese and Hong Kong capital investments into Southern China, creating what Naughton calls the second China Circle (1997: 7). This investment has led to explosive export growth, especially in electronics.

Furthermore, the SOEs that do exist, have become increasingly marketized. Guthrie (1997) studies asset diversification of Chinese SOEs and finds that they respond to market instability and exhibit increasingly market-oriented behaviors. Keister (1998; 2001) shows that Chinese SOEs adopt capitalist-like inter-corporate structures – business groups and interlocking directorates, which also have effects on firm performances similar to that in capitalist economies. Nee (2001) shows that from 1978 to 1991, the investment capital provided to SOEs came increasingly from non central-state sources (retained earnings, loans from state owned banks, and foreign sources). Over this period, the percentage provided by state redistributors fell from 62% to under 7%.[30] Other studies (Groves et al. 1994; Huang and Kalirajan 1998; Cao et al. 1999) have found evidence showing that many SOEs are subjected to market competition and are market integrated. Furthermore, market integration leads to improved performance: greater technical efficiency (Huang and Kalirajan 1998) and higher productivity (Groves

29 See Nee and Cao 1999 on the implications of a "hybrid mixed economy" for social stratification.

30 The OECD (2000) provides some recent data on this process. For instance, in 1999, the central government made the decision to withdraw state control from small and medium-sized SOEs (SOE = State Owned Enterprises). The number of industrial SOEs is expected to fall from the existing nearly 75,000 to at most one or two thousands.

et al. 1994). Another study (Groves et al. 1995) also finds that a managerial labor market is emerging in the state sector and the allocation of managerial resources is increasingly governed by the market. Because these firms remain state owned, but are increasingly market integrated (must buy inputs and sell products on markets) and behave like capitalist firms, we can call this type of property State Capitalism.

The Chinese system is "hybrid" because it is still a long way from becoming dominated by capitalist private property. However, it is capitalist to the extent that markets have flourished, and the private economy continues to expand, while the SOEs decline but behave increasingly like capitalist firms (see Nee 1992 and 2001). By 1993, SOE employment in urban areas declined from 75% to 60%, and in rural areas to around 30% (Cao, Qian and Weingast 1999). This should not be meant to imply that China is particularly neoliberal (see King 2003a). The Chinese transition has been overseen by a strong state (see Nee 2000), which continues to promote "national champions" from the SOEs that constitute Chinese business groups (see Keister 2000).[31] More important for Chinese growth, however, has been the state's massive infrastructural investments, which provides support for new private enterprise formation and growth.

These economic changes have political effects as well. The Communist Party loses its ideological commitment, replaced by a pragmatic approach that emphasizes growth and increasing living standards. China looks less and less like a totalitarian system, and more and more like a bureaucratic authoritarian regime – although it is still clearly totalitarian (because the Communist Party maintains its political monopoly).

Conclusions

The transition to capitalism from communism is rather different from earlier transitions to capitalism. First of all, this is the first time in history when capitalism was formed on the ruins of a society which did not have even in embryonic forms the institution of private property and which did not have therefore a propertied bourgeoisie. Second, socialism had accomplished some of the "historic missions" of capitalism: it completed the process of capital accumulation and industrialization, and, though in contradictory ways, separated the producers from the means of subsistence and production.

These features are consequential, though in different ways, for the nature of capitalism that emerges from communism. Postcommunist capitalisms constitute an "extended family" of capitalisms. In some countries the alliance of the technocracy and intellectuals could smash the power of the communist political apparatus, preventing the development of political capitalism and implementing a postcommunist liberal system that is highly dependent on foreign direct investments, foreign demand, and is sensitive to currency fluctuations. In countries where the technocratic-intellectual alliance and the working class were weaker, the political apparatus retained its power, abandoned the communist ideology and substituted for it nationalism, and implement political capitalism. Finally, in some countries the bureaucracy and technocracy arrived at a balance of power, and under these circumstances capitalism develops from below: the technocracy

31 See Zhou (2001) for an analysis of the state-led process of constructing a national grain market.

delays the political capitalism project of the political bureaucracy, while the communist political bureaucracy limits the liberal reform attempts of the technocracy.

Bibliography

Amsden, Alice H., Jacek Kochanowicz, and Lance Taylor. 1994. *The Market Meets its Match. Restructuring the Economies of Eastern Europe.* Cambridge: Harvard University Press.

Anderson, Perry. 1978. Passages from Antiquity to Feudalism. London: Verso.

Andor, Lazlo, and Martin Summers. 1998. *Market Failure: Eastern Europe's 'Economic Miracle'.* London, Chicago: Pluto Press.

Bernhard, Michael H. 1993. *The Origins of Democratization in Poland: Workers, Intellectuals,and Oppositional politics, 1976–1980.* New York: Columbia University Press.

Baltowski, Maciej and Tomasz Mickiewicz. 2000. "Privatization in Poland: Ten Years After." *Post-Communist Economies* 12 (4): 425–43.

Bernhard, Michael H. 1993. *The Origins of Democratization in Poland: Workers, Intellectuals, and Oppositional Politics, 1976–1980.* New York: Columbia University Press.

Bian, Yanjie. 2002. "Chinese Social Stratification and Social Mobility." *Annual Review of Sociology* 28 (1): 91–116.

Burawoy, Michael. 1996. "The State and Economic Involution: Russia through a Chinese Lens." World Development 24 (6): 1105–17.

Burawoy, Michael. 2001a. "Neo-classical sociology: from the end of communism to the end of classes." *American Journal of Sociology* 106 (4): 1099–1128.

Burawoy, Michael. 2001b. "Transition without Transformation: Russia's involuntary road to capitalism." *East European Politics and Society* 15 (2): 269–290.

Burawoy, Michael and Pavel Krotov. 1992. "The Soviet Transition From Socialism to Capitalism: Worker Control and Economic Bargaining" *American Sociological Review* 57: 16–38.

Burawoy, Michel, Pavel Krotov, and Tatyana Lytkina. 2000 "Domestic Involution: How Women Organize Survival in a North Russian City." In Victoria Bonnell and George Breslauer (eds.), *Russia in the New Century* (Boulder, Co.: Westview Press): 131–161.

Cao, Yuanzheng, Yingyi Qian, and Barry R. Weingast. 1999. "From Federalism, Chinese Style to Privatization, Chinese Style." *Economics of Transition* 7 (1): 103–131.

Chen, Yaobang. 1989. "Tongyi Sixiang, Jiji Tiaozheng, Cujin Xiangzhen Qiye Chi xu Xietiao Jiankang Fazhan." *Chinese Township-Village Enterprises (Zhongguo Xiangzhen Qiye)* 9 (September): 1–8.

Coates, David. 2000. *Models of Capitalism. Growth and Stagnation in the Modern Era.* Cambridge: Polity Press.

Darden, Keith A. 2002. "The Scholastic Revolution: Explaining Nationalism in the USSR." Paper presented at Workshop on Postcommunism, Yale University, Fall.

Davis, Deborah. 2000 (ed.) The Consumer Revolution in China. Berkeley: University of California Press.

Davis, Deborah. 2003. Personal communication.

Ding, X. L. 2000. "Informal Privatization through Internationalization: The Rise of Nomenklatura Capitalism in China's Offshore Businesses." *British Journal of Political Science* 30: 121–146.

Djankov, Simeon, and Bernard Hoekmann. 2000. "Foreign Investment and Productivity Growth in Czech Enterprises." *World Bank Economic Review* 14 (1): 49–64.

Donnithorne, Audrey. 1972. "China's Cellular Economy: Some Economic Trends since the Cultural Revolution." *The China Quarterly* 52: 605–619.

Dyker, David A., and Stanislav Kubielas. 2000. "Technology and Structure in the Polish Economy under Transition and Globalization." *Economic Systems* 24 (1): 1–24.

European Bank for Reconstruction and Development (EBRD). 1996, 1999, 2001. *Transition Report*. London: EBRD.

Ekiert, Grzegorz. 2001. "The State after State Socialism: Poland in Comparative Perspective" Harvard University, Center for European Studies, photocopy. Feb. 1.

Evans, Peter. 1979. *Dependent Development: The Alliance of Multinational State and Local Capital in Brazil.* Princeton: Princeton University Press.

Eyal, Gil. 2000. "Anti-politics and the Spirit of Capitalism: Dissidents, Monetarists, and the Czech Transition to Capitalism." *Theory and Society* 29 (1): 49–92.

Eyal, Gil, Iván Szelényi, and Eleanor Townsley. 1998. *Making Capitalism without Capitalists. Class Formation and Elite Struggles in Post-communist Central Europe.* London: Verso.

Eyal, Gil, Iván Szelényi, and Eleanor Townsley. 2001. "The Utopia of Postsocialist Theory and the Ironic View of History in Neoclassical Sociology." *American Journal of Sociology* 106 (4): 1121–28.

Filer, Randall K., and Jan Hanousek. 2001. "Data Watch: Research Data from Transition Economies." William Davidson Working Paper No. 416., William Davidson Institute at the University of Michigan Business School.

Fligstein, Neil. 1996. "The Economic Sociology of the Transitions from Socialism." *American Journal of Sociology* 101 (4): 1074–1081.

Fodor Éva. 2002. "Smiling women and fighting men: the gender of communist subjects in state socialist Hungary," *Gender and Society* 16 (29): 240–263.

Frank, André Gunder. 1969. *Capitalism and Underdevelopment in Latin America: Historical Studies of Chile and Brazil.* New York: Monthly Review Press.

Garcelon, Marc. 1997 "The Estate of Change: The Specialist Rebellion and the Democratic Movement in Moscow, 1989–1991." *Theory and Society* 26: 39–85.

Gerber, Theodore P. and Michael Hout. 1998. "More Shock than Therapy: Market Transition, Employment, and Income in Russia, 1991–1995." *American Journal of Sociology,* 104 (1): 1–50.

Gligorov, Vladimir. 1995. "Republic of Slovenia: Country Report." *The Vienna Institute for Comparative Economic Studies*. December.

Golovachev, Vitaly. 2002. "Russian Money Goes Around the World." WPS Monitoring Agency, September 13. www.wps.ru/e_index.html.

Gowan, Peter. 1995. "Neoliberal Theory and Practice for Eastern Europe." *New Left Review*. No. 213: 3–60.

Gowan, Peter. 1999. *The Global Gamble: Washington's Faustian Bid for World Domination*. London: Verso.

Granick, David. 1990. *Chinese State Enterprises: A Regional Property Rights Analysis.* Chicago: University of Chicago Press.

Groves, Theodore, Yongmiao Hong, John McMillan, and Barry Naughton. 1994. "Autonomy and Incentives in Chinese State Enterprises." *Quarterly Journal of Economics* 109 (1): 183–209.

Groves, Theodore, Yongmiao Hong, John McMillan, and Barry Naughton. 1995. "China's Evolving Managerial Labor Market." *Journal of Political Economy* 103: 873–92.

Guthrie, D. 1997. "Between Markets and Politics: Organizational Responses to Reform in China." *American Journal of Sociology* 102 (5): 1258–1304.

Haney, Lynne. 2002. *Inventing the Needy. Gender and the Politics of Welfare in Hungary.* Berkeley and Los Angeles: University of California Press.

Hankiss, Elemér. 1990. *East European Alternatives.* Oxford: Clarendon Press.

Hanley, Eric, Natasha Yershova, and Richard Anderson. 1995. "Russia – Old wine is a New Bottle? The Circulation and Reproduction of Russian Elites, 1983–1993." *Theory and Society* 24: 639–668.

Hanley, Eric, Lawrence King and Istvan Janos Toth. 2002. "The State, International Agencies, and Property Transformation in Post-Communist Hungary." *American Journal of Sociology* 108 (1): 129–167.

Hart, Jeffrey A. 1992. *Rival Capitalists: international competitiveness in the United States, Japan and Western Europe.* Cornell University Press.

Helf, Gavin and Jeffrey W. Hahn. 1992. "Old Dogs and New Tricks: Party Elites in the Russian Regional Elections of 1990." *Slavic Review* 51 (3): 511–530.

Heller, Ágnes, Ferenc Fehér, and Márkus György. 1983. *Dictatorship over Needs, An Analysis of Soviet Societies.* London: Palgrave Macmillan.

Hoffman, David. 2002. *The Oligarchs: Wealth and Power in the New Russia.* New York: Public Affairs.

Huang, Yasheng. 1995. "Information, Bureaucracy and Economic Reforms in China and the Soviet Union." *World Politics* 47 (1): 102–134.

Huang, Yiping, and K. P. Kalirajan. 1998. "Enterprise Reform and Technical Efficiency of China's State-Owned Enterprises." *Applied Economics* 30 (5): 585–592.

Jiang, Xiaojuan (Ed.). 2001. *China's Industries in Transition: Organizational Change, Efficiency Gains, and Growth Dynamics.* Huntington, NY: Nova Science Publishers, Inc.

Kaminski, Bartlomiej, and Beata Smarzýńska. 2001. "Foreign Direct Investment and Integration into Global Production and Distribution Networks: The Case of Poland." Working Papers – International Economics, Trade, Capital Flows No. 2646, World Bank.

Karabel, Jerome. 1993. "Polish Intellectuals and the Origins of Solidarity: the making of an oppositional alliance," *Communist and Post-Communist Studies* 26 (1): 25–46.

Keister, Lisa A. 1998. "Engineering Growth: Business Group Structure and Firm Performance in China's Transitional Economy." *American Journal of Sociology* 104 (2): 404–440.

Keister, Lisa A. 2000. *Chinese Business Groups: The Structure and Impact of Interfirm Relations during Economic Development.* Oxford: Oxford University Press.

Keister, Lisa A. 2001. "Exchange Structures in Transition: Lending and Trade Relations in Chinese Business Groups." *American Sociological Review* 66 (3): 336–360.

Kennedy, Michael D. 1987. "Polish Engineers' Participation in the Solidarity Movement." *Social Forces* 65 (3): 641–669.

Kennedy, Michael D. 1992. "The Intelligentsia in the Constitution of Civil Societies in Post-Communist Regimes in Hungary and Poland." *Theory and Society* 21: 29–76.

King, Lawrence P. 2000. "Foreign Direct Investment and Transition." *European Journal of Sociology* 41 (2): 189–224.

King, Lawrence P. 2001a. *The Basic Features of Post-Communist Capitalism: Firms in Hungary, the Czech Republic, and Slovakia*. Westport CT: Praeger Press.

King, Lawrence P. 2001b. "Making Markets: a comparative study of postcommunist managerial strategies in Central Europe." *Theory and Society.* 30 (4): 493–538.

King, Lawrence P. 2002. "Postcommunist Divergence: A Comparative Analysis of the Transition to Capitalism in Poland and Russia." *Studies in Comparative International Development* 37(3): 3–34.

King, Lawrence P. 2003a. "Shock Privatization: The Effects of Rapid Large Scale Privatization on Enterprise Restructuring." *Politics and Society* 13 (1): 3–30.

King, Lawrence P. 2003b. "Does Neoliberalism Work: Testing Sociological and Economic Explanations of Postcommunist Performance." Paper presented at Duke University, Department of Sociology (February): 1–72.

King, Lawrence P., and Balasz Varadi. 2002. "Beyond Manichean Economics: Foreign Direct Investment and Growth in the Transition from Capitalism." *Communist and Post-Communist Studies* 2 (3): 1–21.

Kinoshita, Yuko. 1999. "Technology Spillovers through Foreign Direct Investment." Working Paper No. 221, William Davidson Institute at the University of Michigan Business School.

Klebnikov, Paul. 2000. *Godfather of the Kremlin: The Decline of Russia in the Age of Gangster Capitalism.* New York: Harcourt.

Kojima, Reiitsu. 1992. "The Growing Fiscal Authority of Provincial-Level Governments in China." *Journal of Developing Economies* 30 (4): 315–346.

Konrad, George and Iván Szelényi. 1979. *Intellectuals on the Road to Class Power***.** New York etc.: Hartcourt Brace Jovanovich.

Korbonski, Andrzej. 1999. "East Central Europe on the Eve of the Changeover: The Case of Poland." *Communist and Post-Communist Studies* 32: 139–53.

Kornai, Janos. 1980. *Economics of Shortage.* 1. Volume A. Amsterdam: North Holland Pub. Co.

Kornai, Janos. 1992. *The Socialist Economic System.* Princeton: Princeton University Press.

Kramer, Mark. 1995. "Polish Workers and the Postcommunist Transition, 1989–93." Communist and Post-Communist Studies 28 (1): 71–114.

Kubik, Jan. 1994. "Who Done It: Workers, Intellectuals, or Someone Else? Controversy over Solidarity' Origins and Social Composition." *Theory and Society* 23: 441–66.

Lane, David Stuart. 1981. *Leninism: A Sociological Interpretation.* Cambridge: Cambridge University Press.

Li, Bobai, and Andrew G. Walder. 2001. "Career Advancement as Party Patronage: Sponsored Mobility into the Chinese Administrative Elite, 1949–1996." *American Journal of Sociology* 106 (5): 1371–1408.

Li, Cheng. 2001. *China's Leaders: The New Generation.* Lanham, MD: Rowman & Littlefield.

Li, H. B., and Scott Rozelle. 2000. "Saving or Stripping Rural Industry: An Analysis of Privatization and Efficiency in China." *Agricultural Economics* 23 (3): 241–252.

Liberman, Ira, Stilpon S. Nestor, and Raj M. Desai. eds. 1997. *Between State and Market: Mass Privatization in Transition Economies. Studies of Economies in Transition.* Washington D.C.: The World Bank.

Liberska, Barbara. 1997. "Foregin Direct Investment in Poland." Working Paper No. 7, Polish Academy of Sciences, Institute of Economics, Warsaw.

Lin, Nan. 1995. "Local Market Socialism: Local Corporatism in Action in Rural China." *Theory and Society* 24: 301–354.
Lin, Yin-Min, and Tian Zhu. 2001. "Ownership Restructuring in China State Industry: An Analysis of Evidence on Initial Organizational Changes." *The China Quarterly* 166: 305–341.
Lin, Yin-Min, and Zhanxin Zhang. 1999. "Backyard Profit Centers: The Private Assets of Public Agencies." In *Property Rights and Economic Reform in China,* edited by Jean C. Oi and Andrew G. Walder. Stanford, California: Stanford University Press: 203–225.
Liu, Yia-Ling. 1992. "Reform from Below: The Private Economy and Local Politics in the Rural Industrialization of Wenzhou." *China Quarterly* 130: 293–316.
Linz, Juan and Alfred Stepan. 1996. *Problems of Democratic Transition and Consolidation: Southern Europe, South America, and Post-Communist Europe.* Baltimore: Johns Hopkins University Press.
Lyons, Thomas P. 1986. "Explaining Economics Fragmentation in China: A Systems Approach." *Journal of Comparative Economics* 10 (3): 209–236.
Manchin, Róbert and Iván Szelényi. 1987. "Social Policy under State Socialism." In *Stagnation and Renewal in Social Policy*, ed. by Gøsta Esping-Anderson, Lee Rainwater, and Martin Rein. White Plains, N.Y.: M. E. Sharpe: 102–139.
Marquand, David, and Ramsay MacDonald. 1997. *New Reckoning: Capitalism, States, and Citizens.* Cambridge, UK: Malden, Mass.: Polity Press.
Marquand, Judith. 2009. "Interview with Piotr Chernogrinov." In: Judith Marquand (ed.). *Development Aid in Russia. Lessons from Siberia.* Basingstoke etc.: Palgrave-Macmillan.
McDermott, Gerald. 2002. *Embedded Politics: Industrial Networks and Institutional Change in Postcommunism.* Ann Arbor: University of Michigan Press.
Mencinger, Joze. 1996. "Privatization Experiences in Slovenia." *Annals of Public and Cooperative Economics* 67: 415–28.
Montinola, Gabriella, Yingyi Qian, and Barry R. Weingast. 1996. "Federalism, Chinese Style: The Political Basis for Economic Success." *World Politics* 48 (1): 50–81.
Murrel, Peter. 1993. What is Shock Therapy? What Did It Do in Poland and Russia?" *Post-Soviet Affairs* 9: 111–40.
Naughton, Barry. 1992. "Implications of the State Monopoly over Industry and Its Relaxation." *Modern China* 18 (1): 14–41.
Naughton, Barry. 1994. "Chinese Institutional Innovation and Privatization from Below." *American Economic Review* 84 (2): 266–270.
Naughton, Barry. 1995. *Growing Out of the Plan: Chinesese Economic Reform, 1978–1993* Cambridge: Cambridge University Press.
Nee, Victor. 1989. "A Theory of Market Transition: From Redistribution to Markets in State Socialism." *American Sociological Review* 54 (5): 663–681.
Nee, Victor. 1992. "Organizational Dynamics of Market Transition: Hybrid Forms, Property Rights, and Mixed Economy in China." *Administrative Science Quarterly* 37: 1–27.
Nee, Victor. 1996. "The Emergence of a Market Society: Changing Mechanisms of Stratification in China." *American Journal of Sociology* 101 (4): 908–949.

Nee, Victor. 1998. "Sources of the New Institutionalism" In: *The New Institutionalism in Sociology*, ed. by Mary C. Brinton and Victor Nee. New York: Russel Sage Foundation: 1–16.

Nee, Victor. 2000. "Comment: Controversies and evidence of market transition debate," America Journal of Sociology 105 (4): 1175–1189.

Nee, Victor. 2001. "North's Theory of Institutional Change and State Capitalism in China." Paper presented at the conference "Economic Sociology of Capitalism, " Center for the Study of Economy and Society, Cornell University.

Nee, Victor, and Yang Cao. 1999. "Path Dependent Societal Transformation: Stratification in Hybrid Mixed Economies." *Theory and Society* 28 (6): 799–834.

Nolan, Peter, and Robert F. Ash. 1996. "China's Economy on the Eve of Reform." In *China's Transitional Economy. Interpreting its Significance,* edited by Andrew G. Walder. Oxford: Oxford University Press: 18–36.

Nuti, Mario and Grzegorz Kolodko. 1997. "The Polish Alternative: Old Myths, Hard Facts and New Strategies," available at Social Science Research Network (SSRN).

Organization for Economic Cooperation and Development (OECD). 2000. *Reforming China's Enterprises.* Paris: OECD Publications.

Oi, Jean C. 1999. *Rural China Takes Off: Institutional Foundations of Economic Reform.* Berkeley and Los Angeles: University of California Press.

Ost, David. 1990. *Solidarity and the Politics of Anti-Politics: Opposition and Reform in Poland since 1968.* Philadelphia: Temple University Press.

Pearson, Margaret M. 1997. *China's New Business Elite: The Political Consequences of Economic Reform.* Berkeley & Los Angles: University of California Press.

Popov, Vladimir. 1999. "The Financial System in Russia compared to other Transition Economies: The Anglo-American versus the German-Japanese Model." *Comparative Economic Studies* 41 (1): 1–42.

Popov, Vladimir. 2000. "Shock Therapy Versus Gradualism: The End of the Debate. Explaining the Magnitude of Transformational Recessing." *Comparative Economic Studies*, 42 (1): 1–57.

Qian, Yingyi, and Barry Weingast. 1997. "Federalism as a Commitment to Preserving Market Incentives." *Journal of Economic Perspectives* 11 (4): 83–92.

Reddaway, Peter and Dmitri Glinski. 2001. *The Tragedy of Russia's Reforms: Market Bolshevism Against Democracy*. Washington: United States Institute of Peace Press.

Rodrik, Dani. "Understanding Economic Policy Reform." *Journal of Economic Literature* 34: 9–41.

Rona-Tas, Akos. 1994. The first shall be the last? Entrepreneurship and Communist Cadres in the Transition. *American Journal of Sociology* 100 (1): 40–69.

Rona-Tas, Akos. 1997. "The Czech Third Wave. Privatization and the New Role of the State in the Czech Republic." *Problems of Post-Communism*, 44 (6): 53–62.

Sachs, Jeffery D., and Wing Thye Woo. 1994. "Structural Factors in the Economic Reforms of China, Eastern Europe, and the Former Soviet Union." *Economic Policy* 9 (18): 101–45.

Schroeder, Gertrude. 1998. "Dimensions of Russia's Industrial Transformation, 1992 to 1998: An Overview." *Post Soviet Geography and Economics* 39 (5): 243–70.

Schurmann, Franz. 1964. "China's 'New Economic Policy' – Transition of Beginning?" *China Quarterly* 17: 65–91.

Shlapentokh, Vladimir. 1990. *Soviet Intellectuals and Political Power. The post-Stalin era.* Princeton: Princeton University Press.

Snajder, Aleksandra and Lawrence King. 2002. "Controlled Liberalism: Poland's State-led Transition to Capitalism." Paper presented at the Yale Workshop in Comparative Studies. (www.yale.edu/ccr).

Southworth, Caleb. 2001. "How Russian Industry Works: Worker and Firm Survival Strategies in Six Enterprises in Bashkortosan." Ph.D. diss., University of California, Los Angeles.

Stark, David. 1992. "Path Dependence and Privatization Strategies in East Central Europe." *East European Politics and Societies* 6 (1): 17–54.

Stark, David. 1996. "Recombinant Property in East European Capitalism." American Journal of Sociology 101: 993–1027.

Stark, David Charles and László Bruszt. 1998. *Postsocialist pathways: transforming politics and property in East Central Europe.* Cambridge [England], New York: Cambridge University Press.

Steinfeld, Edward S. 1998. *Forging Reform in China: The Fate of State-Owned Industry.* New York: Cambridge University Press.

Stiglitz, Joseph. 2002. *Globalization and Its Discontents.* New York etc.: W. W. Norton.

Szalai, Erzsébet. 2001. *Gazdasági elit* és *társadalom a magyarországi* újkapitalizmusban. Budapest: Aula Kiadó.

Szelényi, Iván and Balasc Szelényi. 1994. "Why Socialism Failed: Toward a Theory of System Breakdown. Causes of Disintegration of East-European State Socialism." *Theory and Society* 23: 211–31.

Szelényi, Iván, Szonja Szelényi and Imre Kóvach. 1995. "The making of the Hungarian postcommunist elite: Circulation in politics, reproduction in the economy." *Theory and Society* 24: 697–722.

Varese, Frederico. 2001. *The Russian Mafia: Private Protection in a New Market Economy.* Oxford: Oxford University Press.

Vorobyov, Alexander, and Stanislav Zhukov. 2000. "Russia: Globalization, Structural Shifts, and Inequality." CEPA Working Paper Series 1, No. 09.

Walder, Andrew G. 1995. "Career Mobility and the Communist Political Order."*American Sociological Review* 60 (3): 309–328.

Walder, Andrew G. 2002. "Markets and Income Inequality in Rural China: Political Advantage in an Expanding Economy." *American Sociological Review* 67 (2): 231–253.

Walder, Andrew G., Bobai Li, and Donald J. Treiman. 2000. "Politics and Life Chances in a State Socialist Regime: Dual Career Paths into Urban Chinese Elite, 1949–1996." *American Sociological Review* 65: 191–209.

Walder, Andrew G. and Gong Xiaoxia. 1993. "Workers in the Tiananmen Protests: The Politics of the Beijing Workers' Autonomous Federation." *The Australian Journal of Chinese Affairs*, Vol. 0 (29): 1–29.

Walder, Andrew G. and Litao Zhao. 2002. "Political Office, Kinship, and Household Wealth in Rural China." *Working Paper*, Asia/Pacific Research Center, Stanford University, December.

Wank, David L. 1999. *Commodifying Communism: Business, Trust, and Politics in a Chinese City.* New York: Cambridge University Press.

Wasilewski, Jacek and Edmund Wnuk-Lipinski. 1995. "Poland: Winding Road from the Communist to the Post-Solidarity Elite." *Theory and Society* 24: 669–96.

Wedel, Janine R. 2001. *Collision and Collusion: The Strange Case of Western Aid to Eastern Europe.* New York: Palgrave.

Wong, Christine. 1988. "Interpreting Rural Industrial Growth in the Post-Mao Period." *Modern China* 14: 3–30.

Wong, Christine. 1992. "Fiscal Reform and Local Industrialization: The Problematic Sequencing of Reform in Post-Mao China." *Modern China* 18: 197–227.

Woo, W. T. 1994. "The Art of Reforming Centrally Planned Economies – Comparing China, Poland, and Russia." *Journal of Comparative Economics* 18 (3): 276–308.

Woo, W. T. 1994. "The Art of Reforming Centrally Planned Economies – Comparing
Wasilewski, Jacek and Edmund Wnuk-Lipinski. 1995. "Poland: Winding Road from the Communist to the Post-Solidarity Elite." *Theory and Society* 24: 669–696.

Woodruff, David. 1999. *Money Unmade: Barter and the Fate of Russian Capitalism*, Ithaca N.Y.: Cornell University Press.

Yang, Dali L. 1996. *Calamity and Reform in China: State, Rural Society, and Institutional Change since the Great Leap Famine.* Stanford, CA: Stanford University Press.

Zhou, Kate Xiao. 1996. *How Farmers Changed China: Power of the People.* Boulder, CO: Westview Press.

Zhou, Wubiao. 2001. "The Making of an Integrated National Grain Market in China." William Davidson Working Paper No. 397, William Davidson Institute at the University of Michigan Business School.

IV. Critical Theory of Post-Communism

IV.1 Weber's Theory of Domination and Post-Communist Capitalisms

Iván Szelényi

Abstract

This article has four main objectives. First, it introduces the ideal types of domination of Weber. Contrary to the received wisdom, which knows only "three ideal types" (traditional, charismatic and legal rational) I present the "fourth" type of domination, Weber called "*Wille der Beherrschten*" as an important correction of his ideal type of legal-rational authority. Next I make a novel, critical distinction between patrimonial and prebendal types of traditional authority. Third, I discuss various ways that communist regimes tried to legitimate themselves and how they entered eventually a legitimation crisis, leading to the collapse of communism. In the next section, I explore the different ways post-communist capitalisms seek legitimacy (with various combinations of legal rational authority and patrimonialism), and finally I conclude with a trend of re-convergence of some post-communist systems (especially Russia and Hungary, but with signs for similar trends elsewhere) into an illiberal, prebendal quasi-democratic system.

Keywords: Ideal types of domination, Legitimate authority, Post-communist capitalisms, Max Weber, Liberalism, Democratic system, Capitalisms

Introductory notes on Weber's theory of power, domination, and legitimacy

The main purpose of this article is to explore whether post-communist capitalism, at least some versions of it, can be regarded as legitimate authority. The nature of political regimes of certain post-communist regimes, especially the rule by Presidents Putin and Xi and since 2010 that of Hungarian Prime Minister Orbán's government, is often hotly debated, nevertheless the question whether these regimes are legitimate at all and if so on what ground do they claim legitimacy is rarely posed.[1]

1 There is a gigantic literature on this matter, mainly debating whether countries like Russia, Belarus, and Hungary still can be called democracy, or did they turn into "managed democra-

When a system can be called "legitimate" can be debated and the answers to these questions depend to a large extent on our definition of terms. The aim of my article is rather limited. My point of departure is Max Weber's theory of legitimacy and the only question I pose is: Were communist and are post-communist regimes of Putin, Xi, or Orbán legitimate in terms of Weber's theory, and if they are, what are the bases of their claim for legitimacy? Weber's distinction between power (*Macht*) and domination/authority (*Herrschaft*) is crucial to answer this question. The dispute how to translate *Herrschaft* into English is indicative of the controversy about some of the issues of legitimacy. Talcott Parsons offered one of the first – at that time still incomplete – translations of *Economy and Society* into English. He translated *Herrschaft* in a very American way as "authority." [2] The term – which is occasionally also used by Weber – implying the respectability of those who issue commands, rather than emphasizing the asymmetry of power relationships between those who dominate and those who are subordinated to domination.[3] Gerth and Mills just about the same time (Parson was a political conservative, while Mills was on the political left, and Gerth as a native German speaker had an arguably deeper understanding of what "*Herrschaft*" meant) both translated *Herrschaft* as "domination."[4] Whether Herrschaft means authority or domination is of some importance to understanding Weber's work and especially the theory of legitimation.[5] Weber himself was hesitant in his terminology. In the earlier drafts of *Economy and Society,* he used the term "authority" quite often, but as he was redrafting the work for what was eventually published as chapters 1–4 in the version of the book edited by Marianne Weber (Weber 1978), in the chapters written some time between 1919 and

cy" (P. Anderson 2007) or are they already "autocracies" (Kormai 2014), "illiberal democracies" (Zakaria 1997). Some even call those regimes neo-fascist or neo-communist. Nevertheless, the question of legitimacy is relatively rarely posed, which may have a lot to do with the absence of analytical clarity of the concept of legitimacy. After Putin's election to the presidency in 2012, Russian journalists suggested Putin is "illegitimate" (Russian journalists 2012). The former liberal mayor of Budapest, Gábor Demszky, called the Orbán regime illegitimate (See Rádai Eszter 2014). There are also some attempts though to see new types of legitimacy emerging in post-communist "managed democracies" or "autocracies." Daniel Bell saw Confucianism as a new legitimating principle of post-Maoist China (Bell 2008), Ossinovski, in an intriguing MSc dissertation, sees Putin's Russia as a combination of charismatic and legal-rational authority (Ossinovski 2010)

2 Astonishingly, Parsons does not translate the term "*Herrschaft*" even ONCE as "domination." He is in pain when he has to translate "*Herrschaft*" from the German original – see *MWG I/22-4, pp. 126ff.,* MWG I/23, p. 210 – where *Herrschaft* is so obviously not simply authority – a respectable exercise of power – so he invents the difficult concept,"imperative control" (Weber 1947, p. 152). This notion captures the tone of the concept better than authority, but still misses the idea of "subordination" found in "domination."

3 Max Weber, *The Theory of Social and Economic Organization*, 1947.

4 Gerth and Mills, from Max Weber, (1946).

5 The question how to translate *Herrschaft* into English has been debated for some time. Mommsen (1974, p. 74) among others pointed out the difficulties of translation, but in the end he also concluded domination is the most appropriate term.

1920, while the earlier versions were written in 1914 or before,[6] suddenly the word authority almost completely disappears and *Herrschaft* is used almost exclusively.[7]

In order to understand why this is important we need to go back to the distinction between *Macht* and *Herrschaft.* In the later work (1919–1920) Weber defines clearly the difference between the two forms of exercising influence on others. As he puts it so eloquently in the last version of the book: power (*Macht*) is the probability that one actor within the social relationship will be in a position to carry out his own will despite resistance (Weber 2013 Band 23, p. 210).[8] Weber now has a clear definition of *Herrschaft* as well: "Domination (*Herrschaft*) is the probability that a command … will be obeyed." This is about as clear as it can get. Hence *Macht* (power) + legitimacy = *Herrschaft* (domination).

Weber's theory of domination assumes that those subjected to domination do have some degree of "belief" in the system. Those who obey order do so – at least to some extent – "voluntarily." No system of domination can sustain itself if it is just driven by customs, personal advantage or even effectual or idealistic attachment by those subordinated to authority:

> … [E]very genuine form of domination implies a minimum of voluntary compliance, that is, an interest … in obedience…. [C]ustoms, personal advantage, purely effectual or ideal motives of solidarity do not form a sufficiently reliable basis for a given domination. In addition there is ….a further element, the belief in legitimacy.… [E]very system attempts to establish … the belief in its legitimacy (Weber 1978, pp. 212–213).

Many important questions stem from this definition. For me, the crucial question is how to interpret the notion of belief. What kind of, how strong a belief of those subordinated to authority need there be in order to acknowledge domination as legitimate, and who should hold such "beliefs"?

In order to appreciate Weber's sophistication, one has to understand his claim that the privileged groups are not actually "superior." They merely base their claim for obedience in the myth of their superiority. In Weber's words: "Every highly privileged group develops a myth of its … superiority. Under the conditions of stable distribution of power that myth is accepted by the negatively privileged strata" (p. 953).

Hence those who obey orders typically suspect those who dominate justify their superiority by a "myth," therefore their belief is likely to be rather "passive." In other words, the "masses" (my term, not Weber's) are unlikely to have a positive, or affirmative

6 Edith Hanke is uncertain how to date the first formulation, but believes it has to be dated before WWI, *MWG I/22–4*, p. 118.

7 Contrast *MWG I/22–4*, Teilband 4 (written in 1914 or before) and *MWG* I/23 (written in 1919/1920) where the term authority hardly appears. When in the first published version of *Economy and Society* he defined *Herrschaft* he put behind the term *Herrschaft* in brackets and quotation marks "authority" this way: Herrschaft ("Autorität"), see Weber 1978, Vol. I. p.212 or *MWG I/22–4*, p. 449.

8 Already in the draft he wrote before the war, Weber tried to emphasize that *Herrschaft* implies obedience to command: "… in our terminology domination shall be identical with authoritarian power of command" (Weber 1978, p. 946; *MWG I/22–4*, p. 135).

belief in their masters, rulers, leaders, or bosses. They will believe that the domination imposed on them is justified since at this point in time they cannot find a realistic alternative. I do not have to love my master, king, husband, prime minister, CEO[9], Dean, department chair, or whatever: that person will exercise authority as long as I believe this person is better than any of his or her alternatives. If the masses begin to consider a possible alternative ruler/master the system is facing only a "legitimation problem."

Arguably that is a different story for the "staff." In every complex society domination is exercised through a staff and unlike ordinary people (or the masses) the staff is supposed to have a positive, affirmative belief in the myths that justify/legitimate authority. If the staff loses its positive belief in the myth of domination the legitimacy of the system may be in a crisis.

The Shah of Iran was never particularly loved by the people of Iran. They eventually began to hear the message of Khomeini from radical Islamic preachers during the Friday sermons and many Iranians might have believed this to be a better alternative to the rule of the Shah. That created a legitimation problem. But the Shah only fell, when his security apparatus abandoned him. As his staff lost faith in him the legitimation problem turned into a legitimation crisis.

But the road from legitimation problem to legitimation crisis and eventual collapse of the regime is certainly not a one-way street. Most Western liberal capitalist societies faced during the 1960s a serious legitimation problem. As student movements – on rare occasions with some support from labor – began to formulate an alternative to liberal democratic capitalism hence the system faced a legitimation problem – especially around 1968 – but history teaches us liberal capitalism has an extraordinary capacity to survive, not only economically, but also ideologically. Capitalist systems often incorporate "subversive ideologies" into its own world view (for instance, affirmative action for minorities and women and gay rights, which appeared irreconcilable with the world views of liberal capitalism, the "bourgeois social order" before the 1960s are reasonably acceptable now for the middle classes).

As I pointed out before the relationship between "staff" and "ruler" (by ruler I simply mean that person/office that issues command to be obeyed), is quite critical for Weber's theory of history. As history unfolds or "develops"[10] the relationship between the "ruler" and the "staff" changes. Indeed in the most elementary form of social organization (still existent in the family), namely under patriarchal authority the "ruler" has no "staff." In more complex forms, let's call it prebendalism – though Weber' terminology is not carved into stone – the staff has only rather limited claims to appropriate the means of administration (and property). Those are at the discretion of the ruler. In contrast under patrimonialism at least some of the means of administration (and let's foreshadow some of the property rights) are appropriated (though with some limitations) by the staff. In what he calls bureaucratic or legal rational authority no individual (neither the person in

9 CEO = Chief Executive Officer: highest position at any organization.

10 Roth and Schluchter suggests that Weber has no theory of "evolution," he rather conceived "development" over time, see Roth and Schluchter 1979, pp. 195–206; Schluchter 1981, pp. 1–5

authority nor his/her staff) has the rights of coercion, coercive rights are the monopoly of the state (but let us add: the private property rights of all individuals and incumbency of office are secure). I elaborate more about this later in this article.

It is crucial to see: for Weber's interpretative sociology the purpose of the concept of legitimacy is to interpret the various ways domination was operating over human history, to write a genealogy of human history. Much like with the theory of rationality Weber resisted the idea to call a certain type of human action "rational" and others as "irrational". Nothing could have been further from Weber than to limit the uses of legitimate order only to social organization that had existed only during the past hundred or 200 years, hence was "legitimated" by the rule of law or had majoritarian approval, and to designate the rest of human history as "illegitimate." In Weber's theory "irrational" action and "illegitimate" social order were marginal or exceptional cases. The good question was not to ask: is this action rational, or is this social order legitimate, but rather to explore what is the rationality of this action, what is the ground of legitimacy of this order.

Let me try to give examples of illegitimate rule. Illegitimate rule for Weber means the unsustainable system where those in command can obtain compliance only by systematic and actual use of coercion. I put the term "actual" in bold because East European dissidents in the 1980s – who wanted to question the legitimacy of late communist regimes – suggested they are illegitimate since they promise coercion in cases of non-compliance though do not exercise such coercion. In my view this would be unacceptable for Weber. All systems of domination promise coercion: even in a democratically constituted legal-rational authority those who do not comply with the rules/laws will be coerced. In many – if not most – countries people can even be executed. The modern state merely "monopolizes" the power of coercion, but it can never abandon it. Hence a system is illegitimate when those in command have to rely actually on massive coercion, like the mid-to-late 1930 Gulag in the USSR and the Nazi network of concentration camp during the war, arguably even the Kádár regime between 1957 and 1963, with several hundred political prisoners being executed and thousands imprisoned or deported. In an illegitimate system those who issue commands use *Macht*, they are unable to sustain or have lost *Herrschaft*, hence voluntary compliance by those subjected to their command.

In his work on legitimacy Weber also writes about "non-legitimate" types of actions/ systems, which is critically different from "illegitimate rule." If I may use here the Gramscian terminology, "non-legitimate authority" is similar to an emerging "counter-hegemony."

The prime example of non-legitimate authority is the Western city. Interestingly enough in the German original – posthumously published text – Weber did not use the term "non-legitimate authority" (*MWG* I/22–5, p. 59). I assume the term non-legitimate domination was added as a subtitle for Chapter XVI "The City" (Weber 1978, p. 1212) by Marianne Weber, who edited the whole work for publication. Nevertheless the term "non-legitimate authority" (following the logic of non-rational as distinct from irrational) is a sensible one. What is the bottom line in the manuscript *Die Stadt*? My short take on this is: the city that emerges in the West has one exceptional feature: it is an island in the ocean of traditional authority, which introduces a new principle, the principle of *Jus soli* by offering *Bürgertum*, or "citizenship" (and freedom from the master) for all those who spent a certain amount of time in the city. It introduces a new principle of legitimacy – territoriality – that is not accepted as legitimate in the surrounding ocean of traditional authority where everyone's identity is decided *by Jus sanguinis*, by ancestry. "Stadtluft macht frei" (the city air makes you free) is the "non-legitimate" principle of the Western city not known in other cities of history (Weber 1999, *MWG* I/22–5, p. 105). If a serf spent a relatively short period of time in the city and swore allegiance to the city, he became its "*Bürger*," or "citizen" and his master could not reclaim him or her any longer. Non-legitimate authority implies an embryo that begins to grow within the womb of a previous system of domination. It is not legitimate yet, but has a reasonable chance to become legitimate. No determination is implied: non-legitimate authority does not necessarily become legitimate: members of communes of the 1960s might have believed the way they live – which might have involved promiscuity – could eventually become the norm, would become the legitimate way to live. It did not happen – so far – but that does not mean it was not a potentiality.

Let's summarize what we have said so far: systems are legitimate if those subordinated to authority accept their subordination, since they cannot define a better alternative and the staff of the person who issues commands has a firm belief that the master's claims (myths for his superiority) are valid. Those systems are illegitimate that have to coerce the ones subjected to authority to obey orders; hence they have to jail, kill, and torture masses of people in a rather unpredictable way to obtain obedience. Illegitimate authority is unlikely to sustain itself in the long run. Legitimate order always assumes some degree (even if a weak one) of belief and voluntariness. People obey orders from an illegitimate authority merely if they are afraid of what will happen to them if they do not comply; they are concerned about their life and livelihood.

The three (and the fourth) ideal types of legitimate authority

Weber makes distinction between three "ideal types of dominations/authority": traditional, charismatic and legal/rational. Nevertheless, in a lecture delivered in Vienna in the fall of 1917 he considered a fourth possible type of authority, and I will briefly deliberate on this.[11] The distinction between the initial three types serves dual purposes:

1) it is part of his philosophy of history. To put it brutally simple: history develops from earlier stages. It is not "evolution," since a) it is not inevitable, societies can be "stuck" at earlier phases of "development," and b) an interpretative social scientist has no way to claim that later phases are superior to earlier stages. In addition 2) while the typology is mainly historical it is also "trans-organizational." Every actually existing society can be interpreted as a mix of the three types of domination. All actually existing

11 See the review of his lecture in October 25, 1917 in *Neue Freie Presse*, reproduced in *MWG* I/22–4, pp. 752–756).

systems have some elements from all three – and as I try to show: indeed four – ideal types. We may live in a legal-rational social order, but occasionally political leaders may have charismatic appeal and in the family – or in our universities – we may be subjected to patriarchal authority, while fundamentally universities are governed by laws and rules. And to continue with the fourth type of authority: we may live in a legal-rational order where the executive is not in its place by the will of those subordinated to authority (this is the case for instance when a king rules in a constitutional monarchy) or those who exercise political authority may have majoritarian approval but may violate the principles of the rule of law (think of Vladimir Putin).

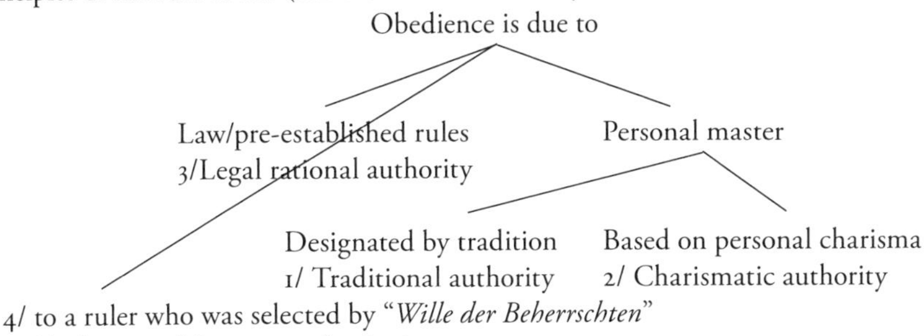

Fig. 1 Obedience and four types of authority

This is very much the essence of the Weberian approach. Our task is to explore the nature of legitimacy in any society: to what extent is a society governed by legal-rational authority? Are there some elements of charismatic or traditional authority present in this social system? It is never either/or, the right question is: what is the empirical mix in any particular concrete empirical case.

First, let me briefly review the three ideal types Weber presents to us in *Economy and Society* and amend it with the "fourth type" at the end of this section of the article. In this article my main task is to explore what is the mix we can find in a communist and post-communist society and how different is it from other societies we are familiar with. The basis of this classification is to whom obedience is due on what grounds in the various systems of domination.

It is important to note that the ontological status of the four types of authority is not quite the same (see Fig. 1). While traditional authority, legal rational authority, and authority based on the "*Wille der Beherrschten*" are stable forms, charismatic authority is a "revolutionary force." Hence I begin the discussion with a brief review of the type of domination with traditional authority (Fig. 2).

Traditional authority

Let us begin with Weber's mature definition of traditional authority:

1. "Legitimacy is claimed for and believed in by virtue of the sanctity of age-old rules …" (p. 226).

2. "The masters are designated according to traditional rule and are obeyed because of their "*Eigenwürde*" (traditional status)" (p. 226).
3. "This … rule is … primarily based on personal loyalty" (p. 227).
4. "The person exercising authority is not a superior, but a "personal master" (p. 227).
5. "Obedience is owed not to enacted rules, but to the person …" (p. 227) [12]

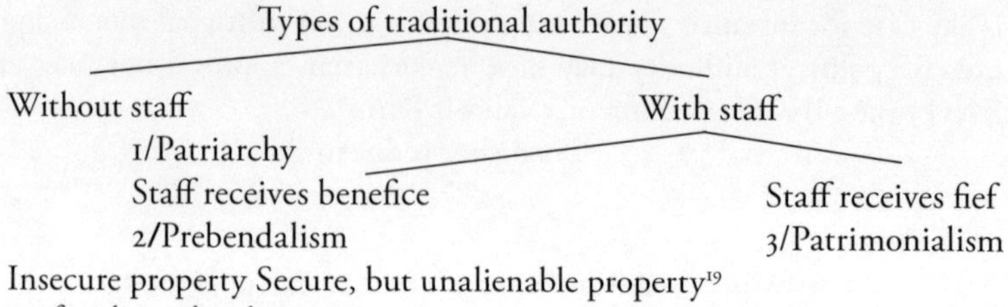

Fig. 2 Types of traditional authority

This seems to be clear enough as an attempt to describe "pre-modern" or "traditional" societies. Weber goes a great deal further and characterizes various types/phases – given his dedication to "developmentalism." I try to avoid terms like "stages" in discussing traditional authority.

Charismatic authority

Not much remains to be said about the second, transitional form of authority: charismatic domination. Its nature is straight forward and it is quite obvious that in some form or degree the charismatic domination concept is applicable not only to archaic societies, but to the world of the twentieth or twenty-first centuries. Weber's definition is clear:

> The term 'charisma' will be applied to a certain quality of an individual personality by virtue of which he is considered extraordinary and treated as endowed with supernatural, superhuman, or at least exceptional powers or qualities. These … are not accessible to the ordinary person, but regarded as of divine origin or as exemplary … (p. 241)

People who subject themselves to charismatic authority consider that person "extraordinary" (almost superhuman, or divine), so charisma is not an innate characteristic of individuals, but it is attributed to them by the followers. But why would they do this? Why would they consider another ordinary person as extraordinary, divine, or exemplary? Weber has a good answer. People "create" charismatic leaders in times of great transformation and crises, when there is a great need for a leader who can deliver miracles and resolve the problems that look almost unresolvable. A charismatic leader offers hope for the hopeless, promises paradise on Earth. And when he cannot deliver? He loses his charisma:

12 All citations are from Weber 1978.

"If proof and success elude the leader for long ... it is likely that his charismatic authority will disappear" (p. 242).

"[The charismatic leader gains and retains his authority] ... solely by proving his powers in practice. He must work miracles.... If the people withdraw their recognition, the master becomes a mere private person ..." (pp. 1114–1115).

No wonder, charisma is the "revolutionary force":

"In traditionalist periods, charisma is the great revolutionary force ..." (p. 245).

"[B]ureaucratic rationalization, too, often has been a major revolutionary force.... But it revolutionizes with technical means ... "from without" ... Charismatic belief revolutionizes men 'from within' ..." (pp. 1116f.).

"In pre-rationalistic periods, tradition and charisma between them have almost exhausted the whole of orientation of action" (p. 245).[13]

Charisma hence is in the "eye of the beholder," not a characteristic of the person who is regarded to be charismatic. The term is borrowed from theology[14] and indeed the "pure types" of charismatic leaders are the founders of great religious movements. Nevertheless there are leaders who strive for and acquire the status of being "charismatic" even in modernity or even under legal-rational authority. Weber considered exceptional individuals in sciences or art to be "charismatic." The question whether they carry "real charisma" or they are pseudo-charismatic leaders or they just carry "fake" charisma is debated.[15] I take an eclectic position here – Weber's theory of charisma is an ideal type; it does not actually exist in pure form therefore it is reasonable to look for signs of charisma in non-traditional settings as well.

It should be crystal clear: charisma is the type of domination that is transitory; basically it is between one of the forms of traditional authority and another form of traditional authority. Hence it is hard or impossible to pass charisma on from one leader to the next. Arguably one exception is the Roman Catholic Church, but transmission of charisma is rather difficult even in the church. When one charismatic leader lost his or her charisma or the leader passed away, it is likely that a certain kind of traditional authority will replace that leader. On rare occasions charismatic authority may be turned into legal-rational authority.

13 All citations from Weber 1978

14 The term was borrowed by Weber from Rudolph Sohm, and from his two volume book on Kirchenrecht, vol. 1 (1892).

15 There is a large literature on this subject. Edward Shils in his "Charisma, Order and Status" (1965) takes off from Weber and tries to adopt it as a broader concept to be applicable to modernity – one may say even to the mundane word; others took a different direction and suggested in modernity charisma can be abused, faked, as, for example, by what Hitler or Stalin did, or it can be abused for commercial purposes, see Bensman and Givant 1975; more recently Costa Pinto et al. 2007

Legal-rational authority

At first glance it appears to be simple and clear what legal-rational domination is and only as we dig deeper do we see that it is a little more complicated. So how is "obedience" attained under this form?

i. "… person in authority, the "superior," is himself subject to an impersonal order …
ii. … the person who obeys authority … obeys only the law …
iii. … members do not owe obedience to [superior] as an individual, but to the impersonal order …" (pp. 217–128).[16]

What is clear that obedience is not due to a personal master but to pre-established laws and rules and the person in authority is subject to the same laws and rules as anyone else. Hence it is legal rather than personal authority. What makes it rational? The fact that it allows rational calculation: the rules have to be pre-established, they cannot change at the discretion of the person in authority and it would follow that legislation can never be retroactive (that would make rational calculation impossible). Rational calculation is critical for Weber: he goes on at great length to explain why traditional or charismatic authority is inconsistent with modern market capitalism. So traditional authority is not conducive to capitalist development, because:

"[T]he general character of the administrative practices [of traditional authority] … restrict the development of rational economic activity … [in the following ways]:

1. Traditionalism places … obstacles in the way of formally rational regulations, which can depended upon to remain stable and hence calculable …
2. A staff …with formal technical training … is typically absent.
3. There is a wide scope for actual arbitrariness …
4. [It had] an inherent tendency to regulate economic activity in terms of utilitarian, welfare or absolute value" (pp. 239–240).

Charismatic authority is not conducive to capitalist development either. It is actually "anti-economic force":

Since it is 'extraordinary,' charismatic authority is sharply opposed to rational and particularly bureaucratic authority.… Bureaucratic authority is … rational … [by] being bound to intellectually analyzable rules; while charismatic authority is specifically irrational in the sense of being foreign to all rules" (p. 244)…. [C]harismatic want-satisfaction is a typical anti-economic force … [it constitutes] an irregular, unsystematic acquisitive act (p. 245).

Hence the only form of domination what is consistent with the requirement of market capitalism is legal-rational authority. It actually could be called a system of "liberalism." But what is the relationship between liberalism and democracy? Weber was called by Mommsen a "liberal in despair." He does not have a clear answer. What matters is that this is a system of rule of law and regulations, which apply equally to all members

16 All citations are from Weber 1978.

including the persons in authority. But where do the laws or rules come from? Weber as late as in 1920 does not have a definite answer to this question:

"Legal authority rests on the acceptance of the validity of the following … ideas:

1. …. norms [laws] may be established by agreement or by imposition, on grounds of expediency or value rationality or both …
2. …. law … [is] … a consistent system of abstract rules which … [was] … intentionally established …" (p. 217)[17].

Hence rules or laws can be established by "imposition" or they can be attained by agreement, though Weber is silent with regard to by whom and how such an agreement has to be reached.

To conclude: legal-rational authority may be a democratic polity or it may not. The question that haunted political science since the seventeenth century, since Hobbes and Locke (namely the question: who is the source of law?) is not addressed in Weber's typology of domination. For him the critical question is: what is the most suitable political system for capitalist development? It has to be liberal, but – by implication – it does not have to be necessarily democratic. Liberal autocratic or authoritarian regimes have a reasonable record in achieving capitalistic aims. Or do they have to turn eventually to democracy? Is the future of China liberal democracy? We can have a strong political commitment to such a project, but as social scientists we do not know. Some political theorists have argued (contested by others) democracy is by far the best shell of capitalism (as Lenin put it[18]), it was actually achieved by the anti-capitalist struggles of the working class, which forced capitalists to political compromises, such as the welfare state and universal suffrage. Whether capitalism needs democracy or not, whether democracy was forced upon capital by labor or it also the most efficient political tool for private gains: Weber is agnostic. But he is certain: there is no capitalist economy without liberalism. This liberalism implies: rule and stability of laws (and inevitably a separation of executive power from legislative power, no matter how legislative bodies are constituted), equality before the law (what requires an independent judiciary) and security of private property rights. Weber is not as specific about these issues as I am now, but this all logically follows from his theory.

The fourth type of domination

But the question of how liberalism is related to democracy – nevertheless was on Weber's mind and this is why in 1917 in his lecture in Vienna he considers a fourth type of domination. (This is rarely noticed in scholarship on Weber[19]). The Neue Freie Presse reports

17 All citations are from Weber 1978.

18 Lenin, V.I. [1917'] 1993. *State and Revolution*, Chapter 1, in V.I. Lenin. Collected Works. Vol. 25 Lenin Institute Archive, pp. 381–492

19 Edith Hanke mentions this in her introduction to *MWG* I/22–4, pp. 86–87, but without elaborating on it. See also pp. 745–46. I could not find any secondary scholarly literature on this subject.

on his October 1917 lecture in Vienna this way: "*Schließlich ging er [meaning the lecturer, hence Max Weber] zu der Darlegung über, wie die moderne Entwicklung der okzidentalen Staatswesen durch das allmähliche Entstehen eines vierten Legitimationsgedankens charakterisiert war, derjenigen Herrschaft, welche wenigstens offiziell ihre eigene Legitimität aus dem Willen der Beherrschten ableitet*" (MWG I/22–4, p. 755; my emphasis). Wow. What a sentence! Unlike in his theory of legal-rational authority now legitimacy may stem from the "will" of the people. But Weber cannot help: he is a liberal in despair. After all these people are the "*Beherrschten*" (they are subjected to domination), the resulting system is still a system of "*Herrschaft*" rather than the realm of freedom and on top of this is "*wenigstens offiziell*" (at least officially) the ground for the fourth type of legitimacy. To conclude: Weber takes no stand about the question what is the best "shell" for capitalism: liberal autocracy or liberal democracy.

In my reading, the fourth system of legitimation is a somewhat ironic definition of democratic legitimacy (after all this is the will of those "subjected to authority, not the will of "free citizens" – hence this is a kind of foucauldian ironic comment about what "will" can be). Nevertheless this is articulated before the collapse of the German largely illiberal monarchical autocracy and before the Weimar experiment with liberal democracy. Let me also add: Weber speaks about "will of those subordinated to authority" before he can see the illiberal autocracy that will emerge as a result of the communist revolution in Russia, hence on October 1917 he might have hoped that in post-revolutionary Russia and post-imperial Germany liberal "democracy" might emerge.

It is telling though that when in 1919–1920 Weber re-writes his theory of legitimacy the "fourth type of legitimacy" disappears. Given the mess that the November 7, 1917 revolution in Russia produced and chaotic nature of the Weimar Republic, Weber – probably wrongly – expected the solution would come from charismatic leaders, rather than "*Wille der Beherrschten.*" What a tragic mistake: charismatic leadership led to disasters, while at least after the Second World War in the Euro-Atlantic region the dominant form of domination became "liberal democracy," hence a combination of legal-rational authority with "*Wille der Beherrschten.*" This arguably is not a perfect, but still the best system of governance – to put it as Churchill did – that humankind has invented so far.

Various types of traditional authority

Let us return to the various types of "traditional authority." This is important for this article. As I pointed out before Weber' distinction among the various types of authority has two purposes: 1/ it aims to offer a typology of social formation over time. In a way it is a substitute for what Marx offered as a history of "modes of production;" 2/ but at the same time it can be used also as an analytic tool to dissect the ways domination operates in any social formation, including "modern" societies. While "modern" societies are primarily legal-rational authorities they may maintain some traditional elements. It is rather uncontroversial to suggest that patriarchal authority exists in "modern societies," even under legal-rational authority. Nevertheless the most provocative hypothesis of this article is to claim that other forms of traditional authority, such as prebendalism or patrimonialism may co-exist with a usually deformed system of legal-rational and democratic authority (hence with the "*Wille der Beherschten*").

Now let me turn to the four "pure" types of traditional authority: patriarchy, sultanism, prebendalism, and patrimonialism. Then I offer a hypothesis as to how these types can be applicable to the analysis of contemporary societies.

Types of traditional authority

1/ Patriarchy

The concept of patriarchy is fairly simple:

> [Patriarchalism is] "... the most elementary form of traditional domination where the master has no personal administrative staff."[20]
>
> "... The decisive characteristic [of Patriarchalism] is the belief of the members that domination, even though it is an inherent traditional right of the master, must definitely be exercised as a joint right ... of all members. Hence the master is still largely dependent on the willingness of the members to comply with his orders.... Therefore the members (Genossen) are not yet really subjects (Untertanen)."[21]

This sounds like a good description of tribal societies or, incidentally, the families we happened to live in. And indeed he elaborates it further to make sure it is clear enough the elementary form of patriarchy can be understood as "domestic authority":

> "[Under] ... elementary Patriarchalism...the patriarch's authority carries strict obligations to obedience only within his own household.... [I]t has only exemplary effect ... or must resort to advice or similar means of influence."[22] This is a sort of "domestic authority ... [Taking its point of departure from] ... the belief in authority [that] is based on personal relations that are perceived as natural. This belief is rooted in filial piety.... The woman is dependent because of the normal superiority ... of the male.... Paternal power ... [is] not primarily based on actual blood relations.... [It] is ... power of disposition over property even after the ... recognition that procreation and birth are connected." [23]

Patriarchy is not merely an "archaic" form from the distant past, the concept – much like almost all other concepts of Weber – is equally applicable for historical analysis or the analysis of contemporary institutional arrangements.

The other forms of traditional authority operate with a staff. He distinguishes three types of traditional domination with staff. His terminology can be somewhat confusing (especially his use of the term "patrimonialism," which often means all three types, by distinguishing primary patrimonialism from patrimonial state and the prebendal form

20 Max Weber, *Economy and Society*, 1978, p.231.
21 Max Weber, *Economy and Society*, 1978, p.231.
22 Max Weber, *Economy and Society*, 1978, p. 231.
23 Max Weber, *Economy and Society*, 1978, p. 1007.

of patrimonialism based on benefices, rather than fief). Let me offer the following simplification of Weber's complex analysis of the three forms of traditional domination. I hope this will bring some clarity in the conceptualization:

2/ Sultanism (a pure case of prebendalism)

In some cases the members of administrative staff "are purely personal instruments of the master.... [When authority] operates primarily on the basis of discretion [of the ruler], it will be called sultanism.... Sometimes it appears that sultanism is completely unrestrained by tradition, but this is never in fact the case. The non-traditional element is not, however, rationalized in impersonal terms, but consists in an extreme development of the ruler's discretion." [24] Under this system the staff possesses the means of administration at the grace of the master and has no security of property rights. Property is not inherited, cannot be alienated, and can be reallocated at any moment at the unilateral decision of the ruler.

Prebendalism is narrowly defined. Under prebendalism the staff appropriates the means of administration of material property only partially. The staff receive benefices:

> "We shall speak of benefices insofar as the forms of maintenance ... are always newly granted in a traditional fashion ... they can be appropriated by the individual, although not in hereditary fashion.... When an administrative staff is ... supported ... in this form, we shall speak of prebendalism."[25]

While sultanism offers no security whatsoever, under prebendalism the incumbent of the office can expect to remain in office and retain property as long as he or she assures the master of loyalty and offers valuable services to the master.

3/ Patrimonialism ("feudalism," vassal compensated by fief)

> "Under patrimonial authority ... the administrative staff appropriates particular powers.... Domination of estate type thus involves (i) ... limitation of the lord's discretion in selecting his administrative staff and (ii) ... often ... appropriation by ... staff of α) the positions ... β) the material means of administration ... γ) the governing power."[26]

How the "material means of administration" are appropriated is crucial. Under patrimonial rule narrowly defined, the staff is rewarded by "fief": "[T]he fief is the vassal's personal property for the duration of the feudatory relationship, however, it remains inalienable, since it is intended to preserve the vassal's service capacity."[27] The property that has been granted as "fief" typically can even be inherited; hence patrimonialism with fief offers quite secure property rights (and also security of office). In patrimonialism, both office and property is relatively secure, though the rights of disposal with

24 Max Weber, *Economy and Society,* 1978, p. 231–232. See, for contemporary applications, Chehabi and Linz 1998.

25 Max Weber, *Economy and Society*, 1978, p.235.

26 Max Weber, Economy and Society, 1978, p.232

27 Max Weber, Economy and Society, 1978, p.1074

property by comparison to private property are still limited. Property is usually inalienable; it usually cannot even be mortgaged. It is only given in order to preserve the vassal's capacity to serve.

Historically speaking sultanism was the form of domination characteristic of the Ottoman Empire. The best approximation of prebendalism in the modern Western world is the Russian service nobility (or *Pomeshchiki*). The ideal type of patrimonialism is West European feudalism. In Russia, boyars owned property and office in a patrimonial way and they were turned into a service nobility after centuries of struggle by Czars from Ivan the Terrible to Peter the Great. In the following sections, I demonstrate the applicability of the concepts of patrimonialism and prebendalism to post-communist capitalisms.

Types of legitimation under communism and post-communism

My main aim now is to pose the question: were communist and are post-communist social orders legitimate and, if so, what is the foundation of their legitimacy?

1/ Can one ever call a communist regime legitimate? If so what kind of legitimation regimes describes such communist rule?

I start this with a brief reference to the question: were communist societies' legitimate orders at all? From the point of view of liberal democracy, it would be easy to dismiss communist societies as "illegitimate," but such a position could be hardly attributed to Weber. If we can find instances of communist social order where there is sufficient "voluntary compliance" by the "*Beherrschten,*" Weber would not hesitate to see that order as legitimate and will ask the question what is the foundation of this legitimacy.

In some communist regimes there was not much "voluntary compliance" and order was maintained by systematic coercion. The most extreme example being Cambodia under Pol Pot (though Pol Pot before he became the supreme leader of Cambodia was seen by many as a charismatic figure, see David Chandler 1999) and arguably certain epochs of Stalinism and Maoism were illegitimate, despotic.

But there are long epochs of communism when order was maintained without coercion, where some kind of communist *Herrschaft* was established. But what kind of *Herrschaft*? Commentators gave various answers. Some communist leaders at least at certain points in time established a charismatic order (most eminent example would be Fidel Castro, but arguably Lenin and following him for certain epochs even figures such as Stalin could establish themselves as charismatic leaders. The same can be argued for Mao). Whether that was real charisma or just pseudo-charisma can be debated (Bensman and Givant 1975). Some described communism as traditional (Heller et al. 1983) or neo-traditional authority (Andrew Walder 1988), Rigby and Fehér (1992) coined the intriguing term "goal rational authority."

All these theories offer insights and are useful tools to explore empirically various cases at various points in the history of communist societies. Arguably some communist orders had a strong charismatic appeal. The propaganda machine, the "personality cult" obviously was important in manufacturing such charisma, in generating enthusiasm and dedication to the leaders who promised to deliver "miracles" through "revolutionary change."

As the leaders failed to deliver miracles or passed away, the system faced the difficult task of institutionalizing charisma or passing it on to another leader. Some communist systems degenerated into illegitimate systems, using massive, systemic coercion (as arguably happened in Cambodia, or during the mid-1930s in the USSR, possibly during the Great Leap Forward or Cultural Revolution in China). On some occasions successors made a bid for carrying on the charisma of the predecessor. The best example may be Stalin during the 1920s, when he faked a "last will" of Lenin that supposedly appointed Stalin as successor. He put the propaganda machine into operation and created a personality cult around himself that did deliver some degree of charisma to the young Stalin. Nevertheless, usually after the passing of the original charismatic leader, communist societies struggled for some other type of legitimacy. In some cases, it is indeed an attempt to create some version of a rather classical traditional authority: such is the establishment of the Kim dynasty in North Korea or an attempt to create some neo-traditional authority, based on elaborate patron-client relationships. In this case, the rulers tried to legitimate the system by claims that the party leadership or the individual leader of the party take better care of things than anybody else could. There were also attempts, and for a while rather successful ones, to claim that communist order – in contrast with the "instrumental rationality, or irrationality of the market" – offers a higher level of legitimacy. The communist system, according to this claim, was based on rationality of the goals rather than rationality of means. Communism in other words is "substantive rationality," compared to market capitalism, which is an inferior type of rationality – it is only formal rationality. Rigby and Fehér formulated it this way originally, but in *The Intellectuals on the Road to Class Power* we also tried to conceptualize the legitimacy of the post-Stalinist USSR and Central Europe in similar terms. "Rational redistributors" claim legitimacy referring to their monopoly on "teleological knowledge" (Konrad and Szelényi 1979).

Hence the investigation of the kind of legitimacy (or illegitimacy) required historically specific empirical investigation. Actually existing socialist societies combined various elements of all of Weberian ideal types. In a concluding remark on the subject, let me make a provocative statement. Communism appeared to be the opposite of legal-rational authority, by its own aspiration the essence of the Marxian project was to overcome the instrumental formal rationality of market capitalism, the "anarchy of the market." Nevertheless, there were elements of legal-rational authority in most phases and forms of communisms. Communist societies felt obliged to draft constitutions. Curiously, often they pretended they operated under the "rule of law": they tortured prisoners, in the worse times, to confess to crimes punishable by laws, though everyone knew they never committed those crimes. Unlike the Nazis who usually just shot enemies, or sent them to gas chambers and did not bother with complicated legal procedures Stalinism, even at times when it arguably was illegitimate, created "show trials." The best known was the trial against Bukharin. Unlike the Jesuit inquisitors who probably mostly believed the accused had actually committed crimes and who tortured the prisoners to "find the truth," Stalinist prosecutors typically knew the prisoners were innocent, so they tortured them to confess invented crimes that could "justify" the prisoners being executed, since execution was what the law prescribed for the confessed crime.

During the despotic rule of Stalin, this was mainly "fake legal-rational authority," people often were murdered without any legal procedure. It is hard to detect any element of legal-rationality, or rule of law under Maoism, especially during the Cultural Revolution. During that time Maoists prosecuted enemies in a way similar to the Nazis. But all communists systems were by definition "illiberal" (hence never genuinely legal-rational). Under post-Stalinist reform communism, the legal-rational component was strengthened, but no communist regime was either liberal or democratic in any meaningful sense of those terms. Those in authority may have been formally elected by somebody, but de facto they were appointed as members of the "nomenclature" under the control of the executive, be it the Central Committee, the Politburo, or some lower level party organization. None of these systems subscribed to any of the key principles of liberalism: separation of legislative, executive, and juridical power, and security/ sanctity of individual property rights. But it is sensible to suggest that such "fake" legal-rational authority was complementing legitimation beyond charisma, traditional authority, or goal rationality, especially in the reform communist epoch.

And now we are ready to face the question of legitimacy under post-communist regimes. Typically, though there are some substantial country-by-country variations, the first stage of transition from communism to post-communism was a transition from some sort of traditional/neo-traditional/goal rational authority to legal rational authority combined with the "fourth system of legitimation" – hence with a system that is legitimated by the "*Wille der Beherrschten,*" hence it was at least to some extent democratic.

2/ Early democracy/liberalism. Legal rational authority in Central Europe (with a patrimonial twist)

Between 1989 and 1991 in most of the formerly socialist countries of Central Europe and in some of the countries of the former USSR, in the Baltic States, and even in Russia, desperate efforts were made to turn these states into liberal democracies with neo-liberal capitalist institutions. Half-hearted reforms were implemented at least during the first few years in war-torn Yugoslavia, Albania, Bulgaria, Romania, Moldova, Ukraine, and the Caucasian republics. Belorussia, the Central Asian former Soviet republics, and certainly the Asian former or still socialist countries, like China and Vietnam are even clearer cases, where no liberal democratic reform took place. But in Central Europe and the Baltic states arguably the dominant form of legitimation was indeed legal rational authority (liberalism) with some form of a democratic polity. The rule of law was accepted, the legislative, executive and juridical powers and the media became reasonably separated from each other. Security of private ownership was acknowledged by the law. Reasonably free multi-party elections were held to constitute the legislative branch. The most critical challenge all these societies faced in the early years was the conversion of public property into private wealth. According to the neo-liberal doctrine, all problems of transition from a redistributive to market economics will be resolved as soon as identifiable private owners are found for the public assets.

The purpose was to "close the commons" in 500 days (as the Russians tried to do it) or in 5 to 10 years, as the Central European countries attempted. That was difficult or impossible to achieve with purely legal-rational and democratic means. In the democratically elected legislatures, elections were free; there was multi-party competition; but voter turn-out was underwhelming, hence the newly elected governments had a somewhat questionable democratic legitimacy. During the electoral campaigns, ideological issues were more often discussed than the crucial question of who will become the private proprietor of assets formerly under public ownership and what will happen with the welfare state.[28] Hence during the early 1990s liberal democracy, even in the countries that were the closest to the "ideal type," like the Czech Republic and Hungary, there was an inevitable patrimonial component in the system of domination. The privatization legislations – especially those that relied heavily on vouchers – gave a great deal of discretion to the executive branch. In countries that tried to use citizenship vouchers, like in the Czech Republic or Russia, or compensation vouchers, like in Hungary, still needed massively subsidized government credits or grossly undervalued property prices to obtain ownership of large corporations without market-tested creditworthiness. So who was creditworthy was decided by an official in governmental and semi-governmental agencies or by banks – in every case through "personal networks." Even when public property was put up for "auction" and the bidders were international, multi-national firms the buyers needed inside information about the "real value" of the firms up for sale. This again could be obtained by privatization agencies or management of those firms but there was just no way to accomplish this by purely market means. And that deviation from legal-rational authority is what I propose calling a secondary "patrimonial principle" of legitimation.

In the most post-communist liberal-democratic regimes this happened by offering special privileged to management or former knowledgeable and trusted government-party officials. Such a patrimonial element was the weakest in Central Europe. The emergent Central European post-communist capitalism basically could have been described with a legal-rational authority, which operated within a reasonably democratic institution. They were as close to "liberal democracy" as one could expect in societies with making a fast transition from communism to liberal capitalism. Nevertheless many commentators tend to over-idealize the 1990s in Central Europe. In comparison with communism, of course, there was a great leap forward to separation of powers, freedom of the media, the "fourth branch of power," and recognition of the legitimacy of private ownership. In most countries there were reasonably free, multi-party elections. The most vulnerable component of this liberal-democracy was the legitimacy of private ownership and the usually miserable voter turnout at elections. The notions of "theft," and "corruption" were attached to the emergent new private property of the nomencla-

28 See Szelényi and Szelényi 1991, and Szelényi et al 1996.

ture-bourgeoisie from day one. Hence private ownership was not as legitimate as one would have hoped. Bálint Magyar coined the term "mafia-state" much later (Magyar 2013), but many ordinary people in Central Europe thought about their new rich as Mafiosi anyway from the very early days of the transition. The separation of power, especially the independence of public media from the government, was also challenged from day one. With this somewhat skeptical note I do accept the fundamentally legal-rational authority and democratic nature of most Central European countries.

3/ Patrimonialism in Russia during the first decade of transition (with some elements of legal-rational authority)

Russia started to diverge from this trajectory very early on. Already in 1998 (Eyal et al. 1998), I called Russia "capitalism from above," a sort of patrimonial order. There may be many reasons for this divergence. Russia has long historical experience with autocratic governments. In addition the new post-communist elites were often recruited from Soviet nomenclature – it was a nomenclature-bourgeoisie. Yeltsin clashed with legal-rational-authority and democratic policy early on. His stated aim was to establish capitalism in Russia in 500 days and the mechanism to achieve this was supposed to be voucher privatization, namely to give a fair share of Russia's "commons" in "vouchers" to every citizen and create millions of owners rather than a few millionaires. But this did not work. Ordinary Russians of course did not know what to do with their vouchers. They were starving, so they sold their vouchers under value to investors/speculators who used them in privatization. What happened next was a classic case of patrimonialism. Yeltsin, the new "czar" had to decide who among the bidders, all with little capital and no credit rating, would acquire the property. He often relied on the advice of his beloved daughter, Tatyana, and she picked the "best people" for the "job." Yeltsin in this way appointed the new grand bourgeoisie. There were "auctions" where property was transformed from public to private, but the Yeltsin regime grossly manipulated these auctions. With these manipulations Yeltsin and his inner circle made sure the people who were defined as "good people" by Tatyana became the new owners (for a colorful and persuasive description of these practices, see Klebnikov 2000). I call the first decade of Russian transition from communism a patrimonial (with some legal-rational components) regime since property was allocated by the "grace" of the ruler. The executive branch had a great deal of autonomy to decide who the new owners would be. The aim of such patrimonial rule, within the framework of a democratic system, was to create a grand bourgeoisie that could be expected to be reasonably loyal to political powers. When the chips were falling, it did work. In 1996 Yeltsin faced re-election as president and he was running behind Zyuganov, the candidate of the Communist Party. The new grand bourgeoisie, the seven largest financiers with the leadership of Berezovsky rallied behind Yeltsin. They hated his opponent, Zyuganov, even more than Yeltsin and since they controlled the media they played a critical role in Yeltsin's re-election. Incidentally the BIG SEVEN claimed just 5 years after the collapse of the USSR that they owned half of the wealth in Russia!

So I call Russia under Yeltsin a patrimonial system. Yeltsin on a few occasions tried to challenge the powers of the new grand bourgeoisie. He had an intense conflict for instance with Gusinsky, but Yeltsin eventually backed down (for the story, see again Klebnikov 2000). Let me just summarize: Russia under Yeltsin was a patrimonial order (property was allocated by the political ruler, but with relatively secure property rights) with some legal-rational authority. It was not quite a liberal system, while private property was defended by law, Yeltsin sent tanks against the legislature, when they went against his will. He operated a somewhat managed democratic system. Elections with stakes were held, but the media was controlled by Yeltsin friendly private owners, so it was hardly a "free media". In contrast most Central-European countries were liberal, legal rational authorities, property was allocated by market mechanism (with some patrimonial management though), with substantial separation of powers. A struggle to bring the media under the control of the executive started very early. This was mostly unsuccessful. Elections were free and to the extent the messy campaign financing law allowed it quite fair, but democracies were not "consolidated." It has taken a long time to form parties which can rotate in power and this process is still under way in every Central European postcommunist country.

Putin's revolution: a turn to prebendalism with illiberal managed democracy

The key characteristics of Putinism

Putin's raise to power represented a major shift in the system of legitimation in post-communist Russia. By the end of the Yeltsin years, the new Russian grand bourgeoisie began to "privatize" the state itself; big money wanted political power. For a while Berezovsky was national security adviser to Yeltsin. For Putin, an ambitious, energetic, able, young, former KGB man, this was totally unacceptable. He wanted to bring big money under political control, to put a leash on the new grand bourgeoisie. He put the new rich under a loyalty test: those who pass the test can stay and get richer, those who fall have an option to emigrate to London or Tel Aviv, or end up in jall in Siberia. The smart ones, like Berezovsky or Gusinsky went to Sheremetyevo airport; the overly ambitious ones, like Khodorkovsky ended up in long jall terms in Siberia. Those who gave up political ambitions and swore loyalty to the new "czar" became "serving nobility" (like Abramovich and Deripaska). They could stay on and become even richer. Even the fact that they belonged to the Yeltsin "family" was forgotten.

But what mechanism is used to redistribute property already allocated? I would call it the process of selective criminalization. No enemies are prosecuted on political, on ideological grounds: they all are accused of having committed economic crimes, such as tax evasion or corruption. Khodorkovsky was not jailed since he had political ambitions, but because he was found guilty of money laundering.... Since the enclosure of the commons took place so fast and usually in a legal vacuum, virtually everyone who is in the class of the nouveaux riches has skeletons in his or her closet. Hence the only question is who controls the prosecuting authority and what skeleton the prosecutor will find in whose closet. This is why I call the system selective criminalization. Those who are found guilty are probably guilty all right, but who is not? The question of who will hold private property was still decided by the political authority, but property rights became less secure. To put it in Weber's terms, "fief" was transformed into "benefices", the boyars of Yeltsin became the *Pomeshchiki* of Putin. The Russian system of legitimation shifted from patrimonialism to prebendalism. Intriguingly this was driven by the apparently democratic nature of policy and the inevitable shift to illiberalism in the system of legitimation.

Even in Putin's Russia, the claim that the system is based on majoritarian rule remains important. The regime needs legitimacy in reasonably free and somewhat fair multi-party elections. Those in positions of authority have to win those elections so they need a constituency that will support them. Big money is an important constituency. But how to create or sustain a loyal big money constituency once all the public property was privatized, all the "commons were enclosed?" Since the property that could be used to create or sustain loyal followers was already allocated during the Yeltsin years, the only way to keep the system going required that property already allocated be redistributed from the non-loyal ones to those Putin hoped would be loyal. This cannot be achieved in a liberal, legal-rational system of authority where property rights are secure, the powers of the executive are checked by the legislature and judiciary, and the media are free. The redistribution of property from the first generation of owners, from the boyars to the *Pomeshchiki* and the corresponding softening of property rights, requires a strengthening of executive power. This can only be achieved with the limitations of powers of the judiciary, legislative powers and the reduction of the independence of the media, hence a shift from legal-rational authority to an illiberal system of powers. It is important to notice the irony of this process: the shift to the prebendal system of illiberal order is driven by the pressure on those who rule to legitimate themselves with the majoritarian principle, hence by their desires to win elections, which at least appears to be free and fair.

This democratic process under Putin is substantially "managed." It needs to retain the appearance of multi-party democracy. As Perry Anderson (2007) noted, such an illiberal democracy – my term not Anderson's – requires "opposition" parties. Hence it is conceivable that in Putin's Russia the Communist Party is kept alive by Putin himself. At some point such a management goes "too" far and turns managed democracy into autocracy, if there is a chance that at elections the ruling party could lose power. Putin created his own party, the United Russia, in 2001 that has dominated the legislature, the Duma, ever since. It won a super majority, which enabled the Duma to change even the constitution in 2007. In 2011, however, it received merely 51 % of the votes. Would he continue electoral democracy once he faces loss or would he turn his system into an autocracy, with no elections or a Soviet type of fake elections where he would again win 99 % of the votes?

Re-convergence of Russian and Central European ways: the move away from liberalism, toward manage democracy and prebendalism in Central Europe. Is China heading in this direction?

Arguably the Putin "virus" is in the system in most if not in all of the Central European systems. Structurally this stems from the system that operates in a democratic framework, where elections at least have to appear to be competitive and fair. Since the "commons were already enclosed," the only mechanism to "buy" votes is through a redistribution of property already allocated.

Undoubtedly Hungary is the vanguard in "Putinization" of post-communism. The Hungarian Prime Minister, Viktor Orbán, astutely called the system he is trying to establish in Hungary "illiberal democracy." I only would add the term "managed" to this, the best description of the emergent system of legitimation in Hungary is "managed illiberal democracy."

Much like United Russia in 2007, the Hungarian ruling party, FIDESZ, achieved a supermajority in parliament in 2010. Having the powers to change the constitution, it passed a new constitution. It can change the composition and rights of the constitutional courts – did both – and manage the electoral system for its advantages. For my argument though, the most important development is the "softening" of property rights. Mr. Orbán's party was briefly in government between 1998 and 2002. When they lost in a close electoral competition, Mr. Orbán acknowledged one mistake he made while prime minister: he did not create his own bourgeoisie. This is a mistake one does not make twice. As he won election comfortably in 2010 and 2014, he made an effort to create and maintain a loyal base and its core had to be a propertied bourgeoisie. During the second term of the FIDESZ government (2010–2014), he reallocated petty property rights. A smart move was to create a retall trade monopoly for tobacco shops. Small grocery stores and gas stations made a great deal of their profits from selling tobacco: now only special stores with tobacco licenses had the monopoly of tobacco retall trade. Obtaining such a license did not make anybody into a billionaire but it was a source of nice profit, so one could anticipate that the recipients of such licenses would reward the ruling party by voting for them and they in fact did so in 2014.

After FIDESZ won the 2014 elections in a rather "managed way" with a new qualified, two-thirds majority, it went one step further and is trying now to put big money "on the leash." As the prime minister said, no tree can grow into the skies. Now the attempt is to limit the power of a few oligarchs and replace them with a whole set of smaller and presumably more loyal oligarchs. This is the classical example what I call prebendalism, the making of a class of "serving nobility." In two by-elections in 2015, FIDESZ lost its two-thirds majority and therefore somewhat limits its illiberal ambitions. The government, for instance, cannot any longer change the electoral rules or the power of the presidency, but it still has absolute majority, so in most legislation the parliament is still just rubber stamping the will of the executive branch.

What we see emerging in post-communism is a novel combination of legal-rational authority operating with a rather or even excessively managed democratic framework combined with some aspects of patrimonialism and, more recently, prebendalism.

Let me be as clear as I can: I am, not writing about any policy error or about a power-grab by one or a few evil individuals. We do see a historically unusual, though not unprecedented, combination of legal-rational authority with some legitimacy claims typically existing under traditional authority. Indeed the managed, illiberal, democratic prebendal states use a substantial dose of "traditionalism" or "conservatism" such as the centrality of religion, patriotism, the traditional family, or the sacredness of life in their ideology. It is illiberal, traditionalistic, conservative, or if you want to put it this way: neo-conservative, or even paleo-conservative. But these practices "inevitably" – if anything is "inevitable" in human history – stem from the accelerated transition from socialism to market capitalism within a democratic framework. Putin and United Russia, Orbán and FIDESZ are reasonably close to being the "pure types" of what I am trying to describe, but the "virus" – no value judgment is meant here to be implied by the term – is in all post-communist democratic societies.

Russian and Hungarian liberal intellectuals tend to demonize Putin or Orbán and these intellectuals do not notice that these politicians have their "twin soul brothers" in virtually all post-communist societies. The Lech and Jarosław Kaczyński in Poland, Vladimir Mećiar and Robert Fico in Slovakia, in some respects Boyko Borisov in Bulgaria, Andrej Babiš in the Czech Republic ... and many others represent the same or similar politics and ideology. What the real aim is of Johannis's anti-corruption campaign in Romania is an intriguing question. Klaus Johannis himself was accused of corruption. Is he "cleansing" Romania or is he involved in selective criminalization? In foreign policy they often are very different. Orbán is the most supportive of Putin, even in the Ukrainian crisis; Kaczyński, while a Euro-skeptic like Orbán, is vehemently opposed to Russia.

What is unique about Putin and Orbán is not so much what they are standing for, but who they are: they have a dose of charisma. Whether this is "genuine charisma" or just "fake charisma" can be debated, but it is hard to doubt that, unlike the other traditionalist leaders I mentioned, they can win and re-win elections. They both have an enthusiastic and loyal following, though we know their charisma can be withdrawn as soon as the leaders stop delivering "miracles."

The most intriguing, China, seems to be conversing with Putinism as well. President Xi is making a bid to become a "charismatic leader"; he allows the official media to call him "Father Xi." He gives long addresses to scientists and writers about what they should do and his campaign against "corruption" sounds very much like the selective criminalization of the "illiberal democracies" of post-communist European countries. Bo Xilai was a Maoist challenger of the current leadership of the Communist Party. Was he convicted for life imprisonment because he was corrupt, or was it a case of selective criminalization? Former Prime Minister Wen's family was reported to own billions of dollars; Bo Xilai was accused of corruption for only a couple of million dollars. The Wen family was not investigated; Bo Xilai got a life sentence. The anti-corruption campaign is suspiciously similar to Putinism. Is China on its way to prebendalism? I do not have enough evidence to tell, but the attack against Bo Xilai and his supporters looks rather similar. Bo Xilai's wife, Gu Kailai, was sentenced also for a life imprisonment for the murder of an English associate (lover? business partner?), Neil Heywood, in a suspiciously short trial, which lasted only for a few days. So who knows what the truth is. But what is certain is that China is moving toward a one-man rule, unknown since the fall of Mao, and the judiciary is being used to catch political enemies. Post-communism from China to Russia to Eastern Europe may be converging on an illiberal prebendal system. The transition from communism has been guided by the principles of legal-rational authority, what I call liberalism and democracy, what I identify as majoritarian selection of the leaders, *Wille der Beherrschten*. Given the challenges of fast pace of transition, especially of the conversion of public ownership to private wealth, liberal democracy was not consolidated in most – or any? – of these countries. All of these countries – or most of them – are pregnant with a dose of patrimonialism, prebendalism, and illiberalism, and such potentialities come to fruition as long as their charismatic leaders deliver miracles by providing at least the impression of security and improving welfare.

References

"Russian Journalists: Putin's Regime is Illegitimate" (2012). Columbia University Press, Institute of Modern Russia www.mrussia.org/en/news/213-russian-journaliszs-putins-regime-is-illegitimate.

Anderson, P. (2007). "Russia's managed democracy", London Review of Books, No. 2, 2–12.

Bensman, J., & Givant, M. (1975). Charisma and modernity: the use and abuse of the concept. *Social Research, 42*(4), 570–614.

Chandler, D. (1999). *Brother number one*. Boulder: Westview Press.

Chehabi, H. E., & Linz, J. (1998). *Sultanistic Regimes*. Baltimore: The Johns Hopkins University Press.

Ciobanu, M. (2010). "Communist regimes, legitimacy and transition to democracy in Eastern Europe." *Nationalities Papers, 38*(1), 3–21.

Costa Pinto, A., Eatwell, R., & Larson, S. U. (eds.). (2007). *Charisma and fascism in interwar Europe*. New York: Routledge.

Eyal, G., Szelényi, I., & Townsley, E. (1998). *Making Capitalism without Capitalists. Class formation and elite struggles in post-communist Central Europe*. London etc.: Verso.

Gerth, H. H., & Wright Mills, C. (1946). *From Max Weber: Essays in sociology*. New York: Oxford University Press.

Heller, Á., Fehér, F., & Márkus, G. (1983). *Dictatorship over needs. An Analysis of Soviet Societies*. London: Palgrave Macmillan.

Klebnikov, P. (2000). *Godfather of the Kremlin. Boris Berezovsky and the looting of Russia*. New York: Harcourt.

Konrad, G., & Szelényi, I. (1979). *The intellectuals on the road to class power*. New York: Harcourt, Brace and Jovanovich.

Kornai, J. (2014)."Fenyegető veszélyek" (Threatening Dangers), Élet és *Irodalom*, May 23.

Lenin, V.I. [1917] (1993). State and revolution, chapter 1, in V.I, Lenin. *Collected Works*. vol. 25 Moscow: Lenin Institute Archive, 381–492.

Magyar, B. (2013). *A magyar polip. A poszt-kommunista maffia* állam. *(The Hungarian Octopus. The post-communist mafia state)*. Budapest: Noran Libro.

Mommsen, W. J. (1974). *The Age of Bureaucracy. Perspectives on the political sociology of Max Weber*. Oxford: Blackwell Publishers.

MWG I/22–3: Wirtschaft und Gesellschaft. Die Wirtschaft und die gesellschaftlichen Ordnungen und Mächte. Nachlaß. Teilband 3: Recht, ed. by W. Gephart und S. Hermes. Tübingen: J.C.B. Mohr (Paul Siebeck) 2010.

MWG I/22–4: Wirtschaft und Gesellschaft Die Wirtschaft und die gesellschaftlichen Ordnungen und Mächte. Nachlaß. Teilband 4: Herrschaft, ed. by E. Hanke, in co-operation with T. Kroll. Tübingen: J.C.B. Mohr (Paul Siebeck) 2005.

MWG I/22–5: Wirtschaft und Gesellschaft Die Wirtschaft und die gesellschaftlichen Ordnungen und Mächte. Nachlaß. Teilband 5: Die Stadt, ed. by W. Nippel. Tübingen: J.C.B. Mohr (Paul Siebeck) 1999.

Ossinovski, J. (2010). Legitimacy of political power in Putin's Russia. London: London School of Economics, MSc dissertation.

Rigby, T. H., & Fehér, F. (eds.). (1992). *Political legitimacy in communist states*. New York: S. Martin Press.

Roth, G. & Schluchter, W. (1979). *Max Weber's vision of history: ethics and method*. Berkeley: University of California Press.

Schluchter, W. (1981). *The Rise of Western rationalism. Max Weber's developmental history*. Berkeley: University of California Press.

Shils, E. (1965). Charisma, order and status. *American Sociological Review, 30*(2), 199–213.

Sohm, R. (1892). *Kirchenrecht*, Erster Band, Leipzig.

Szelényi, I. & Szelényi, S. (1991). "The vacuum in Hungarian Politics. Classes and Parties", *New Left Review*, May-June: 121–131.

Szelényi, I., Szelényi, S., & Poster, W. R. (1996). Interests and symbols in post-communist political culture: the case of Hungary. *American Sociological Review, 61*(3), 466–477.

Walder, A. (1988). *Communist neo-traditionalism: work and authority in Chinese industry*. Berkeley: University of California Press.

Weber, M. (1947). *The theory of social and economic organization. From Wirtschaft und Gesellschaft translated by Talcott Parsons*. New York: The Free Press.

Weber, M. (1978). *Economy and Society. An Outline of intrepretive sociology*, edited by G. Roth and Claus Wittich. Berkeley: University of California Press, 2 vols.

Zakaria, F. (1997). The rise of illiberal democracy. *Foreign Affairs, 76*(8), 22–43.

IV.2 Drifting from Liberal Democracy: Traditionalist/ Neo-Conservative Ideology of Managed Illiberal Democratic Capitalism in Post-Communist Europe

Tamás Csillag and Iván Szelényi

ABSTRACT

Most European post-communist societies after 1989–1991 appeared to be on the road to liberal democratic capitalism. However, a quarter of century after the change of the system, at least some of the countries – Russia and Hungary in particular (arguably setting a trend for many other nations) – began to drift sharply away from liberal democracy. We treat liberalism and democracy as two distinct dimensions of "good governance". We interpret liberalism as separation of powers and security of private property rights. We interpret democracy as majoritarian rule. As the regimes shift to illiberalism, secure private property tends to be converted into "fief" (neo-patrimonialism – like during the rule of Yeltsin), or eventually into "benefice" (neo-prebendalism, this turn happened with the rise of Putin to power). While the principle of majoritarian rule is retained, it is also "managed". But as long as democratic institutions operate, as long as leaders are elected to office the ruling elites of illiberal democracies need a legitimating ideology which can appeal to a broader electorate. We call this post-communist traditionalist/neo-conservative ideology. Post-communist traditionalism/neo-conservatism emphasizes the value of patriotism, religion and traditional family values much like some of the socially conservative Republicans in the USA do.

KEYWORDS: post-communist capitalism, managed and illiberal democracy, transition from communism to capitalism, neo-patrimonial and neo-prebendal forms of ownership, traditionalism/ neo-conservatism.

Introduction: Political system; forms of ownership; ideologies

Formulating the problem

Bálint Magyar, one of the leading Hungarian post-communist liberal politicians expressed his frustration with post-communist politics in the introduction of his 2014-edited book, "The Hungarian Octopus, Volume 2". He stated: "After the fall of the Soviet Empire many of us shared the illusion that communist dictatorships – at least in Europe

– can only be succeeded by Western style liberal democracies" (2014: 7). Many liberal democrats[1] in the former socialist countries of Eastern Europe shared this sentiment with him. Indeed in 1989–91 liberal democracy and market capitalism were the legitimating ideologies of the new political elites in most of the former socialist countries of Europe. Even in Russia, during the first year of Boris Yeltsin's presidency it appeared that Russia might be heading toward liberalism[2]. Yegor Gaidar who was acting Prime Minister of the Russian Federation for the second half of 1992 was widely recognized as a liberal and an advocate of shock therapy, a major neo-liberal economic policy tool. Some basic institutions of liberal democracy and market capitalism were indeed in the making. A multi-party political system was established. Reasonably free and fair elections were held. The media became substantially free in most formerly socialist European countries. The emergent new societies were governed by the rule of law. The executive branch (be it parliamentary or presidential) had to deal with freely elected legislatures. Constitutional courts checked whether the laws passed by the legislature were in accordance with the constitution (even in Russia a powerful Constitutional Court operated between 1991 and 1993). It looked like the three branches of government (the executive, the legislative and the judiciary) were rather autonomous and some system of checks and balances were operating. At the same time, institutions of market capitalism were evolving. Private ownership was sacrosanct and attempts were made to pass legislation regulating the orderly conversion of public property into private wealth. Basic institutions of free market economy (bankruptcy laws, central bank with relative autonomy from the legislature and from the executive, free flow of labor and capital) were also designed.

A quarter of century after "Die Wende", as the above citation from Bálint Magyar indicates, the road to liberal democracy and market capitalism turned out to be rockier than expected. By the middle of the second decade of the 21st century one begins to wonder if the previously widely accepted doctrine "democratic teleology" (Carothers, 2002, Trencsényi, 2014, Levitsky and Way, 2002) is valid at all. "Transitology" and the "third wave of democratization theory" acknowledged that consolidation of democracy may take a long time, but usually it is assumed that deviations in early stages of the transition from models of liberal democracy are only transitional. At one point or another all societies would eventually arrive at the final destination, liberal democracy.

1 In this paper, we use the terms democracy in a narrower definition of the concept. Some authors use the term democracy to write about liberal democracy (rule of law, separation of powers, security of property **and** majoritarian rule), other merely define democracy a system in which leaders were elected by majoritarian rule. We do not cast our vote one way or another in this complex theoretical debate, but we use the term in the second, narrower sense of the term

2 Some East European countries did not experiment with liberal democracy at all. Tudjman's Croatia or Miloševic's Serbia, Bulgaria or Romania in the early 1990s were far from any conception of liberal democracy or even free market capitalism. As Ken Jowitt, a Romanian expert at UC Berkeley pointed out (1996) it was not quite clear, which direction post-communist societies would take: will they become "civic", or "ethnic" (and Jewitt predicted the ethnic turn would be more likely … Unfortunately almost 20 years later we have to concede: he made a good point, valid not only for Romania …)

Francis Fukuyama, who exactly 25 years ago announced the end of history[3], shares Bálint Magyar's anxieties. Fukuyama, in his recent book, Political Order and Political Decay (2014)[4] did not only acknowledge that some countries in transit have not only not proceeded to democracy but he also shows that some even made U-turns and reverted to autocracy. Fukuyama successfully demonstrates that democratic intuitions do not only evolve, but that they can also decay, even in consolidated democracies (hence the title of Berman's review of this book in New York Times: "Global warning").

In this paper, our aim is not as grandiose as Fukuyama's. We merely try to understand the nature of political economies of post-communist countries, which did embark on the road to liberal capitalism and which now appear to be diverging from liberalism. We pay particular attention to Russia and Hungary; however, the phenomenon may be taking place in several other countries as well.

One could of course follow Fukuyama's argument and suggest that such a divergence from liberal democracy is taking place generally on the semi-periphery or periphery of the world system. This may very well be the case, but in this paper we face a challenging enough task to understand this shift in post-communist Europe.

Indeed, the drift from the road to liberal democracy in post-communist Eastern Europe occurs at different points in time, and the degree of deviation varies. Furthermore, the institutions affected by the changes differ from country to country. We also need to note that moving from one system to another is certainly not a one-way street; countries often shift back and forth between trajectories.

We describe the features of the emergent illiberal post-communist systems in political terms. Authors often write about "autocracies"[5], "electoral or competitive autocracies" (Shevtsova, 2000, Levitsky and Way, 2002 and 2010, Levitsky and Way use the term also for some countries in Africa and Latin America), "managed democracies" (Anderson, 2007), "illiberal democracies" (Zakaria, 1997[6] [7] – we wrote about "managed illiberal democracy" combining Gati and Anderson). Some analysts emphasize the features that distinguish these systems economically from free market capitalism. Hence they call it "political capitalism" (Staniszkis, 1991), "state capitalism"[8], "crony capitalism"

3 His book, The End of History, was published only in 1992, but he already presented the same ideas in an article in 1989.

4 For a review of this book see Sheri Berman's work in The New York Times („Global Warning. Francis Fukuyama's 'Political Order and Political Decay'"). http://www.nytimes.com/2014/09/14/books/review/francis-fukuyamas-political-order-and-political-decay.html?_r=0Accessed: 30–10–2014.

5 For a recent sophisticated formulation see Kornai, J. (2014) Fenyegető veszélyek (Threatening Dangers). Élet és *Irodalom*, May 23

6 See also Gati, C. (2013) Hungary's Backward Slide. *New York Times*, December 12. http://www.nytimes.com/2011/12/13/opinion/hungarys-backward-slide.html Accessed: 30–10–2014. Ladányi J. and I. Szelényi (2014) Posztkommunista neokonzervatizmus (Post-communist Neo- conservatism). Élet és *Irodalom*, February 21.

7 See also Gati, C. (2013) Hungary's Backward Slide. *New York Times*, December 12. http://www.nytimes.com/2011/12/13/opinion/hungarys-backward-slide.html Accessed: 30–10–2014.

8 Wooldridge, A. (2012) The Visible Hand. *The Economist*, January 21.

(Sharafutdinova, 2011). Others describe these systems as some sort of "neo-patrimonialism" or "neo-prebendalism" (King and Szelényi, 2005). The most recent formulation of this concept – specifically applied to Hungary – calls the second and third Orbán government "mafia state" (Magyar, 2014, see also for an earlier and broader definition of mafia state Naim, 2012. Naim refers to Russia and Bulgaria, but also to countries in Latin America and elsewhere in the world).

The powerful theory of "mafia state" sees the recent Hungarian postcommunist state not as the organized "under world" but rather as an organized "upper world". In such a system the prime minister acts as a Godfather, (capofamiglia, the Don) and uses public authority to pursue his own economic interests and the economic interests of his real and "adopted" families (composed of all loyal followers) in an unpredictable (un-orthodox), illegitimate and un-ideological way (2014: 10 and 14)[9].

Less attention is paid in the literature to the ideology of the emerging postcommunist system. We call it post-communist traditionalism/neo-conservatism[10]. We will elaborate in the last section of this paper what that ideology is and why it seems to have substantial popular support.

The aim of this paper is to offer a synthesis of various conceptualizations. Our aim is to propose a genealogy of what we call post-communist managed illiberal democracy where property relations shift from private property and market capitalism to neo-patrimonial and eventually neo-prebendal property relations[11]. Rather than dismissing the emergent system as illegitimate[12] we want to understand the mechanisms, how the

9 In this paper, we do not aim at a comprehensive review of the relevant literature, which is far too extensive for a short essay. We only picked some examples from the literature to illustrate the diverse ways post-communist deviations from liberal democracy are conceptualized.

10 We struggled in this paper to find the proper label for the post-communist ideology of "Putinism". Initially we were attracted to the concept of neo-conservatism, but in itself it proved to be too multi-faceted. The term neo-conservatism was coined in the US in the 1960s and its meaning changed over the past half century and is still contested. (See for instance Hunter, J. (2011), What is a Neoconservative? *The American Conservative*, June 23. http://www.theamericanconservative.com/whats-a-neoconservative/ Accessed: 30–10–2014.) The term used for Hungary by Zoltán Gábor Szűcs, 2012. Given the inconsistencies in the term neo-conservatism we also add the concept of "traditionalism", the term Putin's major US supporter, the conservative Buchanan likes to describe himself with. In the relevant section of this paper we will define our use of the terms.

11 In this paper, we use the terms "patrimonial" and "prebendal" in the weberian sense of the terms. Under "patrimonial" authority, property holders receive their property at the grace of their master (fief), but their property rights are usually secure and their property is inherited. Under prebendal authority, property (benefice) given to the followers for their services, but rulers can revoke this property at any time (Weber, 1978:235). We use the terms neo-patrimonial and neo-prebendal to distinguish the postcommunist property relations from traditional authority. Under post-communist conditions property is allocated by political bosses, not by personal masters.

12 Following Max Weber, we regard all domination as legitimate as long as those subordinated to authority obey orders without being coerced to do so. Illegitimate power, involuntary compliance is only a "limiting case" (Weber, 1978: 212–215). Hence we are reluctant to call any political system from Putin's Russia to Orbán's Hungary (or for that sake Kádár's Hungary or Deng Xiao Ping's China) which attracts, or attracted a great deal of "voluntary compliance" and even some degree of "belief" in the system as "illegitimate".

system legitimates itself, hence what the ideology of the system is (that is what we call "post-communist traditionalism"/ neo-conservatism).

We have three sets of "variables": economic institutions, political organization and ideologies. These variables or dimensions interact with each other. To put it with Weber: we want to explore the elective affinities[13] between political systems, economic institutions and ideologies. Most attempts to explain the nature of postcommunist system do focus on one of these dimensions. We, on the other hand, try to explore the interaction of them.

Before we proceed further, we have to define our terminology.

Defining the concept of liberalism and democracy

We make a critical – and we concede: controversial – distinction, much like Montesquieu ([1748] 1989: 157), John Stuart Mill ([1859] 1993: 72–73) or recently Zakaria (1997: 24–25) between democracy and liberalism. In this paper we define democracy and liberalism as two distinct dimensions of "good governance". In fact we make distinction between four types of governance: liberal democracy, illiberal democracy, liberal autocracy and illiberal autocracy (which in extreme cases can be called despotism or dictatorship). These are of course ideal types in the weberian sense of the term. Liberal vs. illiberal; democratic vs. autocratic are two opposing poles on a scale. There is hardly any actually existing system which fits perfectly one of this polar concepts. Hence we are reluctant to use a 2x2 table and fit individual cases into each of the boxes[14], our aim is not to fit individual countries into one of the boxes, but try to estimate the distance of these cases from two or even from each of these boxes.

Democracy

We start this definition of democracy with Samuel Huntington, who offered a "minimalist definition" that can accommodate both liberal and illiberal practices and in this paper we follow Huntington's conception:

> "Elections, open, free and fair, are the essence of democracy, the inescapable sine qua non. Governments produced by elections may be inefficient, corrupt, shortsighted, irresponsible, dominated by special interests, and incapable of adopting policies demanded by the public good. These qualities make such governments undesirable but they do not make them undemocratic. Democracy is one public virtue, not the only one, and the relation of democracy to other public virtues and vices can only be understood if democracy is clearly

13 Weber did not believe in the possibility of causal explanation in the study of social life. Relationship between economic interests and ideologies can be best understood as "elective affinities" (Wahlverwandtschaften, see Gerth and Mills, 1946: 62 and 284)

14 It is useful to use the democracy index of the Economist Intelligence Unit to distinguish between "democracy" and "liberalism". They measure "democracy" in five dimensions: 1/electoral process; 2/functioning of government; 3/political participation; 4/political culture and 5/civil liberties. For this paper we use dimension 1/ as a definition of democracy and especially dimensions 2 and 5 as definition of liberalism. For details, see http://www.eiu.com/public/thankyou_download.aspx?activity=download&campaignid=demo2010 Accessed: 30–10–2014.

> distinguished from other characteristics of political system" (Huntington, 1991:9; cited by Zakaria, 1997: 25).

In agreement with Huntington and Zakaria, we use the term democracy merely to refer to "majoritarian" legitimation of domination, selection of leaders by votes of the majority. Even this simple definition has many complex issues with many miniscule details. Whose majority? What are the rules, which guarantee "open, free and fair" elections?

In the late 18th century, the United States was close to the ideal type of liberal democracy, despite the fact that women and blacks did not have the right to vote. There were severe restrictions even on white men's electoral rights that conditioned the power to vote on property ownership or the ability to pay taxes[15]. There never were and most likely, there never will be elections, which are completely "open, free and fair". Although democracies are generally becoming more inclusive, there are still major fluctuations in terms of fairness and openness of elections, both in the positive and negative directions. At one point, some electoral rules may become so restrictive that one begins to wonder whether this system is still "democratic". In addition, the notion of democracy is relative. In the world today, the liberal form of democracy is hegemonic. Thus, Putin's and Orbán's illiberal democracies are questioned whether they are democratic at all (Levitsky and Way challenged Zakaria and see illiberal democracy as contradiction in terms, 2002 and 2010). Freedom House for the last decade re-classified for instance Russia from democracy to autocracy (indeed there were reasonably credible claims of fraud in recent elections, nevertheless Russia held regular elections and the ruling party at its last elections almost lost its parliamentary majority – hence elections, even in Putin's Russia are not without stakes).

Liberalism

We define liberalism as the political system in which various branches of power (the executive, legislative and judiciary and arguably in our time a fourth branch, the media) are separated from each other and private/individual freedom and property is sacrosanct.

In July 26, 2014, Prime Minister Orbán in the Romanian resort Băile Tuşnad (Tusnádfürdő) called the political system he is dedicated to construct – in our terminology quite accurately – an "illiberal democracy". He used the term "illiberal" in a somewhat different way than we use it. "Liberalism" for Orbán means the excessive emphasis of individual interest over the "national" interest. One can interpret "national interest" as "public interest" (we will explain later the potential difference between "national" and "public" interest). George Schöpflin also criticized what he calls the "liberal consensus" for ignoring "collective identities" (among them "national" identity appears to be the most critical for him) and advocates "illiberalism" (2015: 12; 17).

15 Around 1790 about 60–70 percent of white men had voting rights in the newly formed USA under the arguably most liberal constitution in the history of humankind. No women, no blacks and no people without any property, or at least no people who did not pay any taxes could vote.

Viktor Orbán is quite right: how much emphasis we put on individual liberty and national (public) interest is a key question of good governance.

There are neo-liberals who indeed can be seen as believing that public interest is merely an aggregation of individual interests. Adam Smith is often interpreted as an advocate of this view. Indeed, in The Wealth of Nations he wrote "It is not from the benevolence of the butcher, the brewer, or the baker, that we expect our dinner, but their regard of their own interest" (Smith [1776] 1977:15). This seems to be what Orbán sees as "liberalism".

However, what is "self-interest"? In classical liberal theory (and in the practices of the most liberal political regimes of our times) it is nothing opposed to public interest, as Orbán's speech seems to imply. Smith in his Theory of Moral Sentiments is very clear about this: "No matter how selfish you think man is, it is obvious that there are some principles in his nature that give him an interest in the welfare of others, and make their happiness necessary to him" (Smith [1759] 2006: §1).

The critical point of reference of Smith's "sympathetic theory of human nature" is not the "nation", but it includes into the concept of self-interest the interest of all "others" we interact with, irrespective of their ethnic or national identity. In this sense, such a public interest results from the interest of individuals, rather than from the interest of some "imagined community", like the "nation" (Anderson, 1991). Furthermore, who can question the 20th or 21st century liberalism of the Swedish or Danish state and acknowledge they have a well-developed notion of the "public good", which arguably is consistent with Adam Smith's sympathetic theory of human nature.

The emphatic reference to national interest is of a different order. National interest does not stem from interests of interacting individuals, but from the interests of the "imagined community" of the nation (if imagined communities can have interests) to use Benedict Anderson's theory (Anderson, 1991).

Hence, it is possible to argue that for Putin (or Orbán) the emphasis on national interest drives their desire to achieve the dominance of the executive branch over the other branches of government. It is the executive branch which sees the national interest and should not be bogged down on this effectively by a politically divided legislature or a bureaucratic judiciary. Similarly, the media must also be constrained not to question the national interest in the name of individual liberties.

Let us return to Montesquieu and Mill. The problem of the post 2010 Hungarian regime (or post 2000 politics of Putin) is not so much that it violates the rules of majoritarian (democratic) policy (it actually does do that too). United Russia and Fidesz did manipulate electoral rules and United Russia may have even cheated during the 2011 elections, but the unique feature of these regimes is that they exercise power in an illiberal, non-moderate manner.[16] Are Russia under Putin or Hungary under Orbán illiberal democracies? Even Putin or Orbán would not contest the "illiberal" label, they are

16 The critical question is whether an opposition party, which at least in principle can rotate governmental power, exists or not. In a parliamentary system if the ruling party has a two-third majority, the separation of the executive and legislative branches basically becomes a fiction. If such a supermajority manipulates electoral rules so the ruling party keeps winning elections, the system is on

proudly illiberal. But are their regimes "democratic"? There is no simple yes/no answer to this question. With counter-factual reasoning we would suggest they can be regarded as democratic as long as according to the established electoral rules those in position of authority can be removed from power in regularly held elections.

There are also liberal autocracies, those are typically constitutional monarchies. Zakaria gives the Austro-Hungarian monarchy as an example (1997:29) of a liberal autocracy. Nevertheless even the Hobbesian "good monarch", hence an absolute monarch can act in reasonably liberal (moderate) ways. We are pushing our luck now: for instance the rule of Crown Prince Mohammed bin Zayed al Nahyan, the absolute ruler of Abu Dhabi is quite "moderate". Well, the record of Abu Dhabi on civil liberties is miserable, but it certainly has a sort of "rule of law", it offers a predictable environment to business and security of private property. It is "legal-rational order"... While the ruler is the source of law, the law is upheld, predictable and though Abu Dhabi does not offer much individual liberty it operates with a quite efficient and non-corrupt government. We certainly would not call UAE[17] "liberal", but it is somewhat in between the "liberal" and "illiberal" poles of governance. What about Singapore? Singapore is of course not much of a democracy (though it does have a more and more competitive electoral system), but it certainly has some "liberal" features. It falls short of liberalism in guaranteeing individual liberties, but it performs reasonably well in terms of rule of law, predictability of the legal system and property rights and non-corrupt, efficient functioning of the government. While Putin's Russia and Orbán's Hungary are illiberal managed democracies, Singapore is an autocracy with some liberal features. While we are in some pain in calling any of the existing autocracies in the world today liberal in the full sense of the term, some autocracies tend to have more "liberal" components than some of the "managed democracies".

John Stuart Mill believed that separation of powers, or liberalism, the guarantee of individual liberties is more important for good governance than majoritarian approval of the person in authority. Mill (just like Tocqueville, [1835–40] 2003) was greatly concerned about the "tyranny by the majority", a situation in which a democratically elected leader is not bound by liberal principles and by the separation of powers (J.S. Mill [1859] 1993: 72–73).

By the late 20th and early 21st centuries, however, there is a consensus in the North-Atlantic region: the "best government" is liberal and democratic, a combination of the two dimensions of "good governance" (see Levitsky and Way, 2010 and others[18]). In our view it does not make the analytic distinction between these two dimensions redundant, but explains the hegemony of the ideology of liberal democracy.

---

the verge of becoming undemocratic, or autocratic. Freedom House does not regard Russia since 2004 as democratic, but listed Hungary even in 2014 among the democracies.

17 UAE = United Arabt Emirates.

18 Kornai, J. (2014) Fenyegető veszélyek (Threatening Dangers). Élet és *Irodalom*, May 23

Shift from individual private property rights to neo-patrimonial or neo-prebendal property system.

A critical question of liberalism is that individual/private property rights are sacrosanct. Liberalism turns into to illiberalism, when one questions the security of individual property rights.

In post-communist capitalism, there are at least two challenges for the legitimacy of individual private property. These are arguably unique features of postcommunism, which may not be found in all, or even most semi-peripheral of peripheral economies.

First, the conversion of public property into private wealth happened over a short period of time, 500 days or five years. Especially when there is a legal vacuum, how to do it, upholding principles of legal-rational authority is extremely complex. It is next to impossible to do this in market consistent and legally/morally legitimate ways. Most – if not all of those – whom benefited from this conversion process have a "skeleton in their closet", if not in legal, then at least in ethical terms.

In principle, the conversion of common property into individual wealth could have occurred if the new owners could have purchased the collectively owned assets in competitive bidding at market prices. However, that was often impossible for two reasons. 1/ The domestic bidders did not have the capital to pay the value of common property and 2/ even if they did (foreign large investors certainly did), then they did not have good enough information to evaluate the real value of the property they would have purchased. So even with the best intentions the emergent legal-rational authority, the liberal system needed to rely on some sort of neo-patrimonial support to decide who the new owners would be (domestic investors needed "connections" to get credits, foreign investors needed "connections" to obtain information about the real value of the firms they wanted to purchase).

In this paper, we distinguish between three systems of property right allocation: 1/ A market driven system, supported by a secondary neo-patrimonial mechanism: public property was sold on the competitive market place, but access to credit for domestic investors (with little or no capital) and access to information for foreign investors depended on some neo-patrimonial connection to those who controlled credit/and information. In Central Europe during the 1990's the dominant system of property allocation was mainly market driven.

2/ Neo-patrimonial allocation of public goods to private investors within a legal-rational framework: political authorities operate in a democratic framework (even if it is somewhat already managed) and have to win elections so they need loyal supporters especially among big businesses who controlled the media hence they "appoint" the new grand bourgeoisie, anticipating their loyalty. The property allocated this way was at the grace of political powers. Nevertheless property rights were rather secure. This was like fief, however unlike classical fief this was closer to private property since it was alienable. The new property owners felt empowered by the security of their newly acquired wealth aspired even for political power. The arch-type of this system was Yeltsin's Russia. Some commentators of Yeltsin's Russia suggested that by the end of Yeltsin's rule some oligarchs had de facto privatized the state. This was a case of state capture.

3/ Attempt by a new generation of political leaders to turn neo-patrimonial property into neo-prebendal one: once the "commons were enclosed", there was no more public property to be privatized, nevertheless the (quasi) democratic framework of politics still required the political rulers to create political support. Under such conditions, they had no option but to redistribute property already allocated. They did so by withdrawing property from owners who were not seen as sufficiently loyal, or suspected to have too high political ambitions and reallocating this property (as "benefice") to owners who were believed to loyally serve the political powers. We call this the system of neo-prebendalism, which operates with a much-reduced system of legal-rational authority. It appears to be a system of rule of law, but since the legislative branch is not sufficiently autonomous the laws change easily if the executive branch needs this, occasionally even retrospectively. If the opposition is too weak and rotation of government becomes difficult. The political regime – even if there are regular elections – may cease to be democratic and can turn into an autocracy. Putin's Russia comes close to this type. The Orbán government in Hungary is next in line. Arguably, the road from democracy to autocracy is paved with the "stones" of illiberalism. While illiberalism does not necessarily eliminate democracy, it creates conditions (given the weakness of Constitutional Courts and the legislative branch) for particularly powerful political leaders to flirt with abandoning democratic procedures if they may sense their electoral support eroded and they may not win the next elections.

The ideology, which legitimates the illiberal neo-prebendal system of post-communist capitalism: traditionalism/neo-conservatism

However, as long as the political rulers operate in a democratic framework the elites need more than just the support of big money (they are important especially due to their control over the media). They also need the popular vote. Hence, they have to come up with an ideology, which would appeal to "ordinary people", and especially to people with very strong national (and religious) collective identity.

The extraordinary success Putin and Orbán had at the polls has a lot to do with their ability to formulate an ideology fitting into the world view of a substantial proportion of their electorate. Manipulating the rules of elections is only part of the story. The other part is finding an ideology that is appealing to people who would later vote. We call this ideology post-communist traditionalism/neo-conservatism.

What are the key elements of traditionalism/neo-conservatisms?

These were the major building blocks (and remain so) for all conservative/traditionalist movements: patria, the church and the (traditional) family. What is "neo" or "post-communist" about them?

Mainstream conservatives (such as the CDU in Germany or the "moderate" Republicans in the US) are often critical of left-wing, JFK (= John F. Kennedy), liberalism (especially on their efforts to build "excessive" welfare systems – hence they tend to stand by "small states" – and they were critical of "affirmative action" programs). Classical conservatives however, tend to retain respect for individual liberty and if there is a conflict between traditional values and individual liberties they may defer to individual liberties and stand by the separation of powers. (Ironically the traditional conservative opposition to affirmative action is cast in "liberal" terms": it violates individual liberty of whites against underprivileged African-Americans or Latinos)

As Skocpol and her co-authors (Williamson, Skocpol and Coggin, 2011) pointed out, there has been a revival of conservatism in the US (and we may add, elsewhere in the advanced world). In the US this was especially prominent with the rise of the so called Tea Party (which is of course no "party", just a movement within the Republican Party), especially in its "socially conservative wing"[19]. We call this new conservative revival – and we will argue it has a great deal of affinity with the ideologies emerging in some post-communist countries – as traditionalism/neo-conservatism. In the US the main characteristics of this conservative revival according to Skocpol and her co-authors are: 1/ they identify themselves primarily as social conservatives (Pat Buchanan – one of the forerunners of the movement – as we will show, calls himself paleo-conservative/traditionalist); 2/ they are "populists" in the sense they do inspire a popular movement, stage "culture wars" – extra parliamentarian actions – around socially conservative issues (like abortion, gay rights etc.); 3/ they make a critical distinction between "workers" and "people who do not work" and they oppose only government which gives "hand-outs" to the "undeserving poor" (hence they are not as anti-statist as it appears in their rhetoric); 4/ they are anti-immigrants, most of their support comes from white males and tends to be opposed to racial/ethnic affirmative action; 5/ they tend to be patriotic and religious, advocate teaching of creationism, prayers in school etc.

The value system of post-communist traditionalists/neo-conservatives and the Palinite wing Tea Party values are rather similar[20]. However, there are some differenc-

19 The Tea Party is a multi-faceted movement within the Republican Party. Ron Paul, a libertarian who was in foreign policy matters an isolationist initiated the movement. By 2010 Sarah Palin becomes one of the most influential figures of the Tea Party and she is a rather extreme social conservative and a foreign policy hawk. During the 1960'-1990's, before Palin neo-cons were merely that wing of the Republican Party which were foreign policy hawks and advocated that the US has played its role at the great power of the world, but most neo-cons did not take strong stances in social conservatism. Palin combined now the two and emerged as a Tea Party version of neo-conservatism combined with traditionalism. Nevertheless, Rand Paul retained the libertarianism and isolationism of his father, so the Tea Party movement has two wings: the Palinites and the Paulites. Post-communist traditionalism/ neo-conservatism is the closest to the Palinite version of Tea Party: emphasis on patria and religion combined with social conservatism (See Hunter, J. (2011) What is a Neoconservative? *The American Conservative*, June 23. http://www.theamerican-conservative.com/whats-a-neoconservative/ Accessed: 30–10–2014.), and they are also "hawks" in foreign policy. See Putin's policies in Ukraine or Orbán's position towards the EU and USA and his emphasis on "freedom fight".

20 Clifford Gadddy wrote: "I am sure I could put together a long list of quotes that would make Putin seem like a card-carrying member of the Tea Party" (Cited by Taylor, A. (2013) Pat Buchanan Tells the Truth about Vladimir Putin that American Conservatives Don't Want to Hear. *Business*

es. The Tea Party neo-conservatives/traditionalists are at least rhetorically against "big governments" though they use governmental powers to promote social conservative causes and some universal insurance schemes such social security and Medicare. Post-communist traditionalists/neo-conservatives are rather statist, not only in social issues but also in matters of economic policy.

Challenges of liberal democratic ways to capitalism in Central Europe

As we pointed out earlier, in 1989–1991 the legitimating ideology of the new political elites was liberal democracy and free market capitalism in most European postcommunist societies.

It is important though to see that these societies were at least for the first decade "transitional". These societies struggled with the rather extraordinary challenges to build "capitalism without capitalists" within a very short period of time (Eyal, Szelényi and Townsley, 1998) – a non-trivial task indeed.

While free market capitalism was the hegemonic ideology, even the most liberal countries of the region faced some difficulties to grow up to their ideals. The single most important challenge was the rapid conversion of property rights. Most neo-classical economists believed that the crucial step was to create identifiable private owners for the formerly public property. The Yeltsin-Gaidar team promised to "create" capitalism in 500 days. Central Europe may not have been in quite such a rush but was not far behind. While in England the "enclosure of the commons" took hundreds of years, in post-communist societies the original accumulation of capital took place within a few years. This inevitably brought some "neo-patrimonial" elements even in the liberal version of post-communist systems. While this greatly varied from country to country the legal rules which regulated the conversion from public goods to private property were not sufficiently well defined and left a great deal of room to discretion of political authorities, personal networks to create private ownership.

In countries where vouchers were critical in the process (like in the Czech Republic, Poland and most of all in Russia) there was much more room for clientelistic manipulation of the process. The new private property was secure, but the new owners needed the good will of political powers, bureaucratic office holders to acquire their property. Privatization agencies, banks had to decide who would qualify for loans and they could not use the classical mechanisms of creditworthiness since virtually no one had a credit history.

Even in the case of the most liberal country, Hungary during the 1990s it was useful to have some "patrimonial" connections. We give here two examples (see Kolosi and Szelényi, 2010). One could have had enormous advantage given sufficient inside knowledge what the real value of the public good offered for privatization was. For the purpos-

---

Insider, December 17. http://www.businessinsider.com/is-vladimir-putin-a-us-style-conservative-2013-12 Accessed: 30-10-2014.)

es of privatization, one could borrow up to 90 percent of the purchase price in the form of a very low interest rate government loan. It is obvious that people with authority could "help" that the „right" people would get the privatized assets. Hungary was arguable the weakest or at least one of the weakest cases of neo-patrimonialism. Russia under Yeltsin was the strong case.

We will suggest in the next section that Russia played a leading role in shifting property allocation from one primarily based on the market and turned its democratic system increasingly illiberal. In retrospect, one can see some early signs in a number of Central East European countries – even in the more liberal ones – to move in this direction. The crucial issue was privatization, to what extent governments/political powers can/or shall leave privatization to the "blind" forces of the market. Some "neo-patrimonial" element inevitably played a role[21] hence some office holders (politicians, especially managers) and their "clients" (children, kin, acquaintances) had better than average access to privatized assets (through the mechanisms we just described).

There were also some early "illiberal" attempts to limit the separation of powers. The media was especially an early target. Politicians elected to office (often conservatives) resented the criticism by media, often controlled by people from the socialist times (usually liberals). Hence attempts were made (often nasty fights fought, like under the Antall government in Hungary) to bring the media under governmental control. But with the exception of the South East (Serbia, Macedonia, Albania, Bulgaria, Romania) generally in the region checks-and-balances and the rule of law were the names of the game (even under the rule of Mečiar in Slovakia, Klaus in the Czech Republic or Antall in Hungary).

The neo-patrimonial way to capitalism in Yeltsin's Russia

The privatization practices of Russia during the 1990's were over determined by the desire to "create capitalism" in 500 days. Advocates of vouchers believed that it is a democratic mechanism to achieve fast and fair privatization. The vouchers mailed out to every citizen of Russia were supposed to represent a certain share of the public wealth. When

21 Hence in year 2000 unsurprisingly only two major Central European countries, Hungary (#32) and the Czech Republic (#42) were ranked by Transparency International (TI) among the 50% least corrupt countries (out of the 90 countries they investigated), Poland, Slovakia, Romania, Russia were in the bottom half. The ranking remains the same in 2008 while by 2013 out of 177 countries Poland (#38) overtakes Hungary (#47), but Hungary remains solid #2 since it is ahead of the Czech Republic (#57) and is way ahead of Slovakia and Romania. Russia is close to the bottom all along. Russia ranked as #82–83 out of 90 in 2000. Its ranking improved slightly to # 127 out of 177 by 2013. (www.transparency.org/country). The degree of corruption is substantial, but especially in Poland, Hungary and the Czech Republic rather constant and "mediocre" over the past 25 years. October 29, 2014 Miklós Ligeti the Hungarian director of TI in Népszabadság (p.5) suggested Hungary is now #119 out of 144 countries, but these data are not yet on the official website of TI so we have to take this with a grain of salt. A fall from #44 to #119 in one year sounds like a stretch – if true it would support a rapid fall into the mafia state category very recently.

Yeltsin announced the program, he stated the following: "We need millions of owners rather than a handful of millionaires"[22]. He might have believed that, but that was not the case in reality. In 1996, just five years after the collapse of the USSR Yeltsin was facing a challenging re-election with a serious communist candidate (Zyuganov). The seven biggest financiers of Russia, who otherwise were fighting each other, combined forces to help his re-election, just to prevent the victory of a communist in the presidential elections … and they achieved their aim. The seven claimed – just five years after the collapse of communism – that they owned half of all the wealth in Russia[23]. These seven oligarchs owned most of the media as well …

How could that happen? Yeltsin "managed" the privatization process from the Kremlin. It turned out most Russian did not know what to do with their vouchers (like most Hungarians did not know what to do with the "compensation tickets"– and the story is similar in the Czech Republic and Poland with various types of vouchers) hence they sold those well under nominal value to various investors.

These investors turned up at privatization auctions and the Kremlin had to decide who would win those auctions. When theory turned into practice, Yeltsin de facto "appointed" a handful of billionaires. According to Klebnikov Yeltsin relied mostly on advice from his beloved daughter, Tatyana. When a major auction was coming up Tatyana told Yeltsin: this is a good man, should get the property, this is a bad man, should not get property (Klebnikov, 2000: 202–203). Public property was often grossly undervalued. There were also various mechanisms of manipulating the process of privatization[24]. This was the way in which very young people like Abramovich (who eventually moved to live in the Kremlin, with the "family" as the Yeltsin circle was referred to) and entertained Tatyana for weekends in his dacha. Similar was the trajectory of Deripaska who married Tatyana's stepdaughter, the beautiful Polina Yumashev so he indeed joined the family (Tatyana' second husband was Yumashev, a journalist who became an influential adviser of Yeltsin and Polina was his daughter from an earlier marriage).

Was the Russian state in the 1990s a "mafia state"? Not quite. Klebnikov uses terminology not unlike the one used by Magyar, hence he calls Yeltsin the "godfather" and refers to his circle of protégés as the "family". In some ways it was an organized "upper world", Yeltsin appointed a new grand bourgeoisie, one may be tempted to call it a class of "boyars" – now referred to as "oligarchs" – but he did this in order to consolidate his political power rather than maximize his personal wealth. Under Yeltsin's neo-patrimonial system, the oligarchs did indeed behave like the boyars. They not only felt that their property rights were secure but also they had political ambitions, control over the media, taking public office (like Berezovsky was for a while Yeltsin's national security adviser). How much Yeltsin benefited financially from the system is hard to tell – Tatyana after

22 Cited by Aslund, 1995: 235

23 See World Bank: The Big Seven, 1998

24 Klebnikov gives a detailed description how the Kremlin manipulated auctions. He also gives an interesting example of undervalued assets. According to Klebnikov Gazprom was valued to be worth $250 million when privatized in 1994. It was estimated to be worth $40 billion in 1997 (Klebnikov, 2000: 135)

Yeltsin's fall from power moved to London and lives obviously comfortably but in all likelihood these financial benefits were trivial in comparison with the enormous wealth of the oligarchs Yeltsin appointed.

Russia under Yeltsin started to shift away from the liberal model very early on. Russia did retain to some extent the "democratic system" (if that merely means leaders are elected in reasonably free elections to office – as Yeltsin was in 1996 and as Putin was in 2000 and later two more times). True, the system was "managed"; in 1996 by the oligarchs who controlled the media stood behind Yeltsin (some of them also supported Putin in 2000). The system was turning "illiberal" under Yeltsin not only by overruling the procedural, market driven logic of property allocation by a paternalistic or neo-patrimonial way to do it, but also by limiting the powers of the legislature. In 1993 Russian parliament intended to impeach Yeltsin, Yeltsin counterattacked, stormed the parliament by military force. He adopted a new constitution that gave him greater powers. He dismissed parliament and called a new election. This election (December 1993) did not go his way and resulted in a parliament, which was opposed to many of his policies – an ironic reminder of the importance of "democracy" even in Yeltsin's Russia. Elections in Russia still had a stake. Yeltsin also dissolved the Constitutional Court and when he re-established the Court, he greatly diminished its powers. The key point is this: Yeltsin not only exercised illiberal, non-market ways to allocate property, he also moved in an illiberal direction by reducing the separations of powers of the executive, the legislative and the judiciary … and greatly increasing the powers of the executive. The Yeltsin (and later on Putin) regime was drifting away from liberalism, but was retaining at least some elements of majoritarian rule (hence democracy in our terminology) as the way office holders are selected and as the (most important or at least one of the most important) legitimating principles of the system.

The neo-prebendal turn: Putin's redistribution of property rights and managed illiberal democracy

As Putin came to power, in 1999 as Prime minister and in 2000 as President he was rather uncomfortable with the excessive power of the "boyars" or "oligarchs". While the oligarchs supported him, they did not know whom they supported. They expected another Yeltsin and they anticipated money would stay in power. The dominant oligarch of the Yeltsin's years, Berezovsky learned otherwise really soon and the hard way. Berezovsky was the owner of one of the most popular TV channels. According to one anecdote (whether it is true or not, who can tell? – it is he-told so-she-told so) once Putin was elected as President asked Berezovsky – one of his strong supporters – to visit him in his office. He told Berezovsky who the CEO of TV6 should be. But Mr. President, Berezovsky responded, this is a capitalist society, the owner appoints the CEO … Well, you wanted me to be president; you got me – responded Putin. Berezovsky got the message – unlike Khodorkovsky – so he got on the plane and went to London. He passed away there in 2013 – the circumstances of his death are rather mysterious.

There are two points we would like to raise at this time. 1/ The "oligarchs" were becoming too powerful, Putin wanted to put them on a leash and persuade them to keep out of politics….2/ All the commons were already "enclosed", the only way one could recruit new followers to redistribute to wealth allocated to the first round of oligarchs to a second round of oligarchs… Putin was ready to face both challenges… He was ready to submit the first round of oligarchs to a loyalty test and to dismiss them if they did not pass. He was also ready to redistribute the fortunes confiscated from the disloyal oligarchs to a new set of owners. The political genius of Putin was to convert the neo-patrimonial property relations to neo-prebendal ones. Under Putinism only those who served the political boss well could keep their property. He converted the "boyars" into "pomeshchiks", into "serving nobility." His mission was to complete the transformation started by Ivan the Terrible and Peter the Great: to create an obedient class of property holders… and make property rights much less secure and much more dependent on the political authority: the first, fatal step toward illiberalism.

However, there were major constraints Putin faced in accomplishing what he had set out to do. He was dancing in the chains of "democracy". He tried to combine democratic procedures of election of political leaders with illiberal practices.

Given the worldwide hegemony in 1991 of liberal democracy that was as far as Putin could back-pedal: while he could place severe restrictions on liberalism (such as a stronger executive and weakened legislature and judiciary), he still needed the majority approval of his leadership. He needed regularly held, reasonably free and fair elections to legitimate his rule as prime minister or president.

Putin did stay fairly close to "democracy" or "republican rule" as defined by Montesquieu or Huntington (see description of both in the Introduction) though he tried to "manage" the process as much as possible.

We should acknowledge that democratic processes are "managed" in all "actually existing democracies". In the United States, for instance, if one of the parties gains sufficient electoral majority they often change the boundaries of electoral districts. Criteria of when one can cast a vote are repeatedly renegotiated (can ex-convicts vote – if not, that is clearly a restriction of the Black/Democratic vote[25]), do people have to identify themselves when registering or actually voting with their driver's license (clearly a disadvantage for Black/Democratic voters). Putin "managed" the system not only with such technical procedures. Since the political system was not consolidated, he "manufactured" his own opposition, kept his "opposition" parties, like the communists alive (Anderson, 2007). Zoltán Ripp makes a similar argument about the incorporation of political opposition into the Fidesz system, Ripp, 2014: 97) to make sure the system looks like a genuine "multi-party system" (whether it is or not, is hard to tell).

The main point is this: given the "democratic constraints" on his rule and the iron laws of capitalism and market economy Putin needed a bourgeoisie that would support him unconditionally. While the claim, or "pretense" of democratic/majoritarian legitimacy is so important for "illiberal democracies" would need further elaboration, given

25 Manza and Uggen, 2006

the constraints of space here it should be sufficient to note that in the "third wave of democratization" it is hard or impossible to achieve international reputation without holding regular and apparently free elections of political leaders.

There were various technologies at the disposal of political authority to achieve the aim of redistribution of wealth acquired in the first stage of the accumulation of capital: 1/ the (selective) criminalization of his enemies and 2/ the "transit nationalization" of firms (Békési, 2004:248, also Magyar, 2014: 37). There are some other technologies of power, such as giving concessions of profitable businesses (such as offering monopolistic rights to the sale of tobacco or alcohol to certain merchants) to a network of loyal followers; imposing extraordinary taxes (such as taxes on banks or advertisement, or internet users) – often retroactively, hence contradicting the basic principles of liberal legislation, etc. However, focusing on these two should be sufficient for the time being.

Early in his rule, Putin launched an anti-corruption campaign (noble cause indeed). However, this anti-corruption campaign turned very soon into a campaign against political enemies. This is happening in China, for instance, the campaign against Bo Xilai. His imprisonment is politically motivated, but it was justified by "economic corruption". Bo Xilai received a "present" of $3.5 million from a business person and is now serving a long jall term for this, while the former Prime Minister, Wen Jiabao whose family supposedly accumulated $2.7 billion during his premiership was never investigated and never prosecuted. This is what we mean by "selective criminalization". Authorities use criminalization against oligarchs who grew too big and started to have their own political ambitions. Commentators on Russian politics did see in this more like a change in the nature of corruption rather than a real attempt to eliminate corruption. According to Perry Anderson corruption became the essence of the system (Anderson, 2007). Putin put oligarchs, who acquired billions of dollars under Yeltsin, to a "loyalty test". Those who renounced political ambitions and swore loyalty to the new "tsar" could go on (even people like Abramovich and Deripaska, who were in Yeltsin's "family") who did not face either emigration or jail. Bálint Magyar's mafia state theory makes a similar point. He does not deny corruption existed in previous post-communist regimes, but he claims that after 2010 under the Orbán regime it became government policy, it became the essence of the system.

Undoubtedly, all oligarchs have "skeletons" in their closets. Many nouveaux riches cheated on taxes. They paid high officials for their "help" and even if they did not break laws, at least they certainly manipulated them. Authorities can criminalize anybody. However, criminalization is a system or technology of governance (to put it with Foucault). It is a selective process in which some are prosecuted while others are not. Criminalization as a technology of power creates a sense of fear. You never know when they will come after you, unless you express your loyalty all the time.

The technology of criminalization is not restricted to the very rich. Authorities can criminalize even middle class bourgeoisie or small entrepreneurs. According to some estimates, the number of entrepreneurs in jall in Russia can be several hundreds of thousands[26]. According to other estimates, during the past ten years, up to three million entrepreneurs may have gotten jail sentences[27]. If a small entrepreneur has an appetite for the property of his/her neighbor and does have some connections to the police/ prosecution they may bribe them in order to prosecute their competition/neighbor so they can put their hands on their property. In the system of Putin, corruption – and criminalization of neighbors or competition – became government instruments (Perry Anderson, 2007).

Another technology of redistribution of wealth from "boyars" to "pomeshchiks" is (from the "bad" oligarchs" to the "good" oligarchs) "transitional nationalization" (see Békesi, 2004: 248). The re-nationalization of private property in Russia caught the attention of commentators, but at least according to the data by Perry Anderson during the Putin regime public ownership of productive assets grew only by some 5 percent. While no reliable data are available, it is reasonable to assume that most of the re-nationalized property is re-privatized. The government first works on bankrupting a firm. Once it is in serious trouble, they help the firm out by "nationalizing" it and once this is done it is sold again – often supposedly under-priced – to the new, by now loyal oligarchs.

Putin's firm hand in fighting corruption turned out to appeal to the public. His popularity rose to the stratosphere… into to 70s. It was in part driven by the rising oil prices in the early 2000s, which led to annual GDP growth of 6–7 percent and some improvement in the living standards of most classes, especially of the upper middle class (whose members are the most likely to vote during national elections).

Post-communist traditionalism/neo-conservatism

Nevertheless, even before the global financial crisis there were commentators – mainly on the political right, but not all of them right-wingers – who were reluctant to attribute the popularity of Putin only to high oil prices and increased living standards. Some observers argued that Putin managed to restore the traditional system of domination in Russia: an "autocratic" system in which citizens do not have to take responsibility for public affairs. Instead, they can rely on a caring government that would defend them against some real economic perils and some imaginary foreign enemy. Since this new regime was pro-business, it was more reasonable to see it as retro-tsarist rather than neo-Stalinist (Anderson, 2007; Pipes, 2005; Cannady and Kubicek, 2014). The manufacturing of a common enemy is a common feature of the Central European post-communism neo-conservative right wing parties. The Fidesz regime in Hungary, after 2010 is a rather extreme case of this, blaming the IMF[28], Brussels and more recently the USA for many of the country's troubles. This strategy is not only capable of pacifying

26 Lobello, C. (2013) Why Being an Entrepreneur in Russia Could Land You in Jail? *The Week*, August 9, Accessed: 30–10–2014.

27 Kesby, R. (2012) Why Russia Locks Up So Many Entrepreneurs? *BBC News Magazine*, July 4, http://www.bbc.com/news/magazine-18706597 Accessed: 30–10–2014.

28 IMF = International Monetary Fund.

the public, it is also capable of mobilizing masses and can result in pro-government and anti-foreign enemy demonstrations.

The Russian economy was hit hard by the global financial crisis, hence it is not surprising that Putin and his United Russia party – despite the weaknesses of its opposition and the lack of an alternative view of the future – lost a great deal of support. Under these circumstances, it became more and more obvious that the regime needs an ideological self-justification. In October 2013 Nikita Mikhalkov, a movie director with good ties to the Kremlin demanded a reinvention of a national ideology, what in his view became a "national security question"[29]. Putinism up to this point was sort of latently conservative. It needed an aggressively adopted neo-conservative/traditionalist ideological stance.

Putin began to build his ideological image already when he became prime minister in 1999. He published his "Turn of the Millennium" manifesto (http://www.ng.ru/politics/1999–12-30/4_milleneum), which was the first step to get rid of his KGB past and to create for himself a new political and ideological identity (Cannady and Kubicek, 2014). Already in the Turn of Millennium Putin laid down the principles of his future governance. These were patriotism, order and effective governance (he is reluctant to call it autocracy).

Those who suspect a "communist restoration" behind this project, when the chips come down, may be wrong. The Putin regime is far from being anti-business. The assets of the wealthiest Russians grew fast during the Putin's years. Forbes reports year after year more dollar billionaires in Russia. Today more billionaires live in Moscow than in London. (Perry Anderson, 2007).

At least the appearance of democracy and constitutionalism is also rather important for the Putin regime. Communist regimes also had constitutions and held elections – but none of those were in any way consequential. Under communist regimes, usually no one can sue the executive and the institution of a Constitutional Court typically does not exist[30]. Elections are not competitive and the executive appoints candidates for the legislative branch. That is certainly not the case for Russia under Putin. Putin took the appearance of the constitutionalism so seriously that he did not alter the constitution (though legally he could have done so) to enable him to run for a third consecutive term of presidency. Instead, he swapped places for one term with Medvedev. The emphasis on Christianity or orthodoxy is also important in the constitution of several other Central Eastern European countries, such as Poland, Hungary, Serbia, Croatia, Bosnia and Bulgaria.

Given the weaker performance of United Russia in 2011 and Putin in 2012 (and the subsequent anti-Putin demonstrations), it was indeed justified to call for a stronger ideological appeal. On December 10, 2013 the major Kremlin think-tank The Center for

---

29 Cited by Whitmore, B. (2013) Vladimir Putin, Conservative Icon. *The Atlantic*, December 20.

30 According to Gábor Hamza only Yugoslavia had a Constitutional Court since 1963. Hungary created an "embrionic" Constitutional Court in 1984, followed by Poland in 1985. China also created a Constitutional Court with limited powers in 1982 (Hamza. n.d: 5)

Strategic Communication issued a report entitled Putin: World Conservatism's New Leader (Center for Strategic Communication, 2013)[31].

Putin gave his annual presidential address just two days late [32] and he aggressively followed the ideology proposed by the Center for Strategic Communication. In our times – stated Putin (we do not quote him verbatim but try to capture the essence of his message) – several nations (he does not name any of them, but he obviously has the "West" and especially the USA in his mind) are re-evaluating their moral values. In the name of globalization, they tend to undermine the cultural differences among people and nations. The destruction of these traditional values has significant negative consequences for the societal order. Putin in fact claimed this process is not only destructive but it is also anti-democratic since it attempts to impose the value system of a militantly secular, multicultural and transnational elite. On the other hand, Putin had some good news for his audience: The number of people who are ready to defend those traditional values, the foundation of spiritual and moral values is increasing in every nation. Among those values, Putin names the traditional family. In the address he did not elaborate but given his well known objection to homosexuality he obviously meant family among heterosexuals), he also emphasized the need the defend "life" (likely a somewhat coded objection to abortion) and he emphasized the need to see the primacy of religious life and spirituality over material existence. "This is of course a conservative position" – this is almost a verbatim citation from Putin.

The Center for Strategic Communication and Putin's 2013 presidential address were trying to find an ideology which would unite Putin's supporters and divide his opponents, not only in Russia, but globally. There are two camps in the world: the conservatives (and Putin would like to think in this address even of Merkel as someone belonging to this camp) and the left-liberal "populists". What a fascinating twist in terminology. Neo-liberals normally use this term to discredit opponents on both ends of the political spectrum. However, Putin is explicit who are on his mind: Obama and Hollande, the two politicians who are losing popular support despite their populist promises.

Putin wants to kill two birds with one stone: he wants to gain the sympathy of Western, especially American neo-conservatives and traditionalists and at the same time he wants to offer an ideology for Russia, which restores its messianic vocation faced with the declining West. Russia becomes again the "third Rome", the most dedicated defender of traditional values: the values of religion, orthodoxy, family and patriotism.

However, which are the historical precedents, models for such a leader and such an ideology? (Pipes posed this question already in 2005, and see Cannady and Kubicek, 2014)[33]? None of the Soviet leaders – especially not Stalin with whom Putin, given his

---

31 See also Whitmore, B. (2013) Vladimir Putin, Conservative Icon. *The Atlantic*, December 20. http://www.theatlantic.com/international/archive/2013/12/vladimir-putin-conservative-icon/282572/ Accessed: 30–10–2014.

32 Putin, V. I. (2013) Presidential Address to the Federal Assembly. December 12, 2013. *Johnson's Russia List*. December 12. (Transcript from Kremlin.ru) http://russialist.org/transcript-presidential- address-to-the-federal-assembly-transcript-concluded/ Accessed: 30–10–2014.

33 See also Whitmore, B. (2013) Vladimir Putin, Conservative Icon. *The Atlantic*, December 20.

KGB past, is so often compared – fits the bill. As Pipes already noted (2005) the closest historical precedent is Tsar Nicolas I., the ruler with an iron fist, who mercilessly cracked down on Decembrists and re-established "law and order". Nicholas I in his doctrine released in 1826 legitimated his rule by three principles: orthodoxy, autocracy and patriotism (as Cannady and Kubicek point out Nicholas I is not "nationalist" in the sense of the French revolution, it is the "narod" which constitutes "patria"). Already in 1999, Putin recognized the importance of religion (he now claims his mother secretly baptized him when he was a young boy) and he managed to establish cordial relationships with the Orthodox Church, which has a long history in accepting state authority. It is intriguing that Yelena Mizulina, a representative of United Russia Party in Duma proposed on November 13, 2013 to include in the preamble of the Russian Constitution that Russia is an Orthodox country. Mizulina also proposed the bill to ban gay "propaganda". For her staunch support of Putin President Obama penalized her in March 2014 by freezing her assets in the USA.

Some commentators (Whitman, 2013) interpret the report by the Center for Strategic Communication and Putin's December 2013 address as a call to create a new "International". This time, however, this would be an "International of Conservatives" supposedly led by Vladimir Putin.

Can this become reality, or is (was) Putin daydreaming? Before the Ukrainian crisis blew up Forbes listed in 2013 Putin as the most influential person in the world, ahead of President Obama. Forbes retained his position as #1 even for 2014, after the crisis in the Ukraine. Interestingly on the 2013 and 2014 lists of 10 leaders there are only four politicians and only two were democratically elected (Obama listed as #2 and Merkel, listed as #5). The "free and fair" election of Putin to office was contested in Russia and President Xi has no claim to have democratic credentials. On this list of "ten most influential people in the world" there is only one person who can be vaguely associated with the political left (Obama). The others (with the exception of the popular new Pope, Francis) are representatives of the business world, people like Bill Gates, Bernanke, or Mario Draghi in a way indicating the limited – and arguably weakening – importance of democratically legitimated power in the world.

Even before the explosion of the Ukrainian crisis, Putin had little chance to win the classical conservatives like Merkel or Cameron over into his International. However, the right wing of the American spectrum heard his message. Pat Buchanan, one of the smartest and most articulated voices on the far-right of the Republican Party, expressed sympathy or even admiration for Putin and his presidential address. This is a non-trivial endorsement. Buchanan was adviser to Presidents Nixon and Reagan. He also ran in the Republican presidential primaries in 1992 and 1996 (running against G.H.W Bush he got 23% of the votes at the Republican convention in 1992 and in 1996 he got 21% against Dole). Hence, he is a serious conservative American voice. On December 17, 2013, just five days after Putin's presidential address he put a piece on his blog "Is Putin one of us?" and his answer at that time was: yes. Buchanan sees in Putin the leader in the world who is fighting against militant secularism, abortion, gay marriage, pornography, promiscuity and against the whole "Hollywood panoply". Buchanan sees a new global "culture war" emerging (The term "culture war" is usually attributed to Buchanan, who used it in 1992 in the Republican Convention). In Buchanan's own words: "President Reagan once called the old Soviet Empire "the focus of the evil in the modern world". President Putin is implying that Barack Obama's America may deserve that title in the 21st century". He continued: during the second half of the 20th century, the struggle was vertical: The West fought against the East. In the 21st century, the struggle becomes horizontal: today the conservatives, the traditionalists are fighting the militant secularists, the multicultural and trans-national elite. The similarity of the terminology of Buchanan and Putin is striking. Buchanan poses the question: why don't we call Putin "paleo-conservative" (a term he likes to use to describe himself). In his blog[34] he already acknowledged at the end of December 2013 that his position can be seen as "blasphemy" by Western intellectuals, but if you read Putin's 2013 presidential address, he has a point.

Buchanan did not cross the "red-line" which marks the difference between Republicans and the far-right for the first time in Republican politics. (In fact in 1999 he quit the Republican party, in 2000 he was trying to get a "third party nomination for the presidency", but eventually he decided to endorse in 2004 G.W. Bush and 2012 Mitt Romney as presidential candidates though he is closer to the Tea Party than the Republican main-stream. He did not identify himself as a neo-con. He sees himself as a paleo-conservative, traditionalist independent). Unlike Buchanan, most American conservatives and British Tories were not thrilled to welcome Putin to the family even before the Ukrainian crisis[35].

Nevertheless, it is indisputable that the world is shifting to the Right. The palinite wing of the Tea Party shares almost the same values as Putin on social issues and that is also true for Le Pen's FN, which in May 2014 at the EU parliamentary elections turned out to be the largest party in France and Marine Le Pen is a serious contender for the next presidential elections. There are many indications that Putin is rather close to the traditionalist far-right in Europe (and in the US).

Nevertheless, Republican Party conservatives do not have to be Tea Party social conservatives to express admiration for Putin. Rudy Giuliani, the popular former mayor of New York City noted after Putin invaded Ukraine without debate and deliberation: "That is what you call a leader"[36].

For the time being we focus on the social conservatives within the Tea Party. Indeed if one reads the texts of Putin, he sounds like a card-carrying member of the Tea Party. However, at least in two respects Putinism is sharply different from American social conservative neo-cons in the Tea Party. Sarah Palin may agree on many issues with Putin: on the question of traditional family, gay rights, the role of religion (the need to

34 Buchanan, P. (2013) Is Putin one of us? Patrick J. Buchanan Official Website. December 17, http://buchanan.org/blog/putin-one-us-6071 Accessed: 30–10–2014.

35 Franklin, P. (2013) Vladimir Putin: Not, in fact, a Tory. *Conservative Home: The Home of Conservatism*. December 23. http://www.conservativehome.com/the-deep-end/2013/12/vladimir-putin- not-in-fact-a-tory.html Accessed: 30–10–2014.

36 Krugman, P. (2014) Putin's Bubble Burst. *New York Times*, December 18, http://www.nytimes.com/2014/12/19/opinion/paul-krugman-putins-bubble-bursts.html Accessed: 21–12–2014.

teach creationism in schools). However, at least in two respects there are fundamental differences between the palinite Tea Party and Putinism and that is the question of the state and illiberalism.

The Tea Party – even in its most radical version – subscribes to a Jeffersonian view, anti-federalist, anti-statist position. Skocpol and her co/authors (2011) pointed out that the Palinite wing of the Tea Party has a complex attitude toward the government. Its rhetoric is against "big government", but most Tea Party supporters only object to handouts to the "undeserving poor" and to affirmative action for racial minorities. They support social security and medicare, the "working people" deserve governmental support. Furthermore on ethical issues, such as abortion, prostitution, pornography, drugs, gay rights traditionalists in the Tea Party acknowledge a critical role for governments – there is some "etatism". The formula for Putinism, or to put it more generally the post-communist neo-conservatism is: Tea Party + East European statism.

No matter how much Putin would have loved to, it seems unlikely characters like Thatcher, Reagan or Merkel … would consider themselves part of his International. Putin has better chances appealing to the "new right" of Le Pen or Jobbik in Hungary. There is indeed some evidence that Putin is working hard to attract the anti-EU far-right in Europe to his camp. Some American and British neo-conservatives before the Ukrainian crisis distanced themselves from Buchanan's endorsement of Putin[37]. Some US neo-conservatives also distanced themselves from Putin "autocratic" tendencies" (as David Frum stated, Putin is a coldblooded murderer but at least he hates the gays[38]).

With the confrontation between the West and Russia, the US and Russia the positions have changed somewhat. Now for the "interventionist" subsection of the right wing in the US, Russia is emerging as public enemy number one and they attack the Obama administration not being forceful enough on the issue of Ukraine. But the Tea Party and the right wing of the Republican Party have their "isolationist" elements as well. Pat Buchanan (and Rand Paul, a presidential hopeful for 2016) is one of the leading forces in this respect and Buchanan remains committed to Putin (see his blog: "Is Putting worse than Stalin?" July 28, 2014. Buchanan's answer is: Common … he is no Stalin, he is just playing the geo-political game, only Obama does not understand this). Nevertheless the Ukrainian crisis undoubtedly damaged badly – if Putin ever really had – the ambitions to create a new "conservative International" for short-term benefits (cashing in the support he gained from Russian patriotism for regaining the Crimea for Russia and standing up for Russians in Eastern Ukraine).

However, unlike the West, post-communist Central and Eastern Europe may be much more receptive to that type of conservatism which combines traditionalism, the trinity of "family, patria and God" with some version of statism. Such an ideology is

37 Franklin, P. (2013) Vladimir Putin: Not, in fact, a Tory. *Conservative Home: The Home of Conservatism*. December 23. http://www.conservativehome.com/the-deep-end/2013/12/vladimir-putin- not-in-fact-a-tory.html Accessed: 30–10–2014.

38 See Taylor, A. (2013) Pat Buchanan Tells the Truth about Vladimir Putin that American Conservatives Don't Want to Hear. *Business Insider*, December 17. http://www.businessinsider.com/is- vladimir-putin-a-us-style-conservative-2013–12 Accessed: 30–10–2014.

appealing in the whole region. Many elements of the statist neo-conservatism/traditionalism could be spotted as early as 1990 (in Poland, Slovakia, Hungary) Zoltán Gábor Szűcs is quite correct locating the definite discourse change – using Hungary as a case study – in the 2000s (Szűcs, 2006: 99–128; Szűcs, 2012: 133–141). However, this is far from just a Hungarian receptivity to Putinism. There is virtually no country in the region, which is not open to this idea. Think of Mečiar, Roberto Fico (who is often seen just a more sophisticated version of Vladimir Mečiar), Traian Băsescu, Bojko Borisov, the Kaczińsky brothers and most recently the Czech "Berlusconi", Andrzej Babiš and of course Belarus under Lukashenko and the Ukraine under Yanukovych (and arguably under Poroshenko as well), Serbia under Milošević, Croatia under Tudjman. In terms of their ideology, they are soul brothers of Putin's and of course of Orbán's.

It is reasonable to assume that this may at least in part of some longue-durée effect. Conservatism had a somewhat different meaning during the 19th century or during the inter-war years than in the West. What we consider East or West is another question. Was Bismarck East or West? Certainly Hungarian conservatives by the end of the 19th and early 20th century (István Tisza or Miklós Horthy) were not particularly loved by the Tories or other Western conservatives[39]; even by conservative tastes they were not sufficiently tolerant towards minorities. They also tended to be "statist", especially the Horthy regime during the premiership of Gyula Gömbös. Interestingly the Fidesz ideologues are silent about Gömbös, leaving this heritage to the far-right Jobbik, and searching for their historical precedents more in Horthy, Bethlen and Tisza. However, we can have non-Hungarian examples. Marshall Piłsudski was hardly more acceptable to the Tories in Britain. The Kaczyński brothers would not mind to see Piłsudski as their historical predecessor. Stepan Bandera – a Horthy or Piłsudski kind of Ukrainian politician – is also the hero of the Ukrainian right wing.

Postscript: Is Hungary after 2010 a Case of Putinism?

The Hungarian ruling party and its prime minister, Viktor Orbán (since 2010) deserve special attention. While in world-view, ideology Fidesz is close, at least since 2010 there is one feature that makes Orbán different from Fico, Kaczyński, Borisov etc. (and similar to Putin). Namely, Orbán can win and recently has won elections with overwhelming majorities. No-one can doubt that at least the 2010 election when Fidesz won a two third majority in parliament was free and fair – only Putin's popular appeal can be compared with this (though how "free and fair elections" of Putin and his party ever were is disputed by the opposition and Hungarian and non-Hungarian political scientists). De facto Fidesz only secured 53% of the votes, in an election where only 64% of the electorate voted. With this result – given the curious nature of Hungarian law (never challenged by any of the major political forces as long as it served their interests and not unprecedented in other democracies) Fidesz obtained 68% of the parliamentary seats,

39 Tamás G. M. (2014) Az ellenzéket is le kell váltani. Élet és *Irodalom*, January 3.

hence had a virtually unchecked and almost unlimited power to change laws, pass a new constitution etc. The party, now with a two third majority, passed a new constitution, which expressed the traditionalist/neo-conservative worldviews of the new government – amongst others insisting that Hungary lost its sovereignty on March 19, 1944 when Germany militarily occupied Hungary – hence the country is not responsible for the 600,000 Jews who perished mainly in Auschwitz after the German invasion.

The two third majority of Fidesz in Hungarian parliament was used to legitimate the adoption of a new constitution and to change it at any time since. The political opposition indeed had a good point that the government adopted the new constitution without sufficient consultation with opposition parties and the electorate. Parliament approved it in 18 months.[40] Finally, the new Constitution (now officially called the Fundamental Law) also limited the powers of the Hungarian Constitutional Court.

There were also attempts to bring the judiciary and the media under executive control (see for detailed, outstanding account of the limitations of divisions of powers in Vörös, 2014).

János Kornai in his excellent paper[41] already announced the end of democracy, mainly arguing his case by the limitation of separation of powers. It may be useful to cite Montesquieu, Huntington and Zakaria once again. If democracy (republic) only means the rule by the majority, it is hard to contest that Fidesz acted at least between 2010 and 2014 according to democratic principles (that does not mean it ruled with "moderation"). During the times when Fidesz had a two third majority in parliament Fidesz passed legislation – in accordance with the regulations of existing constitution – what incidentally served its party interest (it is not unheard of in the history of democratic governance when parties when they have legal justification change the boundaries of electoral districts, regulations who is eligible to vote etc.). The change in electoral laws, which had the most significant impact on the election results, was the introduction of the single round elections for individual candidates (previously if a candidate did not win 50%+1 vote in their first round, there was a second round of election between the top candidates). This obviously benefited the party, which had a strong majority … though it is an electoral rule followed in many countries. The Fidesz government also pushed through legislation that gave voting rights for Hungarians living abroad – since the liberal parties and the left wing party opposed such legislation in an earlier plebiscite this also gave an advantage Fidesz. Fidesz supported voting right for all Hungarians irrespective of their residence for a long time. Hence: no one can doubt Fidesz won the 2010 elections by rules accepted by all parties as "democratic". While by 2014 they managed

40 The US constitution was not adopted by a body (Continental Congress) elected by universal suffrage, but the writing of the constitution was a long process and it had to be ratified by all of the 13 members states. Incidentally the US constitution was amended 33 times in its more than 200 years history in a very complicated process. In the first 20 months the Hungarian constitution was amended five times with a simple two third majority again without any requirement of consultation (we should note the first ten amendments to the US constitution also took place in the first year, but each time with a complex process of consultations).

41 Kornai J. (2011) Számvetés (Taking Stock). *Népszabadság*, January 6.

those rules to their own benefit, those new electoral technologies existed in other "democratic" countries and all those changes passed according the legislative and procedural rules. Hence to call this regime "dictatorship" or "autocracy" can only be based on its limitations of liberal separation of powers, but it is hard to question the majoritarian legitimacy of the Fidesz government (which was reconfirmed by three elections in 2014 – one for the national parliament, one for European Parliament and one for local governments – all handsomely won by Fidesz).

If we call the systems of Putin or Orbán "democracy", it is a far cry from calling it "good", or "moderate" governance. Good governance implies a moderate/liberal rule by democratically elected polity.

The bottom line of this paper: Putin's United Russia and Orbán's Fidesz are rather close to each other and it is reasonable to describe them as post-communist neo-conservatism/traditionalism and managed illiberal democracies.

However, there is also a unique feature of Central European traditionalism/neo-conservatism that makes them different from Russia. Putin accused Obama and Hollande to be "left-leaning and liberal populists". Putin is strongly pro-business. One cannot accuse him of being a "populist". The liberal opposition in Central Europe often calls the Orbán regimes "populist" and indeed some of their economic policies (that is especially true for Orbán, but also relevant for Mečiar/Fico, Kaczyński, Borisov or even Klaus) can appear to be "left-wing" (being anti-EU, anti-globalization, nationalist in economic polices). Zsuzsa Hegedűs went so far[42] as to call Mr. Orbán "the true social democrat". In the political mess post-communist Eastern Europe finds itself it is hard to tell who is "left" and who is "right"…

G.M. Tamás[43] (according to the local popular abbreviation "TGM") offered some persuasive arguments and Ágnes Gagyi (2014) echoes his thoughts. The right wing, or center-right parties of Eastern Europe often express more understanding of popular needs and demands rather than the somewhat missionary liberals (see Eyal, 2000). As Gagyi puts it the competition between "democratic anti-populism and anti- democratic populism" is the catch 22 of post-communist politics. The framing of this question as democracy vs. anti-democratic may not be the most accurate but the dilemma is well formulated. There is certainly a strong anti-populist commitment of liberals (and the "left" if it can be called by this name) and the populism of the patriotic right-wing movements. Who will win elections? Of course, the populist, nationalist right (or center right). Why should one vote for a party, which promises only sweat, and blood, while the other party promises to be responsive to popular needs (they will promise to tax banks, rather than the borrowers, will reduce costs of gas, electricity and heating at the expenses of the profit of monopoly companies etc.). Whether the Center right is "populist" or just using a populist rhetoric is another question. The Fidesz government in Hungary for instance proved to be responsive to problems people had on their minds. Eyal is un-

42 Hegedűs, Zs. (2013). Orbán igazi szociáldemokrata (Orbán, a Genuine Social Democrat), *Heti Válasz*, December 4.

43 Tamás G. M. (2014) Az ellenzéket is le kell váltani. Élet és *Irodalom*, January 3.

doubtedly right: the former dissidents turned liberals by insisting to "live in truth" seem to be doing a self-defeating job in democratic politics. They lose elections, and after not knowing how to play the democratic game better, they tend to label their opposition as anti-democratic or even dictatorial. The game of democratic politics is about winning votes, and this practice does not achieve this for them.

Are the right-wing parties genuinely "for the people" and "against business"? Hard to tell. The Fidesz government in Hungary after 2010 certainly impressed the observer as "exemplary student" in "austerity". It reduced budget deficit well beyond 3% required by the EU, reduced inflation, cut welfare spending (in the Clintonian name of workfare from welfare policies) and did not increase the national debt in times of recession when governments are supposed – at least according to Keynes or more recently Krugman[44] – to increase public debts and budget deficits. So "populist" rhetoric's policies were carried out with the anti-populist policies of "actually existing" neo-liberals.

Let us conclude with the question of ideology and search for historical precedents. Image creation is a crucial component of politics. This is one of the fatal weaknesses of theories, which try to label the Centre-right post-communist neo-conservative/traditionalist regimes as "fascist", "dictatorial," "neo-communist", comparing them with Hitler, Mussolini, Stalin or Kádár or just designating them as "mafia". These regimes make a desperate effort to find reasonably respectable historical precedents and a respectable ideology. Traditionalism is at least as important to their self-identity as neo-conservatism. Nothing can be further from truth than the claim: they are unideological… Nicholas I for Putin, Piłsudski for Kaczyński, Admiral Horthy (emphatically before the German occupation of Hungary in March 19, 1944) and especially its roots in Bethlen and Tisza are extremely important ideological exercises. The post-communist traditionalists/neo-cons want to legitimate themselves with the (rather right-wing) conservatives of the pre-communist times, just as US neo-cons want to reach back to Jefferson. These claims require careful analysis and balanced evaluation.

Both for analytical purposes and for political aims it is crucially important to make a distinction between the post-communist traditionalists/neo-cons and the radical far-right, which does not have – at least so far – a chance of electoral victories. Post-communist Central and Eastern Europe is not (yet) the Weimar Republic, ready for a revolutionary radical right (or left). The post-communist traditionalists/neo-cons with their populist rhetoric are capable of winning elections as long as they only have to compete with an anti-populist left/liberal opposition, which can only promise a painful treatment by the good doctor[45].

Post-communist traditionalism/neo-conservatism, a neo-prebendal system of property re-allocation and a managed illiberal democracy is the new model formulated by Putin and Hungary seems to be the closest case to such a system for the time being. The Fidesz government expressed support for Putin on more than one occasion. They

44 Krugman, P. (2014) Putin's Bubble Burst. *New York Times*, December 18, http://www.nytimes.com/2014/12/19/opinion/paul-krugman-putins-bubble-bursts.html Accessed: 21–12–2014.

45 Bokros L. (2014) Kár az orvosra haragudni (Do not blame the doctor). *Vasárnapi Hírek*, October 19. http://www.vasarnapihirek.hu/fokusz/bokros_kar_az_orvosra_haragudni Accessed: 30–10–2014.

supported the "Southern Stream" and even in the Ukrainian crisis tended to side with Russia (Slovakia, Serbia and Bulgaria – and most recently Greece under the new Syriza government – took similar stands). However, who is next in line? While none of the other Central European countries have charismatic leaders who can win elections with such a program – especially not with two third majorities – the potential is there in virtually every country. This is a sobering lesson of history.

References

Aslund, A. (1995) *How Russia Became a Market Economy?* Washington D.C.: Brookings Institution.

Anderson, B. (1991) *Imagined Communities. Reflections on the origin and spread of nationalism*. London: Verso.

Anderson, P. (2007) Russia's Managed Democracy. *London Review of Books*, 29(2): 3–12.

Békési, L. (2014) A maffiaállam gazdaságpolitikája. (The Economic Policy of the Mafia-State.) In Magyar, B. and J. Vásárhelyi (eds.) *Magyar Polip 2*. Budapest: Noran Libro: 241–260.

Berman, S. (2014) Global Warning. Francis Fukuyama's Political Order and Political Decay. *New York Times*, September 11.

Bokros, L. (2014) Kár az orvosra haragudni (Do not blame the doctor). *Vasárnapi Hírek*, October 19.

Buchanan, P. (2013) Is Putin one of us? Patrick J. Buchanan – Official Website. December 17, http://buchanan.org/blog/putin-one-us-6071 Accessed: 30–10–2014.

Cannady, S. and P. Kubicek (2014) Nationalism and Legitimation for Authoritarianism: A Comparison of Nicholas I. and Vladimir Putin, *Journal of Eurasian Studies*, 5(1): 1–9.

Carothers, T. (2002) The End of Transition Paradigm, *Journal of Democracy*, 13(1): 5–21.

Economist Intelligence Unit (2010) Democracy Index 2010. http://www.eiu.com/public/thankyou_download.aspx?activity=download&campaign id=demo2010 Accessed: 30–10–2014.

Eyal, G. (2000) Antipolitics and the Spirit of Capitalism: Dissidents, Monetarism and the Czech Transition to Capitalism, *Theory and Society*, 29(1): 49–92.

Eyal, G., I. Szelényi and E. Townsley (1998) *Making Capitalism without Capitalists. Class formation and elite struggles in post-communist Central Europe*. London: Verso.

Franklin, P. (2013) Vladimir Putin: Not, in fact, a Tory. *Conservative Home: The Home of Conservatism*. December 23. http://www.conservativehome.com/the-deep-end/2013/12/vladimir-putin-not-in-fact-a-tory.html Accessed: 30–10–2014.

Fukuyama, F. (1992) *The End of History and the Last Man*. New York: The Free Press.

Fukuyama, F. (2014) *Political Order and Political Decay. From the industrial revolution to the globalization of democracy*. New York: Farad, Straus and Giroux.

Gati, C. (2013) Hungary's Backward Slide. *New York Times*, December 12.

Gagyi, A. (2014) *Az antipopulizmus, mint a rendszer váltás szimbolikus eleme* (Anti-populism as One of the Symbolic Elements of the Change of Regime). *Fordulat*, 21(6): 298–316.

Gerth, H. H. and C. W. Mills (1946) (eds.) *From Max Weber: Essays in Sociology*. New York: Oxford University Press.

Hamza, G. (n.d.) *Past and Present of Constitutionalism in Central and Eastern Europe*. MS.

Hegedűs, Zs. (2013). Orbán igazi szociáldemokrata (Orbán, a Genuine Social Democrat), *Heti Válasz*, December 4.

Hill, F. and C. Gaddy (2013) *Operative in the Kremlin*. Washington, D.C.: Brookings Focus Book.

Hunter, J. (2011) What is a Neoconservative? *The American Conservative*, June 23. http://www.theamericanconservative.com/whats-a-neoconservative/ Accessed: 30–10–2014.

Huntington, S. P. (1991) *The Third Wave: Democratization in the Late Twentieth Century*. Norman, Oklahoma, University of Oklahoma Press.

Jowitt, K. (1996) Undemocratic Past, Unnamed Present, Undecided Future. *Demokratizatsiya*, 4(3): 409–419.

Kesby, R. (2012) Why Russia Locks Up So Many Entrepreneurs? *BBC News Magazine*, July 5, http://www.bbc.com/news/magazine-18706597 Accessed: 30.10.2014.

King, L. and I. Szelényi (2005) Post-Communist Economic Systems. In Smelser, N. J. and R. Swedberg (eds.) *The Handbook of Economic Sociology*. Princeton, NJ: Princeton University Press: 205–232.

Klebnikov, P. (2000) *Godfather in the Kremlin: The Decline of Russia in the Age of Gangster Capitalism*. New York: Harcourt.

Kolosi, T. and I. Szelényi (2010) *Hogyan legyünk milliárdosok?* (How to Become a Billionaire?) Budapest: Corvina.

Kornai, J. (2011) Számvetés (Taking Stock). *Népszabadság*, January 6.

Kornai, J. (2014) Fenyegető veszélyek (Threatening Dangers). Élet és *Irodalom*, May 23

Krugman, P. (2014) Putin's Bubble Burst. *New York Times*, December 18, http://www.nytimes.com/2014/12/19/opinion/paul-krugman-putins-bubble-bursts.html Accessed: 21.12.2014.

Ladányi, J. and I. Szelényi (2014) Posztkommunista neo-konzervatizmus (Post- communist Neo-conservatism). Élet és *Irodalom*, February 21.

Levitsky, S. and L. A. Way (2002) Elections Without Democracy: The Rise of Competitive Authoritarianism. *Journal of Democracy*, 13(2): 51–65.

Levitsky, S. and L. A. Way (2010) *Competitive Authoritarianism: Hybrid Regimes after the Cold War*. Cambridge: Cambridge University Press.

Lobello, C. (2013) Why Being an Entrepreneur in Russia Could Land You in Jail? *The Week*, August 9, Accessed: 30–10–2014.

Magyar, B. (2014) A posztkommunista maffiaállam rendszerképző sajátossága. In Magyar B. and J. Vásárhelyi (eds.) *Magyar Polip 2*. Budapest: Noran Libro: 7–46.

Manza, J. and C. Uggen (2006) *Locked Out: Felon Disenfranchisements and American Democracy*. Oxford: Oxford University Press.

Mill, J. S. [1859] (1993) On Liberty. In Mill, J. S.: *Utilitarianism, Liberty, and Representative Government*. London: Everyman's Library: 69–185.

Montesquieu, C. L. d. S. [1748] (1989) *The Sprit of the Laws*. Cambridge: Cambridge University Press.

Murray, C. (1984) *Losing Ground: American Social Policy 1950–1980*, New York: Basic Books.

Naím, M. (2012) Mafia States: Organized Crimes Takes Office. *Foreign Affairs*, 91(3): 100–111.

Pipes, R. (2005) *Russian Conservatism and Its Critics: A Study In Political Culture*. New Haven, CT: Yale University Press.

Putin, V. I. (2013) Presidential Address to the Federal Assembly. December 12, 2013. *Johnson's Russia List*. December 12. (Transcript from Kremlin.ru) http://russialist.org/transcript-presidential-address-to-the-federal-assembly-transcript-concluded/ Accessed: 30–10–2014.

Ripp, Z. (2014) Ellenzék a centrális erőtérben: a maffia állam ellenzéke (Opposition in the Centralized Political System: Opposition to Mafia State). In Magyar B. and J. Vásárhelyi (eds.) *Magyar Polip 2*. Budapest: Noran Libro: 97–128.

Schöpflin, Gy. (2015) Europe: An Epistemological Crisis. In Jensen, J. and Miszlivetz, F. (eds.) *Reframing Europe's Future. Challenges and Failures of the European Construction*. Abingdon, Oxon: Routledge: 7–18.

Sharafutdinova, G. (2011) *Political Consequences of Crony Capitalism inside Russia*. Notre Dame: University of Notre Dame Press.

Shevtsova, L. F. (2000) Russia under Putin: Can Electoral Autocracy Survive? *Journal of Democracy*, 11(3): 36–38.

Smith, A. [1759] (2006) *The Theory of Moral Sentiments*. São Paulo: MetaLibri.

Smith, A. [1776] (1977) *The Wealth of Nations*. Chicago: University of Chicago Press.

Staniszkis, J. (1990) "Political capitalism" in Poland. *Eastern European Politics and Societies*, 5(1): 127–141.

Szelényi, I. (2013) Kapitalizmusok a kommunizmus után (Capitalisms after Communism). In Magyar B. and J. Vásárhelyi (eds.) *Magyar Polip 2*. Budapest: Noran Libro: 89–99.

Szűcs, Z. G. (2006) Újkonzervativ forradalom. A nyelvi újítás mint diszkurzív stratégia az 1998-as kormányprogram vitájában (Neo-conservative Revolution. Linguistic Innovation as Discoursive Strategy in the 1998 Debate on the Program of the Government). In Szabó M. (ed.) *Fideszvalóság: diszkurzív politikatudományi* értelmezések (Fidesz-reality. Discoursive Political Interpretations). Budapest: L'Harmattan: 99–127.

Szűcs, Z. G. (2012) A magyar politikai diskurzus változásai 2000 óta (Changes in the Hungarian Political Discourse since the Year 2000). In Boda, Zs. and A. Körösényi (eds.) *Van irány? Trendek a Magyar politikában* (Is There a Direction? Trends in Hungarian Politics). Budapest: MTA TK PTI – Új Mandátum: 128–151.

Tamás, G. M. (2014) Az ellenzéket is le kell váltani. Élet és *Irodalom*, January 3.

Taylor, A. (2013) Pat Buchanan Tells the Truth about Vladimir Putin that American Conservatives Don't Want to Hear. *Business Insider*, December 17. http://www.business-insider.com/is-vladimir-putin-a-us-style-conservative-2013–12. Accessed: 30.10.2014.

Tocqueville, A. de [1835–40] (2003) *Democracy in America*. London: Penguin Books.

Trencsényi, B. (2014) Minek nevezzelek? (By What Name Can I Call You?) In Magyar B. and J. Vásárhelyi (eds.) *Magyar Polip 2*. Budapest: Noran Libro: 49–68.

Vörös, I. (2014) " 'Alkotmányos puces' Magyarországon, 2010–2014." (A Constitutional Coup d'état). In Magyar B. and J. Vásárhelyi (eds.) *Magyar Polip 2*. Budapest: Noran Libro: 49–96.

Weber, M. [1922] (1978) *Economy and Society. An Outline of Interpretive Sociology, ed. by G. Roth and C. Wittich. Vol. I*. Berkeley: University of California Press.

Whitmore, B. (2013) Vladimir Putin, Conservative Icon. *The Atlantic*, December 20. http://www.theatlantic.com/international/archive/2013/12/vladimir-putin-conservative-icon/282572/ Accessed: 30.10.2014.

Williamson, V., T. Skocpol and J. Coggin (2011) The Tea Party and the Remaking of Republican Conservatism. *Perspectives on Politics*, 9 (1): 25–43.

Wooldridge, A. (2012) The Visible Hand. *The Economist*, January 21.

World Bank (1998). *The Big Seven – Russia's Financial Empires*. Washington D.C.

Zakaria, F. (1997) The Rise of Illiberal Democracy. *Foreign Affairs*, 76 (6): 22–43.

IV.3 The Role of Rents in the Transition from Socialist Redistributive Economies to Market Capitalism

Péter Mihályi and Iván Szelényi

Abstract

In this paper we make a critical distinction between inequalities arising from profits and wages on the one hand and inequalities arising from rents on the other following Sorensen (2000) and the 19th century economist, Ricardo. Our new contribution is to show that rents are especially important in postcommunist capitalist transition and without the concept of rents the mechanisms of corruption cannot be understood. We identify three types of rent seeking behavior which can be observed in any capitalist country, but they play a particularly important role in postcommunist transition: (i) market capture by political elites; (ii) state capture by oligarchs; (iii) capture of oligarchs by autocratic rulers through selective criminalization and the redistribution of their wealth to loyal new rich.

Keywords: inequality, capital, capitalism, profits, rents.

Introductory remarks

In the first part of the paper we review how wages, profits and rents are treated in classical social theory. We show the unique contribution of Ricardo to the theory of rent [1817] (2004) and we conclude with a brief discussion of Sorensen's (2000) Weberian re-interpretation and generalization of Ricardo's theory. Like Sorensen, first we define rent as an income gained from closed relationships, from monopolies, cartels and regulatory capture. Then we make two qualifications: (i) while literature in the past 50 years considers whether all or some form of rent seeking shall be interpreted as corruption[1], we use the term in value neutral terms; (ii) we will argue that rents and rent seeking behavior are present in all economies.

1 See e.g. Tullock (1967), Krueger (1974), Posner (1975), Buchanan *et al.* (1980) and Bhagwati (1982).

In the second part of the paper our point of departure is Piketty (2014)[2], [3] and Stiglitz (2012) [4], who see rent as responsible for much of the increases of social inequalities in contemporary capitalist economies, hence the making of patrimonial capitalism. Our hypothesis is that rent seeking was especially present all along in postcommunist capitalisms given the pressure of fast privatization of state owned assets. In some countries (Russia, China or even in Hungary) the significance of rent seeking (and the role of politics in allocation public funds) is increasing. In these countries politics remains in control. It is not big business which captures the state; rather the state captures the market and plays a critical role in the making and unmaking of the new rich.

In our conclusion we evaluate the consequences of increasing rent seeking. Inequalities created by profit and wages are vast, but can be addressed by imposition of progressive taxation. Taxing of rent (taxes on inherited wealth and capital gain being one of the prime examples of such rent) is likely to meet powerful resistance of interest groups.

Part I.

1. Rent in the classical economic theory

Classical economic theory from John Locke to Adam Smith, David Ricardo and Karl Marx struggled with the role labor, capital and rent played in the creation of value, and the determination of prices and incomes. The received wisdom in 18th early/mid19th century economics was the "labor theory of value". Few economists would accept this theory today, but the distribution of revenues exclusively between wages and profits is still often a common point of departure (once rents are defined as a part of profits).

Adam Smith much like Locke explained the origins of rent on land from private ownership of land (and mines), but had a lingering doubt about how much landownership contributed to the creation of new wealth: *"As soon as land of any country has all*

---

2 „.. a society of rentier and a society of super managers – is naive and overdrawn. The two types of inequality tend to coexist: there is no reason why a person can't be both super manager and rentier and the fact is that concentration of wealth today is much higher…" *op. cit.* p. 264.

3 …"Wealth accumulated in the past grows rapidly than output on wages….. The entrepreneur inevitably becomes a rentier…" *op. cit.* p. 573.

4 „.there are two ways to become wealthy: to create wealth or to take wealth away from others. The former adds to society. The later typically subtracts from it… The monopolist, who overcharges for his product takes money from those whom he overcharged… Some… turn to…. rent extraction to garner even more riches…To take just one example, the railroad barons of the nineteenth century provided an important service in constructing railroads, but much of their wealth was the result of political influence – getting large government grants on either side of the railway. Today, over a century after the railroad barons dominated the economy much of the wealth at the top of the United States – and some of the suffering at the bottom – stems from the wealth transfers instead of wealth creation". *op. cit.* p.40.

*become private property, the landlords .... **love to reap where they never sowed** and demand a rent for its natural produce of the earth*".[5] Ricardo moved substantially beyond Locke and Smith: "*The rise of rent is always the effect of the increasing wealth of the country, and of the difficulty of providing food for its augmented population. **It is a symptom, but it is never the cause of wealth.***"[6] While for Locke and Smith wages, profits and rents all contribute to the value and price of the products and to the wealth of the nation, Ricardo only sees such a productive contribution of wages and profits, but rent – at least rent which comes from the scarcity of land – is not the cause of value/price, or wealth, it is the consequence (symptom) of increasing prices/wealth. Smith and Ricardo were liberals; they advocated capitalist transformation of society. As we will elaborate in the following section Smith's lingering doubts about and Ricardo's explicit criticism of rent does not follow from the "general logic of capitalism". Ricardo offered a general – not a historically specific – theory, nevertheless it can be interpreted as a criticism of landed aristocracy. Ricardo's "scarcity rent" is "unearned" income, which does not contribute to wealth creation, it indeed redistributes incomes from wages and profits into rental revenue.

By 1867 Karl Marx was confronted with a different social world, one of industrial capitalism so he attempted to frame a theory of general laws of capitalism. Industrial capitalist and capitalist landowners had to share the profit they expropriated from labor. In Volume I of *Capital* the focus is on wage vs. profit, which should be demonstrated as a negative-sum game (in the long run) in order to offer a scientific explanation why capitalism will have to collapse. This led him to the elegant theory of "exploitation". We try to show that Marx did not achieve this aim. Instead he produced an equilibrium theory of the capitalist economy, which was better suited to explain the iron law of reproduction of capitalism rather than its inevitable collapse.

Marx's point of departure is this: "*The conversion of money into capital has to be explained on the basis of laws that regulate the exchange of commodities, in such a way that the starting point is the **exchange of equivalents***"[7]. But at the end of the production process the capitalist must have more capital than he had when the production cycle began. Marx describes succinctly the logic of capitalist production cycle with a simple formula: 'MCM'. The capitalist production process begins with the capitalist starting it with capital (money), will purchase commodities and eventually selling the product of these commodities for more money, hence accumulating capital. There are two important questions for Marx: (i) If we have to assume that always equivalents have to be exchanged (no one cheats nobody[8]), how can this miracle of gaining more money at the end of the cycle occur? (ii) What can and has to do the capitalist with capital thus accumulated?

For the first question Marx offers an elegant though somewhat Talmudist explanation. The price of labor power is the same as the price of any other commodity: hence the

5 Smith, 1976, p.56, our emphasis.
6 Ricardo [1817] 2004, p. 40, our emphasis.
7 See Part II of Volume I, Marx 1954, p. 161, our emphasis.
8 See *op. cit.* Volume I. p. 161.

costs of its reproduction. The trick is that labor power is the only commodity which produces more value than its own value when consumed. The worker can produce enough value in x hours to cover his costs of reproduction (which even includes the costs of production of the next generation of workers, the costs of raising his/her children), but since his/her labor power is now under the control of the capitalist, the capitalist will require the worker to work $x+y$ hours. Could the capitalist pay less to the worker than the value generated during x hours? No, since in this case the worker will not be able to keep producing himelf and the working class (will starve). Could he pay the worker more than share some of the value created working hours y? (To be a "generous" capitalist?) No, since in this case the worker starts accumulating capital, will eventually become a capitalist and stop selling his/her labor power.

But this leads Marx to the second question. What will the capitalist now do with 'M'? Capitalists compete with each other. If a capitalist would be foolish enough not to invest into expanded production, he will be wiped out by competition. This is indeed the "satanic mills": the worker, derived from the means of subsistence has to sell his/her labor power, cannot collect less or more than the costs of reproduction of his/her labor power and the capitalists have no choice but to use the profit (called surplus by Marx) expropriated from their workers to reinvest, expand production and/or improve productivity. Marx was searching for a scientific theory to explain why capitalism has to fall, but if we eliminate the heated language he used ("money bags"), the exploitation theory of Volume I only explains why capitalism will never fall. John Roemer, arguably the most distinguished "rational choice neo-Marxist" was right on the dot when he stated: "*The neoclassical model of the competitive economy is not a bad place for Marxists to start their study of idealized*[9] *capitalism*".[10] In the third volume of "*The Capital*", Marx made an effort to find the scientific proof for the fall of capitalism. He formulated another fascinating, but logically incomplete and empirically dubious hypothesis of "tendency of rate of profit to decline". Marx was aware that there are "counteracting tendencies" (though surprisingly he did not elaborate on the most important "counteracting tendency": namely that productivity increase from technological innovations can be far greater than the costs of investment into constant capital), so he left the manuscript unpublished and arguably it was Engels who turned the declining rate of profits into a "law" which explains the inevitability of the demise of the capitalist mode of production.

In our reading, since Marx could not persuade himself that he really found the scientific theory he was looking for, he turned his attention to ground rent. While for Ricardo rent for landed property was distinctly different from capitalist profits, Marx's lengthy and somewhat difficult to digest elaboration on rent wants to understand rent as a feature of market capitalism.[11] Nevertheless much to his horror in Chapter 52 he suddenly realized that he is back at Adam Smith: *"The owners merely of labor power, owners of capital, and landowners… constitute then three big classes of modern society based*

9 The term idealized is important. As we know the major shortcoming of neoclassical economics is that there are no perfect markets in any „actually existing" capitalist economies.

10 Roemer, 1982, p. 196.

11 See, especially Marx [1894] 1959, pp. 773–774 and pp. 782–783.

upon the capitalist mode of production".[12] The powerful two class model of bourgeoisie vs. proletariat is now replaced with a three class model where wages, profits and rent are just three different sources of income, hence the inherent equilibrium tendency of the exploitation theory is not resolved. Marx finished the page and broke the manuscript off and left Volumes II and III "*to the gnawing criticism of the mice*"[13].

We believe Marx moved in the wrong direction and lost the important insights Ricardo offered about the differences between profits and rents.

2. Closed and open social relations: Weber offers a new way to think about inequalities generated by wages/profits vs. rent

Max Weber made a captivating distinction between "open" and "closed" relationships. As most Weberian concepts this is in part historical, in part analytical. History tends to move from more closed to more open relations, but even in contemporary societies, closed and open relations coexist and necessarily complement each other. "*Social relationship... will be spoken as 'open' to outsiders if and insofar as its system of order does not deny participation to anyone who wishes to join and is actually in a position to do so*[14]. *A relationship will ... be called 'closed' against outsiders so far as... participation of certain persons is excluded, limited or subjected to conditions*".[15]

In precapitalist, agrarian economies the dominant form of socio-economic organization is based on closed relations, economically speaking it based on "household" economy (*oikos*), (which operates as a budgetary unit). The feudal landlord's or the slave owner's revenue is rent, the prime examples revenue stemming from closed social relationships. Feudal landlords and slave owners "are typically rentiers", who extract products of labor or labor services from serves and slaves and in exchange guarantee their subsistence (slaves and serfs typically do not earn wages, just have the right to grow their own food, or are being fed/closed/housed by the lord or master). The "surplus value" extracted this way is typically not reinvested for profit maximization purposes, but instead it supports the usually luxurious life styles of the court, or household of the landlords or slave owning masters.

Weber's distinction between private wealth, operating as landed estates, as *oikos*, budgetary units and capital, the profit making enterprise, is of far reaching importance. As long as the economy is dominated by landed estates, budgetary accounting – as was the

---

12 *ibid.* p. 885.

13 Marx wrote this about the German Ideology in *A Contribution to the Critique of Political Economy* (1857), but it is reasonable to assume that he found Volume II and III equally incomplete, not ready to be printed. It is especially telling the Volume III, Chapter 52, which was supposed to be the grand conclusion is broken off on the second page.

14 This is a very interesting qualification. Weber tries to avoid the Marxian trap, namely that workers since they do not have capital by definition cannot enter competition. He narrows competition to those own capital and who are wage earners.

15 Weber (1978) p. 43, our emphasis.

case in the ancient world and under Western feudalism (and to some extent under state socialism) the development of the capitalism and dynamic economic growth was greatly limited…. "*The person who is a mere rentier…is…not engaged in profit making*" (Weber 1978, p. 99) and without economy dominated by profit making enterprises the economy will be stagnant. Even the medieval urban economies in the ocean of rural countryside followed a similar logic; the trade and artisanship were organized by guilds, a strictly closed organization. Entering a guild was an arduous and highly selective process, which may last for many years (ridiculously long apprenticeship) and may depend on family connections. Guild members' revenue though can be conceptualized as composed of wages/profit + rent. Most guild members (remember Hans Sachs in Meistersinger) physically produced goods (and earned a "wage" for it), run a business (exploited or even abused their apprentices, collected profits from their work), but since they monopolized the trade, they undoubtedly sold their products over free market determined price, hence they collected rent.

So is it only land or real estate from which such rent can stem? As the example of the guilds show, obviously not. According to Weber closed groups manage to monopolize advantages to their party, by occupying scarce and desirable positions, or by making desirable goods and services scarce through clientelist practices, by creation of cartels, oligopolies or monopolies.[16] Today, such rent is one of the explanations of the very high compensation packages offered to the best specialists.[17] Firms, as well as universities, hospitals, sport clubs, etc. compete with their peers for stars. They don't want to lose a legendary C.E.O., a professor or an athlete to their rivals. It would hurt their prestige and profits. So they pay more and more, especially in those countries where excessively progressive income taxes do not paralyze such incentives.

While the received wisdom from Kuznets (1955) to Piketty (2014) is that inequalities were modest in early stages of development, they increased with industrialization and then began to decline later (this is the inverted U curve of Kuznets) nevertheless, many economists and sociologists, including Piketty detected the reemergence of inequality after 1970s. We do not have reliable data for precapitalist times, but it is safe to assume, that the nature of inequality before capitalism was of different kind (mainly driven by rent rather than by profit) and its extent was substantially higher (and more rigid) than under capitalism. Class inequality under the worst case of capitalism must have been trivial in comparison with inequalities between slave owners and slaves, landlords and serfs.

Let us make a brief remark on socialism. In communist ideology socialism was usually defined as a transition stage between advanced capitalism to communism. This proved to be historically/empirically incorrect. Socialism was rather a transition from feudalism to capitalism. Workers under socialism were neither slaves nor serves, but they were not wage laborers either, selling their labor power on competitive labor markets. They operated in rather "closed" social relations, they were not free to decide whether

16 See Weber [1922] (1978), pp. 43–44. Clearly, all this is very close to the concept of Acemoglu/Robinson (2012).

17 Solow (2014) calls this rent of super managers a „sort of adjunct to capital".

they work or not, they could not negotiate their wages. Under these circumstances there was little if any relationship between their productivity and remuneration. Neither employers, nor employees were actors on the labor market. In classical socialism labor was allocated on a nonmarket trade of labor, to put it with Karl Polanyi. Under socialism social relations were not class relations but rather relations among status groups. Actors were slotted into the hierarchy of status groups according three credentials (education, party membership and position in the nomenclature) and incomes were centrally controlled and defined accordingly.[18]

"Public ownership" while in part was fictional had a rational element. Since the socialist economy was an economy of shortage, not only full employment was guaranteed, but all positions from unskilled workers to top management were practically "tenured". Once you entered a status group (*Stand*) you could not be fired, you had a chance to be promoted to a higher status group, if you received new credentials or were admitted to an ingroup, like you joined the communist party. The employed had *de facto* property right in the assets of the firm/organization they were employed and as proprietors they collected a "rent" even if they did not contribute anything to the productivity of the firm/organization. What one received over that minimum in his/her status group could be seen as wage or profit (with the qualification that given the semifeudal/socialist character of the system this higher income did not necessarily reflect greater contribution to productivity, but might have been a reward for loyalty – hence a special form of rent). We know little about the true extent of inequality under socialism. In most scholarly writing it is probably underestimated, since fringe benefits were not taken into consideration, but all in all socialist economies were relatively egalitarian (more than feudal or most capitalist economies). In terms of the logic of inequality they were closer to precapitalist formations than to market capitalism.

3. Interpretation and generalization of Ricardo's theory of rent by Sorensen

Aage Sorensen (2000) in his path-breaking article reinterpreted and generalized Ricardo's theory of rent. The Sorensen article was cast as a debate with Erik Olin Wright's class theory. Wright in the classical traditions of Marxist theory conceptualizes exploitation – as the basis of fundamental class division – between profits and wages. In this interpretation of Marx profits vs. wages is a zero-sum game, what capitalists gain the workers lose, hence their relationship is antagonistic and will eventually lead to revolutionary overthrow of capitalist order. In contrast, Sorensen sees rents vs (profits+ wages) as a zero-sum game where he defines rent as income stemming from closed relationships (in the Weberian sense of the term), hence as income which is higher than the income would be in perfectly competitive markets (as neoclassical economists would put it). Sorensen calls such rental income exploitation (Stiglitz also uses the term "exploitation rent") and sees it as measure of class divisions.

18 Kornai, 1992, pp. 216–227

In this paper our point of departure is Sorensen's theory of rent, but we do not want to take a position whether rental income is exploitation and therefore the distinction between rent earners and others as class relations, whether relationships between rent seekers and profit maximizers or wage earners are antagonistic or not. Our aim in this section of this paper is much more modest. We follow Sorensen and use a broader notion of rent than it was used in the Ricardian theory. Thus, rents are all incomes stemming from ownership of any assets where access to such assets is closed (be it oligopolies, monopolies, cartels or state regulations) from some actors.

Inequality stemming from profits vs. wages is a moral/political problem. We do not underestimate the importance of these inequalities – in each liberal democracy given the value system of the society the citizens decide how much inequality is acceptable and how much income or wealth from the rich shall be redistributed through taxation to the poor. But inequalities from rents originating from closed relations pose unique challenges: (i) a legitimation problem of liberal capitalism, which claims to be meritocratic and (ii) more importantly, they may undermine the most effective allocation of resources.[19] Mancur Olson (1982) already described historical instances when rent seeking behavior, which captured state regulations or licensing led to the state collapses. To repeat it provocatively: in open social relations (perfectly competitive markets) as long as the sum of profits+ wages is growing, this is a positive-sum game for the society. If rents are growing faster than the sum of profits + wages, this is a negative-sum game (Stiglitz, 2012).[20]

So far we described the Weberian distinction between closed and open relations in historical terms, but as we already pointed out it is also an analytic one. Weber does acknowledge – much like Adam Smith does – that in modern capitalist economies incomes come from three different sources: wages, profits and rents.[21]. His evaluation of the three sources is the most interesting one: "*Of all types of incomes, it is particularly those from business profits and the contracted piece rate or free labor incomes which have a dynamic, revolutionary significance for economic life. Next to these stand incomes derived from free exchange and, in quite different ways, under certain circumstances the 'predatory' incomes.*

Those having a static, conservative influence on economic activity are above all incomes drawn in accordance with a predetermined scale, namely salaries, wages reckoned per unit of working time, gains from the exploitation of office powers, and normally all kinds of fixed interest and rents"[22]

19 Or saying the same in a more modest way: in an economy thoroughly permeated with rents, there is no mechanism which guarantees the most efficient use of assets.

20 „In the aftermath of the financial crisis, no one today would argue that the bankers' pursuit of their selfinterest has led to the well-being of all. At most, it led to the bankers' well-being… It was a negative-sum game, where the gains for winners are less than the losses to the losers. What the rest of society lost was far greater than the banker's payoff…. When the market works well – in the way Adam Smith hypothesized it is because private returns and social benefits are aligned…" p. 41.

21 Weber, 1978, p. 205.

22 Weber, 1978, p. 205, our emphasis.

It is fascinating that these comments by Weber remind Guenther Roth one of the best Weber scholars of Pareto.[23] Pareto in his *The Mind and Society* (1935) made an interesting distinction between "speculators" (foxes) and "rentiers" (lions), hence between those who seek profits and those who seek rent. A balanced market capitalist economy needs both foxes and lions, dynamism and innovation has to be counterbalanced by stability. Hence the proper question is not how much wages/profits vs. rent but how much of what kinds of wages/profits vs. how much and what kind of rents. If some sorts of foxes are too many it may damage the health of economy, but the same goes for certain types and certain numbers of lions. Weber indeed seems to be deeply influenced by this idea of balance between foxes and lions, dynamism and stability, profits and rents.

Rent seeking creates a different kind of inequality than profit maximization and calls for different policy responses. In our reading, Piketty's most innovative contribution in his *"Capital in the 21st century"* is exactly that he is warning about the transformation of modern capitalism into a patrimonial system (which in our reading implies than growing proportion of high incomes and wealth from inheritance and is coming from rent based on monopoly or cartel rather than profits or wages) and that is consistent with the friendly amendments Stiglitz (2015, I, II, III)) and Atkinson (2015) made to the Piketty book. Capitalism in the late 20th and early 21st centuries becomes unequal in a different way: more and more wealth (and privileged social position) is inherited.

* * * * *

A trivially important area of inherited rent revenue comes from *real estate* and generally private wealth. The top 10–20% of society in the United States inherit substantial wealth, mainly in real estate, but also in pension funds and in other accumulated assets. The *educational system* is an important terrain of closures, as defined by Weber. Given the high costs of education, especially of elite education, access to the most highly valued education may not be open to all, but it is closed to youth whose parents cannot afford the often prohibitive costs. The reproduction of almost feudal privileges by the educational is becoming surprisingly strong in postcommunist societies, too. Access to tertiary education of underprivileged strata is much reduced and at least in some countries, like Hungary there is a trend to go back to early "tracking system", hence in the name of "labor market needs" put young people from poorer families on vocational tracks, to make the decision whether one wants to pursue a vocational of academic career as early as age of 14. At the same time, the access to study abroad is the privilege of a very small percent of students born in newly enriched families only.

In the advanced Western democracies, there is an additional mechanism of closure in the educational system and that is *credentialing*. Education is often conceptualized in terms of human capital investment. It is usually assumed that human capital invested into education will lead to productivity gains and higher incomes for the better educated results from such productivity gain. But especially powerful professional associations (such

23 See footnote 67, Weber, 1978, p. 211.

as American Medical Association, or American Law Boards) requiring bar examinations play a role to control the supply of occupations under their jurisdiction, hence they may drive up incomes for those occupations by adding a rent to their income from work.

The emphasis on credentialing (rather just on education or training) may have consequences on what kind of knowledge will be required from candidates seeking valued credentials. Not all knowledge required to pass critical exams will have productivity gains, it may be just knowledge which is useful to screen candidates for such credentials. This is what Bourdieu ([1970] 1977) called "cultural capital" as distinct from "human capital". *Cultural capital* serves more the purposes of the reproduction of the "patrimonial middle class", or "patrimonial upper class" rather than increasing the productivity of the graduate. For parents it may cost as much as $300,000 to $400,000 just to get their children an Ivy League BA or BSc – but the descendants' Ivy League degree will pass on to them the status of "nobility". Employers will seek Ivy League graduate not necessarily since their technical skills are better, but because hiring such people will add to the prestige of their organization.

One of the controversial tendencies in Piketty's work is – as Acemoglu/Robinson (2012) and Atkinson (2015) point it out – that it tends to overemphasize the privileges of the top 0.1 – 1.0 percent and their negative impact and neglecting the inheritance of privileges (such as educational privileges as elaborated above) and wealth on the top 10–20% of the society. In our opinion the privileged position of the top 20% is just as problematic as the top 1% or 0.1 percent.

First, inherited wealth which is common not only in the top 1%, but in the top 20% (and typically not available to underprivileged ethnic minorities (like African American in the US[24]) is seen often as illegitimate by the rest of the society. Moreover, as we already explained above, there is no mechanism (unlike in the case of earning of profits) to allocate the inherited wealth in profitable way. Thomas Mann's "*The Buddenbrooks*" ([1903] 1987) wonderfully illustrates how inherited wealth over the third generation disappears from the process of production, some used for charity, some from conspicuous consumption. Indeed relatively few from the second or third generation of the top 1 percent remain wealthy themselves. [25]

Second, the top 0.1 percent can influence the political process through voluntary donations disproportionately more than others, so it is important to look with scrutiny what happens to their lifelong accumulated wealth at the end: what sort of social objectives do they serve. Even in competitive liberal democracies some individuals in the top 1% virtually capture the state either by using their own wealth to secure office for themselves, or by creating PAC's (see note 26) and supporting candidates who are likely to serve their interest.[26] Campaign finance reform is a burning issue even in the most

24 See Melvin Oliver (1995) and Dalton Conley (1999). Oliver and Conley demonstrated that the major difference between whites and blacks is not in earned income, but in inherited wealth.

25 See e.g. Stanley/Danko (1998).

26 In the United States, a Political Action Committee (PAC) is a type of organization that pools campaign contributions from members and donates those funds to campaign for or against candidates, ballot initiatives, or legislation.

liberal democracies. Nevertheless in advanced market economies many in the top 1% or 0.1% use charitable donation not to capture the state, but supplement the weak or hardly existing "double movement" (think of charitable contributions of Bill Gates or George Soros).

Part II.

The role of rents in postcommunist societies

Introductory remarks. As we argued in the preceding sections, there are some indications that Western type of capitalism may become patrimonial capitalism. In the postcommunist context we do not have the data yet to test Piketty's assertion. Nevertheless, we can accept his general hypothesis, although it is still unclear, whether the children of the highly visible present day oligarchs in Russia and China will have the possibility to pass the entire set of property rights to their children – including the right to sell these assets to foreigners or move the family's financial wealth to foreign countries.[27]

Rent seeking behavior was historically present in all capitalist market economies, even in the most advanced ones. The early high levels of inequalities were driven by two forces: (i) In European countries (especially in England) the privileged estate was able to covert its feudal privileges into privileged positions on the market; (ii) since appropriate mechanisms of market regulations were not in place, it was possible to create monopoly situations, or to create cartel-like agreements. Good examples are the "robber barons" in late 19th century USA (Josephson, 1934, Folsom, [1987] 2010). Some of these robber barons came close to "state capture" until state's elite fought back with antitrust legislations[28].

Interestingly, the transition from socialism to capitalism was often driven or at least colored by similar – and often more extreme rent seeking behavior. Much like during the transition from feudalism to capitalism there was an intense struggle of old elites to retain their power and convert their former privileged position into economic wealth/power. Those who were suddenly converted to the idea of free markets from central planning did not always realize that some regulation (even planning) might be needed to have genuinely free and competitive markets. Similarly private property rights were often (and remain) ambiguous (Stark, 1996). The conditions of law and order, the separation of powers, especially separation of politics from the economy was (and still is) negotiated. It could not be implemented instantly after the disintegration of socialism,

27 We may add to the list the post Soviet Central Asian republics, Belorussia, Ukraine, Hungary – especially, but not exclusively after 2010, Romania, Bulgaria, Serbia, Albania, Macedonia and probably a few more countries.

28 Theodore Roosevelt's antimonopoly legislation during the early 1900 is a prime example of regulating rent seeking.

and even a quarter of century after the transition it is still fought over intensively in many countries. Postcommunist capitalism is a curious system, where in many cases (like Russia at least after 2000, in Hungary after 2010, to some extent in Poland after 2015) "*politics remains in command*". Ironically Mao defined – quite well the essence of socialism with this formulation.

Such institutional inertia of the transition was aggravated by a sense of urgency to convert state property into private wealth as fast as possible (not in China though). Yeltsin after 1991 committed himself to build capitalism in Russia in "500 days". During the early 1990s political elites and their economist advisers tended to believe that once identifiable owners are found for formerly stateowned firms, the free market will resolve everything else. It does not really matter who becomes the first private owner. If the first owner is incompetent (or corrupt), he will be replaced by market competition with competent market actors.

Given the specific circumstances we shall distinguish *three different rent seeking mechanisms.*

1. Market capture by political elites

Market capture by political elites has multiple variants.

a. *Political capitalism: the use of market mechanisms by communist cadres to turn state property into private wealth*

In the early stages of privatization it was often assumed, that the former communist elite converts their political capital into economic wealth.[29] Indeed, it was seen by many commentators that postcommunist capitalism was simply a "kleptocracy" in which the political bosses stole the state assets. Undoubtedly, this occurred in large numbers in Russia[30], the Ukraine, in the Central Asian republics and to certain extent in Bulgaria and Romania, where the elite circulation the first few years was minimal. As Hankiss (1990) and Staniszkis (1991) pointed out communist elites woke up early in Hungary and Poland and tried to convert SOEs into private firms by using the technology called "spontaneous privatization", but in 1989/1990 they lost political power.[31] As far as we can tell neither in Hungary or Poland succeeded the communist political leadership to accumulate substantial wealth before 1989. Nevertheless there is a kernel of truth to the

29 This was the nomenclature bourgeoisie hypothesis of Erzsébet Szalai, 1989, Elemér Hankiss, 1990, and Jadwiga Staniszkis,1991.

30 One good example is Victor Chernomyrdin. In the mid1990s, the CIA estimated his networth at $5 billion, but he claimed to have ownership in a few millions. In 1978 he was already working at the Central Committee of the Communist Party and then back and forth between high government posts (deputy minister, later minister of gas industry) and major managerial positions (chairman of Gazprom). He was prime minister of Russia between 1991–1998. He passed away in 2010 and took his secret into his grave. see Szelényi 2010.

31 For an excellent comparison of Central European postcommunist capitalisms, see Bohle/Greskovits (2012). However, it is important to underscore that none of the Central Europeans who were listed on the Forbes billionaires list is known to have been high communist party official before 1989, see Szelényi 2010.

Hankiss/Staniszkis hypothesis. Some of the postcommunist "new rich" in both countries began to accumulate capital before or just during the transition and it turned out to be a starting point for their future wealth.[32]

b. *Market capture by political elites during privatization of state property for personal enrichment or recruitment of clients*

When mass privatization became the official aim of governments, SOEs (=State Owned Enterprises) were passed into private hands either by vouchers[33] or they were offered for sale on competitive actions.[34] Workers, ordinary citizens or inheritors did not know what to do with vouchers, so they sold them to risk-tolerant young investors under daily changing market conditions. But market did not come from a thin air, as we know from Polanyi. Also in these cases, markets were created by states and/or by political elites. Such a "management" or even "creation" of markets was inevitable for domestic, and even for foreign investors.

Let us begin with domestic investors. During communist times private ownership was outlawed, hence accumulation of private capital was very limited. To enable at least some domestic investors to purchase state property it had to be underpriced. Domestic investors – who did not have any reliable track record or credit rating – needed government guaranteed loans. This required a preselection to be allowed to make bids on auctions. Preselection inevitable relied on possession of personal or political capital. In countries, where communist elites survived (like in China) or where the new elites monopolized political positions (like in Russia, Bulgaria or Romania), the former (or in China still active) communist cadres had advantages.

China is a special case, since market transition in China took place all along until the present day, under the rule of the Communist Party. According the evidence we could find (The Forbes list and Hurun list of Chinese billionaires, See Szelényi, 2010) during the first two decades of the reform wealth accumulation was mainly or exclusively driven "from below". By year 2000 virtually all Chinese billionaires came from humble background, started as rice farmers or bricklayers. Privatization of large SOEs started around 1997 and there is some evidence that during the past decade or so some high communist

32 In Poland for instance Jan Weichert and Mariusz Walter – major owners of postcommunist media – were suspected to have started their business while working for the Polish security services, though they vehemently denied this accusation. In Hungary, Sándor Demján, one of the wealthiest Hungarian today, started his career as a manager of successful cooperative (i.e. semiprivate) ventures in the 1980s. László Kapolyi was a high official during communist times and was listed among the wealthiest Hungarians after 2000 (see Kolosi and Szelényi, 2010). By the time of his death in 2014, however, he lost virtually everything.

33 Vouchers were handed out either for compensation of property lost under communism – like in Hungary, the Baltic states, etc. , or as a share of workers, or citizens in public wealth a method used in Czechoslovakia, Russia and many other countries.

34 Until 1995, Hungary pursued privatization through open tenders and IPOs (= Initial Public Offering = Börsengang), in which foreign investors competed with each other. See Eyal, Szelényi and Townsley (1998), Mihalyi (2001), King and Szelényi (2005).

party cadres and their family did became super rich.[35] The manipulation of markets served either the personal economic interest of the new (or old, surviving) political elites, or the elite may use it as a mechanism to recruit and retain clients. All political elite needs clients, but this is especially important if a regime – like most postcommunists ones, even the Russian – wants to retain at least the semblance of democracy and faces at least apparently competitive elections.

The recent Russian history had partly similar examples, when the wealthiest businessmen started from relatively unimportant (though not humble) positions.[36] These figures were "initiated" into the new grand bourgeoisie, since they were expected to be talented and loyal in exchange for „managed auctions" as described above. Valery Streletsky told in an interview to Klebnikov: "*The key factor in the privatization process was the attitude of Tatyana Dyachenko [Yeltsin's beloved daughter] to this or that banker/oligarch.... She would go to the President and say: this man is a good man and that man is a bad man; this should be supported and that should not be supported... Tatyana Dyachenko is the only person the President listens.*"[37] Boris Berezovsky and Roman Abramovich are prime examples of people who acquired substantial wealth mainly due to their contemporary personal rather than previous political connections.[38]

35 There are contradictory assessments of personal wealth of former Prime Minister Wen Jiabao and current President Xi Jinping. The New York Times reported on both of them that their family wealth may be in the range of $12 billion dollars. If there is wealth in the Xi family, most of it was made by the President's daughter, Qi Qiaoqiao and her husband Deng Jiagui. It is also rumored that many large nominally state owned firms, whose CEO's are "princelings", hence children of former "revolutionary heroes" (President Xi is one of them) are – in reality, entirely privately owned. (Personal communication by Lu Peng.)

36 Vladimir Potanin – a high official who invented to debt swap scheme – was among the few high government officials who were not hiding and are listed among the dollar billionaires and became wealthy after 1991. Mikhall Khodorkovsky is another case. Klebnikov (2000) offers a crisp description of his trajectory: He had a classic career path of a Yeltsin–era business magnate. In 1987, as a top leader of Moscow's Communist Youth League, Khodorkovsky established a trading cooperative financed with Communist Party money; the next year he established a bank. In 1990–93, Khodorkovsky entered the Russian government, serving first as economic adviser to the Russian Prime Minister and then as deputy minister of fuel and energy. In 1999 Khodorkovsky was listed as the 5th wealthiest person in Russia, with an estimated wealth of $500 million.

37 *Ibid* pp. 202–203. Our emphasis.

38 Boris Berezovsky (1946–2013) was one of the first and the most prominent founding member of the club of newly emergent oligarchs. Berezovsky earned in 1983 a Ph.D. in mathematics and at the Soviet Academy of Sciences he became director of one of the laboratories of the Institute of Management. As far as we can tell, there is no indication that Berezovsky was close to high ranking Soviet party officials. He had good relationship with the young reformers, Yegor Gaidar, Anatoly Chubais and Valentin Yumashev. Yumashev was a journalist – eventually became Yeltsin's chief of staff and the second husband of Tanya (or Tatyana) Yeltsin – but during the early 1990s he was just a ghostwriter for the President. He helped Yeltsin to write his 1989 book and was helping him with the "Notes of a President" – eventually published in 1994. It was Yumashev who introduced Berezovsky to Tatyana, who at that time was the wife of Dyachenko (a commodity trader, who became at one point Berezovsky's business partner in Sibneft), but already a good friend of Yumashev. With his newly acquired contacts Berezovsky managed to take major managerial positions and eventually ownership in the car manufacturing firm Avtovaz, in the Russian national

But these "grants" given to the new grand bourgeoisie which was "appointed" by the political boss, anticipated some return to the boss. Indeed, in exchange of Yeltsin's contribution to his growth as a businessmen in 1996, when a Communist Party candidate represented a real threat to Yeltsin's reelection, Berezovsky not only supported the Yeltsin campaign, but managed to persuade six other "oligarchs", the wealthiest of the wealthy at that time, the so called Big Seven[39] to push for the President's re-election. Next to Berezovsky other members of the Big Seven were: Mikhall Fridman, Vladimir Vinogradov, Mikhall Khodorkovsky, Vladimir Gussinsky, Vladimir Potanin and Aleksander Smolensky. The Big Seven claimed already in 1996, just five years after the collapse of the USSR, that they owned half of Russia.

c. *Manipulating markets after privatization either to serve the enrichment of new political elites or to recruit new loyal propertied bourgeoisie*

The suspicion that political office holders may use their office for personal enrichment is still seriously considered in this period. Bálint Magyar (2016), a trained sociologist and former minister in the Hungarian Socialist Liberal government during the 1990s and early 2000s, characterized the rightwing FIDESZ government after 2010 as "*Mafia state*". In his model, Mr. Orbán, the Prime Minister acts as "godfather".[40] It is claimed that government contracts and EU subsidized programs are allocated to family members or members of an "adopted family", hence to loyal clients.

There are many ways markets can be influenced after privatization was completed. Arguably the most important or one of the most important mechanisms is the manipulation of public procurements which by law require competition open to all. Some sectors are particularly suitable for such manipulations (e.g. road constructions, IT services, commercial advertisements of SOEs). By governmental decree such purchases can be declared to be "emergent", hence they shortcut complicated competition and give contracts to clients (occasionally they may be even proxies to government officials). Without competitive bidders, or with reduced numbers of bidders the price for the services the government contracts can be way above what would have been in free competition,

airline, Aeroflot, the major oil company Sibneft. His economic empire also included the aluminium industry and some important media outlets. In 1995 he also acquired TV Channel 1, the most commonly watched TV station which had a tremendous impact on public opinion in the country. Another of these young "talents" discovered by Tatyana was Roman Abramovich. He started out in the shadow economy. It is rumored that he started out his business activities during the late 1980s by selling plastic ducks out of his Moscow apartment and working as a street trader. In 1993, he met Berezovsky, who liked him and introduced him to the "family". In 1995, in the loans for shares program the two men acquired Sibneft. Abramovich paid something like $80 million for the whole company, which must have been worth several billion already at that time. Eventually he even moved to live inside the Kremlin and became a close friend of Yeltsin's daughter Tatyana Yeltsin, who often spent time at Abramovich's dacha. So this is indeed something like the "adopted family", a term coined by Magyar (2016) explaining his theory of the "mafia state".

39 The Big Seven – Russia's Financial Empires, www.worldbank,org/html/prddr/trans/feb98/bigseven.htm

40 It is noteworthy that Klebnikov used this term already for Yeltsin, in year 2000.

therefore those who win such bids collect substantial rent over the profit they would have made on real markets .[41] Government can also limit rewarding licenses, for instance which radio station of TV channel can use frequencies most often listened to or watched.

As the Yeltsin example illustrated, the funding of electoral campaigns needs wealthy supporters who finance the campaign directly and indirectly through the media. Such deals could have been the source of personal income for political bosses like President Putin or Prime Minister Orbán in Hungary.[42] A rather trivial case to collect large number of supporters was the allocation of tobaccoshop licenses in Hungary. Prior to that virtually all stores (including food stores and gas stations) could sell tobacco and a substantial part of their income comes from this trade. In 2013, the government created special tobacco stores, which acquired the exclusive right to sell tobacco, transferring "rent" from other stores to the newly licensed tobacco stores. This was not a major source of income, nevertheless it created a 20year monopoly for some small, medium size businessmen, who according at least to opposition politicians were loyal supporters of the government.

Of course such manipulations of markets are well known in all countries (a famous example for public purchases of military equipment is the United States), but as we showed above these practices are especially widespread in the postcommunist economies. This is not only our opinion; this is one of the reasons why these countries are labelled "corrupt" by Transparency International. Ironically EU money to help the new (postcommunist) member states did more harm in this respect than the progress emanating from newly built transparency mechanism arising from EU membership.

2. State capture by oligarchs

State capture by business elites is most often seen as cases of rent seeking (and corruption) in non postcommunist emergent markets, for instance in late 19th century US or 20th and 21st century Africa. Such rent seeking behavior exists under postcommunism, but it is relatively rare, given the weakness of propertied bourgeoisie and its dependence of the political elite. Those who managed to capture the state in late 19th century US were called "robber barons", their prime example being Rockefeller, Vanderbuilt or Jay Gould. In the postcommunist world they are called oligarchs.

41 For an empirical study of the situation in Romania, see Pirvu (2015).

42 Vladimir Putin's personal wealth is subject of wild speculations. Some commentators claim he is the wealthiest man in the world with a personal property $40–$70 billion. Putin's official disclosure acknowledges his property to be worth of $119,000 (he owns two apartments and one garage place). There are also similarly wild and unconfirmed speculations about private wealth of Hungarian Prime Minister, Viktor Orbán. The personal wealth of current political office holders may be overestimated by political opponents. In any case smart political bosses do not accumulate wealth in their own name, but pass it on to their extended family of friends. Hence if Putin indeed managed to accumulate some wealth of his own, it may be under the name of his daughter Yekaterina and her husband (it is reported the couple owns $2.83 billion just in Silberg Company). Putin's friend, the cellist Sergei Roldugin is also believed to act as his surrogate, when he was reported to move billions of dollars in Panama.

The notion of oligarch is disputed. In this paper we call oligarchs those super wealthy individuals who managed to "privatize the state" itself (to use again Klebnikov's term). Hence these are individuals who did not become wealthy because they occupied political positions or were believed to be loyal followers of political bosses, but who managed to use their wealth to capture the state itself. They were not unlike the "boyars" of early tsarist Russia, a class of wealthy individuals who used politics and the state to gain wealth rather than the other way around. It is only Russia by the end of the Yeltsin years, when we can see cases of such state capture by the new wealthy.

As the Russian state began to collapse, the largest business conglomerates began to build up their own armed security force occasionally with as many as 1,000 mercenaries.[43] Indeed, big businessmen needed security forces, since the city of Moscow was ruled by mafia, usually run either by Russians or Chechens, and without getting protection from one or the other life was virtually impossible for such business figures. Unsurprisingly, two such figures Gusinsky, protected by Russians and Berezovsky, protected by Chechens suspected each other to be behind assassination attempt against them and plot to get them arrests by law enforcement agencies until the two giant oligarchs around 1996 sat down and agreed to cooperate with each other rather than to try to destroy one another.

Berezovsky comes the closest to be called an "oligarch". After the 1996 reelection of Yeltsin as President, he became involved in state affairs, for a while he served as Deputy Secretary of the National Security Council in charge of Chechnya. Since some of his body guards were Chechens he had working relations with the Islamist leaders of Chechen upraising. Even after he left this position he continued negotiations to free hostages taken by Chechen rebels. So he used his business success to gain substantial political power, even political office and many commentators – like Klebnikov – assumed he might have used this office to further his personal enrichment.

3. Capture of oligarchs by autocratic rulers

In 2000, Berezovsky and some other (still surviving members) of the Big Seven (namely Khodorkovsky and Fridman) supported Putin's election, sort of were bringing Putin "into the family" – to use the Mafia language. But Putin was no Yeltsin; he wanted to be Peter the Great and did not want to be bossed around by the "boyars" – i.e. the oligarchs. Though Berezovsky was elected to Duma (the Russian legislature) in 1999, he soon clashed with Putin and fled to England. Later he was sentenced to prison term *in absentia* and was accused of various murders.[44] Berezovsky became Public Enemy Number One for Putin's Russia – it is rumored that there were several attempts by Russian agents to murder him in London.[45] He passed away in 2013 in unclear circum-

43 Klebnikov 2000, p. 151, also *Washington Post*, April 7, 1995

44 While no murder charges were proven against him in any fair court of justice, but he was suspected to be involved in the murder of Vlad Listyev, Russia's most successful TV producer four years earlier. Listyev supported the privatization of TV 1 to Berezovsky, but he advocated a fair competition for advertising time, that clashed with Berezovsky's interest.

45 *The Times*, July 18, 2007.

stances. He might have been killed by Russian intelligence services, or he might have lost so much his previous wealth (most to Abramovich) that he did not want to readjust his life to be "poor", so he rather committed suicide.

Much like Berezovsky, Khodorkovsky was also far too ambitious politically for Putin. Probably he sensed trouble with the new political boss, so in early 2003 he proposed to merge Yukos with the other major Russian oil company, Sibneft. As Berezovsky had to escape Russia, he passed ownership of Sibneft to Roman Abramovich (a solid #2 on the list of wealthiest Russians even in 2009), who regarded Berezovsky as his "mentor". In 2003, Khodorkovsky was put on trial for corruption and sent behind bars. He was only released in 2013, when he moved to Switzerland with a small part of his former wealth (in 1999 he was believed to own $500 million, today, his assets are estimated to be around $100 million). While Khodorkovsky was "eliminated" by Putin, Abramovich is a survivor. This may be due to the fact that unlike Berezovsky or Khodorkovsky, he kept a low profile and assured Putin of his unconditional loyalty. As a "reward" he sort of "inherited" a great deal of property from his former mentor/friend who turned into bitter enemy of Berezovsky.

Excessive rent seeking threatens the legitimacy of the regimes and even private ownership. In response, political elites launch anticorruption campaigns. But it remains to be seen whether the anticorruption drive is indeed aiming at reducing rent seeking or it is merely an instrument to remove political enemies or to reallocate the wealth of oligarchs whose loyalty cannot be trusted. Khodorkovsky was jailed for charges in corruption, but it is hard not to see political motives behind the Putin-Khodorkovsky war. So it is possible that these corruption charges are instruments in a selective criminalization of enemies. Many members of the economic and political postcommunist elites are likely to have "skeletons" in their closets. Businessmen under postcommunist conditions – given the ambiguities of legal regulations and private ownership may be even more likely to offer their gratitude (bribes?) to political office holders than in more established liberal democracies and the political elite may be more inclined to accept appreciations of their services (take bribes?). There are many candidates to be chosen as "corrupt", the question is who will at the end be selected.

In 2012, when the Communist Party of China transferred the power from President Hu to President Xi, the authorities promised to catch "tigers and flies" in a newly launched anti corruption campaign. So far they did catch quite a few flies and some tigers, but those tigers look too much as political enemies to those in the highest position of political power. The first tiger to fall victim to anti corruption was Bo Xilai. Bo was the first secretary of the Communist Party of Chongqing, the largest city in the world and an aspirant for a position in the Standing Committee of the Politbureau. He was a Maoism inspired left-populist politician. He kept speculators out of urban land market and used the profit gained this way to build public housing schools and improve medical facilities.[46] People had to sing songs from the times of the Cultural Revolution, but they received better services. So he looked far too popular and dangerous for the Beijing

46 See Huang (2011) on the Chongqing model.

establishment. He was certainly no saint, but his selection as the first "tiger" may have more to do with his candidacy for the Standing Committee of the Politbureau rather than his deep involvement in corruption. The case against Bo Xilai started with a trial against his wife Gu Kailai. Gu was accused and eventually sentenced for life for the murder of an English business associate, Neil Heywood. She might have been the murderer, but Heywood's body was cremated right after his death. Nevertheless it took the court 7 hours on August 9, 2012 to find her guilty and to sentence her to life imprisonment. [47] Just 11 month after her trial Bo was also out on trial for corruption and abuse of office powers. He was accused and found guilty to have received $3.6 million bribes from two local businessmen. He might very well have taken those bribes, but what is curious why top party leaders, whose family's fortune is in the billions of dollars, are not being investigated how they became so wealthy so fast.

Selective criminalization and "capturing" the *nouveaux riches* is not an exclusively Russian or Chinese phenomenon. Some commentators suspect the anti corruption drive under President Johannis in Romania may be also politically motivated and there is little doubt that witch hunting was also used widely in Hungary, especially after 2010. The new center-right government accused many former socialist and liberal politicians of corruption and quite a few after spending long time in "pre-trial detention" were found not guilty by the relatively still independent courts. There is at least one very interesting case to move against a "new rich" – who was perceived and was probably indeed disloyal by the Hungarian government. Mr. Lajos Simicska, the former treasurer of the post 2010 Hungarian ruling party – a previous winner of many "restricted" competitions for government contracts, hence a great rent collector, suddenly lost the goodwill of the Prime Minister at the end of 2014. In few weeks he was excluded from public procurement tenders, his media firms lost government advertisements. Most recently even his hunting plot which he rented from a state-owned forest farm was taken away from him. As the prime minister put it astutely: "The trees cannot grow into the skies". Unlike Khodorkovsky, Simicska is not in jail, but his business empire is in serious trouble.

Concluding remarks on policy implications

Klebnikov (2000) compared the Russian oligarchs to the American Robber Barons of the late 19th century. They had lots in common. But, as Klebnikov pointed out, the Robber Barons produced something and contributed to economic growth in the US, by operating (a quite) large island of competitive market economy. From the benefit of hindsight, many scholars of the postcommunist economies agree that the Russian oligarchs did not produce much or anything, but deposited their incomes gained just from rent in Swiss banks and accumulated spectacular wealth in real estate in the Riviera,

47 Without a body and murder weapon one would have expected a somewhat longer trial. She confessed, but for murder the usual sentence in China is capital punishment and she got away with a life sentence.

in London or in Florida, not speaking of their yachts and art collections. In the early parts of 1990s, this was not yet clear. Aslund (1995) and others justified their activities by claiming that the brutal behavior of the oligarchs was needed to overcome the resistance of the old *nomenclature*. As of today, it seems that President Putin captured the oligarchs – as we analyzed above – and reversed the positive market reforms of the 1990s.[48]

The purpose of this paper is not to make a case *against* rent seeking and *for* profit seeking. Pareto's observation seems to be insightful: a modern market economy needs speculators and rentiers: foxes and lions. The complex ecosystem of market capitalism needs both animals. Too many foxes, too much speculation, too much unrestrained markets can cause instability and it may require what Polanyi in Great Transformation called the "double movement", it may require transformation of some of the market earned profits or wages into rent to those who cannot provide for themselves on the market (that is what welfare redistribution is). But too many lions, too much rent seeking can suffocate competition. Let's cite one more time John Locke: "*This is to think that Men are so foolish that they take care to avoid what Mischiefs may be done them by Polecats, or foxes, but are content, nay think it Safety, to be devoured by lions.*" (John Locke, [1698], 1988, p. 328, our emphasis). Of course Locke here means "fellow citizen competitors as foxes and the absolute monarch as the lion, but let's translate this into the language of Pareto and we get to the bottom line of this paper: Foxes are fellow competitors, who may outsmart us, lions are rentiers who already outsmarted us, by (ab)using their political connections to restrict competition to their advantage.

Our main inference is that the crucial question is not the extent of measured inequality (income or wealth). Countries with GINI around 0.20 or 0.40 can equally be economically dynamic and socially cohesive. Beyond the ethno-racial, religious and gender-based pay gaps, the key question is: are inequalities stemming from mechanism, which generates competition as free as one conceivably can create between workers vs. workers, capitalists vs. capitalists or it stems from rent seeking, hence exclusion of some players from the competition by the politically connected ones. While we would not go as far as Sorensen and assume an "antagonistic", class division between rent collectors vs. those whose income stems from profit or wages. We share Ricardo's position, namely that it is sensible to tax rents more rather than profits and wages. The current tax rates on property/wealth are rather low in the OECD countries and it allows a huge maneuvering room for future change.[49] This is especially true for some postcommunist countries, like Hungary, where inheritance tax, called "death tax" has just been eliminated. Lower VAT and modest taxes on wages and profits compensated by high taxrates on inheritance and capital gain taxes seem to serve both social justice and economic dynamism.

48 As Aslund himself formulated in a recent article: „Putin's regime has degraded the institutions that are essential to the functioning of a modern economy. The judicial system, for example, is largely in tatters. And above all, the ownership and governance of key assets and resources are almost all in state hands." Aslund – Commander (2016). See also Aslund (2013).

49 In 2012, the combined revenue from all kind of property and (net) wealth as a percentage of GDP was in the range of 0.3% (Estonia, Mexico) and 3.9% (UK). https://stats.oecd.org/Index.aspx?-DataSetCode=REV accessed 9 July, 2015.

Bibliography

Acemoglu, D. and Robinson, J. 2012. *Why Nations Fail. The Origins of Power, Prosperity, and Poverty*, Boston: Harvard University Press.

Åslund, A. 1995. *How Russia Became a Market Economy*, Washington, D.C.: The Brookings Insitution.

Åslund, A. 2013. "Russia Can't Grow and Steal at the Same Time", *Moscow Times*, 27 November.

Åslund, A. and S. Commander 2016. "Russia's Gloomy Prospects", *Project Syndicate*, 9 May.

Atkinson, T. 2015. *Inequality. What Can be Done*? Cambridge: Harvard University Press.

Bhagwati, J. 1982. "Directly Unproductive Profit Seeking (DUP) Activities", *Journal of Political Economy*, 90: 988–1002.

Bohle, D. and B. Greskovits 2012. *Capitalist Diversity on Europe's Periphery,* Ithaca, London: Cornell University Press.

Bourdieu, P. [1970] 1977. Reproduction in education, society and culture. London: Sage Pull.

Buchanan, J. M., R.D. Tollison and Gordon Tullock (eds) 1980. *Toward a Theory of Rent Seeking Society*. College Station: Texas A&M University.

Conley, D. 1999. *Being Black and Living in Red. Race, Wealth, and Social Policy in America*. Berkeley: University of California Press

Eyal, G., I. Szelényi and E. Townsley. 1998. *Making Capitalism without Capitalists. Class Formation and Elite Struggles in Post-Communist Central Europe*. London: Verso.

Folsom, Burton W. [1987] 2010. *The Myth of the Robber Barons*. Herndon, Virginia: Young America's Foundation.

Hankiss, E. 1990. *East European Alternatives*. Oxford: Clarendon Press.

Huang, P. 2011. "Chongqing: Equitable Development Driven by a 'Third Hand'?" *Modern China* 6: 559–622.

Josephson, M. 1934. *The Robber Barons. The great American capitalists 1881–1901*. New York: Harcourt Inc.

King, L. and I. Szelényi. 2005. "Postcommunist Economic Systems", in: N. J. Smelser and R. Swedberg (eds): *The Handbook of Economic Sociology*. Princeton: Princeton University Press, pp. 205–232.

Klebnikov, P. 2000. *Godfather of the Kremlin: Boris Berezovsky and the looting of Russia*. New York: Houghton Mifflin Harcourt.

Kolosi T. and I. Szelényi. 2010. *Hogyan legyünk milliárdosok? (How to become a billionaire) Avagy a neoliberális etika és a poztkommunista kapitalizmus szelleme*. Budapest: Corvina. (In Hungarian).

Kornai, J. 1992. *The Socialist System*. Princeton: Princeton University Press.

Krueger, A. O. 1974. "The Political Economy of Rent Seeking Society", *The American Economic Review*, 64 (3): 291–303.

Krugman, P. 2014 "Why We're in a New Gilded Age", *The New York Review of Books,* May 4.

Kuznets, S. 1955. "Economic Growth and Income Inequality", *The American Economic Review*, 45(1): 1–28.

Locke, John [1698] 1988. *Two Treatises of Governmen*t. Cambridge: Cambridge University Press

Magyar, B. 2016. *Post-Communist Maffia State: The Case of Hungary*. Budapest: Central European University Press.

Mann, T. [1901] 1987. Buddenbrooks. Cambridge etc: Cambridge University Press.

Marx, K. [1867] 1954. *Capital. A Critique of Political Economy, Volume I.* Moscow: Progress Publishers.

Marx, K. [1885] 1956. *Capital, Volume II.* Moscow: Progress Publishers.

Marx, K. [1894] 1959. *Capital, Volume III.* Moscow: Progress Publishers.

Mihalyi, P. 2001. „The evolution of Hungary's approach to FDI in postcommunist privatization", *Transnational Corporations*, 3: 61–74.

Oliver, M. 1995. *Black Wealth/White Wealth. A New Perspective on Racial Inequality.* New York: Routledge.

Olson, M. 1982. *The Rise and Decline of Nations*. New Haven, CT.: Yale University Press.

Pareto, V. [1916] 1935. *The Mind and Society*. (Trattato Di Sociologia General) New York: Harcourt, Brace.

Piketty, Th. [2013] 2014. *Capital in the 21st Century*. Cambridge: Harvard University Press.

Pirvu, D. 2015: "Corruption: Profile of Political Companies in Romania", *Acta Oeconomica*, Vol. 65. Special Issue 1. 65–82.

Polanyi, K. 1966. *Dahomey and the Slave Trade*. Seattle: University of Washington Press.

Posner, R. 1975. "The Social Costs of Monopoly and Regulation", *The Journal of Political Economy,* 83 (4): 807–828.

Posner, R. 2009. *A Failure of Capitalism. The Crisis of '08 and the Descent into Depression*. Cambridge, MA: Harvard University Press.

Ricardo, D. [1817] 2004. *The Principles of Political Economy and Taxation*. Mineola, NY.: Dover Publications.

Roemer, J. E. 1982. *A General Theory of Exploitation and Class.* Cambridge, MA: Harvard University Press.

Smith, A. [1776] 1976. *An Inquiry into the Nature and Causes of the Wealth of Nations.* Chicago: The University of Chicago Press.

Solow, R. 2014. "Thomas Piketty Is Right", *The New Republic*, 23. April.

Sorensen, A. 2000. "Toward a Sounder Basis for Class Analysis", *American Journal of Sociology* 105 (6): 1523–1558.

Stanley, T. J. and W. Danko 1998. *The Millionaire Next Door, The Surprising Secrets of America's Wealthy*, New York: Simon and Schuster.

Staniszkis, J. 1991. "Political Capitalism in Poland", *East European Politics and Societies",* 5 (1): 127–41.

Stark, D. 1996. "Recombinant property in East European Capitalism", *American Journal of Sociology* 101 (4): 993–1027.

Szelényi, I. 2010. "The New Grand Bourgeoisie under PostCommunism. Central Europe, Russia and China Compared", *Working Paper* No. 2010/63. Helsinki: United Nations University, World Institute for Development Economic Research.

Stiglitz, J. 2012. *The Price of Inequality*, New York: W.W. Norton and Company.

Stiglitz, J. 2015. *New Theoretical Perspectives on the Distribution of Income and Wealth among Individuals, Part I, II and III. NBER Working Papers* Series. Cambridge, Ma: National Bureau of Economic Research.

Szalai, E. 1989. "The New Elite", *Across Frontiers* 5: 25–31.

Tullock, G. 1967. "The Welfare Costs of Tariffs, Monopolies and Theft", *Western Economic Journal* 5: 224–32.

Weber, M. [1922] 1978. *Economy and Society. An Outline of Interpretive Sociology*, edited by G. Roth and C. Wittich. Berkeley, CA.: University of California Press.
Weber, M. [1922] 2013. *Wirtschaft und Gesellschaft. Soziologie.* Tübingen: J.C.B. Mohr (Paul Siebeck), MWG 1/23.
Weber, M. [1908] 1986. *The Agrarian History and Ancient Civilization.* [Agrarverhältnisse im Altertum (3. Fassung), London: Verso. (MWG I/6: 320–751).

IV.4 Karl Polanyi a Theorist of mixed Economies

Iván Szelényi and Péter Mihályi[1]

Abstract

Karl Polanyi's scholarship is interpreted in radically different ways. The "hard" reading of Polanyi sees him as a radical socialist, the "soft" reading presents him as a theorist of mixed economy. The paper sides with the soft interpretation. It uses his biography to explain his theoretical "elusiveness", presents a novel interpretation of his three types of economic integration, claiming all economies are "mixed". While it acknowledges Polanyi as one of the major sources of world system theory, it claims that Polanyi saw not only the dangers, but also the necessity and positive consequences of globalization. Finally, it shows that in spite of Polanyi's life-long commitment to the political left, his scholarly work did not offer an apology of socialism. Instead this paper uses Polanyi's theory of economic integration to build a critical political economy of state socialism.

Keywords: world system theory, rent, rent seeking, mixed economies introduction

Introduction

It is not easy to locate Polanyi on the intellectual landscape of his times. All of his life, he was on the unorthodox Left (Dale, 2016), but exactly due to his resistance to all orthodoxies, he never found a real theoretical/political "home" for himself. Luban (2017) accurately writes about "the elusive Polanyi" rejected by liberals *and* neo-liberals (is there a difference between the two?) for his criticism of "market fundamentalism" (Block and Sommers, 2016) *and* by revolutionary Marxists as a revisionist social democrat.

There are two conflicting readings of Polanyi' works. Lacher (2019) distinguishes a "soft" and "hard" version of his theory. The soft version sees Polanyi as an early theorist of the "mixed economy", where market failures are compensated by government intervention (Szelényi, 1991, Block and Somers, 2014, Stiglitz, 2001). Others see him as a radical socialist (Kari Polanyi-Levitt 1994, Hann, 2019). It is notable that the hard reading of Polanyi typically comes from soft evidences: unpublished materials, like correspondence, lecture notes from his archive (Lacher, 2019), rather than the text he considered to be publishable in respectable academic outlets.

1 Péter Mihályi, Professor of Macroeconomics, Corvinus University of Budapest and Central European University. Iván Szelényi, William Graham Sumner Emeritus Professor of Sociology and Political Sciences , Yale University, Max Weber Emeritus Professor of Social Sciences, NYUAD.

In section 1, we offer a contrast between these two interpretations while reminding the readers of his biography. Polanyi's elusiveness arguably had a lot to do with his challenge to navigate between two individuals he clearly loved, his younger brother an anti-communist; and his wife who was for big chunk of her life a "Marxist-Leninist revolutionary". In Sections 2, 3 and 4, we revisit three themes of Karl Polanyi's *œuvre: The Great Transformation* (1944) and his contributions to *Trade and Market in the Early Empires* (1957).

In Section 2, we propose a somewhat unorthodox interpretation of his distinction between three forms of economic integration, enriching it with our own rather novel theory of *rent*. While the hard interpretation of Polanyi sees him as a complete rejection of the market economy (and a radical socialist critique of capitalism), our central point is that he mainly advocated a mixed economy in which – in modern economics – markets are likely to play a dominant role. In 1944 the fall of Fascism was becoming clear and the question was what will be the shape of the postwar societies. In our "soft" interpretation Polanyi wanted capitalism to transcend what it was in the 1920s, but the book is consistent with Keynesianism, the New Deal and economic policies of postwar Scandinavian-type of Social Democracy.

Then, in Section 3, we make a few comments on his views about globalization and the world market. In some ways, Polanyi laid the foundation what became to be known as "world system theory". Indeed, Polanyi saw the world history as moving from redistributive empires to world markets. Polanyi and Wallerstein overlapped at Columbia. Wallerstein was in his early work an Africanist, and Africa was also a specialty of Polanyi. While Wallerstein in the first volume of world system theory (1974) did not acknowledge the Polanyian origins of the theory, that was understandable. In the early 1970s, Polanyi was not *comme il faut*, since he was not a Marxist and the early version of world system theory was driven by Frank's (1966) radical revolutionary Marxism. The hard reading of Polanyi saw him as a world system theorist. In the soft reading it is hard to see in Polanyi any signs of a "development of underdevelopment" theory, or a program to overthrow the system of "global capitalism", though this is exactly why Polanyi is so attractive to the early 21st century radical, revolutionary, anti globalist left.

Finally, in Section 4 we try to use Polanyi to develop the political economy of "really existing socialism"[2], knowing that Polanyi himself never offered a political economy of socialism. Here again the hard and the soft readings of Polanyi clash. For the hard reading, reform communism of the János Kádár type is interpreted as "market socialism" consistent with Polanyi's vision of operating double movement, correcting the fault of pure markets (Hann, 2019). The first author of this paper in his 1979 book with George Konrad offered a radically different (and soft) reading of communist political economy. The Konrad-Szelényi book used Polanyi's theory of redistribution to offer a radically

2 We use the terms socialism and communism interchangeably. In our view, in the communist ideology this distinction is merely an ideological construct. Well, some call themselves „democratic socialists" (like Bernie Sanders), but since they do not want to eliminate private ownership and accept markets as dominant coordinating mechanism, and just manage it, they are basically social democrats.

critical theory of the socialist economy. The lesson learned from socialism was simple. Redistribution is not the solution, it is the problem.

The elusive Polanyi or the two Polanyis: the biographical background

From his published scholarly work it is indeed hard to tell who the "real" Polanyi was. Was he a radical whose aim was to overthrow the capitalist market system or was he the advocate of a mixed economy? What was his take on the USSR and Maoist China, or for that sake on Kádár's "goulash communism"? There are no clear answers.

But from the extensive literature about his life, we know that during his adult life he was caught in a cross fire between the people he loved most, his younger brother (who early turned into a conservative and vehemently anti communist philosopher) and his wife (a dedicated communist revolutionary for a great deal of her life).[3] Karl Polanyi was born in Vienna in 1886 in a well-to-do Jewish family (called at that time Polacsek, eventually he adopted the more Hungarian sounding name of Polanyi). Karl grew up in Budapest. He was, of course, bilingual. He was "transnational", as well, often referred to as an Austrian-Hungarian social scientist and that is what he was, though you may add to this "English" and "American".

His younger brother, Michael (who became at least as influential as Karl in physics and philosophy) was born in 1891 in Budapest.[4] Karl and Michael became involved in the so-called *Galileo Circle*, a left-leaning, liberal group of young intellectuals, flirting even with Marxism. The Polanyi family, like most Jewish families in the Austro-Hungarian Empire at that time was rather secular, one even may say assimilated (their grandfather was a rabbi, but the Polanyi-children grew up without religion). Karl was a better fit with the Galileo Circle, Michael was seen by other members of the circle as an "independent thinker", probably a bit too conservative (Nagy, 2018: 83) and very early on he had an interest in the Christian religion. Karl also had his "religious turn". He served during World War I in the Austro-Hungarian army, but in 1917 he fell ill with typhus, read the New Testament while in hospital (Dale, 2016), but what captured his attention was the assumed affiliation between socialism and Christianity. So, one brother, Michael was led by Christianity towards conservativism/liberalism (are they different? what a mess of political science terminology ...), while the other, Karl tried to combine Christianity with socialism.

In 1918, they were both sympathetic to the democratic revolution led by Count Mihály Károlyi.[5] Michael, despite his fresh medical degree, became Secretary of Health

3 We have done no primary research on his life, so this section of our paper relies on information from the secondary literature. If we can claim any new contribution in this section of the paper it would be merely the claim that his "elusiveness" was deeply rooted in his personal struggles to build a bridge between conservative reformism and a radical revolutionary project.

4 He died in 1976, surviving his brother by 12 years.

5 Károlyi was a vehement opponent of the Great War. When the previous Prime Minister who took Hungary to the war, István Tisza was murdered on October 31, 1918, the King, Charles IV appoint-

in Károlyi's government, but left it on the day the Hungarian Bolsheviks took over power. Then he returned to medical practice. Later, he was the only person in the medical school who refused to join the Red Army. Karl gave the benefit of the doubt to the Hungarian communism (which took over power from Károlyi in March 1919 in order to establish a Hungarian Soviet Republic). But he soon became disappointed. Already in May 1919 he left Budapest for Vienna. He claimed that this was for "health reasons" – a good excuse for political disappointment. Michael, an advocate of Károlyi's republicanism was strongly opposed to the communist turnover (and for the Leninist *coup d'état* 1917 in Russia). Ironically he did stay in Hungary until December 1919 when he found out that he as much opposed to anti-communist, nationalist counter-revolution as he had opposed earlier the communist revolution. Karl and Michael remained loving brothers, but in collision in terms of their worldview for the rest of their life (Congdon 1997).

There is another biographical detall we have to mention to appreciate the personal/intellectual tension in which Karl developed his intellectual/political identity. In 1920, Karl Polanyi fell in love with a young, but married woman, Ilona Duczyńska (1975). Soon she got divorced, then they were married and had a long and happy married life.[6] Ilona was also born in Vienna in 1897. Her father was a politically radical who belonged to the upper Polish nobility. Her mother was an equally wealthy Hungarian noblewoman. Ilona commuted between Vienna and Budapest, studied engineering in Zürich and was close to the anti-war circle of Lenin. She also joined the *Galileo Circle* but became a revolutionary communist. In May 1917, she was ready to murder the already mentioned Hungarian Prime Minister, Count István Tisza, who was held responsible for Hungary's entry into the Great War. She even carried a gun with her to a public meeting of Tisza when the news came that Tisza was ousted by the king, so she abandoned her murder plan. Nevertheless she was arrested and sentenced to two years in jail, but the October 1918 revolution liberated her.

She joined the Hungarian Communist Party in 1918. She represented the Hungarian communist government in 1919 in Zürich and of course after the fall of the communist regime she had no choice but to move into emigration to Red Vienna in 1919. Given her independent way of thinking, she was expelled from the Hungarian Communist Party in 1920 for "revisionism". She was nevertheless attracted by the radical working class movement in Vienna in the 1920s and early 1930s, joined briefly the Austrian Communist Party in 1934, but just again to be expelled at the order of Moscow given her increasing doubt of the show trials in the USSR. One odd consequence of post-WWII anti-communism in the US was that Ilona – a former communist party member – could not enter the US. Hence, the couple had to live at the Canadian side of the US-Canada border and after Karl got jobs in the US (first in Bennington College, later at Columbia

ed Károlyi as Prime Minister. Two weeks later, Hungary declared itself as "People's Republic" (it meant a "liberal state", but not a monarchy any more), and Károlyi became President. On March 21 of 1919 he resigned and passed the power on to a communist regime, which transformed Hungary into a Soviet-type communist dictatorship.

6 She died in Canada, in 1978, surviving her husband by 14 years.

University) he had to commute to his US jobs from there. This US law was absurd: Ilona who in Vienna earned a doctorate in physics at Vienna College of Technology in the 1930s, during the WWII served in the British defense industry as a Fellow of the Royal Astronomical Society and was involved in developing the British air-force. Nevertheless, the situation was that she did not qualify for a US visa since earlier in her life she was a member of a communist party.

This is the biographic background to Polanyi's "elusiveness". He lived in cross-fire between his conservative, anti-communist brother and his wife who for a very long time was a "democratic Bolshevik", if that combination of terms was meaningful at all. The greatest challenge for Karl was to evaluate the USSR. He could not be critical enough to satisfy his anti-communist brother, but could not be sufficiently appreciative of the Soviet experience to please his wife. This colored his views about markets and redistribution. The way out was supposed to be "Christian socialism" (at least early in his career), influential enough at the turn of the 19th-20th century, but disappearing after WWII, giving way to conservative *Christian Democracy.*

After the Great Depression, and especially after 1945, it became evident to many of the great thinkers of the time that *capitalism and classical liberalism cannot continue to exist* the way they did (especially during the 1920s). John Maynard Keynes was of course one of the revolutionaries, who came with a vision for a future world order, but many others with (very) different political persuasion followed this line of analysis, let's just mention the "conservative" Karl Mannheim (1940) and the "neo-liberal" Schumpeter (1943). Where does Karl Polanyi fit into this? In our soft reading Polanyi was very close to the ways Keynes, Mannheim, Schumpeter imagined the rebuilding of the world after the defeat of Fascism, but given his wife's radicalism, in his diary and in personal communications his political views were a bit more radical. Indeed, Karl Polanyi tried to find excuses for the show trials of the 1930s. In 1956 after October 23, finally he was on the same side with his brother against the Russian invasion of Hungary. Interestingly, he was mainly enthusiastic about the "workers council" movement which emerged late in the game, in December 1956. On the other hand, Polanyi had little to say when Imre Nagy, the communist Prime Minister who had liberal tendencies was executed – the most horrendous crime committed by the Kádár regime.

In our soft reading of Polanyi, his explicit political avowals had almost no effect on his scholarly work. He remained an economic anthropologist, never turned into a political scientist. True, he made a few errors when it came to political statements, but to regard him as a supporter of Kádárist reformism is untenable. Kádár turned from a blood-handed dictator into a communist reformer in 1963. Polanyi passed away in 1964 when "goulash communism" was hardly on the horizon.

The hard reading of Polanyi is mainly based on soft evidence, personal diaries from the Polanyi archive and his correspondence. This archive is currently under the control of Polanyi's daughter, Kari Polanyi-Levitt (b. 1923), a fine scholar who became close to classical world system theory (sort of development of under development type). We respect her admiration for her father and the extraordinary work she put into sustaining the legacy of Polanyi. But she clearly has a scholarly (and political) agenda, which is missing the "elusiveness" of her father. We do not deny the attraction in Polanyi for a hard, revolutionary approach, but we would like to bring attention to his soft theory of mixed economies.

The three forms of economic integration: reciprocity, redistribution and market

We have a long standing interest in Karl Polanyi's theory of various forms of economic integration (Konrad and Szelényi, 1979, and Szelényi, 1978). Our aim now is to offer (not an exegesis, but) a (not radically) novel interpretation of Polanyi. As an "economic anthropologist" Polanyi was critical of formal economic theories and offered instead a substantive view of the economy. Economies can be integrated in more than two ways: the dualist model of capitalism or non capitalism is a misleading simplification.[7] When a society is composed by symmetrical groups their economic integration is based on *reciprocity*. Ancient empires were held together by *redistributive mechanisms* (they are based on asymmetrical political and legal relations between rulers/masters and their subjects) just like modern economies operate through *market interactions* (based also on asymmetrical economic relationships between employers and employees – to put it with Weber – and owner of capital and owners of labor – to put it with Marx). Arguably the most innovative contribution of *The Great Transformation* was the claim that none of these coordinating mechanisms (even not the market) are "natural", but they are all social constructions.

Usually, these three forms of integration are defined at various historical instances. To put this in the Marxist way, reciprocity sounds much like tribal society, redistribution like feudalism (or slave society) and market integration is *the* "capitalist mode of production". But Polanyi was more Weberian than Marxist. Yes, his concept can be used to describe macro structures, but they are also useful to characterize micro systems. And we arrived now to our somewhat unorthodox interpretation of Polanyi.

Notes to Figure 1:

* See Malinowski (1922). While in *kula* trade, each transaction exchange is based on gift (reciprocity) and therefore economically meaningless or even irrational, after the whole cycle is completed, it turns out to be economically rational. The first island receives goods they need, though during their journey it looks like all action is 'irrational' or ruled by 'tradition'.

** Anderson (1985).

*** Max Weber (1978) makes this point in the chapter on The City in *Economy and Society* (Volume II, Chapter XVI) where he notes "non-legitimate" authority within the increasingly market oriented medieval city.

**** Anderson (1985) sees this as a critical distinction between slavery and Western feudalism.

7 This was more fully developed in his *Trade and Market in the Early Empires* (1957).

FIGURE 1: The main sources of income inequality in history from tribal to feudalism to slave society and to classical capitalism

1. Tribal societies		
Markets	Redistribution	Reciprocity
(3) Tertiary	(2) Secondary	(1) Dominant
In tribal, circular trade (Trobriand Islanders) boat owners may collect rents, and sailors may collect wages.	If a tribe is larger than extended kinship, the chief is likely to collect rents disguised as gifts.	In smaller, symmetrical, kinship based societies some trade is possible and the chief may have to allow some market exchange between slaves and non-slaves and he may collect rent.
2. Classical Slave Societies (Egypt, Greece and Rome)		
Markets	Redistribution	Reciprocity
(2) Secondary	(1) Dominant	(3) Tertiary
Non-slave, free citizens (even some slaves) operate profit-oriented businesses.	Slave owners appropriate the entire output of slaves, but may have to allow some trade among slaves (and even earning non-slaves to make the economy moving).	Though kinship is broken, network of slaves can offer mutual help.
3. Patrimonialism (West-European Feudalism)		
Markets	Redistribution	Reciprocity
(3) Tertiary	(1) Dominant	(2) Secondary
Urban citizens may employ wage labor and generate profit***.	Landlords collect rent from serfs in exchange for protection and agricultural land use, but allow some market among serfs and non-serfs.	Serfs are allowed to have their own households and produce means for their survival****.
4. Liberal, Market Capitalism (All Stages and forms)		
Markets	Redistribution	Reciprocity
(2) → (1) From secondary to primary	(1) – (2) From primary to secondary	(3) Tertiary
In colonial times, within the core nations, some wealth is generated by profit-oriented businesses. In the globalization period, profit- seeking is the main source of income and wealth.	In colonial times, incomes of large private business often came from colonies as rents. In the globalization period, the rent seeking capacity of core countries is reduced. Oligopolies and monopolies also collect rent, which can be restricted by anti-monopoly laws.	Important for families (child-rearing), but in advanced and modern capitalist countries, some or most of mutual help tends to be institutionalized and commodified.

In Figure 1 and Figure 2 we offer in a historical comparison of a great number of economies with several combinations of Polanyi's three integrative mechanisms, but we interpret them as *three drivers of inequality* (which are particularly useful to conceptualize microlevel variations within a given system of integration). In our recent books (*Rent-seekers, Profits, Wages and Inequality: The Top 20%*, Palgrave, 2019 and *Varieties of Post-communist Capitalism: A Comparative Analysis of Russia, Central Europe and China*, Brill, 2020) we explore various sources of inequalities – both wealth and income. Inequalities can be created by wages/profits, by rents and by gifts. In these Figures our dependent variable is income inequality. Wealth inequality diverges from this somewhat. But our Figures are already complex enough, so we reserve some of our comments about distribution of wealth for our narrative after Figure 2.

In liberal market economies wages (income and wealth from work) and profits (income and wealth from capital) are typical drivers of inequality. But what about rent? Is it the major driver of inequality in redistributive economies? Are there rents in market economies and do they reduce market induced inequalities? Is it the source of inequality in redistributive empires (or even in patrimonial systems)? And what about *gifts*? Is that unique for reciprocity or can gifts be the source of inequality in redistributive and market economies?

Adam Smith ([1776] 1976), the classical – in a way "ultimate" – theorist of modern capitalism believed that there are three sources of the wealth of nations, wages, profits and rents[8]. Marx disagreed with Smith. He saw labor as the only source of wealth, but for Marx both profit and rent were merely value appropriated from labor. Rent was just another form of profit.

In our work on rent, our inspiration comes primarily from Ricardo ([1817] 1911), and from the more recent literature from Aage Sorensen (2000). Ricardo disagreed with Smith and interestingly Marx did not appreciate his interesting insights. His argument was cast in terms of rent on land. Ricardo's major point was that the quantity of land available to produce agricultural goods is limited, while the demand for food is increasing, given the increases in the population. An owner of land does not have to produce more or better quality food in order to have a higher income. Nevertheless the question whether the incomes generated by those, who have monopolistic/oligopolistic ownership of productive assets may earn a higher income than those who compete on free markets remains relevant. He claimed that rent is not the source, it is only an indication of wealth. This proved to be false, since the productivity of agrarian land was growing at least as fast as the world's population. Agrarian production grew fast, actually faster than the population. There is still hunger in the world today, but not because we could not

8 Smith sensed that there may be a difference how much contribution each of the members of the holy trinity gives to the wealth of nations: „As soon as the land of any country has all become private property, the landlords, like all other men, love to reap where they have never sowed and demand a rent for its natural produce" (Smith, p. 56). This may be interpreted as a hint that landlords collect a rent without adding to the wealth (hence they obtain "unearned" income), while Smith believed that those who collect wages or profits all earn (and therefore morally deserve) their income.

produce more food, but due to unequal distribution of incomes and the incompetence of state redistribution.

Nevertheless during the last fifty or so years the question of *rent seeking* was increasingly applied to other productive assets than agricultural land. The most obvious example is real estate, especially real estate in central cities. The price and value of real estate in desirable urban location grew much faster than inflation and incomes, hence those who inherit or just sit on such real estate long enough, see their wealth skyrocket without work or further investment.

Aage Sorensen (2000) expanded the notion of rent radically. He defined rent as income, which is earned above incomes what one would earn on competitive markets. Therefore, if one leases a house to a tenant at a price, which covers the investments and improvements (plus market defined interest), the owner collects a "profit" even if in common language it may be called "rent". The same applies to pensions: the income of a retired person is derived from life time savings (and interests) is often called "rent", though it is merely post-retirement "postponed wages plus profits". In the way Sorensen uses it rent comes from either the market (monopolies, oligopolies, cartels) or state induced restrictions of the markets (in Sorensen's logic welfare payments, excessive income). Stiglitz (2013) comes close to this view. He states: "…there are two ways to become wealthy: to create wealth or to take wealth away from others… [S]ome genuine wealth creators often are satisfied with the wealth that their innovation or entrepreneurship has reaped. Some eventually turn to abusive practices like monopoly pricing or other form of rent extraction." He calls this "wealth transfer instead of wealth creation" (p.40).

This citation is important for our analysis. It confirms that rent seeking can deeply root in market integration, though the key argument in this paper will be that the major source of income/wealth inequality is a characteristic of redistribution and state limitation of competition. Well, not that Stiglitz disagrees. He sees government restriction of markets also as another source of rent seeking: "Rent seeking takes *many forms*, [our emphasis[9]] hidden and open transfers and subsidies from the government …This is often a negative-sum game, which is one of the reasons, why on average, economies have grown more slowly…" (pp. 48–49). Stiglitz calls this "regulatory capture" (following Stigler, 1971, see Stiglitz, 2013, p. 59).

And he continues: "Another form of rent seeking is… selling to government products at above market prices "(p. 50). When regulatory capture (we called it "state capture of markets" in Mihályi and Szelényi, 2020) becomes dominant, we face a marginal case between markets and redistribution, some call it "crony capitalism" (M. Pei, 2016 and Anders Åslund, 2019) or "mafia state" (Bálint Magyar, 2016), which to put with Polanyi is between market and redistributive integration. But in any case, we make an attempt to integrate our rent-based approach to inequality in the model of all societies in history by distinguishing between the sources of income on the one hand, and wealth on the other.

9 This is critical for this paper. While the major source of inequality under redistribution is rent, some rents are generated by the very market integration. For instance over accumulation can yield to rent or "extra profit" not as a result of political/state/government intervention (that would be redistribution), but due to the lack of state action to protect free competition.

We assert that all economies in the past and the present tend to be mixed systems (Szelényi, 1991, Stiglitz, 2001). But it is possible and reasonable that we categorize an economic system by identifying which of the coordinating mechanism is dominant, which is secondary, which is tertiary. This is the approach we used already in Figure 1. If market integration is dominant we tend to call that system capitalism. Polanyi calls economies dominated by redistribution as "ancient empires" (by extension we will try to apply its logic to patrimonial or West European feudalism as well). Societies organized by extended kinship ties, or "tribal societies" are predominantly based on reciprocity.

Nevertheless dominant economic mechanisms cyclically produce failures, in cases of failures a secondary or tertiary mechanism kicks in to counteract the failures of the dominant mechanism. Polanyi in his studies of market economy (capitalism) writes about countervailing tendencies. He calls this as "double movements". If uncontrolled, or not sufficiently controlled, markets produce excessive inequalities of incomes and wealth, which may threaten social stability. Under popular pressure government may intervene with welfare measures, hence with redistribution. Government may impose high taxes on high incomes or even wealth and relocate it to low income groups who cannot earn enough income on the market to make ends meet. Some families, especially the poorest of the poor – think of poor Roma families in Eastern Europe – may fall out of the reach of welfare state so they have to rely on reciprocity, short, or often long term help by kinship groups. But reciprocity may be present in affluent strata as well and intriguingly can be the source of transfer of privileges to the next generation. If I give support to my granddaughter to finish college it is merely a gift and it usually does not involve any market consideration. I do not consider by making such a gift any future possible return on my "investment". Such gift can become especially important if for welfare considerations a government imposes too high inheritance taxes. In this case reciprocity is counteracting excessive redistributive intervention in the allocation of wealth.[10]

In small scale societies if one kinship group may turn out to be too small and they may not be able to produce everything they need they may be engaged with more extended kinship network in market like trade. Take as an example the Trobriand Island (Malinowski, 1922). On each of the small islands, small tribes existed in economies dominantly integrated by reciprocity. But none of these small islands could produce a sufficient diversity of produce necessary for survival. Hence Trobriand islanders were engaged in extensive "trade", what Malinowski called "*kula trade*". Well, this "trade" was not quite market, since the islanders on their sailing trips exchanged the "gifts" (Mauss, 1954) [11]. On no island they visited, they received the equivalents of what they gave. It was set by tradition what they had to give and accept. Nevertheless, at the end of their journey, they returned home with goods, which were equal to what they took on their trip, hence the whole *kula* cycle was like a market. In this case failures of reciprocity

10 It is „excessive" to the extent it is seen as „unfair" by the wealthy.

11 According to Mauss (1925/1954) gifts can be traded, but they are not commodities. Commodities have to be exchanged as change of equivalent values, gifts are regulated by tradition and when given or received their value is not evaluated. To put it with Polanyi, trade of gifts is "non-market trade".

were corrected by trade. In large, extended kinship groups, tribal societies occasionally a Chief (who may have been seen of having magical powers, special access to gods or spirits) emerges and members of the group may have to give tributes to the Chief without expecting reciprocity. One may consider calling such a tribute "rent" in the definition we will provide below.

In ancient empires the ruler tried to extract as much produce from the local communities (or slave owners from their slaves, or landlords from the serfs) as possible (you may call it taxes, we will call them rents and will explain shortly why). If such a "tax-collection" or "rent seeking" is too excessive and threatens the well-being of people they either compensate for this by establishing local markets or rely on gifts from more fortunate kin by invoking "tradition", based on the principles of reciprocity. The best-described examples were the Hydraulic Empires, like ancient China (Wittfogel, 1957). Legitimated by flood control and irrigation needs the emperor appropriated a great deal of products from the village communities, nevertheless these communes survived given extensive reciprocity in the communes and in addition a highly developed system of market towns.

This critical change of transformation from antique slave society to medieval feudalism occurred when slaves turned into servants (Perry Anderson, 1985). As Anderson with his rather unorthodox Marxism points out, the fall of the Roman Empire cannot be explained by class struggles within the empire, it rather came from invasion from Germanic tribes, which brought into the system a novel system that moved property relations. Slaves were replaced by serfs, who in exchange for labor on the feudal estate had their own family estates (and families), hence the great empires were replaced by economies where family organization played a crucial role. Landlords still took rent from serfs (forced labor on their estate), but in exchange their allowed families to produce their own food and even permitted their surplus products to sell on self-regulating market.

Economies where market is the dominant coordinating mechanism we call "capitalist". Most market coordinated economies are "mixed ones"; in our reading they were the major objects of Polanyi's analysis. Pure markets would be dysfunctional; they have to be complemented by welfare redistribution and some degree of reciprocity.

In section 4 of this paper, we shall return to this theme, and we also raise the question of communist economies. Were they modern (or "rational", rather than "traditional") versions of redistribution[12] and if so, what was the role of the market on the one hand and reciprocity on the other, to limit the social and economic damage caused by "redistributive failures"? To the extent redistribution can correct market failures, markets (or reciprocity) may correct redistributive failures.

12 Konrad and Szelényi (1979) were often criticized for calling the communist economy „rational redistribution", while its opponents emphasized the irrationality of the communist system. Our intention in this book was to underline the differences in the legitimacy claims of ancient and communist redistributive systems. Ancient systems were legitimated by tradition; the legitimacy claim of communism was „scientific communism".

Globalization and the world market: the tendency towards dis-embedding. Polanyi's basically pro-market critique of market fundamentalism

Modern capitalism was identified with the emergence of the world market at least since Adam Smith ([1776], 1976). For Smith, global capitalism was a win-win situation. As long as there is free trade, all parties will pursue the most efficient activity for them (*op. cit.* p. 401). He was a fervent critic of mercantilism, which aimed to maximize national wealth by imposing export-import duties. Instead, Smith advocated free international trade (hence his famous recommendation of the "invisible hand").

Marx, in many ways, followed Adam Smith's line of analysis. Capitalism was a global system, but for Marx, it was a system of exploitation of the working classes wherever they lived and worked (it was win-win only for the bourgeoisie). Capitalism has to be overthrown globally: "Workers of the world unite!". The question of core-periphery, imperialism and colonialism were not central for Marx's analysis. Marx considered the global variation in modes of production (social formations) in the *Grundrisse* ([1857–58], 1973, pp. 471–514). Anti-globalization and world system Marxists have little inspiration from Marx. They mostly refer to Chapter 14 of Volume III of *The Capital* where Marx offered an analysis of export of capital or to Engels' 1892 preface to his splendid *Condition of Working Class in England*[13], where he wrote about the "industrial monopoly" of England over the world, paving the way to the theory of uneven development and eventually imperialism.

With Rosa Luxemburg and Lenin, the theory of capitalism was substantially changed. Interestingly both theorists came from the semi-periphery or periphery of the world system, from Poland and Russia respectively, hence their understanding of the problems of capitalism was much less West-European centrist than the theory of Marx or even Engels. Rosa Luxemburg's 1913 book on *The Accumulation of Capital* (1951) with her emphasis on "uneven and combined development" foreshadowed later Marxist works on "dependent development" (Evans, 1979) or "development of underdevelopment" (Frank, 1966) and Immanuel Wallerstein's world-system theory (1974).[14] The real breakthrough was, of course, Lenin's book on imperialism (1917), which in turn laid the foundation of a theory (or practice) dislocating the attention from the most developed capitalist

13 This is the preface to the second German edition of the book ([1845/92] 1969, pp. 19–29).

14 Frank generalized out of the South American experience of the 1950s and 60s and argued that in the „third world" development means only deepening the „underdevelopment". This was, of course, later contradicted by successful development stories especially in East Asia (like South Korea, Singapore or Taiwan) and eventually even in some South American countries (e.g. Brazil or Mexico), where Evans' theory is a better fit. Frank was an important inspiration for the early work of Wallerstein. But his ideas lead to an absurd conclusion: the only way out is a "counter-systemic" jump. Hence countries, which isolated themselves from the world market, like Albania or North Korea, adopted the only viable way to break the logic of the "capitalist world system".

countries to countries of the periphery. From here, it was just a small step to Stalin's interesting innovation of "socialism in one country".[15]

Polanyi, in our reading, kept an equal distance from Smith and the Marxist theory. Like Smith and the Marxists, he dated the emergence of capitalism with the making of the world market. But he did not share Smith's optimism about the "invisible hand" of the market. Polanyi was a radical critic of market fundamentalism. Markets tend to become unregulated, but as this happens – as Stiglitz pointed out in his introduction of *The Great Transformation* –, markets can become self-destructive. This was not all that different from Schumpeter's intriguing argument that capitalism will not survive since it is too successful.

This is why "double movement", or "counteracting tendencies" are so central to Polanyi's thinking. Markets have to be disciplined; they have to be "re-embedded" (more about embeddedness later). Pure markets would cause unmitigated social – and even economic – disasters. But Polanyi was careful not to spell out exactly what combination of the three integrative mechanisms would really "work". There is no clear blueprint of the society – to use now Mannheim's (1940) terminology – "in the age of reconstruction".

But Polanyi was at least as far removed from the dependency theory and the development of underdevelopment view of the world, as he was from market fundamentalism. The transition from ancient redistributive empires to global market economy is central for Polanyi's view of history.[16] As this is happening, there is a tendency for "disembedding" – i.e. the separation of spheres. Polanyi, much like Weber, was not an "evolutionist". Markets replacing redistribution, moving away from deeply embedded economies towards disembeddedness is just the way the world is changing. Granovetter (1985) in his wonderful work on "embedded" economy did not acknowledge the historical trend toward disembedding, though already in the "strength of the weak ties" (Granovetter 1973) he saw that in a market economy too much embeddedness can – and is likely to – have damaging consequences. E.g. on the job market in recruiting personnel, one cannot rely on "strong ties": you cannot hire the nephew of the boss. But given information shortages about job applicants, you cannot proceed fully bureaucratically either. You need letters of recommendation from earlier employers or teachers whom you trust, but who were not too close to the candidate.

We may use the terminology Weber scholars use to describe Weber's historical philosophy: Polanyi was not an "evolutionist"; he was a "developmentalist". What is disembedding in Polanyi is rationalization in Weber. Weber saw rationalization as inevitable but acknowledged its downside (the iron cage of bureaucracy). Around 1914, he began to use

15 Stalin used this term for the first time in December 1924, see Carr (1958), Chapter 12.

16 The idea that the capitalist world system replaces „empires" was critical for Wallerstein as well. Wallerstein and Polanyi were colleagues at Columbia (and both were experts on Africa). Hence it is not unjustified to see Polanyi as a predecessor of world system theory. But when in the early 1970s, Marxism became a major new force, making references to Polanyi, who was mostly seen – in the soft interpretation – as a welfare-statist, social-democratic liberal was inappropriate. So, unsurprisingly there is little reference to Polanyi in the first volume of Wallerstein.

a new term, „disenchantment" (*Entzauberung*) to capture especially clearly what was lost with rationalization (while being fully aware what is being gained from it, see Szelényi 2015). In our soft reading of Polanyi, he believed that when disembedding became excessive, the economy had to be re-embedded to avoid the economic and socio-political catastrophes – like the Great Depression, Fascism-Nazism and Stalinism. *The Great Transformation* is a book about an "age of reconstruction". As Stiglitz pointed out in the introduction to the book we have already quoted above, these were fairly radical ideas in 1944. But today it is old news for most institutional economists, like Stiglitz himself.

With our experiences of state socialism, we have to push Polanyi's analysis a little further. Yes, Polanyi was a theorist of a mixed economy, where markets co-exist with other forms of integration. But which form is the dominant one? We believe – and assume Polanyi would be comfortable with such an interpretation – that in a globalized, complex world, the dominant coordinating mechanism *has to be* the market. Polanyi did see the danger of market failures from time to time and the need to complement markets with regulations, some welfare redistribution and/or even on more reliance on reciprocity. The 2008 Great Recession and collapse of financial markets was not the beginning of the end of the global capitalist order. These events called for some regulation which was achieved – in the US for example – through the 2010 Dodd-Frank Consumer Protection Act. It can be debated whether Dodd-Frank went too far, or not far enough, but except for a few orthodox market fundamentalist, most economists blamed the 2008 financial crisis for excessive, previous deregulation. For Polanyi – who started his adult life as a Christian socialist -, the fundamental task would have been to create enough non-market mechanisms to provide well-being for everyone. Markets often create too much inequality, too much poverty and segregation. Hence we need well-targeted policies to counteract them. To achieve this, we need social movements and (above all) a liberal democratic system. This was the way he thought about the world.

As this must be clear for the readers of this paper by now, we challenge the hard interpretation of Polanyi. We see him primarily as an advocate of the welfare state and social democracy, and not as a revolutionary socialist who aimed to break up the world system and replace a market integrated society with one integrated by redistribution. True, he was extremely naive politically (Saval, 2016), he was inexcusably soft during the purges in the USSR during the 1930s and not standing up against the Hitler-Stalin pact either. Probably, these were gestures to his formerly revolutionary wife. But unlike his brother, who wrote a careful book about the inefficiencies of the early Soviet economy[17], he did not offer an analysis of the economic system of the USSR. Polanyi was a great economic anthropologist but was a lousy politician. Let's not damage his scholarly contribution by his often naïve and not well informed political views.

17 Polanyi, Michael (1940).

Concluding remarks: an attempt to apply Polanyi's economic anthropology to socialism

Polanyi never attempted to develop a political economy of state socialism/communism. In what follows we try to offer a critical political economy of such systems.

FIGURE 2: The main sources of income inequality in socialist and postcommunist economies

1. State Socialism (All Stages)

Markets	Redistribution	Reciprocity
(3) → (2) From tertiary to secondary	(1) Dominant	(2) → (3) From secondary to tertiary
During the classical stage, the attempts to eliminate private businesses were prevalent, but not fully successful. In the reform period, private organizations within state firms and small businesses outside the firms were tolerated.	Redistributors (planners) disposed with the entire "surplus" supposedly in the public interest.*	During the classical period, family networks corrected redistributive failures (e.g. family food production and housing construction); in the reform period production for markets is allowed to a certain extent.

2. Post-Socialist, Illiberal Capitalist Regimes (All Varieties)**

Markets	Redistribution	Reciprocity
(1) → (1.5) From dominant to supplementary	(1.5) → (1.) supplementary to dominant	Tertiary
In the quasi-liberal stage, profits and wages are important. As the system moves to illiberalism and competition is restricted, it loses importance.	The dominant trend in illiberalism is rent allocation to those who are loyal to the executive power.***	The welfare state, which was underdeveloped under socialism, is further cut back. Kinship becomes more important again (childcare and care of the elderly).

Notes: *Konrad – Szelényi (1979). ** Szelényi – Mihályi (2020). *** Mihályi – Szelényi (2017)

The first author of this paper (Iván Szelényi) took on himself this unaccomplished task and used Polanyi's theory to develop the political economy of the actually existing, state socialism (with George Konrad ([1974] 1979) and in many later publications). Ilona Duczynska read this book, *The Intellectuals on the Road to Class Power* when it was still in manuscript (and before its authors were put in jall for it) and she was thrilled: "This is Polanyi, this is Polanyi".

The bottom line of the book was that socialist[18] economies were "modern" versions of redistribution. Their integration was redistributive since all the surplus which could be used for expanded reproduction was first concentrated in a central hand and was then redistributed to various actors. In archaic empires, redistribution was legitimated by tradition, in 20th-century socialist economies it was supposed to be guided by the rationality of central planners, or "redistributors". But this system was greatly distorted, in part, given the information shortages of planners and even more fatally that these economies were "deeply embedded". To put it with Mao: under socialism "politics was in command".[19] Even if economists had had sufficient information and fast enough data processing to respond in time to the changes in the economy, they could have been – and often were – overruled by political considerations.

Tamás Bauer (1978), in a splendid analysis showed how this system created repeatedly redistributive failures. The "central hand", the "redistributors" were under pressure from state-owned enterprises (SOEs) for investment funds. Given the political pressures to satisfy as many "consumers" as possible, they tended to allocate too broadly those funds. But funds were still insufficient to finish all ongoing investment projects. So, the center run out of money, they had the freeze incomplete investments, which therefore could not generate any income for years. The economy entered into an "over-investment" crisis. Funding had to be cut back until projects were completed, generated revenues, which could be appropriated by the central hand. Once the central hand accumulated enough resources again, the economic cycle of socialism began again, and the redistributor began to throw money at clients.

János Kornai in his *Economics of Shortage* (1980) – arguably one of the most important books ever written on the political economy of socialism – identified the essence of socialism to have tendency for chronic shortages. Much like Bauer, he saw an economic cycle in socialist economies, producing extreme shortages, and when it causes severe crises by reducing those and moving into the next stage of shortages. This is a deeply institutionalist analysis, which offers a comparative analysis of capitalist and socialist economies. While a capitalist economy is driven by a tendency towards *overproduction*, a socialist economy is driven by a trend to *chronic shortages*.

Neither Bauer nor Kornai used the distinction between markets and redistribution, though they were both familiar with Polanyi and our earlier attempts to use his ideas for developing a new political economy of socialism as a redistributive economy. Kornai considered this possibility, but rejected it, mainly because "redistribution" refers to the welfare state, "redistribution" of resources from rich to poor. Hence, he instead used the

18 Some call it state socialist, communist, state capitalist – the name is not of major concern for us, as we have already indicated in an earlier footnote.

19 In a widely publicized talk during the Cultural Revolution, when Mao and Lin Piao "reviewed 600,000 revolutionary students and teachers and Red Guards" marching at Tiananmen Square, Mao gave the following instruction to his closest followers: „You should put politics in command, go to the masses and be one with them and carry on the great proletarian revolution even better (…)". *Peking Review*, Vol. 9. #47, Nov. 18. 1966. https://www.marxists.org/subject/china/peking-review/1966/PR1966–47b.htm, Last time visited: 29 January, 2020.

term "bureaucratic coordination". Terminology is of little or no significance[20], nevertheless there is a fundamental agreement that socialist economies – be they redistributively integrated or bureaucratically coordinated – kept producing bureaucratic or redistributive failures in economic efficiency and also in social inequalities.[21]

To follow our soft interpretation of Polanyi, all actually existing societies of Eastern Europe were mixed economies (though their dominant coordinating mechanism was redistribution). Except very short, exceptional periods, when attempts were made to eliminate the market altogether, socialist economies needed some market mechanisms to correct redistributive failures (much like market economies need some welfare redistribution and market regulation to control market failures). For instance, even in Castro's Cuba, Stalin's Russia or Mao's China when collectivization of agriculture created unbearable food shortages, some concessions were made to food production by family organizations or even some farmers' markets. After 1963, Kádár's Hungary went quite far in allowing the "second economy" first in agriculture, next in other sectors of the economy, but of course, the party-state retained firm control on the industrial enterprise sector of the economy. With such a mix they substantially reduced – though never eliminated – the shortage economy.

In a mirrored comparison – as David Stark (1996) called it – between capitalism and socialism, it is primarily the dominant coordinating mechanism which creates inequality, and the secondary one compensates for this. This is also true for excessive fluctuations in the business cycle. Excessive inequalities in a socialist redistributive economy are created by redistribution and those who are "felt out" (for instance the unskilled rural working class" have to take care of themselves on the market place). This is true also for the capitalist business cycle (in 2008 in market capitalist countries' governments with taxpayers money had to ball out banks "which were too large to fail").

Finally, one last comment on market socialism and democratic socialism. The idea of *market socialism* has been with us for a long time. One of its early formulations came from Oscar Lange (1936) a committed socialist, who saw the inherent inefficiencies of the Soviet economy, and believed that it could be fixed by turning it into a market economy. Michal Kalecki (1972), a Keynesian economist, who returned to communist Poland after World War II, was advocating reforms along the same lines, by turning socialism into a "mixed economy". One of the most radical theorists along these lines was the Hungarian

20 Szelényi (2009) challenged Kornai by drawing a clear line between „welfare redistribution" (reallocation of market earned incomes) and redistribution of *capital goods* in a dominantly redistributive economy, where the surplus at the disposal of the central hand is not defined by the market. In addition, Weber had a good point when he called "rational bureaucracy" the ideal type of legal-rational (hence capitalist) authority. Szelényi was critical of Kornai's suggestion about the "prematurely born welfare state" theory under socialism which had to be reduced in market transition. According to Szelényi, the problem within socialism was not too much welfare state, but too much redistribution of capital goods.

21 We seem to believe – without hard data – that socialist economies might have produced lower level of inequalities than capitalist ones. The question, however, is what inequality is generated by which mechanism. If inequality is acceptable by the society, the next question is which inequality calls for correction and in what ways (Szelényi, 1978)?

Tibor Liska (1988[22]), who went as far as suggesting that market economy is only possible under socialism, since private ownership *per se* is a limitation of free competition.

A related question is whether socialist democracy is conceivable and the debate about this also goes back to the classics. Marx in his journalistic work (before 1843–44) was a *bourgeois* liberal advocating universal suffrage. He sifted to a revolutionary view of the transition to socialism, but had little to say about the relationship between the "dictatorship of proletariat" and "democracy". In fact, in his 1875 *Critique of the Gotha Program,* he took a stance against a dictatorial transition. By his *State and Revolution* in 1917, Lenin was less shy and took a harder line on the "dictatorship of proletariat". He eventually ended up with the idea of "socialist democracy", which is a hundred times more democratic than the bourgeois one, which – according to him – is the dictatorship of the minority over the majority, while dictatorship of the proletariat is the dictatorship of the majority over the bourgeois minority.

As far as the relationship between democracy, markets and property rights are concerned, Kornai (1992) persuasively pointed out that socialism was a system, based on three legs:

- public ownership of the means of production,
- redistributive (or in his terminology bureaucratic) coordination of the economy and
- one-party rule, legitimated by Marxism-Leninism.

This is a fixed menu, not *à la carte*. These three components not only logically hung together, but we have not experienced in the last almost one hundred years of experiments, where any of these components could have been separated from the rest. This leads us back to our soft interpretation of Polanyi. The critical question is: which is the dominant coordinating mechanism? If it is redistribution, it will come with state-ownership and one-party rule. This is a critical question for our theoretical-ideological political debates today. Chris Hann (2019) regarded Kádárist Hungary as "market socialism", and suggested that it should be shown to socialists around the world that there was a possibility for a functioning socialist dream. While we agree, that the Kádárist regime skillfully combined the dominant redistributive mechanism with some market elements, and created something that the Hungarians used to call "the merriest barrack in the socialist camp", this "something" was burdened with terrible political (and to many members of the society even economic) inequalities, which are unacceptable.

We do appreciate that some older people in rural communities who suffered a great deal during the managed transition from redistribution to a market economy, are nostalgic about the previous regimes. But there is no reason for the young generation of left-leaning social analysts to be nostalgic about this epoch.

Many of us – including the first author of this paper – hoped (much like Polanyi himself) during the early 1960s, in the Soviet reform plans, the 1968 Hungarian economic reform and especially during the Prague Spring of the same year, that "socialism with a human face" may be possible. But history proved us wrong. Kornai was right logically

22 The manuscript was written some 20 years earlier, just not published due to censorship.

and historically: public ownership goes hand in hand with redistribution and one-party rule. China today is somewhat an exception. There is indeed a great deal of private ownership and arguably quite a bit of market. But given the monopoly of the Communist Party, both are limited and after all China is still a communist country. But this needs more discussion than this paper allows. It is certainly true that the Chinese leaders today allow more private ownership and market than any previously existing communist regimes did.

With the fall of communism it appeared that "liberal capitalism" is in the making. And it was, but the forms communist economies were far too "embedded" to allow a liberal system to emerge. As a result emergent capitalism was to a large extent deeply embedded in social and political relations, and given the deep roots in political connections then emergent new postcommunist system was more oriented to rent seeking than profit maximization. Today, most of the post-communist economies are on the verge of capitalism and re-feudalization.

References

Anderson, Perry. 1985. *Passages from Antiquity to Feudalism*. London: Verso.

Åslund, Anders. 2019. *Russia's Crony Capitalism: the Path from Market Economy to Kleptocracy*. New Haven, CT.: Yale University Press

Bauer, Tamás (1978): "Investment Cycles in Planned Economies", *Acta Oeconomica*, No. 3, 243–260.

Block, Fred L. and Margaret Somers. 2016. *The Power of Market Fundamentalism: Karl Polanyi's Critique*. Cambridge: Harvard University Press.

Carr, Edward H. 1958. *Socialism in One Country*. London: Penguin Books.

Chebani, Houchang and Juan Linz (eds). 1998. *Sultanist Regimes*. Baltimore: Johns Hopkins University Press.

Congdon, Lee. 1997. "Between brothers: Karl and Michael Polanyi on fascism and communism", *Society and Economy in Central and Eastern Europe*, 19 (1): 114–123.

Dale, Gareth. 2016. *Karl Polanyi: a Life on the Left*. New York: Columbia University Press.

Duczyńska, Ilona. 1975. Der demokratische Bolschewik: zur Theorie und Praxis der Gewalt. München: List.

Engels, Friedrich [1845/1892] 1969. *Condition of the Working Class in England*. Marx-Engels internet Archive, www.Marxists.org/archive/. Moscow: Institute of Marxism Leninism.

Evans, Peter D. 1979. *Dependent Development. The Alliance of Multinational State, and Local Capital in Brazil*. Princeton: Princeton University Press.

Frank, André Günder. 1966. The Development of Underdevelopment. New York: *Monthly Review Press*, 18 (4): 17–31.

Granovetter, Marc. 1973. "The Strength of the Weak Ties", *American Journal of Sociology*, 78(6): 1360–1380

Granovetter, Marc. 1985. "Economic action and social structure: the problem of embeddedness", *American Journal of Sociology*, 91 (3): 481–510.

Hann, Chris. 2019. *Repatriating Polanyi. Market society in the Visegrad States*. Budapest: CEU Press.

Kalecki, Michal. 1972. *Selected Essays on Economic Growth of the Socialist and the Mixed Economies.* Cambridge: Cambridge University Press.

Konrad, George and Iván Szelényi. [1974] 1979. *The Intellectuals on the Road to Class Power.* New York: Harcourt, Brace and Jovanovich.

Kornai, János. 1980. *Economics of Shortage.* Amsterdam: North Holland.

Kornai, János. 1992. *The Socialist System. The Political Economy of Communism.* Princeton: Princeton University Press.

Lacher, Hannes. 2019. "Karl Polanyi, the 'always embedded market economy' and the re-writing of The Great Transformation", *Theory and Society* 48 (5): 671–707.

Lange, Oscar. 1936. "On the economic theory of socialism", *The Review of Economic Studies*, 4 (1): 53–71.

Lenin, V. I. 1917. *Imperialism, the Highest Stage of Capitalism*, Petrograd: Life and Knowledge Publisher.

Liska, Tibor. 1988. Ökonosztát. (The economic state), Budapest: Közgazdasági és Jogi Könyvkiadó (in Hungarian).

Luban, Daniel. 2017. "The elusive Karl Polanyi", *Dissent* 64 (2): 68–78.

Luxemburg, Rosa [1913] 1951. *The Accumulation of Capital.* London: Routledge Classics.

Magyar, Bálint. 2016. *Post-Communist Mafia State. The Case of Hungary.* Budapest: CEU Press.

Malinowski, Bronislaw. 1922. *Argonauts of the Western Pacific.* London: Routledge and Kegan Paul.

Mannheim, Karl. 1940. *Man and Society in an Age of Reconstruction.* London: Harcourt, Brace.

Marx, Karl [1857–58]. 1973. *Grundrisse.* London: Penguin Books.

Marx, Karl. [1867]. 1954. *Capital.* Volume I, Moscow: Progress Publishers.

Marx, Karl. [1885]. 1965. *Capital.* Volume III. Moscow: Progress Publishers.

Mauss, Marcel [1925]. 1954. *The Gift: Forms and Functions of Exchange in Archaic Societies.* London: Cohen and West.

Mihályi, Péter and Iván Szelényi. 2017. "The role of rents in the transition from socialist redistributive economy to market capitalism", *Comparative Sociology*, 16 (16): 13–38.

Mihályi, Péter and Iván Szelényi. 2019. *Rent-seekers, Profits, Wages and Inequality: The top 20%.* Cham (Switzerland): Palgrave – Macmillan.

Nagy, J. Endre. 2018. *Keserédes testvérség. Polányi Károly* és *Polányi Mihály.* (Bittersweet brotherhood, Karl Polanyi and Michael Polanyi), Szombathely: Savaria University Press (in Hungarian only).

Pei, Minxin. 2016. *China's Crony Capitalism. The Dynamics of Regime Decay.* Cambridge, MA: Harvard University Press

Polanyi, Karl. 1944. *The Great Transformation.* New York: Farrar and Rinehart.

Polanyi Karl. 1957. "The economy as an instituted process', in: Karl Polanyi, Conrad M. Arensberg and Harry W. Pearson (eds). *Trade and Market in the Early Empires: Economies in History and Theory.* Glencoe, Ill.: The Free Press: 243–270.

Polanyi, Karl. 1963. "Ports of trade in early societies", *The Journal of Economic History 23* (March*)*: 30–45.

Polanyi, Karl. 1966. *Dahomey and the Slave Trade: an Analysis of an Archaic Economy*, Seattle: University of Washington Press.

Polanyi-Levitt Kari. 1994. "Karl Polanyi as Socialist", in: K. McRobbie (ed). *Humanity, Society and Commitment: on Karl Polanyi.* Montreal: Black Rose, 115–134.

Polanyi, Michael 1940. *The Contempt of Freedom. The Russian Experiment and After.* London: Watts.

Ricardo, David [1817]1911. *The Principles of Political Economy of Taxation.* London: J. M. Dent and Sons.

Saval, Nikil. 2016. "Polanyi in our time", *The Nation*, December 22.2016, www.thenation.com/issue/january-16–23-2017.

Schumpeter, Joseph A. 1943. *Capitalism, Socialism and Democracy.* London: George Allen and Unwin.

Smith, Adam [1776] 1976. *The Wealth of Nations.* An inquiry into the nature and causes of the wealth of nations. Chicago: The University of Chicago Press.

Sorensen, Aage. 2000. "Towards a sounder basis of class analysis", *American Journal of Sociology* 105 (6): 1523–1558.

Stigler, George. 1971. "The theory of economic regulation", *Bell Journal of Economics and Management Science* 2 (1): 3–21.

Stiglitz, Joseph. 2001. "Foreword" in Karl Polanyi, *The Great Transformation.* Boston: Beacon Press, vii-xvii.

Stiglitz, Joseph. 2013. *The Price of Inequality.* New York: W.W. Norton and Company.

Stark, David. 1996. "Recombinant Property in East European Capitalism", *American Journal of Sociology,* 101 (4): 993–1027.

Szelényi, Iván. 1978. "Social inequalities in state socialist redistributive economies – dilemma for social policy in contemporary socialist societies of Eastern Europe", *International Journal of Comparative Sociology,* No.1–2, 63–87.

Szelényi, Iván. 1991 "Karl Polanyi and the theory of a socialist mixed economy", in: Marguerite Mendell and David Salee (eds.), *The Legacy of Karl Polanyi: Markets, State and Society at the end of the 20th Century.* New York: St. Martins Press, 231–248.

Szelényi, Iván. 2009: "János Kornai: From Socialism to Capitalism", *Czech Sociological Review* 45 (3): 611–615.

Szelényi, Iván. 2015. "*Entzauberung*: Notes on Weber's Theory of Modernity", *International Political Anthropology,* 8 (1): 5–14.

Szelényi, Iván. 2018. *Building Nations with Non-nationals.* Budapest: Corvina.

Szelényi Iván and Péter Mihályi. 2020 *Varieties of Post-Communist Capitalism. A Comparative Analysis of Russia, Eastern Europe and China,* Leiden, The Netherlands: Brill.

Wallerstein, Immanuel. 1974. *The Modern World System. Capitalist Agriculture and the Origins of the European World Economy in the Sixteenth Century.* New York: Academic Press.

Weber, Max. 1978. *Economy and Society. An Outline of Interpretive Sociology,* edited by G. Roth and C. Wittich. Berkeley: University of California Press.

Wittfogel, Karl August. 1957. *Oriental Despotism: a Comparative Study of Total Power.* New Haven: Yale University Press.

V. Revolt of the Masses and the Ukrainian Crisis

V.1 Back to Max Weber: the concept of "Der Wille der Beherrschten"

Introduction

In October 1917, Max Weber made a surprising statement in a lecture in Vienna. After he described his three types of authority (traditional, charismatic, and legal-rational) he added that there is a fourth type of authority, the "Wille der Beherrschten", too. We only know a report on this from an Austrian newspaper, the *Neue Freie Presse*, dated from Oct. 25, 1917[1]. That is all: we do not have the original Weberian text, so we can only guess what he actually said or wanted to say.

We have been struggling with the translation of this German term into English for quite a while[2]. Verbatim it could be translated as "will of the rul*ed*" which is accurate if we regard the other three systems of domination as various forms of "will of the rul*ers*". But it misses the anti-authoritarian content of the concept. Hence, in this paper, we use as a translation the term "revolt of the masses" for *Wille der Beherrschten*.

There are three data points in Weber's own writings we know for sure:

1. By 1920, when he was finishing his final draft of the theory of domination, he did not mention this "fourth type" at all.
2. In the interpretation of the 1917 text[3], the editor in the preface to that volume, Edith Hanke traced back the origins of modern democratic thinking to Weber's earlier essay on the Western city in the Middle Ages. According to this account, the concept of "modern democratic thinking" was first formulated in 1914 in the first version of the paper on cities,[4] but at this point the idea of "democratic legitimacy" as a part of theory of domination was still missing.
3. In the second version of the paper on the city Weber did not use the term of *Wille der Beherrschten.* He defines the non-legitimate authority in medieval Italian cities as "the opposed reinterpretation of charismatic domination" but neither as a "fourth system of domination", nor as a "democratic system of domination". The will of the ruled is not identical with modern democratic thinking. Far from it. There is just no democratic system of domination in Weber. All four systems of domination may

1 Reproduced in MWG I/22-4: 752ff.

2 With Péter Mihályi we discussed this at some length in our book *Varieties of Post-communist Capitalism. A Comparative Analysis of Russia, Eastern Europe and China* (Brill, 2020): 25-26.

3 Which is included in the MWG I/22-4: 752-763.

4 See Breuer 2006, and Hanke (2022): 28.

have a "democratic" element that it may reflect the wish (or will) of the "people", or of the "majority". It is certainly true for traditional and legal-rational authority and it is conceivable for the revolt of the masses. As we will show Zelensky was elected obviously in free and fair elections by a landslide, but this election was a rare instance of majority approval of a leader based on the revolt of the masses. Revolt of the masses claims legitimacy alone because a sufficiently large, desperate population is unwilling to accept one of the other three systems of domination. In general traditional or even legal-rational authority can be legitimate without majority approval, some legal-rational domination is autocratic (a good example is Singapure). Even government that came to power by a putsch, even a military coup can gain legitimacy if at one point people typically begin to obey order without systematic coercion. After initially brutal repression Augustino Pinochet – who implemented with the help of Milton Friedman an undoubtedly liberal economic system with dictatorial politics in Chile – could reduce coercion. By somewhat improving living conditions obedience was expected by most Chileans.

Let's turn now from the non-legitimate authority of medieval Italian cities to 21st century Ukraine. Ukraine has never been a liberal democracy, but it is a country where a substantial part of the population desperately desires to be a Western type of democracy.

When in Januaty 2014 pro-Western masses had started demonstrations – the so called Maidan Revolution in central Kyev – and demanded the resignation of Victor Yanukovych, the rather corrupt Russian friendly president, he responded violent, murderous attacks by the army and secret police. But the masses did not relent in spite of the death of more than 100 protesters. This stubborn resistance undermined the moral of the police and army. As Yanukovych realized that he was losing the support of his own staff (using an important Weberian *terminus technicus*), he had no choice but to escape to Russia. Yanukovych was not removed by democratic means, free and fair elections, but – if our Weber interpretation is correct – by the revolt of the masses.[5]

Back to the Ukrainians: they had the choice between two rather corrupt politicians, Yulia Timoshenko and Petro Poroshenko. More generally, they elected the lesser evil, Poroshenko. His corruption and his lukewarm relation with the West disappointed the Ukrainian electorate. People lost their faith in professional politicians. To everybody's great surprise, next time they elected a young comedian whose mother tongue is Russian and who is of Jewish descent in a country with long standing antisemitic traditions. This 2019 election was as far as we can tell a free and fair election, but a far cry from the usual democratic process. Volodymyr Zelenskyy had no political experience and no political party backing him. This was a vote against politicians, Zelenskyy was elected as president by the revolt of the masses.

5 This was not a unique event in post-1945 history. The same happened – *inter alia* - to Mohammad Reza Pahlavi, the former Shah of Iran. The masses rebelled against his almost 40-years of uninterrupted rule. Within weeks his traditional system was overthrown by the Iranian Revolution on 11 February 1979. In a number of countries, the events of the Arab Spring unfolded according to similar scenarios in the early 2010s: Algeria, Egypt, Lebanon, Morocco, etc.

We must acknowledge that the revolt of masses has something to do with charisma. Firstly, not all charismatic leaders are brought to power by "the people". But once they are in power, they often claim to be charismatic, deliver "miracles" to subordinated people who are desperate for a better life. They remain charismatic as long as they do deliver those "miracles". If they do not deliver, people may revolt and if the staff is sufficiently concerned, they may fall (like Yulia Timoshenko or Poroshenko). But not all charismatic leaders are brought to power by the revolt of the masses. Some may be rulers on claims of traditional authority, others may be "appointed" by a bureaucrat or elected in reasonably free and fair elections. But they may eventually gain charisma. There are rulers who become rulers by the "*Gnade*" of the ruled since they were charismatic to begin with, since they offered "miracles" and they may use their status by the revolt of the masses if they fail to deliver those miracles. Secondly, the leadership struclure created after the revolt of the masses is inherently unstable (see my remarks on pp. 197ff. in this book). There is not the slightest institutional guarantee of the calculable and peaceful transfer of power from the first generation of rulers to the second – unlike as it happens in traditional or legal-rational systems.

The Russian president, Vladimir Putin certainly was not brought to power by "the people". He was a basically unknown former KGB agent in 1999, Yeltsin appointed him as the next president in exchange for amnesty from prosecution for protection for himself and for his daughter Tatyana. During many years Putin was lucky, international prices of oil and gas increased steadily between 1998 and 2008, and he managed reasonably well the Russian economy. He improved living standards, in a way he delivered "miracles" one could not expect after the devastating 1990s. Now the question is, will he be able to keep his"charisma" with an ugly war in the Ukraine and serious economic problems at home. If he loses his charisma, his staff may get the courage to strike against him. As we write this commentary in March 2022 the future of Russia may depend how this works out.

V.2 Sovereignty: Uses and abuses

Introduction

In our last book (Szelényi and Mihályi, 2020), we attempted to come forward with a synthetic analysis of the coexisting and rival social arrangements of today, and within them, the forms of domination in post-communist countries. Francis Fukuyama's theory of the "end of history" seemed to be an interesting starting point. Fukuyama (1989) argued that, since the socialist-capitalist conflict that dominated the world's conflicts until 1989 had disappeared, the whole world was on the road to liberal capitalism. But Fukuyama's Harvard mentor Samuel Huntington already warned in a 1993 article that although the struggle between the two great ideologies was over, certain conflicts remained. These he called conflicts between civilizations. And indeed, after the collapse of socialism there were conflicts between states of different ideologies - mostly over the borders of the new states. These included the wars in the former Yugoslavia (1991-2001) and the two wars of Russia in Chechnya (1994-1996, 1999-2000), or the brief skirmishes between the post-Soviet successor states in Central Asia (e.g., between Armenia and Azerbaijan). In a more recent article (Szelényi/ Mihályi, 2021), we argued, following Max Weber, that at the beginning of the 21st century, six regimes of power are competing with each other: liberalism, conservatism, illiberalism, autocracy, dictatorship and despotism. We have also written that history is not a one-way process, and that liberal democracy is not necessarily a permanent state of affairs. In fact, in some post-communist countries in 1990 liberal regimes were in the making, but by 2010 some turned into illiberal political systems. Some of these regimes then became autocracies. But there is also a way 'backwards'. In many places, illiberal regimes have been able to move in a conservative or even liberal direction.

What is and will be a sovereign Ukrainian state?

But neither Fukuyama, nor Huntington, nor ourselves have attached any particular importance to the question of sovereignty and connection to the outside world. It is precisely in this dimension that the course of world history has taken a new direction today. As the world was suddenly informed overnight, Putin - or formally the Russian legislature - recognized as sovereign states two miniature puppet states, Luhansk and Donetsk, created on the territory of Ukraine by Russian agents and not recognized by anyone. Frankly speaking, we ourselves considered these two tiny states, which declared themselves as "people's republics" and which for 8 years (!) were not recognized by anyone, not even Putin's Russia, as a bad joke.

A few days after the recognition of the sovereignty of these vassal states, Putin went even further: he questioned whether Ukraine was a sovereign state. And on 23 February 2022 (tellingly, on the birthday of the Red Army), Russia launched a full-scale invasion into Ukraine - attacking even the territories on which Ukraine's sovereignty had not been formally questioned by Moscow for 8 years.

Putin made two important arguments. One is historical, the other linguistic-cultural. According to him, Ukraine has never been an independent state from Russia, its borders were arbitrarily drawn during the Soviet Union. Furthermore, the Russian language and culture are dominant in the region, and therefore a Ukrainian government that does not accept this does not represent a significant part of the population, and therefore cannot be accepted as a sovereign state. Putin is, of course, deliberately slip-sliding, since what he says about Ukraine applies to most of the states of the former Soviet empire that became sovereign in 1991. On the other hand, the Russian argument is not without precedent. The borders of practically all African states are disputed because the borders of these states were defined by former colonial powers 50 to 100 years ago.

To understand what has changed now, it is necessary to recall the definition of sovereignty in terms of foreign relations. A state is sovereign if its sovereignty is unconditionally recognized by other sovereign states. In the last four months, Russia has made it clear to the outside world, with a great deal of force and with the deployment of almost 200 000 troops, more forcefully than ever before, that it does not recognize Ukraine's right to join NATO, even though the then Russian President Yeltsin had no such reservations when Ukraine declared its independence in 1991. At that time, Russia accepted the results of the referendum in the whole of Ukraine, after 54% of the citizens who voted even in Crimea wanted to be part of Ukraine and only 42% of the population there wanted to be part of Russia. What is more, well before the breakup of the Soviet Union was even in existence, in 1975, the Helsinki Final Act was signed by the Soviet Union and the socialist countries of Eastern Europe, thus reaffirming the doctrine of 'sovereign equality', a principle enshrined in the UN Charter, which gives each state the right to freely determine not only its foreign policy but also the alliance system to which it adheres.

The history of the Crimea also offers compelling arguments against Putin's 'historical' appeal. Crimea was an autonomous, multilingual and multi-ethnic province (*kanate*) of the Ottoman Empire more than 200 years ago. In 1785, the census counted 84 per cent of the population as Tatars and only 2.2 per cent as Russians. Even in 1897, the Tatar population was still larger than the Russian population. When Russia won the war against the Turks in 1783, Crimea was annexed by the Tsarist regime. In 1921, in the process of the formation of the Soviet Union, the Constitution recognized Crimea as an autonomous Soviet socialist republic, still multilingual and multi-ethnic, although the Russian-speaking population was then the largest. In 1946, one of Crimea's still important ethnic groups, the Tatars (who still made up 20% of the population), were exiled *en masse* (some 230,000 people) to Siberia. Most of them perished (although no proper figures are available), so Ukrainian governments often refer to this dark chapter in Soviet history as a genocide - and rightly so. Borders and maps were redrawn at this time. The Crimean territories were downgraded to an *oblasty* (territory) of the Russian Federation, with similar powers to those of the Hungarian counties in Romania. To the outside world, and presumably to the surprise of the Russian public, in 1954 Khrushchev recognized Crimea as part of Ukraine. It is still unclear how much of this was motivated by Khrushchev's Ukrainian nationalism or his guilt over the atrocities against the Tatars. Khrushchev was of Ukrainian descent, spoke with a strong Ukrainian accent throughout his life, but was also the first Soviet leader to point out the horrors of Stalinism. The Soviet state's justification for annexing the peninsula to Ukraine was based on the cultural similarities and close economic ties between Crimea and Ukraine, including the fact that there was no direct land connection between Crimea and the Russian Federation at the time. Therefore, the Crimea had, indeed, more economic ties to Ukraine than to Russia.

But all these considerations were by and large suspended for many long decades after World War II in the name of the protection of the *status quo*. The majority of the developed and/or influential countries, including the Soviet Union and its successor state, the Russian Federation, accepted that any attempt to renegotiate the borders between states on the basis of historical arguments is bound to lead to endless disputes, including war. This is why most countries (especially Ukraine itself) considered the 2014 seizure of Crimea by Putin's Russia as a violation of Ukrainian sovereignty and did not accept it as legitimate. An important detail is that this is also the view of the current Turkish political leadership, which intervenes in the Russian-Ukrainian dispute and even supports the exiled Crimean Tatar National Assembly (*Majilis*) on the grounds that Crimean Tatars belong to the Sunni sect of Islam and that their language, which belongs to the Kipchak-Turkic language family, is not very far from the spoken Turkish language.

The principle of the inviolability of borders is therefore important and can be said to be the "dominant" approach in the resolution of international conflicts, but it is not exclusive. Examples include the break-up of Yugoslavia and the birth of independent Kosovo, but also counterexamples are when borders are redrawn through peaceful agreements between elites (see the peaceful separation of the Czech Republic and Slovakia in 1993). Unfortunately, this is not the case in Ukraine.

Sovereignty, citizenship and democracy in history

The modern state as we know it today has evolved over centuries of struggle. The state has had and still has a claim to two types of monopoly. On the one hand, the state has a monopoly on the use of force. But this does not apply only to physical violence (the slave-owner could kill his slaves), but also to legal coercion (the feudal lord could impose his standards of behavior on his serfs and punish them if they violated them). The modern state applies these monopolies within a geographically defined territory - unlike monarchies, whose borders are not physical. Those who owe obedience to the ruler are those who are subjects of the ruler. It is now forgotten, but the last Habsburg rulers, the kings of Hungary, historically called themselves, among other titles, Kings of Jerusalem, and this is how they were taught in schools.

Following Weber, we can say that, in contrast to the feudal state, territoriality played a prominent role in the development of the modern bourgeois state. As early as 1914, Weber had already raised the question of the role of Western (mainly Italian) cities in the development of modern societies in the Middle Ages, when he sought to explore the historical content of the idea that *Stadtluft macht frei.* The fact is that many cities in the European Middle Ages took in refugees from serfdom, and if they were not claimed by their feudal lord within a certain period of time, they became citizens of the city.

States that consider themselves sovereign also claim the exclusive right to determine who the citizens of the state are. Rogers Brubaker, in his magnificent treatise *Citizenship and Nationhood in France and Germany* (1998), distinguished between citizenship based on "blood or ethnicity" and citizenship based on territoriality. He argues that Germany is the country that applies citizenship based on blood. According to this concept, a citizen is one whose parents were German, regardless of where he or she was born. This idea was already in use in the 19th century. It was especially important during the Cold War years, when anyone who lived in the Soviet Union or in an allied communist country but could prove German ancestry was considered and accepted as a German citizen in West Germany – i.e., the Federal Republic of Germany (FRG). However, non-Germans born in the FRG had to "naturalize" their German citizenship.

In France, by contrast, anyone born in France could become a French citizen. The same was - and still is - the case in the United States. Looking at the changes over time, it is worth pointing out that the German-French comparison is more complex than that, and is also important for the interpretation of Hungarian history. In 1804, the Code Napoleon defined citizenship on an ethnic/cultural basis, as the French Revolution had sought to homogenize France, which had previously been ethnically and linguistically multicultural. But given the influx of people from the former French colonies - often people of different languages, religions and ethnicities - this cultural/linguistic definition of citizenship has become untenable. This is what has happened in the UK and, with increasing immigration, in the US and Australia.

There are also multilingual, ethnically and religiously diverse, multicultural countries - perhaps most countries are. Some work, some don't. India has long been seen as a model multicultural state, but with Narendra Modi's rise to power (2014), religious divisions have erupted, with Hindu authorities in some states even challenging the citizenship of Muslims. The issue of granting citizenship is also a highly controversial topic in Hungary. Conservatives and right-wingers tend to define "nation" on the basis of language. FIDESZ has succeeded in making this principle legally binding. Hungarian-speakers in neighboring countries were not only offered Hungarian passports (accepted by 1 million of them), but were also allowed to vote in Hungarian elections. Whether citizens living abroad can vote varies from country to country. In Australia, only those who have a permanent residence in Australia can vote, but any US citizen, wherever he or she lives, can vote in national elections - even by mail. The Hungarian citizenship and voting rights acts are extraordinary - perhaps unprecedented - because it not only grants citizenship to those who were not born in Hungary today, or who have never lived here, but also allows those to vote who do not have a Hungarian residence. It is as if every Jew who was neither born nor lived in Israel, and does not even have a home in Israel, could vote in Israeli elections.

So far, we have only argued that sovereignty is an important principle for the maintenance of world peace, but we must also recognize that the notion of sovereignty is often misused to justify the very principle and practice of dictatorship. In practice, a state is not sovereign because there was a democratic agreement on its borders and laws at some point in the past. Many - perhaps most - of the states that we without hesitation regard as sovereign today are dictatorial or even despotic in their internal order (e.g. Cuba, North Korea, Myanmar or Saudi Arabia). China's sovereignty is also difficult to question, although the most populous state on earth has no (or almost no) democratic legitimacy. According to the criteria of liberal democracies, China can hardly be considered a state based on the rule of law by the criteria of liberal democracies. Neither in the Mao era nor since 1976 were free and fair elections ever held. Nevertheless, the Chinese state mostly observes and enforces its own non-legitimate laws. This is very important to stress because some states defend their undemocratic laws, which violate human rights and are incompatible with the legal order of democracies, by claiming that their state is sovereign and that other states have no right to interfere. It is interesting that even the sovereignty of Hitler's Germany was not much questioned at the time, although anti-humanist, racist and sexist laws were passed. War broke out six years after Hitler came to power, when Germany violated the borders of Poland and occupied one half of the country (the other half was "given" to Stalin). There are also many important examples of how the international community of democratic states, while never for a moment contesting the borders or internal laws of a non-democratic state, insists on controlling and limiting the military development programs of autocracies, dictatorships and despotic countries if those programs represent a danger for the global security (as it was the case of the Cuban missile crisis back in 1962 or today with respect to the Iranian nuclear weapon program).

The importance of language and religion

Returning to the starting point of this chapter, the Russian-Ukrainian conflict, we cannot escape the fact that there are linguistic arguments justifying the seizure of Crimea and even the Russian annexation of the whole of Ukraine. There is no doubt that language and religion have a 'nation-building' significance. But language and national identity are not necessarily the same. According to public opinion polls, there are many people in Ukraine who, although Russian speakers, consider themselves Ukrainian (the current president of the state, Volodymyr Zelenskyy, a Russian native speaker, seems to be one of them). In the former Yugoslavia, there are also successor states whose language is Serbian. That said, it is a generally accepted principle in international diplomacy that crossing the borders of a neighboring state on the sole ground that "our language is spoken" in the area near the border is a serious violation of sovereignty.

A further problem is how to define '"language". Is there a Ukrainian language or is it just a dialect of Russian? This could be an important argument for annexing Ukraine to the Russian empire. The Yugoslav ("southern Slavic") state under Josip Broz Tito did not recognize a separate Croatian language either: a single Serbo-Croatian language was the accepted "scientific" position. When Croatia tried to recognize itself as a sovereign state, despite the opposition of a good part of the Serbs, efforts were made to emphasize the specificity of the Croatian language. The same happened with the Czech and Slovak languages after the break-up of Czechoslovakia. The nation-building role of language also played a major role in Hungary. As early as the 18th century, the Habsburgs, under the influence of the Enlightenment, recognized that modern science and politics could not be conducted in Latin and, not surprisingly, considered German to be the common language. This, however, clashed with Hungarian nationalism, and in 1844-45 the Hungarian diet declared Hungarian the official language of the Hungarian Kingdom, even though native Hungarians were a minority of the country's population. This was strongly protested by the other native speakers, especially the Croats, but it became a tense issue when the language of school education became the subject of debate.

In addition to language, religion is also a 'nation-building' factor. Croats not only speak a different language from Serbs, but are mostly Roman Catholic, while Serbs are Orthodox Christians. The only difference between Bosnians and Serbs is that Bosnians are Muslims and may well speak Serbian. This is also important in Ukraine, as Western Ukraine - the most anti-Russian part of the country - is Greek Catholic, unlike the Eastern Orthodox Russians living in the eastern part of the country.

Intranational and supranational sovereignty

Another contentious area of sovereignty is the right of federal states to legislate within a confederation and within member states. This issue is - more or less - resolved in the United States of America or the Federal Republic of Germany. Both countries have a constitution that applies to the federation as a whole, but member states can make their own laws as long as they do not contradict the common constitution. In the US, for example, there are states where even the death penalty is allowed (and often used) because it is not directly prohibited by the constitution. There is a big debate today about whether a federal electoral law is possible or necessary, which does not allow member states to make electoral rules that restrict the voting rights of minorities. In Germany, too, there was a recent debate about the extent to which member states (*Länder*) should abide by a provision made by the federal government in Berlin that restricts individual freedoms in the name of protecting against Covid. In the case of the Russian Federation, the official name of the state implies that it is a federation of legally equal states, but the reality is so far removed from this that the whole issue is not even a matter of debate in Russian politics.

The unexpected focus on the question of sovereignty has a special connection with the resolution of disputes within the European Union. It is well known that the EU has no constitution. What there is, the Lisbon Treaty, is merely an implicit agreement on what should be considered an electoral or judicial system that meets 'European standards'. Disputes over this are decided by the European Court of Justice, but member states challenging its rulings (in this case Hungary and Poland) have not entirely without merit argued that the courts have no business legislating. A European constitution would therefore be needed, but many Member States would rebel against this, as it would be seen as an infringement of their sovereignty. It is true: in a federal state system, Member States must give up part of their sovereignty. This is why some EU Member States are opposed to the vision of a United States of Europe. Another problem in the EU is that the separation of legislative and executive powers is not clear. While the European Parliament can make laws, the European Council (the body of heads of state and government) can veto them and refuse to implement them, even if only one country vetoes them. Can the EU then be called a democratic federation?

Is it an analysis or a choice of values?

The task of the social scientist is analysis, not judgement. Max Weber's cogent argument: the job of the social scientist is not to tell people what to do, it is to find out what they can do. Under normal circumstances, the primary task is to uncover the facts and to present the resulting ethical-political decision alternatives. It is then up to citizens to decide democratically which alternative to choose. But these are not the times we live in.

As far as Russia and Ukraine are concerned, principles of democracy have been violated in both countries over the last three decades and the economic performance of both countries was disastrous. Many say that Ukraine is one of the most corrupt countries in Europe. It is true. Ukraine ranks 122nd in Transparency International's (TI) list. But Russia is ranked even lower by TI (136th). In the ongoing war against Ukraine, it is obvious the Russians are clearly in flagrant breach of international law. It is also a fact that over the last three decades, the Ukrainian state has not behaved fairly towards its own minorities - the Russians, the Belarusians, the Poles and the Hungarians, or even the Crimean Tatars - claiming their own sovereignty. But that is no reason for Moscow to force neutrality on Kyev and forbid Ukraine to join NATO and the EU, either now or later. It was even more absurd that during the war with Ukraine, Moscow seemingly seriously "warned" Sweden and Finland not to give up neutrality and instead think about joining NATO any time in the future. In the case of the two Nordic countries, Putin's arguments at the beginning of the invasion about language and history have no basis whatsoever. In principle, it is not impossible for Ukraine to 'return' to the Russian empire. But that is a decision for Ukraine's citizens to make, not for another country, and not for social scientists looking on from the safe confines of a NATO and EU member state 900 kilometers westward from Kiev.

Of course, this is a very abstract answer and a feeble conclusion. We know it. If the Ukrainian public opinion is divided, then neither a parliamentary decision nor a referendum is a guarantee of a fair, just and quick solution. The cases of England and Scotland, Spain and Catalonia are examples of the fact that there is no sure recipe for dealing with ethnic conflicts – no matter how spectacularly the world is moving forward in the process of globalization.

References

Breuer, Stefan. 2006. "Nichtlegitime Herrschaft", In: S. Breuer, *Max Webers tragische Soziologie*, Tübingen: Mohr Siebeck, 149–167.

Brubaker, Rogers. 1998. *Citizenship and Nationhood in France and Germany.* Massachusetts: Harvard University Press.

Fukuyama, Francis. 1989. "The End of History", *The National Interest* 16, Summer, 3-18.

Hanke, Edith. 2022. *Max Webers Sprache. Neue Einblicke in das Gesamtwerk*, Wiesbaden Harrassowitz.

Huntington, Samuel. 1993. „The Clash of Civilízations?", *Foreign Affairs*, Vol. 72. No. 3. Summer, 22–49.

Szelényi, Iván and Péter Mihályi. 2020. *Varieties of Post-communist Capitalism. A comparative analysis of Russia, Eastern Europe and China*, Boston: Brill.

Szelényi, Iván and Péter Mihályi. 2021. "The six competing types of domination in the early 21st century", *International Political Anthropology* 14 (2): 175–189.

Weber, Max. 1978. *Economy and Society. An Outline of Interpretive Sociology*, ed. by Guenther Roth and Claus Wittich, 2nd ed. Berkeley, Los Angeles, London: University of California Press, 2 volumes. (ES).

Weber, Max. 2005. *Wirtschaft und Gesellschaft. Die Wirtschaft und die gesellschaftlichen Ordnungen und Mächte.* Nachlaß, Teilband 4: Herrschaft, ed. by E. Hanke, in cooperation with T. Kroll. Tübingen: J.C.B. Mohr (Paul Siebeck). (MWG I/22-4).

Weber, Max. 2006. "The Three Pure Types of Legitimate Rule", In: *The Essential Weber. A Reader*, ed. by S. Whimster. Abington/Oxon, New York: Routledge, 133–145.

Kultur- und sozialwissenschaftliche Studien / Studies in Cultural and Social Sciences

Herausgegeben von / Edited by Stefan Breuer, Eckhart Otto und Hubert Treiber

20: Hubert Treiber

Max Weber unter Anhängern des Altphilologen Hermann Usener

Religionswissenschaft auf philologischer Basis im Heidelberger Gelehrtenkränzchen „Eranos" 1904–1909

2021. VIII, 260 Seiten,
31 Abb., 1 Tabelle, br
170x240 mm
ISBN 978-3-447-11571-1
⊙E-Book: ISBN 978-3-447-39100-9 *je € 58,– (D)*

Hubert Treibers Monographie befasst sich mit dem Heidelberger religionswissenschaftlichen Gelehrtenkränzchen „Eranos", dem Gelehrte verschiedener Disziplinen angehörten, um Vorträge zu Fragen der Religion(en) zu halten und zu diskutieren. Mitglieder waren u.a. die Theologen A. Deissmann und E. Troeltsch, der Altphilologe und Schwiegersohn H. Useners, A. Dieterich, der Kulturwissenschaftler E. Gothein, der Jurist G. Jellinek, der Philosoph W. Windelband und der Kulturwissenschaftler Max Weber, der in diesem Kreis über den 2. Teil der *Protestantischen Ethik* referierte.
Die Eranos-Mitglieder werden portraitiert, es wird auf kollegiale respektive freundschaftliche Beziehungen untereinander eingegangen, einige Vorträge werden ausführlich dargestellt wie diskutiert und auch dahingehend befragt, inwieweit sie Einfluss auf Webers religionssoziologische Schriften ausübten. Ein gesondertes Kapitel befasst sich mit der Frage nach „Takt" in der wissenschaftlichen Tätigkeit, ein zentraler Streitpunkt zwischen Hermann Usener und Max Weber. Ein vollständiger Abdruck des Eranos-Protokollbuchs inklusive Transkription sowie mehrere Übersichten zur Usener-Schule wie z.B. Lehrstuhlbesetzungen durch Usener-Schüler vervollständigen die Darstellung des „Eranos".

21: Edith Hanke

Max Webers Sprache

Neue Einblicke in das Gesamtwerk

2022. VIII, 206 Seiten, 4 Abb.,
3 Graphiken, 4 Tabellen, br
170x240 mm
ISBN 978-3-447-11775-3
⊙E-Book: ISBN 978-3-447-39239-6 *je € 49,– (D)*

Max Weber (1864–1920) ist weltweit bekannt als Soziologe, Nationalökonom, Kulturwissenschaftler, Historiker und Methodologe. Für viele Fachdisziplinen ist Weber ein Kategorienpräger, aber auch die Alltags- und Mediensprache greift auf seinen Begriffsfundus zurück. Weber war ein Meister der präzisen Sprache, der Schachtelsätze, Gedankenstriche und Anführungszeichen, ein Beherrscher der Schriftsprache, ein charismatischer Redner und ein bildungsbürgerlicher Briefeschreiber. Seine Sprache ist daher nicht nur Arbeitsinstrument, sondern auch Kommunikationswerkzeug, Ausdruck von politischen Überzeugungen und tiefverankerten Werthaltungen. Edith Hankes Untersuchung der Sprache Max Webers eröffnet einen neuen Zugang zu den unterschiedlichen Facetten seines Werks und seiner Persönlichkeit: reflektiert-distanziert, brutal, männlich, aber auch humorvoll, spöttisch und sensibel.
Die Studie basiert auf der nunmehr abgeschlossenen Max Weber-Gesamtausgabe, die alle Werkteile mit philologischer Sorgfalt aufgearbeitet hat. Als langjährige Mitarbeiterin an diesem Editionsprojekt gibt die Autorin anhand der verschiedenen Textgattungen Einblicke in die Sprach- und Gedankenwelt Max Webers bis hin zur internationalen Übersetzungsarbeit. Das Buch versteht sich als Einladung, Max Weber neu zu lesen – auch aus Freude an seinem großen Sprachreichtum.

Kultur- und sozialwissenschaftliche Studien / Studies in Cultural and Social Sciences

Herausgegeben von / Edited by Stefan Breuer, Eckhart Otto und Hubert Treiber

22: Stefan Breuer

Max Weber in seiner Zeit

Politik, Ökonomie und Religion 1890–1920

2022. XII, 448 Seiten, gb
170x240 mm
ISBN 978-3-447-11764-7
⊙E-Book: ISBN 978-3-447-39244-0 je € 89,– (D)

Max Weber (1864–1920) zählt zu den Gründervätern der Soziologie, doch greift sein Werk weit über die Grenzen dieses Faches hinaus in Disziplinen wie Nationalökonomie und Politikwissenschaft, Rechts- und Religionsgeschichte. Stefan Breuer untersucht im ersten Teil des Buches zunächst die für Webers Frühwerk prägenden Einflüsse von Hermann Baumgarten, Theodor Mommsen und Rodbertus und befasst sich anschließend mit seinen agrarpolitischen Interventionen der 1890er Jahre, seinem Engagement in der Evangelisch-sozialen Bewegung und im Alldeutschen Verband. Der zweite Teil kreist um seine Analyse des zeitgenössischen Kapitalismus und dessen Verhältnis zu Neomerkantilismus und Imperialismus, erörtert seine Stellung zu den verschiedenen Erscheinungsformen des Sozialismus und des modernen Parteiwesens und unternimmt anschließend den Versuch einer Positionsbestimmung seiner politischen Theorie im Rahmen des Liberalismus. Im dritten Teil behandelt der Autor Webers Beiträge zu einer Entwicklungsgeschichte der Religion innerhalb und außerhalb des Okzidents, teils unter historischen und systematischen Gesichtspunkten, teils im Wege eines Vergleichs mit den Konzeptionen Oswald Spenglers, Erwin Rohdes und Ernst Troeltschs.

23: Gerhard Wagner

Gesammelte Aufsätze zur Wissenschaftslehre Max Webers

2022. XII, 138 Seiten,
7 Abb., 12 Tabellen, br
170x240 mm
ISBN 978-3-447-11776-0
⊙E-Book: ISBN 978-3-447-39238-9 je € 48,– (D)

Max Webers *Gesammelte Aufsätze zur Wissenschaftslehre* zählen seit ihrer ersten Auflage 1922 zu den faszinierendsten, aber auch dunkelsten Kompendien der Wissenschaftsphilosophie der Kultur- und Sozialwissenschaften. Die im vorliegenden Buch enthaltenen Aufsätze sind als Begleitforschung zur Edition von Band I/7 der Max Weber-Gesamtausgabe entstanden. Sie ergänzen diesen Band insofern, als sie die neu erschlossenen, bisweilen in der Ästhetik und in den Naturwissenschaften liegenden Quellen zentraler Konzepte wie Erklären, Handeln, Gesetz, Idealtypus, Kausalität, Typus, Verstehen usw. explizieren und an den heutigen Forschungsstand anschließen. Damit leisten sie nach einem Jahrhundert einen wichtigen Beitrag zur Erhellung der immensen Komplexität und verblüffenden Aktualität von Max Webers Wissenschaftslehre.